DIGITAL JOURNALISM STUDIES

Digital Journalism Studies: The Key Concepts provides an authoritative, research-based "first stop-must read" guide to the study of digital journalism.

This cutting-edge text offers a particular focus on developments in digital media technologies and their implications for all aspects of the working practices of journalists and the academic field of journalism studies, as well as the structures, funding and products of the journalism industries.

A selection of entries includes the topics:

- Artificial intelligence;
- Citizen journalism;
- Clickbait;
- Drone journalism;
- Fake news;
- Hyperlocal journalism;

- Native advertising;
- News bots;
- Non-profit journalism;
- User comment threads;
- Viral news;
- WikiLeaks.

Digital Journalism Studies: The Key Concepts is an accessible read for students, academics and researchers interested in Digital Journalism and Digital Journalism Studies, as well as the broader fields of media, communication and cultural studies.

Bob Franklin was Foundation Chair in Journalism Studies at Cardiff University from 2005–2018, founding editor of the journals *Digital Journalism* (2013–2018), *Journalism Practice* (2007–2018) and *Journalism Studies* (2000–2018) and editor of Routledge's book series *Disruptions: Studies in Digital Journalism*. Recent publications include *The Routledge Handbook of Developments in Digital Journalism Studies* (2019, with Scott Eldridge II).

Lily Canter is a hybrid journalist–academic. She balances working as a senior lecturer at Sheffield Hallam University with her freelance career as a consumer affairs journalist writing for the *Guardian, Metro, Moneywise* and digital native news websites. Her academic research, published in international journals, examines journalism and social media, local newspapers, education and freelancing.

DIGITAL JOURNALISM STUDIES

The Key Concepts

Bob Franklin and Lily Canter

LONDON AND NEW YORK

First published 2019
by Routledge
2 Park Square, Milton Park, Abingdon, Oxon OX14 4RN
and by Routledge
52 Vanderbilt Avenue, New York, NY 10017

Routledge is an imprint of the Taylor & Francis Group, an informa business

© 2019 Bob Franklin and Lily Canter

The right of Bob Franklin and Lily Canter to be identified as authors of this work has been asserted by them in accordance with sections 77 and 78 of the Copyright, Designs and Patents Act 1988.

All rights reserved. No part of this book may be reprinted or reproduced or utilised in any form or by any electronic, mechanical, or other means, now known or hereafter invented, including photocopying and recording, or in any information storage or retrieval system, without permission in writing from the publishers.

Trademark notice: Product or corporate names may be trademarks or registered trademarks, and are used only for identification and explanation without intent to infringe.

British Library Cataloguing-in-Publication Data
A catalogue record for this book is available from the British Library

Library of Congress Cataloging-in-Publication Data
Names: Franklin, Bob, 1949- author. | Canter, Lily, author.
Title: Digital journalism studies : the key concepts / Bob Franklin and Lily Canter.
Description: London ; New York : Routledge, 2019. | Includes bibliographical references and index.
Identifiers: LCCN 2019004029 (print) | LCCN 2019008820 (ebook) | ISBN 9781315406107 (ebook) | ISBN 9781138223059 (hardback : alk. paper) | ISBN 9781138223066 (pbk. : alk. paper)
Subjects: LCSH: Online journalism. | Digital media.
Classification: LCC PN4784.O62 (ebook) | LCC PN4784.O62 F73 2019 (print) | DDC 070.4–dc23
LC record available at https://lccn.loc.gov/2019004029

ISBN: 978-1-138-22305-9 (hbk)
ISBN: 978-1-138-22306-6 (pbk)
ISBN: 978-1-315-40610-7 (ebk)

Typeset in Bembo
by Swales & Willis, Exeter, Devon, UK

Printed in the United Kingdom
by Henry Ling Limited

CONTENTS

Introduction	vi
Acknowledgements	xv
List of key concepts	xvi

THE KEY CONCEPTS 1

References 277

INTRODUCTION

This relatively small book addresses big issues and concerns. We have designed and written *Digital Journalism Studies: The Key Concepts* to provide students of journalism, journalism studies, media, communication and cultural studies, as well as public relations and marketing, with a uniquely, accessible and authoritative guide to the central concepts and ideas informing the innovatory and rapidly expansive scholarly field of Digital Journalism Studies.

In writing the book our ambition has been to deliver a "first-stop – must read" text which offers an invaluable, high quality and research-based resource for students enrolled on undergraduate and postgraduate programmes which mostly focus on digital journalism or Digital Journalism Studies. The book identifies, analyzes and presents key ideas and concepts in Digital Journalism Studies, explores their interconnections and offers recommendations for further reading and study.

Alternative but similarly formatted "keyword collections", "dictionaries" or "glossaries" exist, although their earlier publication prevents them from capturing and addressing more recent and significant developments in Digital Journalism Studies triggered by the affordances of digital media: see for example, Zelizer and Allan (2010), Franklin, Hamer, Hanna, Kinsey and Richardson (2005), Harcup (2014).

From journalism and journalism studies to digital journalism and Digital Journalism Studies

The worlds of journalism and Journalism Studies have changed markedly since the late 20th century, and at some considerable pace! With hindsight, the transition from the world of newspapers as "news" printed literally on "paper" to the digital and online world has often seemed uneven and characterized by a series of fits and starts. Occasionally, however, there has been what might be termed "disruptive moments" in which the redundancy

INTRODUCTION

of analogue technologies, journalistic practices and the editorial products which they delivered became apparent. Simultaneously, these moments revealed the potential for a new digital world and a new digital journalism. On these occasions, the conflict between current practice and future prospect has seemed irreconcilable and stark. Let's briefly consider one such moment.

On 14 September 1987, *The New York Times* published its largest ever edition, which boasted a staggering 1,612 pages and weighed in at a startling 12 pounds. Given the paper's editorial mission to publish "All the News That's Fit to Print", emblazoned daily on its masthead, the publication of such a record-breaking newspaper was perhaps unsurprising. Intended to underline the authority of legacy "newspapers of record", this monstrous mash-up of printers' ink and pulped trees risked looking like a dinosaur. Despite its record-breaking girth, the print monolith offered readers only a modest fraction of the many thousands of pages of news promised by news online.

Print newspapers, moreover, delivered neither the **immediacy** of online news, whether *The New York Times* was actually read in New York, Nigeria or Nanyang, nor the opportunities to read "any one of a million blogs, online fanzines, discussion sites, hobby forums, gossip mills and conspiracy exchanges, all of them capable, in theory and quite often in practice, of offering what a reader might take 'as news'" (Meek, 2018: 11). Three other "costs" were underscored by this edition of *The New York Times*. First, notwithstanding the size of this particular issue, *The New York Times* remained a single newspaper, while, in a multimedia world, readers online might access news on every news-paper around the globe, along with news delivered by radio and televisual news organizations, online news ignited nothing less than a global explosion in the reach of news. Second, online news delivered *interactivity* along with *immediacy* which meant readers might access the user comment threads of other readers and also contest evidence and opinions expressed in articles by journalists. Finally, but crucially, at a time which predated paywalls, news online was free. Proprietors, globally, argued that the news must be "Fit to Print" but also "Free to Read". The extent and depth of these changes in journalism have been nothing less than remarkable and have attracted both advocates and critics. And it is at these disruptive moments that awareness of the potential of a new digital journalism arises while the implausibility of continuing to print "news" on "paper" in a highly competitive market with an anticipation of generating profit is revealed.

Digital Journalism Studies: The Key Concepts examines these develop-ments in digital media technologies, the emergence of mobile telephony and social media and explores their radical implications for journalism. Without implying any deterministic unravelling of events, these changes have undoubtedly initiated substantive shifts in all aspects of the professional practices and newsroom cultures of journalism, the academic field of journalism studies which monitors and critically interrogates such changes, as well as the structure, funding, organization, staffing, regulation and products of the journalism industries. A comprehensive and fundamental rethinking of key concepts, theoretical approaches and research methods has proved necessary to untangle and explore these far-reaching developments in journalism and journalism studies. In an age of citizen journalism and blogging, in tandem with the emergence of "semi-journalistic" organizations such as WikiLeaks, there is a need to revisit and reconsider even fundamental questions such as "What is Journalism?" and "Who is a Journalist?" These are turbulent times, described by Domingo, Masip and Costera Meijer (2015) as a "moment of mind blowing uncertainty in the evolution of Journalism".

Adopting more sober language, other commentators articulate the radical implications of such changes. So many elements of contemporary journalism professional practice have become normalized as part of everyday newsroom practice, they suggest, that we are witnessing nothing less than "the emergence of Digital Journalism Studies as a new field of scholarly inquiry" (Franklin and Eldridge, 2017: 1).

As noted above, however, the pace of these developments in digital media, as well as their engagement with journalism, has often been uneven and erratic. In some phases the transition from journalism to digital journalism has certainly taken longer than many observers imagine or understand. Why not experience an early "taster" of how useful this book might prove by turning now to the entry on "Digital Journalism" on page 73. Once there you can read, for example, that journalism historian William Mari (2019) argues that the pre-internet introduction of computers into legacy media newsrooms occurred in three phases running from as early as the 1950s through to the 1990s. The mainframe computer arrived in the 1950s to late 1960s; minicomputers were introduced between the 1970s and 1980s, with the first journalistic uses of the microprocessor stretching from 1982–1992. Then

> the pace of change from **legacy media** to digital media and digital journalism quickened with the arrival of the internet, increasingly sophisticated software packages, the **affordances** of **Web 2.0, (live) blogs, smartphones, tablets, social media, algorithms,**

INTRODUCTION

news bots, live streaming, mobile news and the enhanced and varied uses of **Artificial Intelligence** (AI) in news journalism.

(Franklin and Canter: 73)

Continue reading and you will see that journalism scholars Malik and Shapiro (2017: 16–21) suggest that Digital Journalism "is born [eventually] … when the author–audience relationship becomes more interactive and engaged" (cited in Franklin and Canter, 2019: 75).

In this way, we hope that *Digital Journalism Studies: The Key Concepts* will help you to address, understand, and learn about the fundamental developments in digital media technologies that have transformed the landscape from journalism to digital journalism.

Pedagogy and publishing

The academic study of journalism has expanded rapidly since 1971 when the first year-long postgraduate Diploma programme in Journalism was launched at Cardiff University, UK under the direction of Sir Tom Hopkinson. Initially, the programme was intended to provide training, as well as an education, in the skills, knowledge and practical understanding necessary to work as a journalist (typically) in a local newspaper newsroom. Eventually more academic elements were introduced into the curriculum, which required students to study course components focused on journalism ethics, law, government and public administration. Subsequently, university based courses have burgeoned and typically attract high student applicants and enrolments; the number of higher education institutions offering journalism programmes has similarly grown along with teaching and research staff in journalism.

Intellectually, the discipline of Journalism Studies is still relatively new, multi-disciplinary, derives scholarly inspiration from the cognate fields of media, cultural and communication studies, but has developed at a considerable pace since the mid-1990s, especially since the new millennium (see **journalism studies**).

Initially, the number and range of scholarly and practitioner based book titles published to support student learning in the field was limited. This situation has changed markedly. The very striking growth in publishers' interests in this field is illustrated by recollecting that the first and only research-based book to be published with "Journalism" or "Journalist" in the title, following Jeremy Tunstall's classic *Journalists at Work* (1971), was Brian McNair's *News and Journalism in the UK* in 1994; an unbelievable famine of titles which lasted almost a quarter of

ix

INTRODUCTION

a century. A plethora of journalism studies' titles is now published each year with all major publishers producing independent subject catalogues to announce their journalism titles.

Publishers' enthusiasm for this relatively new field of study is not limited to books to inform students' work and to provide illustrative case studies. Three new peer reviewed journals – *Journalism Studies* (2000), *Journalism Practice* (2007) (Routledge, Taylor and Francis) and *Journalism; Theory, Practice, Criticism* (2000) (Sage) – were launched in the first decade of the new millennium. The journals resource and support student learning and enjoy both critical and financial publishing success. Article downloads run into many hundreds of thousands each year.

A second wave of new journals has accompanied the proliferation of scholarly and pedagogic interest in Digital Journalism Studies, including *Digital Journalism, Mobile, Media and Communication* and the online-only journal *Social Media and Society*. This flow of scholarly research in academic journals is further supplemented by publications emanating from a host of newly established research centres. Two examples illustrate rather than capture the full range. The Tow Centre for Digital Journalism, for example, is located in the Columbia School of Journalism in the USA while The Pew Centre is a non-partisan, independent "Fact Tank" based in Washington.

Aims and objectives

It is intended that *Digital Journalism Studies: The Key Concepts* will provide an extensive, detailed and useful reference or "source" text for students and others with interests in Digital Journalism Studies. The book's aims and objectives are:

- To provide a detailed, research-informed, up-to-date, unique, authoritative but highly accessible account of the key concepts in Digital Journalism Studies, written by senior academics in the field, one of whom also trained and currently works both as an academic and a journalist;
- To explore the relationship between Digital Journalism Studies and the cognate intellectual disciplines of media, communication, cultural studies and, to a lesser degree, public relations;
- To indicate the plurality and range of new theoretical stances evident in Digital Journalism Studies, as well as the way that "legacy" concepts have been refashioned and reformulated for relevance in the new digital setting;

INTRODUCTION

- To introduce and illustrate some of the key, distinctive methodological approaches which inform Digital Journalism Studies, while also re-evaluating the suitability of traditional research designs in an age of digital media;
- To reveal the relevant interconnections between key concepts and ideas by using **bold** "hyperlinks" across the alphabetically listed entries;
- To provide extensive bibliographical guidance to facilitate further study by citing a wide range of primary and secondary literature including research findings from recent articles in leading peer reviewed journals;
- To illustrate the multidisciplinary character of Digital Journalism Studies and the degree to which it builds on the traditional social science and humanities disciplines of sociology, politics, economics, history, psychology, literature and linguistics, alongside natural science disciplines such as mathematics, computing science and statistics;
- To alert readers to recent debates involving Digital Journalism Studies, including the diverse speculations about the future of journalism, allegations concerning fake news, issues arising from the lack of civility in online reader comment threads, the growing number of entitlement claims for "The right to be forgotten" and the charge by the US President that the press – especially CNN – is "the enemy of the people";
- To outline the impact of recent policy developments on the organizational structures, financial resources and business strategies, as well as the ethical and regulatory environment of digital media within which journalism is conducted, along with their consequences for journalism products and professional practice.

These are considerable ambitions. We hope that we have met them and that readers will find this a highly readable, academically useful and thought provoking read, which is informative, enlightening and, like all good journalism, contains a modicum of wit.

Structure and content

We decided that the most accessible and readily understood way to structure the contents of this book was to construct a simple alphabetical listing of the key concepts involved in Digital Journalism Studies, followed by a lengthy alphabetical listing of references and sources cited in the text.

But this seemingly simple procedure immediately generates an important question concerning what might be termed "criteria of inclusion"; that is, which concepts are to be included? And equally important, of course, which are to be excluded? Different authors would undoubtedly generate distinctive listings of entries. Moreover, not all entries are of equivalent significance for discussions of Digital Journalism Studies. Entries on the growth and prevalence of **listicles**, for example, may not seem to warrant the more extensive consideration offered in our selection of topics to **business models, Facebook** or **Digital Journalism Studies**. Worse, the expansive nature of Digital Journalism Studies combined with the pagination and word budgets within which this (and every other) book project has been conducted means that the selection of entries involves considerable compromise. It is, therefore, important to make clear the considerations which have informed our decision making – our "criteria of selection" – although in doing so we are aware that such a procedure risks stoking potential controversy as much as achieving any agreement.

Entries were selected:

(1) On our assessment, as academics with a long-standing interest and engagement in the fields of Journalism and Digital Journalism Studies, of those matters which seem to have proved most significant, influential and shaping in their consequences and implications for this new scholarly field. Hence, consideration of **business models, "crisis" of journalism** and **social media** rank highly);

(2) To reflect a concern to include the broadest possible range of competing voices engaged in the various debates (both professional and scholarly) concerning digital journalism (the changing role of **subeditors** alongside the growing role of research design based on **visual ethnography**);

(3) because of the importance and prominence of particular ideas and concerns expressed in scholarly literature and debate (the continued relevance of significant concepts like **agenda setting**, for example, but also the emergence of ideas about **gatewatching** and **gatecrashing** to complement traditional but significant notions of **gatekeeping**);

(4) to reflect the need to address public concerns and debates articulated in more public forums such as news media (public concerns with privacy and confidentiality in the context of **social media, the right to be forgotten**, as well as lack of civility in **user comment threads**);

(5) to prioritize and include entries which focus upon *change within journalism*, either because ideas or themes were key agents triggering

INTRODUCTION

change or because they were themselves a new feature of the landscape of Digital Journalism Studies (for example, the expansive role of **algorithms** and **artificial intelligence (AI)** in journalism as well as the emergence of **automated content, data journalism, immersive journalism** and **robot journalism**).

The resulting alphabetical listing of concepts ranges from Actants through Citizen Witnessing, Drone Journalism and Facebook to Paywalls, Tweets, WikiLeaks and YouTube: along the way Crowd Sourcing, Digital War Reporting, Legacy Media, Metasources, Non-Profit Journalism, Snapchat and Viral Media are discussed and analyzed. Entries also embrace discussion and analysis of new conceptual and theoretical approaches to digital journalism studies as well as innovative research methods and research design.

Each entry is between approximately 250–1,800 words (reflecting complexity, significance and the range of existing scholarly literature requiring review and inclusion), makes extensive connections between related entries and concludes by suggesting bibliographical references to allow readers opportunities to follow up subjects of interest in greater detail.

Explore, engage, but mostly enjoy!

A major ambition for the book has always been to whet readers' appetites. In our drafting of entries, we have tried to offer an engaging and well informed "first word" about a particular topic, without any claims to have offered the last. Entries have been written to encourage further reading and study around the topics addressed and to provoke further thoughts and reflection. To that end, we hope that *Digital Journalism Studies: The Key Concepts* provides an accessible and engaging resource for readers seeking a single text which offers cross-disciplinary references to a wide range of ideas, concepts and cutting edge research findings which are central to understanding the culture and professional practices of Digital Journalism as well as the academic and scholarly requirements of Digital Journalism Studies.

We anticipate that *Digital Journalism Studies: The Key Concepts* will generate further questions but also provide some answers to the issues and concerns raised not exclusively by us as authors, but by the students, teachers, academics, researchers and journalists that we hope will read this book. We believe the book will prove to be a helpful and early pioneer within the field of Digital Journalism Studies expanding the student and scholarly readership of work in the Digital Journalism

Studies' field across the world. Such an ambition may seem rather grandiose. But given the global reach of digital journalism today, it is certainly appropriate.

References

Domingo, D., Masip, P. and Costera Meijer, I. 2015 "Tracing Digital News Networks: Towards an Integrated Framework of the Dynamics of News Production" *Digital Journalism* 3(1): 53–67.

Eldridge, II, S. and Franklin, B. 2019 *The Routledge Handbook of Developments in Digital Journalism Studies.* London: Routledge

Franklin, B., Hamer, M., Hanna, M., Kinsey, M. and Richardson, J. E. 2005 *Key Concepts in Journalism Studies.* London: Sage

Harcup, T. 2014 *A Dictionary of Journalism.* Oxford: Oxford University Press

Malik, A. and Shapiro, I. 2017 "What's Digital? What's Journalism?" in Franklin, B. and Eldridge, II, S. (Eds) *The Routledge Companion to Digital Journalism Studies.* Abingdon: Routledge, 15–24

Mari, W. 2019 *A Short History of Disruptive Technologies 1960 to 1990; Introducing the Computer in the Newsroom.* London: Routledge

McNair, B. 2003 *News and Journalism in the UK.* London: Routledge

Meek, J. 2018 "The Club and the Mob" *London Review of Books* 6 December: 9–16

Tunstall, J. 1971 *Journalists at Work.* London: Constable and Robinson

Zelizer, B. and Allan, S. 2010 *Keywords in News and Journalism.* Maidenhead: McGraw Hill, Open University Press

ACKNOWLEDGEMENTS

We would like to acknowledge the enthusiastic support and advice of editorial colleagues at Routledge, especially Margaret Farrelly, Natalie Foster, Kitty Imbert and Jennifer Vennall. We would also like to thank the many hundreds of scholars of Digital Journalism Studies we have cited and referenced when making our own arguments in the pages that follow. Additionally …

Thanks to Sheffield Hallam University for giving me the time and space to research and write, and to my husband Mark Dayman for never complaining when I take on yet another project.

Lily Canter

Love and thanks to Annie for all her help with everything, but mostly for sharing her life with me.

Bob Franklin

LIST OF KEY CONCEPTS

actants 2
Actor Network Theory
 (ANT) 2
advertising 3
advertorial 5
affordances 6
agenda setting 7
aggregators 9
algorithmic journalism 10
algorithms 11
alternative journalism 13
Amazon 14
ambient news 16
application programming
 interface (API) 17
apps *see* smartphones; tablet 18
artificial intelligence (AI) 18
audiences 20
audiences: creative and
 quantified 23
audience repertoires 23
automated content 25
automated content analysis 26

BBC 29
Blogosphere 32
blogs/blogging 34
brand studios 36
breaking news 37
British Digital Corporation 39

business models 40
BuzzFeed 42

censorship 44
churnalism *see Flat Earth News* 46
circulation *see* downloads 46
citizen journalism 46
citizen witnessing 49
clickbait 50
columnist 51
comments *see* user
 comment threads 54
computational journalism 52
computer assisted reporting
 (CAR) 54
content farms *see Flat
 Earth News* 54
convergence 54
copyright 56
creative cannibalism 58
creative destruction 59
"crisis" of journalism 60
crowdfunding 62
crowdsourcing 63

data journalism 64
data visualization *see*
 infographics 67
deadline 67
defamation 68

LIST OF KEY CONCEPTS

democratic deficit 71
digital journalism 73
digital journalism education 75
digital journalism and
   the environment 78
digital journalism ethics 79
Digital Journalism Studies 81
digital war reporting 85
disruption 87
diversity 88
downloads 90
drone journalism 91

editor 93
email 95
embargo 96
entrepreneurial journalism 97
ethnography 99

Facebook (WhatsApp,
   Instagram) 101
fact checking 105
fake news 106
filter bubble 110
Flat Earth News 111
Flickr 113
freelance 113
freemium paywall 115
Future of Journalism
   Conference 116

gatecrashing 117
gatekeeping 118
gatewatching 120
geo-social news 121
global journalism 122
Google 124

hacks 125
hacks/hackers 126
hamsterization 127

The *Huffington Post*
   (*HuffPost*) 128
huffinization 130
hyperlocal business
   models 131
hyperlocal journalism 132
hypertext 134

immediacy 135
immersive journalism 136
impartiality *see* transparency 137
in-betweeners 137
(The) *Independent* 139
infographics 141
information subsidies 142
infotainment 144
Instagram *see* Facebook 145
interactivity 145
interview 146
inverted pyramid 147
investigative journalism 149

journalism 152
journalism studies 154
journalist 157
journalistic cultures 160
journalists' identity 161

legacy media 163
Leveson Inquiry 165
lifestyle journalism 167
like 168
liquid news 169
listicles 170
live blogging 171
local media 174
local newspapers 176
long form narrative 178

magazine journalism 179
mashup 180

xvii

LIST OF KEY CONCEPTS

metasources 181
metered paywalls 182
Metro 183
mobile news 184
MOJO journalism 185

native advertising 187
network journalism 189
news 189
news agency 191
news beats 193
news bots 195
newsroom 196
news updating *see* deadline;
  liquid news 197
news values 197
newszak 199
non-profit journalism 199

online firestorms 200
online journalism 201

paywalls 203
the people formerly known as
  the audience 204
the people previously known as
  the employers 205
personalization of news 207
photojournalism 208
platforms 211
podcast, podcasting 211
precision journalism 213
produsage 213
propaganda model 214
ProPublica 216
public service 217

reciprocal journalism 218
Reddit 219

revenue streams *see* advertising;
  business models; crowdsourcing;
  paywalls 221
right to be forgotten 221
robot journalism *see* algorithmic
  journalism; artificial
  intelligence;
  news bots 222
RSS feeds 222

scarecrow journalism 223
shovelware 224
Skype 225
slow journalism 227
smartphones 228
Snapchat 229
social influence 230
social media 232
social media editor 233
social media guidelines 234
sources 235
style guide 237
subeditor 238
subscription 239
surveillance 240
syndication 242

tablet 243
transparency 244
Tumblr 246
tweet 248
Twitter 249
Twitter and news 252
Twitter and personal
  branding 254
Twitter and political
  reporting 256
Twitter and uses by
  journalists 258

user comment threads 260
user-generated content
  (UGC) 262

viral news 263
visual ethnography 265
vlogs 267

Web 2.0 268
web analytics 269
WikiLeaks 271
Wikipedia 273

YouTube 274

DIGITAL JOURNALISM STUDIES

The Key Concepts

ACTANTS

In a special issue of the journal *Digital Journalism*, focused on reconceptualizing key theoretical changes reflecting the development of **Digital Journalism Studies**, Seth Lewis and Oscar Westlund seek to clarify the role of what they term the "four As" – namely the human actors, non-human technological actants, **audiences** and the involvement of all three groups in the activities of news production (Lewis and Westlund, 2014). Like Primo and Zago, Lewis and Westlund argue that innovations in computational software require scholars of digital journalism to interrogate not simply *who* but *what* is involved in news production and to establish how non-human actants are disrupting established journalism practices (Primo and Zago, 2015: 38).

The examples of technological actants that they offer embrace **algorithms,** networks and content management systems. Their broader concern is to create a research agenda with a "sociotechnical emphasis" which more fully emphasizes the role of technology in news production processes not by downplaying the role of human actors but by foregrounding "technologies and technologists as key aspects of study." Such an emphasis does not imply a technologically determinist view, however, since the technological actants are programmed by human actors who are "socially constructed" to meet journalistic, commercial and technological purposes within news organizations (Lewis and Westlund, 2014.

See also **actor network theory**.

Key Sources
Lewis, S. C. and Westlund, O. 2014 "Actors, Actants, Audiences and Activities in Cross-Media News Work: A Matrix and Research Agenda" *Digital Journalism* 3 (1): 19–37
Primo, A. and Zago, G. 2015 "Who and What Do Journalism?" *Digital Journalism* 3(1): 38–52

ACTOR NETWORK THEORY

Actor Network Theory (ANT) emerged in the 1980s through the work of Bruno Latour (1987). Concerned with examining technological innovation and broader sociotechnical processes, ANT emphasizes the historical context in which scientific innovations emerge and, significantly, it assigns agency to human and non-human actors in networks where non-human agents or **actants** include machines, animals, networks, texts and **algorithms**. Actors and actants are assigned equal agency and integrated into the same conceptual framework. John Law describes ANT as,

> ... a disparate family of material-semiotic tools, sensibilities and methods of analysis that treat everything in the social and natural worlds as a continuously generated effect of the webs of relations within which they are located. It assumes that nothing has reality or form outside the enactment of those relations.
>
> (Law cited in Banks, 2011)

ANT is often counter posed to accounts of scientific development that overemphasize the role of individual human actors while disregarding actants and their network context. Attributing the theory of gravitation to Newton, for example, ignores his social context, his scientific colleagues, his use and reliance on "Euclidean geometry, Kepler's astronomy, Galileo's mechanics, his tools, the details of his lab, cultural factors and environmental restrictions on him" (David, 2007), along with a host of other technical and non-technical elements which ANT would describe and consider closely.

ANT has been "scathingly criticized" for: assigning agency to nonhuman actors; assuming that all actors are equal within the network: being anti-humanist; being managerialist; and representing the powerful while ignoring the impact of race, gender and class (Crawford, 2004).

Key Sources

Banks, D. 2011 "A Brief Summary of Actor Network Theory" *Cyborology* 21st December https://thesocietypages.org/cyborgology/2011/12/02/a-brief-summary-of-actor-network-theory/

David, L. 2007 "Actor-Network Theory (ANT)" *Learning Theories* 23rd March https://www.learning-theories.com/actor-network-theory-ant.html

Latour, B. 1987 *Science in Action: How to Follow Scientists and Engineers through Society*. Cambridge, MA: Harvard University Press

ADVERTISING

Until early in the new millennium, advertising revenues provided the life blood for all commercial media and constituted an essential resource to

ADVERTISING

finance the researching, writing and distribution of news and other editorial content. By offsetting production costs, advertising also reduced the price of access to media for audiences. Across the 20th century, **legacy media** enjoyed expansive advertising revenues to fund their activities; advertising, for example, accounted for an average 80 per cent of local newspapers' revenues and 100 per cent of the burgeoning free **local newspapers** (Franklin, 2006: 8). Advertising constituted the crucial element in the profitability of national, regional and local newspapers, delivering profits of 25–35 per cent on investment; exceptionally high rates of return compared to many other industries (Franklin, 2008: 13).

But developments in digital media technologies disrupted (see **disruption**) this "advertising led" **business model** and created intensely competitive pressures for advertising revenues from news organizations publishing online, news updates on mobile devices, news aggregators such as **Google** News and micro blogging sites such as **Twitter** – and all this in the context of declining circulations and readers, as well as growing concerns with the legitimacy and credibility of news organizations and **fake news** (Chyi, Lewis and Nan, 2012; McNair, 2018; Starr, 2009: 28). These trends have been exacerbated and accelerated by the economic recession beginning in 2007. Pew's *State of the News Media 2013* report optimistically suggested that newspapers' advertising revenues were "stabilizing but still threatened" despite a fall in print advertising for a sixth consecutive year and by a substantial $1.8 billion (8 per cent) in 2013. Measured by revenues, the newspaper industry in the USA has shrunk to 60 per cent of its size a decade ago (Edmonds, Guskin, Mitchell and Jurkowitz, 2013: 8).

Despite this sustained decline in advertising revenues since the emergence of online news media, there seems to be no consensus within the academy or journalism industry about advertising's role in resourcing a viable journalism or the consequences of declining advertising revenues for such a prospect. Picard, for example, celebrates the massively enhanced plurality of revenue sources which have replaced or supplemented advertising as news providers become "less dependent on any one form of funding than they have been for about 150 years" (Picard, 2016: 12–22). These multiple revenue streams include "readers and advertisers, events and e-commerce ... foundations and sponsors, and from related commercial services such as web hosting" (Picard, 2016: 12–22). By contrast, Bakker argues that the much diminished revenues from advertising oblige news organizations to produce cheaper news content using "aggregation, content farms and **Huffinization**" which have given rise to a new "low pay and no-pay journalism" staffed by "part timers and amateurs" (Bakker, 2012: 627).

One unequivocal trend since the decline of media reliance on traditional advertising has been the rapid growth of **native advertising**, although this raises serious journalistic concerns about the proximity, independence and veracity of editorial when the "wall" between advertising and journalistic content collapses so totally (Lynch and Sirrah, 2018).

See also **native advertising**.

Key Sources

Bakker, P. 2012 "Aggregation, Content Farms and Huffinization: The Rise of Low Pay and No-Pay Journalism" *Journalism Practice* 6(5–6): 627–637

Edmonds, R., Guskin, E., Mitchell, A. and Jurkowitz, M. 2013 "Newspapers: Stabilizing but Still Threatened" *The State of the News Media 2013* PEW Research Center's Project for Excellence in Journalism, http://stateofthemedia.org/2013/newspapers-stabilizing-but-still-threatened/

Franklin, B. (Ed) 2008 *Pulling Newspapers Apart: Analysing Print Journalism.* London: Routledge

Lynch, L. and Sirrah, A. 2018 *Native Advertising: Advertorial Disruption in the 21st Century News Feed.* London: Routledge

Picard, R. 2016 "Twilight or New Dawn of Journalism? Evidence from the Changing News Ecosystem" in Franklin, B. (Ed) *The Future of Journalism: In an Age of Digital Media and Economic Uncertainty.* London: Routledge, 12–22

ADVERTORIAL

The word Advertorial is a neologistic hybrid formed from the words "**advertising**" and "editorial." Advertorial is a paid advertisement that is disguised as editorial copy by adopting the house graphic and layout formats. On occasion it may also use a journalistic byline. In this way, advertorial misrepresents the nature of the text and suggests to readers that they are reading a news story or feature researched and written by a **journalist** and therefore constrained and shaped by the journalist's ethical and professional commitments to objectivity, impartiality and truthfulness.

The mutual advantages for both parties are obvious. For the organization, company or individual buying the advertising space, the advertorial, with its allusions to journalistic authorship, confers authority and credibility on the arguments and claims made in the advertisement which advertising copy could not match (Franklin and Murphy, 1998: 245–247). For the newspaper, advertorials enable **editors** to allocate a greater part of the editorial space to advertising copy which, in pre-digital times, generated the majority of many newspapers' revenues and which remain a significant revenue source for digital media. Given the mutual benefits enjoyed by advertisers and media owners/managers, it is perhaps unsurprising that the popularity of advertorials grew rapidly during the 1980s, although they also triggered conflict between the journalistic and advertising sections of the news organization because they seemed to breach the "firewall" which journalists believe should separate advertising from editorial (Carlson, 2014; Eckman and Lindlof, 2003: 66).

More recently, scholars of **journalism studies** have raised objections to the practice of **native advertising**, which similarly blurs the strict division between advertising and objective news reporting (Carlson, 2014; Ferrer Conill, 2016; Lynch, 2018).

Key Sources

Carlson, M. 2014 "When News Sites Go Native: Redefining the Advertising–Editorial Divide in Response to Native Advertising" *Journalism* doi:10.1177/1464884914545441

Eckman, A. and Lindlof, T. 2003 "Negotiating the Gray Lines: An Ethnographic Case Study of Organisational Conflict between Advertorials and News" *Journalism Studies* 4(1): 65–79

Lynch, L. and Sirrah, A. 2018 *Native Advertising: Advertorial Disruption in the 21st Century News Feed*. London: Routledge

AFFORDANCES

The concept of affordances (Hutchby, 2001) has its origins in the conscious attempt to construct a conceptual middle ground between the "rock" of *technological determinism* and the similarly "hard place" of *technological constructivism*. The former views new social relations as a consequence of the emergence of particular forms of technology, while the latter assumes technological artifacts to be entirely socially shaped. To find a way forward, Hutchby defines affordances as the "functional and relational aspects which frame, while not determining, the possibilities for agentic action in relation to an object." Consequently, new technologies become artefacts which are "both shaped by and shaping of the practices humans use" in their interactions with them (Hutchby, 2001: 444). Stripped of the complex language in which this division is expressed, affordances articulate new possibilities for human action which developing technologies provide.

In Graves' application of the concept of affordances to his analysis of **blogging**, he understands them as "the features of a technology that make certain actions possible"; affordances are essentially enabling and facilitating (Graves, 2007: 332).

Graves' exploration and interpretation of blogging does not argue that blogging technologies simply came along and created a new practice of blogging, but that they "facilitated" an activity which was already beginning to take place much "in the same way" as the development of the telephone and telephone usage. Graves' research catalogues the development of blogs from simple web pages to the current software that automatically arranges posts in reverse order. Consequently, blogging emerged at the "intersection of technology and society" where "technology and sociocultural practice evolve together, each feeding back into the other" (Graves, 2007: 343).

The extent and pace at which new technologies are adopted – or alternatively are contested, challenged and rejected – reflect a range of factors including cultural, ideological, social or economic concerns; for example, the extent to which the new technologies promise to promote or threaten to diminish the interests of particular socio-economic communities. Remember the Luddites!

Key Sources
Graves, L. 2007 "The Affordances of Blogging: A Case Study in the Culture of Technological Effects" *Journal of Communication Inquiry* 31(4): 331–346
Hutchby, I. 2001 "Technology, Texts and Affordances" *Sociology* 35(2): 441–456

AGENDA SETTING

Agenda setting has proved to be among the most influential and widely discussed concepts employed by **Journalism Studies** scholars. Maxwell McCombs and Donald Shaw published their initial paper in 1972, drawing on their research study to establish what a hundred undecided voters regarded as the most import issues for the election and how these identified issues were represented in the news media, during the Presidential election in Chapel Hill, North Carolina (McCombs and Shaw, 1972). Their substantive conclusion, which forms the basic premise of agenda setting theory, is that the way in which news media report particular issues influences and helps to shape public perceptions and debate. Some 30 years later and in his own words, McCombs claimed the "principal finding in Chapel Hill" was that "those aspects of public affairs which are prominent in the news become prominent among the public." Moreover, this finding has been "replicated in hundreds of studies worldwide" (McCombs, 2006: 543). Significantly, since these early beginnings, agenda setting has offered a nuanced assessment of media influence that eschewed any propagandist implications. In a classic formulation of agenda setting, the suggestion is that while the media "may not be successful much of the time in telling people what to think ... it is stunningly successful in telling its readers what to think about" (Cohen, 1963: 13).

Online and **digital journalism**, however, generate communication innovations which may disrupt this established theorizing of agenda setting (Bro, 2017; Singer, 2019). McCombs himself poses some of the challenging questions which digital journalism poses for agenda setting theory. The internet, for example, radically changes the communications eco-structure and generates many more diverse and plural sources of news and opinion. Additionally, the emergence of **blogs** and **citizen journalism** provide **audiences** with their own voice in communications networks and McCombs concedes that "there are many agendas in contemporary society and many more of these are now readily available to a large segment of the public" (McCombs, 2006: 545).

Consequently, some scholars of **Digital Journalism Studies** predict a diminished significance for agenda setting as audiences increasingly fragment and confront "a unique external media agenda that is a highly individualized composite constructed from this vast wealth of online **news** and information" resulting in a public agenda characterized by "considerable diversity and the scattering of public attention" (McCombs, 2006: 545). Bro (2017), for example, confirms that "in an era with an abundance of news media, news material and news providers ... it is increasingly difficult for news organisations to set the agenda outside newsrooms" (Bro, 2017: 78). Similarly, Meraz's study of political blogs reveals that the agenda setting potential of legacy media has reduced to become "just one force among many competing influences" (Meraz, 2009: 701). Significant in this latter respect is the overwhelming influence of **social media** in agenda setting public discussion.

Key Sources

Bro, P. 2017 "Gatekeeping and Agenda Setting: Extinct or Extant in a Digital Era?" in Franklin, B. and Eldridge, II, S. (Eds) *The Routledge Companion to Digital Journalism Studies*. London: Routledge, 75–84

Cohen, B. C. 1963 *The Press and Foreign Policy Princeton*. NJ: Princeton University Press

McCombs, M. 2006 "A Look At Agenda Setting: Past, Present and Future" *Journalism Studies* 6(4): 543–557

Meraz, S. 2009 "Is There an Elite Hold? Traditional Media to Social Media Agenda Setting Influences in Blog Networking" *Journal of Computer-Mediated Communication* 14(3): 682–707

Singer, J. 2019 "Theorizing Digital Journalism: The Limits of Linearity and the Rise of Relationships" in Eldridge, II, S. and Franklin, B.. (Eds) *The Routledge Handbook of Developments in Digital Journalism Studies*. London: Routledge, 487–500

AGGREGATORS

The curation and gathering of **news** and other content has always been a central task for **journalism**. Under the direction of the news **editor**, following a tip from a **source** or perhaps after reading a story in a rival paper, a **journalist** would leave the office "to get a story." This might involve interviewing a source at the town hall or police station, attending a session at a local law court, interviewing a witness to a newsworthy event, or all of these news gathering activities. Returning to the newsroom, the journalist would write the story for the next issue or bulletin of the news organization. This is one way to gather news but it is costly in terms of time, resources and the journalist's salary.

News organizations such as **Google** News, however, use **algorithms** to systematically scan online news organizations and **blogs** to deliver news and news updates and make them available at a single dedicated online location. Definitions, however, have "never been blurrier" (Friedman, 2014). Decisions about which **sources** of news to scan and represent on a dedicated site were initially made by editors (i.e., human actors) but such decisions are increasingly made by non-human **actants** (i.e., algorithms).

This is a very different form of news aggregation which is much faster, capable of drawing together news from a much wider range of news sources than a journalist could consult and which involves effectively no paid human labour costs measured by wages. In this sense aggregators *gather* news but they do not *originate* news stories. Journalists write stories and aggregators gather them into a single online space where they can be read and consulted without charge. It is easy to see why news aggregators have created such financial difficulties for **legacy media** (Bakker, 2012). Legislators in some countries have considered enacting laws to oblige aggregators such as Google News to compensate the original publishers when aggregators repurpose and republish stories (Friedman, 2014). It is, moreover, not clear whether the monetizing of content by aggregating news deriving from multiple online sources and representing it in distinctive ways on a single site is legal (Isbell, 2010).

See also **Google**.

Key Sources

Bakker, P. 2012 "Aggregation, Content Farms and Huffinization: The Rise of Low Pay and No-Pay Journalism" *Journalism Practice* 6(5–6): 627–637, doi:10.1080/17512786.2012.667266

Friedman, A. 2014 "We're All Aggregators Now: So We Should be Ethical about It" *Columbia Journalism Review*, 23rd May https://archives.cjr.org/realtalk/rules_for_ethical_aggregators.php

ALGORITHMIC JOURNALISM

Technological change has always triggered consequences for **journalism** and the activities of **journalists** (Mari, 2017; Pavlik, 2000). But recent developments in computer software, especially **algorithms** and natural language generation (NLG) – which automatically produces human (natural) language from a computational representation of information – have increasingly supplanted many of the day-to-day tasks of journalists (Dorr, 2016). Algorithms are increasingly automating the researching, editing, aggregating, writing and distribution of news and other content, especially sport and financial news, weather reports and even investigative reporting (Broussard, 2014). The financial gains, including the savings on journalists' salaries, deliver the motive for this increasing use of what has variously been dubbed "machine written news" (Van Dalen, 2013), **"robot journalism"** (Clerwall, 2014), and "algorithmic journalism" (Dorr, 2016).

When Van Dalen conducted focus groups with sports journalists using copies of machine written news as stimulus materials, the journalists were able to distinguish the algorithmic written content from the copy written by journalists but they acknowledged that the algorithmic copy was well written, presented a good deal of factual information and, in some cases, was superior to copy written by journalists. The sports journalists suggested this last outcome was explained by sports journalism's high reliance on **churnalism** and the use of **news subsidies** as sources of copy in the sports journalism field (Van Dalen).

Key Sources
Clerwall, C. 2014 "Enter the Robot Journalist: Users' Perceptions of Automated Content" *Journalism Practice* 8(5): 519–531
Dorr, K. N. 2016 "Mapping the Field of Algorithmic Journalism" *Digital Journalism* 4(6): 700–722
Dorr, K. N. and Hollnbrucher, K. 2017 "Ethical Challenges to Algorithmic Journalism" *Digital Journalism* 5(4): 404–419
Van Dalen, A. 2013 "The Algorithms Behind the Headlines: How Machine-Written News Redefines the Core Skills of Human Journalists" in Franklin, B. (Ed) *The Future of Journalism: Development and Debates*. London: Routledge, 144–154

ALGORITHMS

An algorithm is a detailed, sequential, step-by-step set of instructions for completing a task or solving a problem. In this sense, algorithms are more commonplace than might be imagined and are routinely used as guides to the various stages involved in completing everyday tasks. A recipe in a cookbook, for example, identifies the necessary ingredients and details in a very specific order the instructions required to complete the baking of your favorite cake successfully.

The Tynker blog (Tynker, 2018) offers a simple example and an ordered algorithmic listing of sequential tasks necessary for children to complete their daily morning routine:

When alarm rings:

Switch off alarm or hit snooze button;
If latter, when alarm rings again, switch off or hit snooze button;
Get up;

Shower;
Get dressed;
Eat breakfast;
If sunny walk to school
If raining go on the bus or ask parent for a lift.

The type of algorithms used with computers for the completion of various tasks in digital or **algorithmic journalism** – such as making calculations, interrogating large data sets, automated reasoning and then, with the assistance of natural language programming, writing news and other content – can still be understood by the simple definition above, but the instructions used to guide the computer are infinitely more complex and to instruct the computer, programmers write them in computing code (Dorr, 2016; Linden, 2019).

The efficiency, speed and accuracy with which these algorithms (**actants**) are able to accomplish operations or problem solving, compared to human actors, along with their relative cheapness compared to journalists' salaries, is striking and explains their growing use in digital journalism not only to write news stories, but to identify which types of news content appeal to particular categories of readers. Carlson observes that automated **journalism** has become "algorithmic processes that convert data into narrative news texts with limited to no human intervention beyond the initial programming" (Carlson, 2015: 417).

But Linden advises that **journalists** should not necessarily assume an attitude of "technology panic" because of the growing role of algorithms in journalistic **news** writing since they

> are already surrounded by algorithms taking care of everything from web searches to photo and text editing, mostly using them unconsciously and seamlessly. [Removing] … these items of software would reveal the extent to which journalists and **editors** are already dependent on automated decision systems.
>
> (Linden, 2019: 240)

But Linden suggests that humans and algorithms remain closely connected since human intentions are deeply embedded into algorithms informing their choices and decisions. In this way, "algorithms … are neither entirely material nor entirely human – they are hybrid" (Linden, 2019: 240).

Key Sources

Carlson, M. 2015 "The Robotic Reporter: Automated Journalism and the Redefinition of Labor, Compositional Forms, and Journalistic Authority" *Digital Journalism* 3(3): 416–431

Dorr, K. N. 2016 "Mapping the Field of Algorithmic Journalism" *Digital Journalism* 4(6): 700–722

Linden, C.-G. 2019 "Algorithms Are a Reporter's New Best Friend: News Automation and the Case for the Augmentation of News" in Eldridge, II, S. and Franklin, B. (Eds) *The Routledge Handbook of Developments in Digital Journalism Studies*. London: Routledge, 237–250

Tynker 2018 "How to explain Algorithms to Kids" https://www.tynker.com/blog/articles/ideas-and-tips/how-to-explain-algorithms-to-kids/

ALTERNATIVE JOURNALISM

In the UK setting, **alternative journalism** flourished briefly during the 1970s nourished by a diet of radical and community politics but died towards the end of the 1980s on the "iron rations" of Thatcherism (Harcup, 2013: 32). Early researchers of the local alternative press suggested that "perhaps more poignantly than any other aspect of the **local media**" the demise of the alternative press illustrated "the power of the market in marginalising ideological debate" (Franklin and Murphy, 1991: 26). Alternative journalism and alternative media always proved elusive to definition, partly reflecting the wide range of their editorial concerns – community matters, politics, feminism, gay rights, football fanzines, cultural and literary subjects as well as protest issues around ecology and racial politics – but also because they were not defined in terms of their direct concerns but in polar opposition to "mainstream" journalism (Atton, 2002; Harcup, 2003, 2013).

Contra mainstream journalism, alternative journalism has always pursued an alternative **news** agenda, used and cited distinctive news **sources**, sought out different **audiences**, organized editorial production in a more democratic and inclusive way, adopted a distinctive **business model** and assumed a critical editorial posture to authority and established political structures. In aggregate, these features of the alternative press identified a distinctive notion of news and journalistic working (Atton and Hamilton, 2008).

With great prescience, at the time of the apparent collapse of alternative journalism of the 1970s and 1980s, Harcup highlighted the "discernible irony" that the "demise of these newspapers coincided with the arrival of computers and desktop publishing technology which might have made their production cheaper, quicker and less labour intensive" (Harcup, 1998: 115). But while the revolution in digital journalism has not encouraged a resurgence in alternative journalism as understood during its initial iteration, the arrival of low cost and global distribution of online news via the web, the emergence of **citizen journalism** and opportunities for more plural voices in both the sourcing and drafting of news stories, the emergence of **blogs** and even **live blogging**, along with the growth of **social media** as sources of news for journalists (professional and citizen), all attest to the presence of alternative voices in public debate to a degree which was previously inconceivable. Moreover, Harcup's 2015 study of *The Leeds Citizen*, an alternative blog organized and written by a single retired journalist, illustrates the effectiveness of alternative journalism and monitorial citizenship in criticizing local decision makers and the local policy process, while establishing a distinctive relationship with local audiences (Harcup, 2016).

Key Sources
Atton, C. and Hamilton, J. F. 2008 *Alternative Journalism*. London: Sage
Harcup, T. 2013 *Alternative Journalism, Alternative Voices*. London: Routledge
Harcup, T. 2016 "Alternative Journalism as Monitorial Citizenship? A Case Study of a Local News Blog" *Digital Journalism* 4(5): 639–657

AMAZON

Amazon is a global success story. A pioneer of internet shopping which launched as an online "book shop" in July 1994 and rapidly morphed into a "general store" selling everything from DVDs to washing machines, drum kits, computing hardware and services and, more recently, foodstuffs. As the Amazon logo signals, with its arrow which travels from left to right from the first to the fourth letter, Amazon sells everything from A to Z. Significantly, Amazon web services control 45 per cent of the world's Cloud Computing capacity and it is currently the largest internet based retailer measured by revenue (Neate, 2018). Amazon was worth $740 billion and in 2018 the company announced that sales increased by 40 per cent, or $50 billion, in the first three months of the year (Neate, 2018). This company success has made its founder and owner Jeff Bezos extremely wealthy. Indeed, in April 2018, Forbes magazine announced that his $100 billion fortune made him the wealthiest person in the world and the world's first "centibillionaire" (Forbes, 2018). On 3rd September 2018, following a two percent rise in values the previous day, Amazon joined Apple as the second company to be valued by Wall Street at $1tn (Davies and Rushe, 2018).

While all this may be interesting, it was not clear how germane this business success might be for developments in **Digital Journalism Studies** until October 2013 when Bezos purchased the *Washington Post* for $250 million, ending 80 years of continuous ownership by the Graham family dynasty (Haughney, 2013). The *Post* was suffering from the financial difficulties that plagued many of even the largest **legacy media**. Bezos acknowledged his lack of **journalism** experience, but argued that understanding the internet was more important and set about reinventing the paper as a "media and technology company" (Kim, 2016). The *Post* has subsequently redesigned its website and mobile Apps and created software which delivers superior analytics and marketing features for the *Post* (Gutsche and Hess, 2019). In October 2015, the *Washington Post* surpassed *The New York Times* for US unique web visitors.

At the time of purchase, some *Washington Post* **journalists** publicly expressed doubts about the impact of the sale to Bezos on the quality, range and independence of editorial content. Competitor and rival *The New York Times* described the sale as a "shock," suggesting that "one of the crown jewels of newspapers [had been] surrendered by one of the industries' royal families." The enhanced market success of the *Washington Post*, driven by the employment of digital marketing techniques is, however, beyond doubt.

Key Sources

Davies, R. and Rushe, D. 2018 "World's Richest Man Delivers Amazon to $1tn Mark" *Guardian*, 5th September, 27

Forbes 2018 "Profile; Jeff Bezos" https://www.forbes.com/profile/jeff-bezos/

Gutsche, R. E. and Hess, K. 2019 *Geographies of Journalism: The Imaginative Power of Place in Making Digital News*. London: Routledge

Neate, R. 2018 "'Too Much Power in the Hands of Too Few': The Rise and Rise of a Retail Behemoth" *Guardian*, 25th April, 8–11

AMBIENT NEWS

The phrase "ambient news" was first used by Ian Hargreaves in *Journalism: Truth or Dare* (2003) to suggest that the emergence of digital media technologies in tandem with the growing economic, social political and cultural value of information, have made **news** more accessible to **audiences** to the point where it is omnipresent or ambient. News which was previously difficult and/or costly to obtain, "today surrounds us like the air we breathe." And indeed, "much of it is literally ambient: displayed on computers, public billboards, trains, aircraft and mobile phones" (Hargreaves, 2003: 3).

The emergence of **social media** platforms, especially **Twitter** since 2006, have led scholars such as Hermida (2010, 2013) and Bruns (2010) use the term "ambient journalism" to refer to the constant stream of tweets which represent a fragmented "mix of news, information and comments, usually connected to current reality, but without an established order" (Hermida, 2012). This new "para-journalism form" to which everyone can contribute is distinguished by the immediacy of access it offers and its use of official and unofficial **sources** of news. "These broad, asynchronous, light weight and always-on communication systems" Hermida claims "are creating new kinds of interactions around the news, and are enabling citizens to maintain a mental model of news and events around them, giving rise to ... ambient journalism" (Hermida, 2010: 298)

Key Sources

Bruns, A. 2010 "Oblique Strategies for Ambient Journalism" *M/C Journal* 13(2) http://journal.media-culture.org.au/index.php/mcjournal/article/viewArticle/230

Hargreaves, I. 2003 *Journalism, Truth or Dare?* Oxford: Oxford University Press

Hermida, A. 2010 "Twittering the News: The Emergence of Ambient Journalism" *Journalism Practice* 4(3): 297–308

Hermida, A. 2013 "#Journalism: Reconfiguring Journalism Research about Twitter, One Tweet at a Time" *Digital Journalism* 1(3): 295–313

APPLICATION PROGRAMMING INTERFACE (API)

API is the common acronym for Application Programming Interface, which is a type of software that allows two applications to communicate with one another. In the broadest of terms, an API enables users to access data on the internet via an application. It is a set of functions and procedures that allows an application to connect to the internet and send data to a server. The server then retrieves that data, interprets it and sends it back to the phone, **tablet** or computer to present it in a readable manner (MuleSoft, 2018).

Most large digital companies have built APIs for their customers and many of them are open source so they can be developed and adapted into third party apps. **Twitter** provides free API software that enables the online community to develop its own Twitter tools, which has led to a whole host of associated applications starting with Twitterrific in January 2007, followed by HootSuite, TweetDeck and Twitterfall. Twitter's API consists of two different parts: Search API and REST API. REST API enables Twitter developers to access the core Twitter data including **tweets**, timelines, and user data. Search API enables the developer to query the tweets and provides information about trending topics (Dermidas, Ali Bayir, Akcora, Yilmaz and Ferhatosmanoglu, 2010). Developers have created external apps to use API to access data on Twitter's operating system that is then sent back to the app and presented in the desired format, such as a list of selected key terms or hashtags. Journalists are able to use these third party tools to search, gather, curate, produce and disseminate tweets (Hermida, 2013). These API enabled tools allow journalists to quickly spot trends and source **user-generated content** from specific places using geolocation without having to scroll through millions of live posts. These applications interact with multiple social media channels but Twitter remains the most popular platform, having become an essential part of the digital journalist's everyday toolkit (Cision, 2013).

This access to a stream of data made available via APIs has been leapt upon by academic researchers (Boyd, 2013) who have been quick to recognize the value in studying Twitter data to "gain a better understanding of its users, uses, and impacts on society and culture from a variety of perspectives" (Zimmer and Proferes, 2014: 251). An analysis of 351 Twitter-based academic research studies found that the majority relied on various Twitter APIs to retain research data, including popular sites TwapperKeeper and 140kit. A change in

Twitter's API terms of service in 2011 limited researchers' access to Twitter data and shut down these two sites, but in their place emerged new online aggregation tools to capture Twitter research data – allowed under Twitter's new policies. These included qualitative data analysis software NVivo, which released a plugin in 2012 allowing researchers the ability to automatically capture and analyze Twitter data (Zimmer and Proferes, 2014).

Recognizing the significance of Twitter in cultural research, the American Library of Congress announced in 2010 that every public tweet ever published since Twitter's inception in March 2006 would be archived digitally. This was continued until the beginning of 2018 when it shifted to archiving tweets on a selective basis. In doing so, the library has been able to secure a tweet text documenting the first 12 years of Twitter, in particular its "emergence, applications and evolution" (Osterberg, 2017).

Key Sources

Cision 2013 "Social Journalism Study" http://www.cision.com/us/2013/12/how-journalists-view-pr-and-social-media/

Dermidas, M., Ali Bayir, M., Akcora, C., Yilmaz, Y. and Ferhatosmanoglu, H. 2010 "Crowd-sourced Sensing and Collaboration Using Twitter" IEEE International Symposium on A World of Wireless, Mobile and Multimedia Networks Montreal, QC, 2010, 1–9

MuleSoft 2018 "What Is an API?" https://www.mulesoft.com/resources/api/what-is-an-api

APPS *SEE* SMARTPHONES; TABLET

ARTIFICIAL INTELLIGENCE (AI)

The catch-all term for the use of machines to mimic cognitive human functions such as learning and problem solving. Computers that can survey and gather data within a particular environment, taking action to maximize the chance of successfully achieving a goal, are said to be acting as intelligent agents. Within the context of digital journalism, artificial intelligence (or AI), is realized via **automated content, newsbots** and **robot journalism**. News organizations use intelligent tools for a range of tasks previously conducted by staff. AI can be used to automate mundane tasks, such as Reuter's News Tracer, which tracks down breaking news, giving journalists more time for investigation with less needed for grunt work. Intelligent software can also be used to correlate information quickly and efficiently, such as the *Washington Post*'s Knowledge Map, or to crunch data fast, as shown by *The New York Times* Research and Development Lab's editor application. Machines can even use **algorithms** to automatically generate reports and stories from raw data, such as the quarterly corporate earnings reports from the Associated Press (Galily, 2018).

In the future, publications may replace people with augmented software to carry out simple fact-finding or checking tasks and it is highly likely that journalists will see further encroachment of AI into the **newsroom** to save companies both time and money. There is still debate over how much human input is required in the production of journalism, with some analysts arguing that narratives are difficult to program and trusted journalists are needed to understand and write meaningful stories (Rizzo, 2018). A 2018 report from PricewaterhouseCoopers claimed that AI could potentially create as many jobs as it destroys, but this does not mean that those who lose their jobs will be equipped to take on the new technological positions.

Economist and Nobel Prize winner Joseph Stiglitz warns that although AI has the potential to increase the productivity of the economy and make everybody better off, this will only happen if it is well managed (Sample, 2018). And while AI can be used to deliver a more personalized service, it is also used against consumers in the collection of their data for marketing and advertising purposes.

Key Sources

Galily, Y. 2018 "Artificial Intelligence and Sports Journalism: Is It a Sweeping Change?" *Technology in Society* 54: 47–51

Rizzo, A. 2018 "3 Facts You Need to Know about Artificial Intelligence in Journalism" *Reuters* https://agency.reuters.com/en/insights/articles/articles-archive/3-facts-you-need-to-know-about-Artificial-Intelligence-in-journalism.html

Sample, I. 2018 "Joseph Stiglitz on Artificial Intelligence: 'We're Going towards a More Divided Society'" *Guardian* www.theguardian.com/technology/2018/sep/08/joseph-stiglitz-on-artificial-intelligence-were-going-towards-a-more-divided-society

AUDIENCES

Developments in digital media technologies and the emergence of **Digital journalism** have generated far reaching consequences for the audience for **news** journalism, which require a radically revised conception of the role of audiences in news making, alongside the highly varied and expansive ways in which scholars of **Digital Journalism Studies** have conceptualized peoples' relationship and engagement with news (Anderson, 2011a, 2011b; Groot Kormelink and Costera Meijer, 2016; Schroeder, 2014).

The **affordances** of digital media technologies, for example, triggered a radical redistribution of media-based communicative power that had previously been exercised (largely) in monopoly by **journalists, editors** and other professional news workers employed in mainstream and **legacy media. Web 2.0** technology, **social media**, as well as the mobility and computing facilities of **smartphones**, empowered individual citizens to metamorphose from merely passive recipients (readers, listeners and viewers) of news to more active roles (Gillmor, 2004) which encouraged writing comments (often critical) to online threads about the editorial work of professional journalists (Ksiazek and Springer, 2019), curating and publishing their own blog(s) (Bruns, 2008), contributing to – or even launching – a hyperlocal or community newspaper (Harte, Howell and Williams, 2018), or even writing and publishing work as **citizen journalists** in legacy media alongside the work of professional journalists.

These various forms of more active audience engagement with news media prompted journalism academic Jay Rosen to coin his now celebrated phrase concerning **"the people formerly known as the audience"** (Rosen, 2006). Other scholars neologized distinctive words or phrases to capture this new relationship between audiences and digital media. Axel Bruns, for example, preferred his word **"produsage"** to identify the shifting roles of those who previously either "produced" or "used" or consumed the news (Bruns, 2008), while the title of Dan Gillmor's book *We The Media* made his view of the enhanced role for the public in news making unequivocal (Gillmor, 2004).

Like Bruns, Gillmor and Rosen, most scholars, news workers and members of the public believed that the old broadcast model of communications which invested the role of news writing and transmission solely in the journalist – the "one to many" relationship between journalists and audiences – had been superseded by the digital communication address of "many to many." Audiences were no longer excluded from journalism or consigned to the passive roles of reading the news and, of course, paying for its production.

It is not only audiences' contribution to the sourcing and writing of news which has changed in the age of digital journalism, but also the ways in which users engage with, respond to, and consume media. In their significant paper published in *Digital Journalism* (2015), Irene Costera Meijer and Tim Groot Kormelink analysed findings from quantitative and qualitative research studies of audiences across the decade between 2004 and 2014 using a "synthesizing analysis" to "gain a better understanding of peoples' changing news consumption and to broaden and deepen the existing professional and academic vocabulary about news use" (Costera Meijer and Groot Kormelink, 2015: 675).

They identified 16 distinctive styles of engagement with media and described each of them by using a verb (for example, reading, sharing or liking), not least because this is how the people involved in their research understood their engagement with news media: as an activity rather than anything passive. These styles of engagement include: "Reading, watching, viewing, listening, checking, snacking, monitoring, scanning, searching, clicking, linking, sharing, liking, recommending, commenting and voting" (op cit: 666).

"Reading" involves more than simply the activity of reading newspapers, magazines or websites. Reading journalism involves more than "knowing" what happened and involves "understanding" what the event is about. Reading is about depth and requires time. They also suggest that the digitization of journalism has led to a decline in reading (Costera Meijer and Groot Kormelink, 2015: 667). "Watching" is "a fairly intense activity" and watching the news requires people to be attentive and to watch without interruption, although digital media technology makes it possible to stop the programme or bulletin and return to it later. "Viewing," however, is characterized by a more "laid back" style of watching, a second order activity undertaken when the viewer is cooking or mending socks and peering up only occasionally (op cit: 668). "Listening" was mostly overlooked by research respondents and featured as a lesser activity perhaps as part of the activity of driving a car (op cit: 668–669).

"Checking" in the news setting is a "habitual activity" rather like checking **email**; it involves finding out whether anything interesting has happened since the last check, while "snacking" is "geared towards getting a basic overview of the day's events." Research respondents claimed it was like a tapas meal involving choosing between a range of news options. "Scanning" eschews getting an overall picture of the day's events in favor of seeing whether there are new developments in the unravelling of a particular story (op cit: 670–671). "Monitoring" reminds one of Michael Schudson's suggestion that for democracy to work it might be sufficient for citizens to monitor and keep a watchful eye on the news for possible dangers rather than being fully informed, while "searching" involves finding answers to particular queries ranging from policy issues to personal matters. "Clicking" is the practice of "hitting news items or links for more information" with crime, sports news and entertainment achieving the highest "clicks" (op cit: 672–673).

Finally, "linking" (copying and pasting the URL of a news story), "sharing" (clicking on Share), "recommending" (clicking on recommend), "commenting" (posting comments to online threads), and "voting" (in response to an online news poll) are distinctive activities but respondents offered similar reasons for engaging (or not) in them; often they did not use them frequently if they did not wish to appear too often on social media. Engaging in these activities is driven less by what respondents wished to do than the anticipated response of others if they did (op cit: 674).

See also **the people formerly known as the audience**.

Key Sources

Anderson, C. W. 2011a "Deliberative, Agonistic and Algorithmic Audiences: Journalism's Vision of Its Public in an Age of Audience Transparency" *International Journal of Communication* 5: 529–547

Gillmor, D. 2004 *We the Media: Grassroots Journalism By the People, For the People.* Sebastopol: O'Reilly Media

Groot Kormelink, T. and Costera Meijer, I. 2016 "Tailor Made News: Meeting the Demands of News Users on Mobile and Social Media" in Franklin, B.. (Ed) *The Future of Journalism in an Age of Digital Media and Economic Uncertainty.* London: Routledge, 296–305

Ksiazek, T. and Springer, N. 2019 "User Comment in Digital Journalism: Current Research and Future Directions" in Eldridge, S. and Franklin, B. (Eds) *The Routledge Handbook of Developments in Digital Journalism Studies.* London: Routledge, 475–487

Rosen, J. 2006 The People Formerly Known as the Audience PRESSthink, 27th June http://archive.pressthink.org/2006/06/27/ppl_frmr.html

AUDIENCES: CREATIVE AND QUANTIFIED

In his highly influential article, "Between creative and quantified audiences: Web metrics and changing patterns of newswork in local US newsrooms," Chris Anderson argues that the advent of **digital journalism** technologies and **Digital Journalism Studies** have created distinctive but paradoxical ways of understanding the essential character of the **audience** for **news**; Anderson terms it a "provocative tension" in "journalistic visions of the audience" (Anderson, 2011a: 505).

On the one hand, the interactive **affordances** of digital journalism technologies have empowered news users and have significantly enhanced their active and participative role in generating and co-creating news; they can no longer simply be characterized or even marginalized as **"The people formerly known as the audience"** (Rosen, 2006). For Anderson, audiences are "productive and generative" (Anderson, 2011a).

On the other hand, the ability of web metrics to deliver concise, precise and detailed descriptions of the audience facilitates and promotes a very different characterization of the audience as a highly quantified and passive entity; a "largely consumptive aggregate" (Anderson, 2011a: 550). Anderson concludes that this more active and participative view of the audience increases **journalists'** reliance on audience metrics to help inform their own perceptions about **news values** and news judgments more generally.

Key Sources
Anderson, C. W. 2011 "Between Creative and Quantified Audiences: Web Metrics and Changing Patterns of Newswork in Local US Newsrooms" *Journalism* 12(5): 550–566
Rosen, J. 2006 The People formerly Known as the Audience PRESSthink, 27th June http://archive.pressthink.org/2006/06/27/ppl_frmr.html

AUDIENCE REPERTOIRES

Uwe Hasebrink's discussion of **audiences** and media repertoires begins with a seemingly obvious point: media audiences cannot be considered as "a concrete and quantifiable group in the way that is possible for the audience in a theatre or cinema." They simply cannot be measured in that quantitative manner. While the media industries and advertisers have long since constructed a model of audiences which identifies them as primarily "countable and tradeable commodities," the reality of audiences' diverse, cross media and individualistic needs for information, undermines this "media-centred approach." Analysis of audiences' uses of **news** media is more complex (Hasebrink, 2017: 364–365; see also Hasebrink and Domeyer, 2012; Schroeder, 2014).

The development of convergent digital media, moreover, has exacerbated this inherent complexity in perhaps predictable ways. Hasebrink uses the data set in the *Reuters' Institute Digital News Survey 2015* (Newman, Levy and Nielsen, 2015) to illustrate audiences' expansive use of **social media** as **sources** of **news**, the explosive growth in the use of **smartphones** and **tablets** for accessing news, as well as audiences' tendency to reject trusted news brands, whether a particular radio bulletin or newspaper, in favor of **email** alerts, news **aggregator** sites, notifications from **app**s, search engines and, of course, social media to discover news. (Hasebrink, 2017: 366). A survey-based study of news consumption across multiple media platforms in three highly developed media markets in China confirmed these shifting patterns of media use (Yuan, 2011).

Hasebrink has challenged this "media centred" approach to audiences because it focuses "on describing the audiences uses of particular media based on the size and composition of the audiences they reach" (Hasebrink, 2017: 365). He advocates an approach based on media repertoires that offer a "more holistic approach to information oriented practice" (op cit: 368). A person's media repertoire comprises "the entirety of the media" they use routinely and consequently includes "the relatively stable cross-media patterns of media use" (op cit: 368).

In an earlier work, Hasebrink and Domeyer (2012) suggest that the concept of media repertoires was intended to overcome two difficulties plaguing research on media use. First, it emphasizes that individual's engagement with media involves a range of media and argues that how these distinctive elements interrelate is central to understanding individual media uses. Second, it involves a conceptual framework that allows the incorporation of both quantitative and qualitative data, thereby bridging the divide between the more general findings offered by quantitative work on media use and qualitative research delivering subjective insights into particular engagements with media (Hasebrink, 2017: 368; Hasebrink and Domeyer, 2012: 757).

The repertoire approach also identifies four levels of information needs that shape individuals' media repertoires: needs for concrete problem solving, group related needs, thematic interests, and undirected information needs (Hasebrink, 2017: 370). *Undirected information* needs reflect an individual's ambition to stay informed about any relevant public agenda, while *thematic interests* trigger people to look for specific information media exploring their particular interests. *Group related needs* reflect what an individual's particular reference group think about particular topics, while *problem oriented needs* specify particular information needed to resolve specific problems. Hasebrink concludes that the objective of the repertoire approach is significant since it aims to provide nothing less than, "a simple analytical tool that helps describe and understand transforming communication practices within the digital environment" (op cit: 373).

Key Sources

Hasebrink, U. 2017 "Audiences and Information Repertoires" in Franklin, B. and Eldridge, II, S. (Eds) *The Routledge Companion to Digital Journalism Studies.* London: Routledge, 364–374

Hasebrink, U. and Domeyer, H. 2012 "Media Repertoires as Patterns of Behaviour and as Meaningful Practices: A Multimethod Approach to Media Use in Converging Environments" *Participations: Journal of Audience and Reception Studies* 9(2): 757–783

Newman, N., Levy, D. A. and Nielsen, R. K. 2015 *Reuters Institute Digital News Report 2015: Tracking the Future of News.* Oxford, UK: Reuters Institute for the Study of Journalism

Schroeder, K. 2014 "News Media Old and New: Fluctuating Audiences, News Repertoires and Locations of Consumption" *Journalism Studies* 18(11): 1343–1362, doi:10.1080/1461670X.2014.890332

Yuan, E. 2011 "News Consumption across Multiple Media Platforms: A Repertoire Approach" *Information, Communication and Society* 14(7): 998–1016

AUTOMATED CONTENT

Automated content is one of a growing number of synonyms for editorial content which is produced without any human involvement or agency in the actual writing of the content: such synonyms include automated writing (Carlson, 2014b), robo-journalism (Clerwall, 2014), automated journalism (Casswell and Dorr, 2018: Thurman, Dorr and

Kunert, 2017) and "machine written news" (Van Dalen, 2013). These new forms of journalism are reliant upon the involvement of **actants**, including **algorithms**, which operate in tandem with natural language programmes (NLPs) with instructions to interrogate substantive data sets in specified ways in order to produce text for publication (Casswell and Dorr, 2018; Thurman, Dorr and Kunert, 2017).

Critics suggest that automated content in journalism simply extends the idea and practices of "churnalism" to their logical conclusion in a digital age, while advocates argue that the automated writing of editorial content liberates journalists from the routine reporting of non-contentious issues, enabling them to focus on more important journalistic concerns which may arise within the investigative journalism beat. Broussard has even designed an algorithm which searches for, and generates, a list of potential issues for local journalists to consider, investigate and report (Broussard, 2014).

Key Sources

Casswell, D. and Dorr, K. 2018 "Automated Journalism 2.0: Events Driven Narrative: From Simple Descriptions to Real Stories" *Journalism Practice* 12 (4): 477–496

Clerwall, C. 2014 "Enter the Robot Journalist: Users' Perceptions of Automated Content" *Journalism Practice* 8(5): 519–531

Thurman, N., Dorr, K. and Kunert, J. 2017 "When Reporters Get Hands-On with Robo Writing: Professionals Consider Automated Journalism's Capabilities and Consequences" *Digital Journalism* 5(10): 1240–1259

Van Dalen, A. 2013 "The Algorithms Behind the Headlines: How Machine-Written News Redefines the Core Skills of Human Journalists" in Franklin, B. (Ed) *The Future of Journalism: Development and Debates*. London: Routledge, 144–154

AUTOMATED CONTENT ANALYSIS

The development of digital media technologies has resulted in far-reaching changes in all aspects of the professional practices of **journalism**, the journalistic products resulting from this professional work and ultimately in **Digital Journalism Studies**, the academic and scholarly field of inquiry that critically addresses these professional changes. The consequences for the academic study of journalism have involved revisions of its dominant research agendas (Franklin, 2016), the need to reconsider the basic concepts and theoretical frameworks informing analysis (Steensen and Ahva, 2015b), as well as a reappraisal of existing approaches to research design and (where necessary) to develop new methods to explore journalism in an age of digital media (Karlsson and Sjøvaag, 2016a; Karlsson and Strömbäck, 2010).

Ahead of the digital revolution in journalism, content analysis proved a remarkably useful and popular element in the research designs of journalism scholars trying to systematically explore the salient features of news related texts in **legacy media**, as well as other consistencies or divergences in patterns of editorial content, sometimes in comparative settings across time and space. In the 1950s, Berelson offered what has proved to be the classic definition of this research method, specifying that "content analysis is a research technique for the objective, systematic and quantitative description of the manifest content of communication" (Berelson, 1952: 263), although journalism scholars have long since come to recognize the utility and nuanced exploration of content offered by qualitative approaches (Brennen, 2013).

Examples of content analysis abound in the scholarly literature. Across the 1970s, for example, the Glasgow Media Group became closely associated with this approach to research design. The Group published a series of studies of *Bad News*, using the technique to identify a systematic skew in news coverage of the economy and industrial relations which favored the interests of the owners and managers of industry against those of workers, especially when they engaged in industrial action. Later book titles – *More Bad News* and *Really Bad News* – reporting follow-up research studies based on content analysis offered similar findings (Eldridge, 2000). Content analysis has remained a widely deployed, centrally significant and analytically useful research technique for studies of journalism.

But the emergence of digital and **online journalism** in the new millennium has prompted novel methodological problems but also further opportunities for content analysis. Three particular problems required resolution. First, journalism in the online setting was no longer constrained by the limitations of space inherent in print journalism and consequently the number of news stories for analysis in research studies grew apace. Content analysis had always been labor intensive, required considerable training of researchers to guarantee reliable coding of data, making research studies lengthy and costly, which, in turn, imposed limitations on sample sizes and, therefore, the kinds of questions which researchers could address (Flaounas, Omar,

Lansdall-Welfare, De Bie, Mosdell and Lewis, 2013: 102). A study by Len-Rios, Rodgers, Thorson and Yoon (2006), for example, required three research assistants to code articles from only 42 issues of two newspapers.

Second, online **news** stories proved more ephemeral and increasingly "liquid" because of their "ability to mutate and sometimes disappear" (Zamith, 2019). Online news is constantly changing via updates that may begin within minutes of the journalist uploading the initial version of the story. Worse, the revised update of the story may leave no observable trace of its earlier iteration, which can be lost as drafts "begin to bleed into each other" (Zamith, 2019: 95–97).

Third, it is not only the liquid and ephemeral nature of the content of particular news stories which makes content analysis problematic in the online environment, but also the frequent reordering of news stories in the news agenda. News editors frequently change the order in which stories are presented on screen, reflecting reader metrics across the previous hour or a shorter time period. News organizations also use algorithms which interrogate reader metrics and reposition news items in the news agenda to reflect these dynamics (Karlsson and Sjøvaag, 2016a; Zamith, 2019).

This constant flux which characterizes online news prompted Karlsson and Strömbäck to suggest that it was necessary to "freeze the flow of online [liquid] news" to enable the capture of a consistent and representative sample of stories for analysis; researchers must examine the same corpus of "frozen" news content if traditional failsafe mechanisms such as intercoder reliability are to operate effectively (Karlsson and Strömbäck, 2010: 2). They identify a number of possible techniques: for example, taking a screenshot of the content using a computer program or relying on the systems "print screen" function, although each generates problems. More recently, journalism researchers such as Zamith have advocated the development of new computational techniques for content analysis, involving content retrieval software such as Wget, HTTrack, CasperJS and Selenium WebDriver (Zamith, 2019).

Automated content analysis brings significant **affordances** for scholarly research, as analysis is increasingly based on "state of the art AI techniques including data mining, machine learning and natural language processing techniques" (Flaounas, Omar, Lansdall-Welfare, De Bie, Mosdell and Lewis, 2013: 103). The scale, scope and longitudinal reach of recent content studies are impressive and exciting for the potential it suggests for the academic field of Digital Journalism Studies. Flaounas et al.'s (2013) study of "massive scale automated analysis of news content" published in the launch issue of *Digital Journalism*, for example, was based upon

2,490,429 articles and stories derived from 498 online English language new sources, from 99 countries, stretching back across a year (Flaounas, Omar, Lansdall-Welfare, De Bie, Mosdell and Lewis, 2013: 103). The scale of research studies continues to grow with Malik and Pfeffer's 2016 article, published in *Digital Journalism*, based on a sample of 1.8 billion journalists' Tweets gathered across four months in 2014 analyzing 6,103 hashtags for journalists and news organizations using **automated content** techniques (Malik and Pfeffer, 2016: 955).

The potential for research in our field – given the development of automated text analyses – where **news bots** can write the news, but others can read and analyze its content (both quantitatively and qualitatively), based on these staggeringly large and barely conceivable samples, is incredibly exciting. Automatic text generation and content analysis makes Michael Frayn's *Tin Men* – who merely drafted headlines – look like uneducated illiterates.

Key Sources

Flaounas, I., Omar, A., Lansdall-Welfare, T., De Bie, T., Mosdell, N. and Lewis, J. 2013 "Research Methods in the Age of Digital Journalism: Massive Scale Automated Analysis of News Content – Topics, Style and Gender" *Digital Journalism* 1(1): 102–116

Karlsson, M. and Sjøvaag, H. 2016 "Research Methods in an Age of Digital Journalism" *Digital Journalism* 4(1): 1–8. Introduction to a Special issue of Digital Journalism devoted to reconsidering research methods in Digital Journalism Studies

Karlsson, M. and Strömbäck, J. 2010 "Freezing the Flow of Online News: Exploring Approaches to the Study of the Liquidity of Online News" *Journalism Studies* 11(1): 2–19

Malik, M. M. and Pfeffer, J. 2016 "A Macroscopic Analysis of New Content in Twitter" *Digital Journalism* 4(8): 955–979

Zamith, R. 2019 "Innovation in Content Analysis; Freezing the Flow of Liquid News" in Eldridge, II, S. and Franklin, B. (Eds) *The Routledge Handbook of Developments in Digital Journalism Studies*. London: Routledge, 93–104

BBC

The monolithic public service broadcaster evolved from humble beginnings almost a century ago when it began filling the airwaves with music, drama, news and "talks" for just a few hours a day. Today, the

British Broadcasting Corporation is known for its original, impartial and global reporting but at its inception news content was supplied by an agency rather than by the organization itself. As the world's oldest and largest national broadcaster its **public service** model is emulated by many countries and it has played a prominent role in British culture, being known affectionately as The Beeb and Auntie. The BBC began as a private venture in the Strand, London when a group of leading wireless manufacturers, including Marconi, formed the British Broadcasting Company on 18 October 1922. Within five years, the organization recognized its public significance and established itself as the British Broadcasting Corporation in January 1927 under a Royal Charter. The charter defined its objectives, powers and obligations with Sir John Reith, a Scottish engineer, becoming the first Director-General responsible for fulfilling these policies. He set out the directive to "inform, educate and entertain" which underpins the BBC to this day. The broadcaster was originally funded via a tax on the sale of wireless sets but is now principally financed by the annual television licence fee, which is set by government. A further quarter of its revenue comes from its commercial arm, BBC Studios Ltd., which sells programmes and services internationally. As a result, there is no advertising on BBC radio, television or online.

The BBC, with its 21,000 employees, now operates radio, television and news websites regionally, nationally and internationally, broadcasting in 40 languages via BBC World Service. In the UK, the BBC reaches 93 percent of UK adults and BBC World Service has a global weekly audience of 279 million. Its portfolio of products also includes BBC iPlayer, BBC Sounds and BBC News. The corporation's official headquarters are at the purpose-built Broadcasting House in Portland Place, London and its secondary operational base is in MediaCity, Salford, where many staff were relocated following a decision taken in 2004 and in a bid to better service northern audiences. In recent years, the BBC has had to make significant cutbacks due to the licence fee freeze in 2010, which has included thousands of redundancies and the sharing of content between stations and channels. In 2017–2018 it made annual savings of £160 million. Although the organization does not have to generate advertising revenue as its rivals do, it has come under immense pressure due to commercial competition, audience fragmentation and the emergence of alternative digital delivery platforms (Hermida, 2009). Younger audiences satisfy much of their news and entertainment needs via **social media** networks, on demand streaming services, instant messaging apps and video sharing websites such as **Instagram**, Netflix,

Snapchat and **YouTube**, questioning the continued relevance of a global public service broadcaster. More recently, the broadcaster has also come under fire for its gender pay gap, which was brought to the fore in 2018 when China editor Carrie Gracie resigned from her post when it emerged she was being paid considerably less than men in similar roles. All that being said, the BBC remains the most trusted news brand in the UK and remains Europe's most successful public broadcaster with an impressive weekly reach online of 43 percent and 64 percent via television and radio (Newman, Fletcher, Kalogeropoulos, Levy and Nielsen, 2018). Meanwhile the BBC's research and development department continues to innovate with digital storytelling technology to secure the future of the audio–visual producer.

The longevity of the BBC has in part been due to its ability to adapt in terms of technology and practice. From radio, to television to digital, the BBC has invested in each new medium and become world renowned for its non-partisan reporting across all of its brands. The BBC Charter requires it to treat news with due impartiality and due accuracy, which has caused challenges in the digital era as reporting has become more personalized. The first major shift was the explosion of the **blogosphere**, which began outside established media but was soon appropriated by professional journalists. The BBC began incorporating **blogs** into its online platform BBC News in the mid noughties and these quickly became popular with users and influential in setting the news agenda. In October 2008, economics editor Robert Peston broke one of the biggest stories of the financial crisis when he revealed on his blog that the UK's leading banks were seeking a government bailout. However, the adoption of blogging as a core part of the corporation's news output led to internal debates about the impact on editorial values of accuracy, impartiality and fairness, which appear at odds with unmediated, personality-led blogs. Research by Hermida (2009) suggests that, despite these concerns, blogs emerged as a key mechanism for communicating analysis and commentary that maintained journalistic norms and BBC integrity, only differing in style rather than substance. This is supported by Bennett (2016), whose later analysis of BBC live blogging concluded that although the incorporation of eyewitness accounts initially increased the inclusion of non-official sources in BBC coverage, this was a temporary shift. As more official sources adopted social media into their communication practices, the BBC returned to these traditional actors, meaning that in the long term live blogs have only slightly widened the inclusion of multiperspectival sources and the editorial approach towards news values has not shifted.

A similar approach has been taken with regard to the integration of **user-generated content (UGC)** which the BBC carefully scrutinizes and verifies in order to ensure it is accurate, non-partisan and fits its own traditional news values. By 2011, journalists had become more comfortable and effective at integrating UGC into their news output, working more closely and collaboratively with the creators (Hänska-Ahy and Shapour, 2013). In her observation of the 24-hour BBC UGC hub, set up following the 2005 London bombings, Harrison (2010) noted that UGC was being utilized for multiple reasons which did not fit the cynical view that it was a means to save money, since managing UGC was labour intensive. Similarly, in her assessment of the BBC's use of UGC in war reporting, Johnston (2016) found that verification processes were complex and lengthy, taking time to develop. Rather than a money saver, UGC is a means for the BBC to meet its obligations toward inclusivity and mass reach, a way to combat viewer disengagement with mainstream news and a response to increasing competition for audiences, plus technological advances. However, there is some evidence that the extensive use of UGC has encouraged the increasing use of soft news rather than reporting matters of public concern (Harrison, 2010).

Key Sources

Bennett, D. 2016b "Sourcing the BBC's Live Online Coverage of Terror Attacks" *Digital Journalism* 5(7): 861–874

Hänska-Ahy, M. T. and Shapour, R. 2013 "Who's Reporting the Protests? Converging Practices of Citizen Journalists and Two BBC World Service Newsrooms, from Iran's Election Protests to the Arab Uprisings" *Journalism Studies* 14(1): 29–45

Harrison, J. 2010 "User-Generated Content and Gatekeeping at the BBC Hub" *Journalism Studies* 11(2): 243–256

BLOGOSPHERE

The blogosphere is the name given to all existing **blogs** and their authors and readers, understood as a distinct community or network. Bruns and Jacobs define the blogosphere as, "the common term to describe the overall community of blogs and bloggers, which is interlinked through a large number of cross references between individual blog entries" (2006: 5). It is this interconnected nature of the blogosphere that underlies its significance rather than any particular blog or grouping of blogs. As Hiler observes,

> it's ... when you tap the collective power of thousands of weblogs that you start to see all sorts of interesting behaviour emerge. It's a property of what scientists call complex adaptive systems and its enabling weblogs as a collective to become more than the sum of the parts.
>
> (Hiler, 2004)

It is this collective voice of the blogosphere which makes it a significant element in what Dutton dubbed the "fifth estate" and which the *Guardian* described as "the Commentariat": A term previously constituted by professional political **journalists** and commentators but now joined by the amateur bloggers (*Guardian*, 2005).

The term "blogosphere" was coined initially in the late 20th century as an allegedly humorous play on the Greek word "logosphere," which conjoined "logos" and "sphere" to imply the "world of words." At around the same time, the blogosphere began to grow rapidly, reflecting the availability of accessible and free software such as "blogger," which enabled individuals to establish their own blogs. There was a perfect storm of factors contributing to growth in the blogosphere: barriers to entry were low, there was effectively no control or regulation of content and bloggers were provided with opportunities to link and connect with others to promote or respond to particular ideas. From less than three million blogs in 2003, the blogosphere had grown massively to 42 million blogs by 2006 – figures which show the blogosphere doubled in size every six months (Joust and Hipolit, 2006). With this proliferation, the blogosphere came to comprise a number of specialist areas of blogger interest and activity such as news, politics, fashion, food, health and science. Some bloggers, such as Salam Pax, the Iraq war blogger, was widely read and eventually secured his own column at the *Guardian*.

Key Sources

Bruns, A. and Jacobs, J. 2006 *The Uses of Blogs*. New York: Peter Lang

Dutton, W. H. 2009 "The Fifth Estate Emerging through the Network of Networks" *Prometheus* 27(1): 1–15

Guardian 2005 "The New Commentariat", www.theguardian.com/media/2005/nov/17/newmedia.politicsandthemedia 17 November 2005

Hiler, J. 2004 "Borg Journalism: We Are the Blogs. Journalism Will be Assimilated" *Micro-Content News* (1 April 2002) www.microcontentnews.com/articles/borgjournalism.htm cited in Bruns and Jacobs 2006: 8

BLOGS/BLOGGING

The word blog was initially an abbreviation for "web – log" a feature of the new and emerging online world of news and comment facilitated by **web 2.0** technology. Blogs were an early manifestation of "amateur journalism" and typically assumed the form of a highly personalized diary or journal with entries listed in reverse chronological order (at the head of the blog), which constituted a "log" of these brief comment pieces. But, increasingly, blogs assumed the form of highly opinionated essays expressing views about particular issues and events in the news.

Blogs presented readers with opportunities to become producers or contributors to debates about news online, instead of merely "consumers" of news texts. Axel Bruns (2008) noted this emerging, dual role for people as producers and users of news and promptly dubbed them "**produsers,**" probably the most often cited neologism in the lexicon of **Digital Journalism Studies**. But as prominent, even public service, news organizations such as the **BBC** came to appreciate the value of blogs for attracting readers and site traffic, established political and economic correspondents at the BBC began to incorporate blogging into their job brief and, in this way, blogging became "normalized" and routine in day-to-day journalism practice. Blogs written by senior BBC correspondents offered them opportunities to draft a distinctive form of news narrative, which routinely attracted huge readerships, proved influential in setting the news agenda and shifted blogging from an activity "largely taking place outside established media to a practice appropriated by professional journalists" (Hermida, 2009: 268).

The study by Messner and DiStaso (2008) of the reliance of **legacy media** and blogs on each other as a **source** of news revealed – in their analysis of 2,059 articles across 6 years from *The New York Times* and the *Washington Post* – that the newspapers increasingly legitimized blogs as credible news sources. Similarly, their study of 120 blogs highlighted that they relied heavily on legacy media as sources of news. These two sets of findings prompted them to hypothesize a "news source cycle" in which news content ricochets between blogs and mainstream media (Messner and DiStaso, 2008).

Significantly, bloggers' contribution to news narratives has generated "**boundary disputes**" and what Carlson and Lewis (2015) termed "blurring boundaries," when bloggers claimed their new-found involvement in the news warranted them assuming the mantle of "journalist"; professional journalists contested these claims to professionalism suggesting bloggers were merely "interlopers" (Eldridge, 2015). Singer (2006) itemized the differences between the two groups, claiming journalists were involved in gathering, organizing and reporting information, which was informed by concepts such as objectivity, balance and fairness, cited sources for the facts they included in their stories and, consequently, the reporting of professional journalists enjoyed public credibility. By contrast, highly controversial and opinionated blogs lacked any cited sources for their (often exaggerated) claims and displayed little concern for objectivity which, to date, had been the central professional value of journalism and was the sheet anchor of journalists' professional identity. Singer's summary claim was that, "while all journalists ... publish information, not all publishers of information are journalists."

A more recent development has been the arrival of **live blogging** which, in their study of Live Blogging at the *Guardian*, Thurman and Walters (2013) suggest involves journalists relaying comment and information relating to (perhaps) a breaking news story such as the London Bombings in July 2005, or a sporting event, which unravels in real time and incorporates audience feedback into the news text. Live blogging is consequently understood as "a single blog post on a specific topic to which time-stamped content is progressively added for a finite period – anywhere between half an hour and 24 hours" (2013: 83). The blogs contain multimedia, video, still images and hypertext links, which makes them increasingly popular with readers; at the *Guardian* they attract more visitors for longer periods than standard articles on the same subjects. Live blogging is growing rapidly as an editorial format (Thurman and Walters, 2013: 83).

In summary, blogs continue to offer readers news, comment and information in popular formats and an opportunity for non-professional writers to contribute to the online debate about news. Their formats have changed considerably to embrace live blogging and, increasingly bereft of their opinionated style, blogs have concomitantly become notice boards for breaking news articulated in traditional journalistic language and style.

See also **live blogging**.

Key Sources

Bruns, A. 2008 *Blogs, Wikipedia, Second Life and Beyond: From Production to Produsage.* London: Peter Lang

Carlson, M. and Lewis, S. (Eds) 2015 *Boundaries of Journalism: Professionalism, Practices and Participation.* London: Routledge

Hermida, A. 2009 "The Blogging BBC: Journalism Blogs at the World's Most Trusted News Organisation" *Journalism Practice* 3(3): 268–284

Messner, M. and DiStaso, M. 2008 "The Source Cycle: How Traditional Media and Weblogs Use Each Other as Sources" *Journalism Studies* 9(3): 447–463

Thurman, N. and Walters, A. 2013 "Live Blogging – Digital Journalism's Pivotal Platform? A Case Study of the Production, Consumption and Form of Live Blogs at Guardian.co.uk" *Digital Journalism* 1(1): 82–101

BRAND STUDIOS

The rapid establishment and growth of brand or content studios has been central to the expansion of **native advertising** and consequent profitability of many **news** organizations across the last decade. But these financial gains have incurred a particular cost in terms of the close marrying of editorial and advertising, the increase in the opacity of journalistic practices and ethics and a changing relationship between news organizations and their readerships (Ferrer Conill, 2016; Lynch, 2018).

Lynch claims that brand studios such as T Brand at *The New York Times* and many other news outlets such as **BuzzFeed**, the *Wall Street Journal*, the *Guardian* and the **BBC**

> have embraced the idea of producing their own native content for advertisers, shifting from an arms-length relationship with those advertisers to a client or partnership relationship, and (in some cases), taking on all of the functions of a conventional advertising agency in the process.
>
> (Lynch, 2018)

This means that at "data-driven news outlets such as the *Washington Post*, the same **algorithms** that are used to generate ideas for editorial content are used to suggest topics to advertisers" (Lynch, 2018: Ch. 2) and consequently the separation between editorial and **advertising**, so vital to a responsible and democratic journalism, is not simply blurred so much as killed at birth.

The resources that brand studios enjoy in terms of number of **journalists** employed, technical equipment, back up and support and economic resources, are substantial. "At many media outlets" Lynch observes, "the 'shiniest toys in the room,' for storytelling – such as video and virtual reality production studios, exist because of their advertising potential, not their editorial potential" (Lynch, 2018: Ch. 2).

The T Brand native advertising studio at *The New York Times*, for example, was launched in 2014, has expanded rapidly and to good financial effect: A \$14 million loss early in 2016 was converted into a \$13 million profit by early 2017. Chief Executive and ex BBC Director-General, Mark Thompson, claimed that across the same period native advertising had helped to generate a 19 percent growth in digital advertising. Since 2014, *The New York Times* has shrunk its editorial staff but the T Brand Studio is continuing to grow, with more than 100 employees. In 2016, *The Times* established T Brand International to create native advertising for global markets, with offices in London, Paris and Hong Kong (Lynch, 2018: Ch. 2).

Increasingly, native advertising is seen as the most effective way to restore the advertising revenues which sustained the journalism industry ahead of the crisis in **journalism** and the collapse of the traditional journalism **business model**. In turn, the establishment of a brand studio to develop advertising campaigns and copy to promote products and producers, as well as political and social campaigns, is seen as a precondition for economic stability, if not growth.

Key Sources

Lynch, L. and Sirrah, A. 2018 *Native Advertising: Advertorial Disruption in the 21st Century News Feed*. London: Routledge

Ferrer Conill, R. 2016 "Camouflaging Church as State: An Exploratory Study of Journalism's Native Advertising" *Journalism Studies* 17(7): 904–914, doi:10.1080/1461670.2016.1165138

BREAKING NEWS

Journalists' obsession with **deadlines** illustrates the central importance of time in both the mythology and reality of **journalism. News** is judged to be valuable and worthy to the extent that it is new or recent. According to the old journalistic adage, nothing is older than yesterday's news. Hence, journalists ascribe great value to breaking news stories as quickly as possible: Live coverage of breaking news, which allows audiences to watch as events literally unravel before their eyes, is considered to be the most desirable kind of news. Editorial genres such as live reports, with a journalist reporting from the actual site of a clash between demonstrators and the police, for example, is judged more exciting than a filmed report of events from earlier in the day. The message which **journalists** wish to convey about live reporting is simple: this news is so new, so fresh, that it is being reported in real time while it is actually happening. Inevitably, the keenest competition between news journalists has always been a contest about being the first to break a story, about the "Thirst to be first," as Lewis and Cushion (2009) called their study of breaking news.

Developments in media technologies have typically brought with them increasing possibilities for reducing the gap between the occurrence of an event and its reporting by journalists. With the advent of 24-hour news channels and the possibility of sustained live coverage of newsworthy events such as hostage situations, for example, breaking news came into its own. But in an early study, Lewis and Cushion (2009) found that the relatively new 24-hour news channels spent little time actually "breaking" news and, in their "rush" to report, failed to provide the necessary context to make news stories meaningful and intelligible. Moreover, since many of the stories labeled as "breaking news" were incorrectly badged, they concluded that "a viewer is much better off … watching a conventional news bulletin like the Ten O'Clock News" (Lewis, Cushion and Thomas, 2006). In their later research based on content analyses of SkyNews and BBC News 24 channels, between 2004 and 2007, Cushion and Lewis (2009), argued that while breaking news had become increasingly frequent and important compared to conventional coverage for these 24-hour news channels, such news was less well informed and featured less independent coverage than conventional reporting. Consequently, they concluded that the decision to cover more breaking news actually "impoverishes the quality of Journalism" (Lewis and Cushion, 2009: 304–318).

More recently, with the advent of digital media technologies and **social media, citizen witnessing** of events provides journalists with much of their raw source materials, which further accelerates the possibilities for "breaking" news stories and facilitates **immediacy**. In her study of the reporting of the London riots in summer 2011, Farida Vis illustrates how journalists Paul Lewis (*Guardian*) and Ravi Somaiya (*The New York Times*) used **Twitter** as a reporting tool for breaking news about the riots by analysing the 731 **tweets** the journalists posted across the four days of the riots. (Vis, 2013: 31).

Key Sources

Lewis, J. and Cushion, S. 2009 "The Thirst to be First: An Analysis of Breaking News Stories and Their Impact on the Quality of 24-Hour News Coverage in the UK" *Journalism Practice* 3(3): 304–318

Lewis, J., Cushion, S. and Thomas, J. 2006 "Immediacy, Convenience or Engagement? An Analysis of 24-Hour News Channels in the UK" *Journalism Studies* 6(4): 461–477

Vis, F. 2013 "Twitter as a Reporting Tool for Breaking News: Journalists tweeting the 2011 UK Riots" *Digital Journalism* 1(1): 27–47

BRITISH DIGITAL CORPORATION

In his "alternative MacTaggart Lecture," delivered in August 2018 as part of the annual Edinburgh Television Festival (Franklin, 2005), the Labour party leader Jeremy Corbyn proposed establishing a digital broadcasting corporation (British digital corporation, or BDC) funded by a "digital licence fee" to be levied on the leading tech companies, **Facebook, Amazon**, Netflix and **Google**. Corbyn described the large tech companies as "digital monopolies that profit from every search, share and like that we make," enabling them to "extract huge wealth from our shared digital space" and create a problem for democracy (Corbyn, 2018; Waterson, 2018b). The idea for a BDC was not yet Labour policy. Corbyn's ambition was to generate debate.

To that end, he offered "four big ideas" to help "build a free and democratic media in the digital age." These included: (1) "Support for public interest journalism"; (2) "A more democratic, representative and independent **BBC**"; (3) "Empowering private sector **journalists** and **audiences**"; (4) establishing "a publicly owned British Digital Corporation as a sister organisation to the BBC" (Corbyn, 2018).

Achieving these goals would require the levying of a "digital licence fee" which would, in turn, involve a new and permanent legal status for the BBC abolishing the current requirement for periodic negotiations between the BBC and the government concerning the level of the licence fee. Other proposals for reforms included elections for representatives from among licence fee payers to serve on the BBC's governing board as critics and watchdogs on the Corporation's practices and programming; the introduction of charitable status and tax breaks for **not-for-profit** news organizations, with a particular focus on the radically diminished local news organizations; the establishment of an independent fund to finance other forms of public service broadcasting, again financed by the larger tech companies; and routine BBC publications of equality data, especially social class, for all content creators, whether in house or external to the BBC (Corbyn, 2018; Waterson, 2018b).

In part, Corbyn's "big ideas" reflect a bourgeoning public and parliamentary concern with the emergence of **fake news**, and the Cambridge Analytica scandal involving the company's use of personal data in 87 million Facebook accounts ahead of the 2016 General Election in the UK guaranteed an increasingly critical attitude among parliamentarians towards **social media**. Earlier in 2018, a report of the House Select Committee for Culture, Media and Sport's investigation into fake news identified a levy on tech companies as the major funding source for education programmes and data regulation (Waterson, 2018b). Corbyn himself acknowledges that the idea for the BDC was initially floated by James Harding, then Director of Home News at the BBC, in his Hugh Cudlipp Lecture in January 2018.

Corbyn concludes that the "public realm does not have to sit back and watch as a few mega tech corporations hoover up digital rights, assets and ultimately our money." The BDC would "use all our best minds, the latest technology and our existing public assets not only to deliver information and entertainment to rival Netflix and Amazon, but also to harness data for the public good" (Corbyn, 2018).

Key Sources

Corbyn, J. 2018 Alternative MacTaggart Lecture available at: https://labour.org. uk/press/full-text-jeremy-corbyns-2018-alternative-mactaggart-lecture/

Franklin, B. 2005 *Television Policy: The MacTaggart Lectures*. Edinburgh: Edinburgh University Press

Waterson, J. 2018a "Cambridge Analytica Scandal and Fake News Have Left Social Media Firms Ripe for Atbooktack" *Guardian*, 23rd August, 4

Waterson, J. 2018c "Tax Facebook and Netflix to Fund the BBC, Says Corbyn" *Guardian*, 23rd August, 1

BUSINESS MODELS

The emergence of digital media technologies such as **web 2.0**, mobile telephony and online **news** media disrupted the traditional business model for news organizations, which relied greatly on advertising revenues to fund the production and distribution of news. The initial consequences of this disruption for the **journalism** industries are well rehearsed in the scholarly literature: Collapsing circulations, closure of print titles, fewer editions, reduced pagination, **advertising** revenues and jobs for **journalists**. These cuts in resources and journalists prompted a curtailment of certain kinds of "public service" coverage which are central to the provision of information necessary to keep **audiences** (citizens) well informed and able to participate fully in the public sphere and informed public decision making. Consequently, a key concern has been – and arguably remains – to develop a new business model to fund and resource a viable, sustainable and democratic journalism in the digital age (Franklin, 2011: 3–9, 2013b: 2–8, 2015: 2–9).

The initial response of news media was to develop and produce online versions of newspapers, available to readers for free. But the evident dilemma with making online news access free is that, since many sites will each broadly report the same big news stories, there is no economic reason why readers should buy the print version of any of the competing newspapers and incur the cost of the copy price; proprietors quickly realized that they were losing the value of copy sales which contributed to even further revenue falls (Starr, 2009). In 2009, Rupert Murdoch announced his intention to charge for online content in all News Corporations titles. Explaining this policy shift in his MacTaggart Lecture in August 2009, James Murdoch claimed that "it is essential for the future of independent **digital journalism** ... that a fair price can be charged for news to people who value it" (Murdoch, 2009: 16).

The Times and *The Sunday Times* erected **paywalls** and began charging for online access in May 2010. The industry judged this policy shift to be significant and broadly followed Murdoch's lead. Not everyone has been persuaded, however, that paywalls alone will guarantee sufficient revenues to fully resource news journalism in the way that **advertising** had previously (Brandsetter and Schmalhofer, 2014: 23–33; Myllylahti, 2017: 166–175).

There is little consensus, and distinctive business models stress alternative and/or supplementary suggestions to complement advertising and paywalls to fund journalism. These include **crowdsourcing** (Aitamurto, 2017) and **crowdfunding** (Carvajal, Aviles and Gonzalez, 2013), **hyperlocal** and community journalism (Hess and Waller, 2017), public subsidies (Downie and Schudson, 2010; McChesney and Nicholl, 2010), levies on the profits of corporate media industries, especially mobile telephone companies, as well as proposals for the growing use of "robo-journalists" and **news bots** to draft articles – especially in the areas of sport, finance and weather – at dramatically reduced costs (Carlson, 2015; Clerwall, 2014). Most business models for digital media enterprises include a mix of these various resource-generating elements as news organizations (Corporate, hyperlocal or public/private sector), in an increasingly competitive environment, urgently seek a surrogate source of funding to replace the collapsed advertising revenues that resourced journalists and journalism until the 21st century.

See also **revenue streams, advertising, paywalls** and **crowdsourcing**.

Key Sources

Brandsetter, B. and Schmalhofer, J. 2014 "Paid Content? A Successful Model for Publishing Houses in Germany?" *Journalism Practice* 8(5), doi:10.1080/17512786.2014895519

Carvajal, M., Aviles, J. A. and Gonzalez, J. L. 2013 "Crowdfunding and Non-Profit Media: The Emergence of New Models for Public Interest Journalism" in Franklin, B. (Ed) *The Future of Journalism; Developments and Debates*. London: Routledge, 101–110

Downie, L. and Schudson, M. 2010 "The Reconstruction of American Journalism" *Columbia Journalism Review* www.cjr.org/reconstruction/the_reconstruction_of_american.php

McChesney, R. W. and Nichols, J. 2010 *The Death and Life of American Journalism: The Media Revolution that Will Begin the World Again*. Philadelphia: Nation Books

Murdoch, J. 2009 "The Absence of Trust" The James MacTaggart Annual Lecture at the Guardian/Edinburgh international festival, 28 August www.google.co.uk/search?hl=n&source=hp&q=james+murdoch+mactaggart+lecture+transcript&meta+&aq=0&oq=james+murdoch+mactaggart=lecture

BUZZFEED

Best known for its **listicles**, quizzes, memes and pop culture articles, BuzzFeed is now an award-winning global media and technology company worth around $1.5 billion. Founded as a side project in 2006 by *HuffPost* (formely **Huffington Post**) co-founder Jonah Peretti, it was originally set up as instant messaging bot BuzzBot to link users to popular content on the web. The site had no writers and simply acted as an **algorithm** tracking and curating **viral news**. In 2011 political journalist Ben Smith was hired as **editor**-in-chief to expand the site into serious **journalism** and investigative reporting. In 2016, BuzzFeed formally separated its news and entertainment content into BuzzFeed News and BuzzFeed Entertainment Group, and by 2018 BuzzFeed News had won the National Magazine Award and been a Pulitzer Prize finalist. The company has around 1,700 employees worldwide and editions in ten countries including the USA, UK, Australia and Japan. It generates **advertising** revenue through **native advertising** that matches its own editorial content rather than via traditional banner ads.

BuzzFeed now shares a significant part of the online news market across Europe and the Americas with 6–14 percent of users accessing the site at least once a week, depending on their country of origin (Newman, Fletcher, Kalogeropoulos, Levy and Nielsen, 2018). The website continues to emphasize virality and shareability and the success of its content is measured by its "social lift" rather than number of views or hits. Stories are shared via **social media** and BuzzFeed concludes that the content that proves most popular relies on identity, emotion, conversation, aspiration and global reach (Jones, 2015). The organization, which has a relatively young staff base, has also made a conscious effort to tackle **diversity** issues and report on non-elite topics, including immigration and transexuality, often using innovative **app** development technology to tell untold stories (Warren, 2015). More controversially, the organization has been accused of breaching ethical media boundaries and working outside of traditional norms. In 2017, the site posted unsubstantiated documents about President Donald Trump's purported behavior in Russia prior to his inauguration, with a warning that the information contained errors and was unverified and potentially unverifiable. Other media outlets, including the *Guardian* had seen the documents but had declined to publish them because they were unable to independently verify the contents.

Despite these high-profile reports, some scholars continue to dismiss digital native platforms including BuzzFeed (Canter, 2018) claiming they contain soft news and are proliferated with "funny cat videos" (Bednarek, 2016: 232). Yet, conversely, evidence shows that journalists working for traditional news organizations positively welcome BuzzFeed's entry into the journalistic field and see it as reinforcing existing professional norms, and acting as a transformative force to preserve future **journalism** (Tandoc, 2017; Tandoc and Jenkins, 2017). The news articles produced by BuzzFeed largely play by the rules, although there is some departure from traditional journalistic practice (Tandoc, 2017) as the leaked and unverified Trump dossier demonstrates. Meanwhile, BuzzFeed journalists themselves believe they are more attentive to **audiences** and more willing to experiment than those working in traditional news organizations (Tandoc and Foo, 2018).

See also **news values**.

Key Sources

Canter, L. 2018 "It's Not All Cat Videos: Moving beyond Legacy Media and Tackling the Challenges of Mapping News Values on Digital Native Websites" *Digital Journalism* 6(8): 1101–1112, doi:10.1080/21670811.2018.1503058

Tandoc, E. 2017 "Five Ways BuzzFeed Is Preserving (or Transforming) the Journalistic Field" *Journalism* 19(2): 200–216

Tandoc, E. and Foo, C. 2018 "Here's What BuzzFeed Journalists Think of Their Journalism" *Digital Journalism* 6(1): 41–57

Tandoc, E. and Jenkins, J. 2017 "The Buzzfeedication of Journalism? How Traditional News Organizations Are Talking about a New Entrant to the Journalistic Field Will Surprise You!" *Journalism* 18(4): 482–500

CENSORSHIP

The history of **journalism** has perhaps inevitably unraveled in close parallel to the history of censorship. A perennial and primary concern for journalism has been to disseminate political **news**, information and comment while news media have traditionally offered a forum to host and conduct significant policy debates; such activities and commitments have not always matched the ambitions of powerful economic and political elites. In liberal democratic societies, which place great emphasis on the values of freedom of political thought and speech, however, censorship is considered at best a "necessary evil" which should be strictly limited and employed only in closely specified circumstances (Steel, 2011).

Despite these liberal commitments, censorship remains concerned with controlling speech and written information which might: (1) incorporate elements of hate speech against identified minorities; (2) risk betraying "official secrets" which might damage the national interest, especially at times of war (Miller, 2004); or (3) offend public taste and decency (for example, in portrayals of explicitly violent or sexual activity in literature, theatre or the public arts).

Public perceptions of "censors" tend to underestimate their number and range. As Woolmar observes,

> censors are not just people with big black pens cutting out information from books or letters which they don't like, or with scissors chopping out bits of film or video. As well as government officials, they can be owners of publications, judges, editors, advertisers or

even the writers themselves. Nor are they always in far-off countries ruled by dictators.

(Woolmar, 2000)

Herman and Chomsky argue for the pervasiveness of censorship in liberal democracies, as well as more authoritarian state systems, because, while there may be fewer formal, legal and politically censorial constraints on news media, the corporate and monopoly structures of ownership of media institutions and the activities of advertisers limit the diversity and range of expressed views by "manufacturing consent" (Herman and Chomsky, 1988).

The arrival of digital media technologies such as **Web 2.0** in tandem with the ready availability of personal computers, however, was initially greeted with considerable political optimism. The **affordances** of digital media, it was suggested, would create an era of digital democracy, transforming citizens into active creators rather than passive recipients of political news. Citizens could interrogate online documents and data sets and report the insights of an enhanced plurality of news sources. **Citizen journalists** could generate a genuinely open political conversation in an online public sphere via **blogs, live blogs** and **social media**. Additionally, citizen journalists might access facilities for live and networked streaming to report political events, from debates to demonstrations and even riots, as they occurred and without any mediation by journalists, editors, politicians or police reports (Artwick, 2019). In such an open, digital public sphere, there would be few opportunities for censorship (Sullivan, 2008). This is what Coskuntuncel skeptically labels "the digital democracy discourse" (Coskuntuncel, 2019: 503)

Alissa Richardson's research illustrates how the growth of smart cameras and especially small networked cameras for "sousveillance" and the live streaming of political news – for example, the protests following the shooting of Trayvon Martin – created what she terms "the oppositional gaze" and enhanced public perceptions of minority communities, as well as the growth of the Black Lives Matter Movement (Richardson, 2019: 390). Digital citizen journalism offers disintermediated coverage of political events.

These new affordances of digital media, however, can be used in authoritarian states, such as Turkey, to deliver highly repressive systems of censorship. The Turkish Governing Party (AKP), for example, recruits digital media teams to "propagate, harass and deter critics and journalists, surveil citizens and drive the discussion online." Coskuntuncel cites *The Wall Street Journal's* claim that following riots in 2013, the Turkish government recruited a 6,000 strong social media team to "disseminate pro government propaganda, intimidate dissidents and create a network of informants," while a senior party official told the *Wall Street Journal* that the teams would focus on **Twitter, Facebook, YouTube** and **Instagram** to "promote the party perspective and monitor online discussions." Access to **WikiLeaks'** services are sometimes cut in line with the US Government's interests, and Facebook and Twitter accounts are routinely monitored (Coskuntuncel, 2019: 507–508).

Digital media and citizen journalism seemingly offer no guarantees of free and open political discussion and debate when confronted by a determined and authoritarian government. It is not the nature of the technology, but what governments do with it, that determines the quality of open public debate and the extent and forms which censorship assumes.

Key Sources

Artwick, C.. 2019 "Social Media Livestreaming" in Eldridge, II, S. and Franklin, B. (Eds) *The Routledge Handbook of Developments in Digital Journalism Studies.* London: Routledge, 296–310

Coskuntuncel, A.. 2019 "Outsourcing Censorship and Surveillance: the Privatization of Governance as an Information Control Strategy in Turkey" in Eldridge, II, S. and Franklin, B. (Eds) *The Routledge Handbook of Developments in Digital Journalism Studies.* London: Routledge, 501–514

Herman, E. and Chomsky, N. 1988 *Manufacturing Consent: The Political Economy of the Mass Media.* New York: Pantheon

Richardson, A. 2019 "The Movement and its Mobile Journalism: A Phenomenology of Black Lives Matter Journalist–Activists" in Eldridge, II, S. and Franklin, B. (Eds) *The Routledge Handbook of Developments in Digital Journalism Studies.* London: Routledge, 387–400

Woolmar, C. 2000 *Censorship.* London: Wayland

CHURNALISM *SEE FLAT EARTH NEWS*

CIRCULATION *SEE* DOWNLOADS

CITIZEN JOURNALISM

There is limited agreement over the definition of citizen journalism, which has many iterations around the world and does not have a unified set of practices. However, it is this lack of tangibility that sets it apart from professional journalism, which operates within a more clearly defined set of norms and ideologies. For some, citizen journalists are simply unpaid individuals who carry out journalism within a similar set of boundaries to professional journalists and are perhaps former or retired journalists, students or those working in adjacent fields (Ahva, 2017) such as non-profits producing media content. For others, citizen journalists are merely amateur bystanders or witnesses who participate in accidental acts of journalism because they are present when extraordinary events take place (Allan, 2013). Then there are those who actively participate in the production and dissemination of journalistic content without payment as a form of political activism to invoke social change. Another subset comprises volunteers who produce content in their local community in collaboration with news organizations (Canter, 2013b) to gain a wider audience.

The term citizen journalism is often debated with a lack of consensus among scholars over the differentiation between this and **alternative journalism**,participatory journalism, grassroots journalism, interactive journalism, meta-journalism, **networked journalism**, mass self-communication, open and closed journalism and **user-generated content** (Atton, 2002; Bowman and Willis, 2003; Castells, 2007; Deuze, Bruns and Neuberger, 2007; Goode, 2009). Allan (2007) defines citizen journalism as a process whereby non-professionals collect news content for amateur and mainstream media distribution while Hermida and Thurman (2008) define this as user-generated content. For others, citizen journalism can only exist and be published in a non-professional environment (Nip, 2006) and cannot be labeled citizen journalism if it appears in the mainstream media or has any involvement from professional journalists. Charman (2007) further complicates the picture by referring to citizen journalism as more than submitting user-generated content, but also investigating through Freedom of Information requests, fact-checking the work of professional journalists and asking for input into professional stories in the development stage. Meanwhile, Goode (2009) understands that citizen journalism has a wide definition and suggests it could include rating stories, commenting, and tagging stories online, in a term he calls metajournalism. All of these forms of citizen journalism come together in **social media** platforms such as **Twitter** to become a melting pot of citizen and professional news content in this hybrid information space (Hermida, 2013).

Technologically, citizen journalism is associated with **smartphones**, mobile internet and social media and undoubtedly these tools and platforms have opened up global public communication to the masses on a scale never seen before. Nonetheless, citizen journalism is not a 21st century phenomenon and has occurred before digitization and the inception of the World Wide Web. The capture of the assassination of

American President John F. Kennedy on November 22, 1963 on a home video camera by spectator Abraham Zapruder is arguably the first case of documented citizen journalism. From that moment onwards, citizens have been capturing newsworthy events on analogue stills and video cameras before moving over to blogs, digital devices and ultimately smartphones. In 1991, a resident video-recorded LAPD officers brutally beating Rodney King and sent the footage to a local television news station. The incident was covered by news media around the world and was the catalyst for the 1992 Los Angeles riots. Meanwhile, blogger Matt Drudge broke the news of the decade when he revealed the affair between President Bill Clinton and his intern Monica Lewinsky, on his blog *The Drudge Report* in 1998. A landmark moment for citizen journalism in the UK was the 2005 London bombing, which saw the BBC receive 1,000 amateur photographs, 20 pieces of video, 4,000 text messages and 20,000 emails within six hours of the terrorist attack. The next day, the main BBC television newscast began with a package edited entirely from videos sent in by the public. Then, in 2008, the web, in particular social media, came to the forefront of citizen journalism following the Mumbai terror attacks. Within minutes of the attack bloggers were updating a local news website, a page was entered into **Wikipedia** and a Googlemap was created showing locations of the attacks. A man grabbed his camera and went onto the streets before uploading 112 photos to **Flickr**; meanwhile, hundreds of people tweeted events on Twitter as they were held hostage. Today there is an expectation that citizen journalists, or simply citizens, will upload eyewitness accounts, video, photo and audio clips to the internet, predominantly via social media, as breaking news events unfold.

See also **journalists' identity, in-betweeners**.

Key Sources

Bowman, S. and Willis, C. 2003 "We Media: How Audiences Are Shaping the Future of News and Information" Hypergene. www.hypergene.net/weme dia/weblog.php

Charman, S. 2007 "The Changing Role of Journalists in a World Where Everyone Can Publish" *The Freedom of Expression Project* www.freedomofexpression. org.uk/resources/the+changing+role+of+journalists+in+a+world+where +everyone+can+publish

Goode, L. 2009 "Social News, Citizen Journalism and Democracy" *New Media & Society* 11(8): 1287–1305

Nip, J. Y. M. 2006 "Exploring the Second Phase of Public Journalism" *Journalism Studies* 7(2): 212–236

CITIZEN WITNESSING

A term conceptualized by Stuart Allan in his book *Citizen Witnessing* (Allan, 2013), in which he deals with the "fractured and fraught debates about **citizen journalism** and its impact on journalism" (Ewart, 2014: 252). In his thought-provoking and provocative text, Allan introduces citizen witnessing in order to rethink familiar assumptions surrounding the amateur and the professional **journalist**. He argues that citizen journalism should be reconceptualized through the lens of citizen witnessing and embraced as a public service that can reinvigorate journalism's responsibilities within democratic cultures.

Rather than focusing on the debate of whether citizen journalists are a passing fad, another name for **user-generated content** or a useful contribution to democratization (Ewart, 2014: 252), Allan explores the role of the everyday citizen in **news** reporting and the spontaneous actions of ordinary people caught up in extraordinary crisis events. These individuals bear witness to what they see, engage in unique forms of journalistic activity generating eyewitness accounts via video footage, digital photographs, tweets and blog posts. Allan argues that citizen witnessing is usually organic, often accidental and only occasionally proactive and although the citizen may be the first witness on the ground, it is the journalist who will shape the raw material into a story, fact check it, and distribute it. The journalist–citizen relationship is a mutual one of "respectful reciprocity" and the two cannot exist in isolation as "us and them" (Allan, 2013: 201). Allan also asserts that journalists have a responsibility to bear witness rather than just simply report the facts. Furthermore, when both parties bear witness, the roles become fluid with the journalist-as-citizen and the citizen-as-accidental-journalist.

Similarly, Andén-Papadopoulos, in her paper on citizen-camera witnessing (2013), interrogates the emerging modes of civic engagement connected to the smartphone in countries such as Burma, Iran, Egypt, Libya and Syria. She discusses the "camera-wielding political activists and dissidents who put their lives at risk to produce incontrovertible public testimony to unjust and disastrous developments around the world, in a critical bid to mobilize global solidarity through the affective power of the visual" (2013: 754). By performing rituals of bearing witness, these dissenting bodies capture videographic and photographic testimony while risking their lives on camera, reactivating the idea of martyrdom.

Key Sources

Allan, S. 2013 *Citizen Witnessing: Revisioning Journalism in Times of Crisis.* Cambridge: Polity

Andén-Papadopoulos, K. 2013 "Citizen Camera-Witnessing: Embodied Political Dissent in the Age of 'Mediated Mass Self-Communication'" *New Media and Society* 16(5): 753–769

Ewart, J. 2014 "Citizen Witnessing: Revisioning Journalism in Times of Crisis" *Digital Journalism* 2(2): 252–253

CLICKBAIT

Ever clicked on an online headline that ends in a question mark? Then chances are you have been drawn in by the powers of clickbait, which exploits readers' curiosity gap and entices them to click through to the linked content. Features of clickbait headlines include a specific style of writing including the use of questions, numbers, lists, forward referencing, spectacularization and negativity (Kuiken, Schuth, Spitters and Marx, 2017). The techniques used by clickbait writers are considered to be a derivative of yellow journalism in America or tabloid journalism in the UK, which present exaggerated, sensationalist news with eye-catching headlines, often with little or no legitimate research behind the stories. *Wired* magazine's 2015 explanation of the clickbait phenomenon featured the satirical headline "YOU'LL BE OUTRAGED AT HOW EASY IT WAS TO GET YOU TO CLICK ON THIS HEADLINE" and concluded that clickbait is "annoying, but by god, it works – even when readers recognize it for what it is" (Gardiner, 2015). The technique is used to drive **advertising** revenue, which is often based on the number of hits – or click rate – a story, page or website receives. However, over time, the use of click rate as an advertising metric has become less popular as websites have moved towards sponsored content and **native advertising**.

The ubiquity of clickbait led to a backlash in recent years, with the satirical newspaper the *Onion* launching ClickHole in 2014 to parody digitally born websites **BuzzFeed** and Upworthy who favor this type of headline writing. The same year, **Facebook** announced it was taking measures to reduce the impact of clickbait. The semantic device has also been linked to **fake news** and utilized for political ends, often via the spreading of false information on **social media**. Katharine Viner, editor-in-chief at the *Guardian* wrote that chasing down cheap clicks at the expense of accuracy and veracity undermined the value of journalism and truth (2016).

See also **infotainment, newszak, web analytics**.

Key Sources

Gardiner, B. 2015. "You'll Be Outraged at How Easy It Was to Get You to Click on this Headline" *Wired* www.wired.com/2015/12/psychology-of-clickbait/

Kuiken, J., Schuth, A., Spitters, M. and Marx, M. 2017 "Effective Headlines of Newspaper Articles in a Digital Environment" *Digital Journalism* 5(10): 1300–1314

Viner, K. 2016 "How Technology Disrupted the Truth" *Guardian* www.theguardian.com/media/2016/jul/12/how-technology-disrupted-the-truth

COLUMNIST

Loved and loathed in equal measure, the newspaper columnist is often hired for their controversial, vitriolic opinion which is given a public platform in a daily or weekly column. Personal **journalism**, comment, opinion or op-ed is another name for this form of writing, which developed from the traditional essay and burgeoned under mass newspaper consumption between the two world wars. Appearing in tabloid, broadsheet and online newspapers, columnists respond to contemporary events and issues extolling their "wisdom" to educate or simply entertain the reader. Celebrities often front columns in tabloid newspapers for a handsome fee, although the actual words are usually ghost written by a staff **journalist**. MacArthur suggests that the best definition of a column is a "good read" and that they "set us up for the day, help to define our views ... or they utter thoughts we might agree with but are ashamed to own up to ... or we read them because we can't stand them" (2004: 39).

The ubiquity of self-publishing online via **blogging, social media** posts and **user comment threads** has not deterred **news** organizations from hiring their own opinion writers, who often set the agenda for the day and become talking points and news stories in their own right. Despite the wealth of public opinion online, columnists still hold weight and have become more frequent as media outlets desire an increasing amount of personalized content. They use social media to their advantage, building a following on platforms such as **Twitter**, where they are able to continue voicing their views to the masses. However, this does make them vulnerable to trolling, where they come under attack from people in the online community who post vulgar, aggressive or inflammatory remarks about them. Similarly, columnists have fallen foul of the law themselves and been accused of trolling other users due to their provocative tweets. In 2017 *Mail Online* columnist Katie Hopkins was successfully sued for defamatory comments she posted on Twitter about food writer and poverty campaigner Jack Monroe. She was required to pay £24,000 in damages and £107,000 in legal costs, which led to her filing for insolvency (Oppenheim, 2018). Hopkins had previously left the *Sun* after writing a column that compared migrants to "cockroaches" and "feral humans."

Although there is still a substantial place in the market for paid columnists, many online news websites have introduced sections hosting blogs or comment pieces from the public. *HuffPost* (formerly the ***Huffington Post***) built a large proportion of its business on the back of this type of free content and the *Guardian* has a vibrant Comment is Free section which features the opinions of academics, experts, laypeople and professional writers. Indeed, the argument of whether column writing constitutes as "real journalism" continues today. In 2018, the *Guardian*'s left-wing columnist Owen Jones was accused of not being a "qualified journalist" and earning a living from "writing polemic" by regional political editor Jennifer Williams, after Jones attacked journalism as a socially exclusive profession. He responded by claiming that opinion writing was a subset of journalism (Sharman, 2018).

Key Sources
MacArthur, B. 2004 "Ego Trips Full of Passion that Set the Tone for Newspapers" *The Times* 27 February, 39

COMPUTATIONAL JOURNALISM

The descendent of precision **journalism** and **computer assisted reporting**, computation journalism involves the "application of software and technologies to the activities of journalism" drawing from the field of computer science (Flew, Spurgeon, Daniel and Swift, 2012:

157). The practice goes beyond the daily use of computers since journalists have been using them since they first replaced typewriters in the **newsroom**. Instead, computational journalism is utilized for large-scale manipulation of data and the organization and presentation of said information. It also brings together information technology specialists and journalists in order to develop new computer tools to tell stories in the public interest.

Coddington argues that computational journalism is not simply another name for **data journalism** because it goes beyond the use of a particular set of tools and is instead "centred on the application of computing and computational thinking to the practices of information gathering, sense-making, and information presentation, rather than the journalistic use of data or social science methods more generally" (Coddington, 2015a: 335). It also goes beyond computer assisted reporting, popular in the 1990s, due to its ability to aggregate, automate and abstract information.

Flew, Spurgeon, Daniel and Swift (2012) argue that the potential value of computational journalism is increasing due to three key factors. First, the amount of data publicly available, particularly from government sources, but also unofficial leaks and whistle-blowing websites such as **Wikileaks**. Second, the accessibility of free open source software and **Web 2.0** applications that enables greater experimentation. Finally, the explosion of online participation on social media sites provides greater opportunities for collaboration between professional journalists, citizen journalists and the wider public. An example of this is the *Guardian*'s response to the MPs' expenses scandal first published by the *Telegraph* in 2009. The *Guardian* made publicly available the data surrounding MPs' expense claims, enabling readers to search by MP, constituency or item, and send findings to the newspaper's staff for further investigation. This **crowdsourcing** technique was relatively inexpensive and over 20,000 consumers participated with 170,000 documents reviewed in the first 80 hours.

Key Sources

Coddington, M. 2015 "Clarifying Journalism's Quantitative Turn: A Typology for Evaluating Data Journalism, Computational Journalism, and Computer-Assisted Reporting" *Digital Journalism* 3(3): 331–348

Flew, T., Spurgeon, C., Daniel, A. and Swift, A. 2012 "The Promise of Computational Journalism" *Journalism Practice* 6(2): 157–171

CONVERGENCE

COMMENTS *SEE* USER COMMENT THREADS

COMPUTER ASSISTED REPORTING (CAR)

Expressed broadly, computer assisted reporting is the use of computers to gather and analyze data in order to create and write **news** stories. Once a niche, investigative reporting method that grew out of social science-influenced **precision journalism**, CAR is now routinely used by journalists (DeFleur, 1997). Reporters, particularly those involved in **data journalism**, regularly collect information in databases, analzye public records with spreadsheets and use geographic information system mapping to study demographics and political change. At its most basic, CAR is integrated into the daily practices of all journalists in the use of email to conduct interviews and the searching of the web for background information.

The term is less widely used today, due to the ubiquity of computers, but had its heyday in the 1990s (Garrison, 1998) when a vast amount of information was made available to the American public under freedom of information legislation.

See also **computational journalism**.

Key Sources
DeFleur, M. 1997 *Computer-Assisted Investigative Reporting: Development and Methodology*. Mahwah, NJ: Lawrence Erlbaum
Garrison, B. 1998 *Computer-Assisted Reporting*. Mahwah, NJ: Lawrence Erlbaum

CONTENT FARMS *SEE FLAT EARTH NEWS*

CONVERGENCE

Convergence describes the instance of the coming together of opinions or effects and was first applied to media by Pool (1983: 24), who offered an early conceptualization of media convergence as a process "blurring the lines between media." When used in the context of "convergent journalism," convergence describes a type of **journalism** that sees the coming together of different news media, most often print, broadcast and online. The term became particularly popular in the mid-2000s with Convergent Journalism degrees popping up at universities. Quinn (2005) maintains that convergent journalism has a broad scope of definitions varying from country to country and culture to culture, which also varies within countries and within companies. Convergent journalism can be divided into different types, including ownership, tactical, structural, information gathering and storytelling or presentation (Quinn, 2005). It usually sees the coming together of different news platforms in terms of both production and ownership, hence incorporating both journalistic and economic convergence.

Paulussen (2011) refers to the economic model of convergence that evolved at the end of the 20th century when print media companies embraced convergence in the hope of finding salvation from readership and **advertising** decline. This media convergence strategy was "guided by old economic motives of cost efficiency, productivity and profit consolidation" (Paulussen, 2011: 60) and enabled companies to produce more **news** for the same or little more money across multiple platforms. This convergence of production practices had a dramatic impact on journalists as it required them to become multi-skilled and for news desks to think about presenting a story in more than one medium. This led to the **MOJO journalism** that we see today, whereby reporters are expected to produce written copy for the newspaper, a different version for the website and photographic, video and audio content for the website and **social media**. There has been widespread criticism that economics has driven technological convergence rather than a normative desire to create better journalism and service the public. Therefore, there was initially great reluctance among journalists to embrace convergence. A major report by Williams and Franklin (2007) within the largest British regional publisher Trinity Mirror in 2007 discovered that journalists felt convergence had brought about a greater workload, but had not introduced extra pay or extra staff to offset this and that there was insufficient training and the resultant journalism was poor quality.

Convergent journalism has also brought about a change in the relationship between journalists and audiences. Non-professional content by audiences has now come together with the work of professional journalists, in the form of **user-generated content** raising questions about the quality and accuracy of such journalism and whether it is being utilized for democratic and journalistic means or for economic benefit. Jenkins (2008) argues that it is possible for the two to exist together, albeit often in conflict. He describes a landscape where top-down corporate convergence, which sees the merger of companies and content for profitable gain, coexists alongside bottom-up grassroots convergence, where audiences become involved in the production of media. These, he argues can reinforce one another and create closer, more rewarding relationships but at other times the two forces are at war.

Key Sources

Jenkins, H. 2008 *Convergence Culture: Where Old and New Media Collide*. New York: New York University Press

Pool, I. D. S. 1983 *Technologies of Freedom*. Cambridge, MA: Harvard University Press

Quinn, S. 2005 "What Is Convergence and How Will It Affect My Life?" in Quinn, S. and Filak, V. F. (Eds) *Convergent Journalism: An Introduction*. London: Focal Print, 3–19

Williams, A. and Franklin, B. 2007 "Turning around the Tanker: Implementing Trinity Mirror's Online Strategy" http://image.guardian.co.uk/sys-files/Media/documents/2007/03/13/Cardiff.Trinity.pdf

COPYRIGHT

This law gives the creators of literary, dramatic, musical and artistic works the right to control the ways in which their material may be used. It is an automatic right when an individual or organization creates a work that is regarded as original, and exhibits a degree of labor, skill or judgment. For work to be protected by copyright law it must be tangible and expressed in a physical form, meaning you cannot copyright an idea. The period of time a piece of work is protected for depends on a range of factors such as what type of work it is and when it was made. Each country has its own copyright law but most will protect works created in other countries in the same way. Some forms of creativity are also protected by intellectual property laws.

In **journalism**, issues of copyright breach arise when content such as photographs or entire sections of **news** text or broadcast footage are used without permission. However, in the UK, it is lawful to use or reproduce work without permission under the fair usage, or fair dealing, rule. This is allowed when the use of the work is for research or private study, is used for the purposes of criticism, review or quotation, or it is utilized for the purposes of reporting current events – although this does not apply to photographs. The rather ambiguous nature of this defence has created an online environment where news organizations cannibalize content from one another's websites in the interests of "reporting current events." This is a largely untested legal area and has become somewhat of an accepted norm among news outlets (Phillips, 2010b).

Since photographs are not protected by fair dealing, photographers have become more vigilant in pursuing media organizations for breach of copyright. In the US, there were more than 200 private settlements in 2017 for copyright infringement as a growing number of independent photographers launched lawsuits against moguls such as AOL, CBS, NPR and Yahoo! (Van der Sar, 2017a). In one peculiar case a photographer and an online media company found themselves locked in a counter legal battle. Jon Tannen filed a lawsuit accusing CBS Interactive of using his copyrighted photos in an article on *247 Sports* without his permission, demanding $150,000 for each infringed photo. In response, CBS filed its own copyright infringement lawsuit against Tannen accusing the photographer of posting screenshots from a 1958 CBS TV series on his social media accounts without permission, seeking $150,000 in damages (Van der Sar, 2017b). These kinds of lawsuits for the reproduction of protected images have led to an eruption of attribution and copyright free image galleries such as Morguefile, Pixabay and Splash and the creation of American non-profit organization Creative Commons to license material for free.

In Europe, media publishers could be due billions in payouts due to a controversial change to copyright rules. Article 11 of the European Copyright Directive, known colloquially as the link tax, would force news aggregation and search engine sites such as **Google** and **Facebook** to pay publishers for showing news snippets or linking to news stories on other sites (Sweney, 2018b). At the time of publishing, the proposal was heading for a final vote in the European parliament.

See also **creative cannibalism**.

Key Sources

Sweney, M. 2018b "EU Copyright Law May Force Tech Giants to Pay Billions to Publishers" *Guardian* www.theguardian.com/law/2018/sep/12/eu-copy right-law-may-force-tech-giants-to-pay-billions-to-publishers-facebook-google

Van der Sar, E. 2017a "CBS Sues Man for Posting Image of a 59-Year TV-Show on Social Media" *TorrentFreak* https://torrentfreak.com/cbs-sues-man-for-posting-image-of-a-59-year-tv-show-on-social-media-171030/

Van der Sar, E. 2017b "Pirating Mainstream Media Outlets Haunted by Photographers in Court" *TorrentFreak* https://torrentfreak.com/pirating-main stream-media-outlets-haunted-by-photographers-in-court-171028/

CREATIVE CANNIBALISM

A strange contradiction exists in **journalism** whereby journalists strive for exclusive scoops yet appear to spend most of their time following the pack and making sure they have the same content as their rivals (Crouse, 1973). Rather than creating **diversity**, competition breeds uniformity in the fields of cultural production (Bourdieu, 2005) and this has never been truer than in the digital age. The internet and 24-hour rolling news has ratcheted up the competitive pressure as reporters desperately scramble around trying to ensure they have not missed anything on rivals' websites (Phillips, 2010a).

This has exacerbated the drive for churnalism as journalists can easily and speedily repackage and repurpose material found elsewhere on the web in a "manic recycling of copy" (Phillips, 2010a: 96). The more stories a reporter is expected to churn out per day, the more likely they are to borrow content from other news media, including spurious material from the public relations industry and, at times, **fake news**. It is now widespread practice for reporters to rewrite stories from other news organizations' websites without contributing any additional material or verifying the sources, and usually not attributing the original story. This has put an end to the scoop – the exclusive story – because as former *Guardian* editor Alan Rusbridger noted in 2010, most scoops now have a life expectancy of about three minutes before they are pilfered by another news organization. This cannibalism of content also ignores copyright law but, as Phillips found (2010a) in the British press at least, there appears to be a mutual tolerance of lifted material that breaches copyright. By comparison, American newspapers tend to credit the source of the repurposed material.

Qualitative research by Phillips (2010b) revealed that quality British newspapers such as the *Daily Telegraph* were just as likely to be guilty of this practice as the tabloid press. Journalists on the *Daily Telegraph* were the most frequent to describe using stories and material, unattributed, taken directly from other newspapers. As the only national newspaper to be taking a web-first approach in 2008, the *Daily Telegraph* appeared to set the questionable rules of what was to follow, with a third of their stories at that time being directly lifted from another news organization. Today, cannibalization is an accepted norm within the news media as time and budgetary pressures continue to push journalists to create content fast.

As well as further homogenizing content, cannibalization has a negative impact on **freelance journalists** who find that their work is lifted without any attribution or additional payment. Canter (2017a) discusses how international newspapers and digital native news sites regularly cannibalize exclusive freelance content without acknowledging where the story originates, including trusted brands such as the BBC (Canter, 2017b), leaving freelances out of pocket with limited recourse. See also *Flat Earth News*.

Key Sources
Phillips, A. 2010a "Old Sources: New Bottles" in Fenton, N. (Ed) *New Media, Old News: Journalism & Democracy in the Digital Age*. London: Sage, 87–101
Phillips, A. 2010b "Transparency and the New Ethics of Journalism" *Journalism Practice* 4(3): 373–382

CREATIVE DESTRUCTION

The creation of a new industry that in the process destroys an older one is an economic phenomenon referred to as creative destruction. Also known as Schumpeter's gale, the concept is associated with Austrian economist Joseph Schumpeter, who derived it from the work of Karl Marx and applied it to economic innovation and the business cycle in his 1942 book, *Capitalism, Socialism and Democracy*. This pattern of creation and destruction of wealth can be readily applied to the media industry, which has been subject to the greatest disruption of its history in the past three decades. The emergence of the web and with it digital native news websites such as *HuffPost* and social media platforms such as **Facebook** has led to the creative destruction of the traditional newspaper. Employment in the newspaper business in the US fell from 455,700 in 1990 to 225,100 in 2013, while internet publishing and broadcasting grew from 29,400 to 121,200 over the same period. Similarly, in the UK, 198 local newspapers closed between the beginning of 2015 and the end of 2016. And yet the number of journalists working in the UK rose by 12 percent between 2012 and 2018, in part due to the job demand from digital and online platforms (Spilsbury, 2018). However, such is the cyclical nature of creative destructionism that this innovation in digital journalism is likely to be a source of temporary market power as new technological inventions will ultimately erode the profits of these digital media firms as new entrants take over the market.

Key Sources

Schumpeter, J. 1942 *Capitalism, Socialism and Democracy*. New York: Harper Perennial

Spilsbury, M. 2018 *Journalists at Work*. www.nctj.com/downloadlibrary/JaW%20Report%202018.pdf

"CRISIS" OF JOURNALISM

In their 2013 study of how the *Wall Street Journal*, the *New York Times* and *USA Today* framed reporting of the newspaper industries' financial difficulties as a "crisis" – and, on occasions, even a permanent crisis – Chyi, Lewis and Zheng argued that coverage focused unduly on specific newspaper closures, "short term drama over long term trends," lacked sufficient background and context and "invoked a 'death' imagery" (Chyi, Lewis and Nan, 2012: 305–307). To paraphrase the distinguished American writer Mark Twain, however, while reports of the "death of newspapers" may have been greatly exaggerated, it was difficult to deny that newspapers were facing serious and compelling financial difficulties resulting from the collapse of their existing **business model** based on **advertising**, which resulted in lost **journalism** jobs, reduced publication schedules, in some cases the transition to online only publications and in others to the closure of long-standing and highly respected newspapers (Chyi, Lewis and Nan, 2012). These events carried clear implications for the ability of the press to report the democratic process (Starr, 2009).

Political communication scholar Jay G. Blumler suggests that it is best to untangle the crisis of journalism into two distinct crises, which are separate and reflect particular histories; what Blumler describes as "a crisis with two legs" (Blumler, 2011: xv).

The "crisis of viability" is essentially a financial crisis that is threatening the resources necessary to fund and sustain the reporting and news making activities of **journalists** working in mainstream journalistic organizations. The second crisis, which involves what he terms a crisis of "civic adequacy," concerns the "impoverishing [of] the contributions of journalism to citizenship and democracy." Significantly, while these two crises are interconnected (using Blumler's metaphor, the "two legs" are attached to the same body), they are also distinct, which suggests that even if the crisis of financial or resource viability was resolved, this would not "automatically" fix the crisis of civic adequacy. Indeed, Blumler argues that the history of each crisis is illustrative here. The crisis of viability, for example, is relatively short-lived while the "civic crisis has been building for some time" (Blumler, 2011: xv).

In the longer term, however, is it likely that the newly developing forms of internet-based, online and **hyperlocal** news media will (to extend Blumler's metaphor to breaking point) "step into the shoes" of their **legacy media** predecessors and resolve the crisis of civic adequacy. Blumler's definitive "no" to this question is informed by two observations. First, there is little, if any, evidence to suggest that journalists' reporting of public affairs is reorienting into more civic or citizen oriented modes in the new digital environment. Second, features of the emerging digital media ecosystem – competition, the clamor for public attention, the brevity of Tweets through which political conversations are increasingly conducted, as well as the growing incivility of those conversations (Ksiazek and Springer, 2019) – militate against any likely resolution of the crisis of civic adequacy.

This view was endorsed by Fico, Lacy, Wildman, Baldwin, Bergan and Zube (2013) in their study of 48 **citizen journalism** sites, 86 weekly newspapers and 138 daily newspapers in the US to explore how well the citizen journalism sites might work as effective "information substitutes and complements" for the dwindling newspaper coverage of local government as traditional newspapers increasingly lost staff and in some cases closed (Fico, Lacy, Wildman, Baldwin, Bergan and Zube, 2013). They concluded that "citizen journalism sites are, at best, imperfect information substitutes for most newspapers" (Fico, Lacy, Wildman, Baldwin, Bergan and Zube, 2013: 154).

Key Sources

Blumler, J. G. 2011 "Foreword: The Two Legged Crisis of Journalism" in Franklin, B. (Ed) *The Future of Journalism*. London: Routledge, xv–xvii

Fico, F., Lacy, S., Wildman, S., Baldwin, T., Bergan, D. and Zube, P. 2013 "Citizen Journalism Sites as Information Substitutes and Complements for Unites States Newspaper Coverage of Local Government" *Digital Journalism* 1 (1): 152–168

Ksiazek, T. and Springer, N. 2019 "User Comment in Digital Journalism: Current Research and Future Directions" in Eldridge, S. and Franklin, B.

(Eds) *The Routledge Handbook of Developments in Digital Journalism Studies*. London: Routledge, 475–487

Starr, P. 2009 "The End of the Press: Democracy Loses Its Best Friend" *The New Republic* 4 March, 28–35

CROWDFUNDING

The collapse of **journalism** industries' traditional **business model**, based around advertising during the first two decades of the new millennium, witnessed a frantic search by news organizations for resources to fund journalism in the digital age which included **pay-walls**, online **advertising**, as well as new **not-for-profit** news organizations. A significant new mechanism for funding and sustaining the production of news, especially public service or investigative news, was crowdfunding (see also **crowdsourcing**).

Crowdfunding is a way of raising finance to fund a specific project or activity by using the internet to invite a potentially global **audience** to contribute sums of money which may range from modest amounts to more substantial sums. The motives for contributing to a crowdfunded project may similarly vary from people who simply believe in a particular cause or charitable ambition to those who anticipate a financial return on their "investment." Those seeking funds typically establish a profile of their project on a website such as *Kickstarter* (www.kickstarter.com/), before publicizing the site on **social media**, via networks of friends, family and work acquaintances.

An early crowdfunded project dates back to 1997 when fans of rock band Marillion raised $60,000 to fund the band's tour of the US. Subsequently, the band has adopted crowdfunding techniques to fund the production of three of its albums. Similar crowdfunding strategies have has been widely adopted to fund the production of journalism (Aitamurto, 2017: 185–193) with sites such as the Global Investigative Journalism Network (https://gijn.org/resources/crowdfunding-for-journalists-2/) and Through the Cracks (http://throughcracks.com/) offering opportunities to fund specific projects.

Aitamurto identifies four types of crowdfunding in journalism; fundraising for a single story, perhaps an issue which a **journalist** or organization feels that mainstream media ignores or offers too little attention; the more costly journalistic project of sustained coverage of a topic such as environmental reporting or establishing a new journalistic **beat**; fundraising to create a new **blog, platform** or publication and, finally, fundraising for a service that supports journalism. Funding requests were initially to cover a single story but, increasingly, crowdfunding seeks resources to sustain coverage across a new beat (Aitamurto, 2017: 188).

Key Sources

Aitamurto, T. 2017 "Crowdsourcing in Open Journalism: Benefits, Challenges and Value Creation" in Franklin, B. and Eldridge, II, S. (Eds) *The Routledge Companion to Digital Journalism Studies.* London: Routledge, 185–193

UK Crowdfunding. "What is Crowdfunding" www.ukcfa.org.uk/what-is-crowdfunding/

CROWDSOURCING

While **crowdfunding** makes broad appeals to the general public for resources to fund journalistic projects, crowdsourcing seeks to tap into the aggregated wisdom, experience, knowledge and beliefs of the "crowd" to inform those journalism projects (Muthukumaraswamy, 2010). Crowdsourcing allows **journalists** "to harness the crowd's knowledge for journalism" by channelling "information to journalists quickly and from a large number of people thus contributing to the journalistic process in several ways" (Aitamurto, 2017, 2015). Crowdsourcing offers an example of what Aitamurto calls "an open journalistic practice" because of its conscious effort to "open up" the previously closed professional world of **journalism** to the public (Aitamurto, 2017: 186).

When journalists wish to crowdsource a particular story, they publish a request online, similar to crowdfunding, inviting members of the public to offer the information they are seeking from the crowd (Capati, 2015). The **Guardian's** 2009 investigation into MPs' expenses claims is perhaps one of the most well known crowdsourced stories; "thousands of people" were recruited to examine and comment on Parliamentarians' claims for expenses, which many readers judged to be false and unwarranted claims. Subsequently, crowdsourcing has been used by news organizations to investigate other possible cases of corruption and scandal. Aitamurto offers an example. In 2013, Swedish newspaper *Svenska Dagbladet* crowdsourced an investigation into mortgages and about 50,000 readers "submitted their information on a crowdmap on the newspaper's website and dozens of stories were written based on their crowdsourced data" (Aitamurto, 2017: 187).

Crowdsourcing stories bring many benefits to the news organization. For journalists, crowdsourcing involves "knowledge discovery and peer learning" (Aitamurto, 2017: 188). There are other advantages for the news organization. First, the online crowd is potentially unlimited and offers the journalist a substantial pool of information. Second, journalists can access the collective views and insights of the crowd to inform their journalism. Third, the data generated may be delivered very quickly but certainly – and fourth, very cheaply (Aitamurto, 2015). Muthukumaraswamy concludes that crowdsourcing offers a further example of how the lines between journalists and readers are blurring (Muthukumaraswamy, 2010).

Key Sources

Aitamurto, T. 2015 "Crowdsourcing as a Knowledge Search Method in Digital Journalism: Ruptured Ideals and Blended Responsibility" *Digital Journalism* 4 (2): 280–297

Aitamurto, T. 2017 "Crowdsourcing in Open Journalism: Benefits, Challenges and Value Creation" in Franklin, B. and Eldridge, II, S. (Eds) *The Routledge Companion to Digital Journalism Studies.* London: Routledge, 185–193

Capati, M. K. 2015 "5 Crowdsourced News Platforms Shaping the Future of Journalism" *Crowd Sourcing Week* 30th June. https://crowdsourcingweek. com/blog/5-crowdsourced-news-platforms/

Muthukumaraswamy, K.. 2010 "When the Media Meet Crowds of Wisdom: How Journalists Are Tapping into Audience Expertise and Manpower for the Process of News Gathering" *Journalism Practice* 4(1): 48–65.

DATA JOURNALISM

The meaning of data **journalism** seems uncertain and is, consequently, often contested: So is the timing of its origins. Scholars and journalism professionals, moreover, sometimes hold distinctive views. Borges Rey, for example, acknowledges "the plethora of ... often competing conceptualizations of data journalism" but "defines" it as "the type of **news** reporting through which **journalists** engage with computerized data to inform their publics" (Borges-Rey, 2015: 284). Simon Rogers, **editor** of the **Guardian** Data **Blog**, however, suggests that data journalism involves journalists in little more than the shift from using words to using "the power of data to tell stories" (Rogers, 2013a). Borges-Rey, moreover, sees data journalism emerging "across the last decade" (2015: 284), while Rogers claims that a table of data on the back page of the launch issue of the *Guardian* on May 5th 1821, exploring the cost of educating pupils in different Manchester schools, offered the first example of data journalism at the *Guardian* (Rogers, 2013b). At times, it seems that data journalism might be reducible to the tautological statement that it is simply journalism that involves data. To cite Rogers again, "So what is data journalism? If you ask me, it is just journalism" (Rogers, 2013b). More forensic definitions do exist. Coddington, for example, cites Howard's suggestion that data journalism involves, "gathering, cleaning, organizing, analyzing, visualizing, and publishing data to support the creation of the acts of journalism" (Howard, cited in Coddington, 2018: 230).

The various definitions offered by journalists and scholars typically include the following elements which can be composited into a more holistic view in which data journalism becomes (1) a specialist and emerging field of journalistic activity which (2) has grown across the new millennium and involves (3) journalists (as content producers, investigators, curators and story tellers), (4) computer scientists, programmers and statisticians (as specialists in the interrogation and interpretation of data and data sets), as well as (5) digital designers (as skilled specialists in web design, data visualization and **infographics**), to create (6) significant, data rich stories and (7) to present them in accessible, engaging and compelling ways for readers. Fink and Anderson discovered "considerable variety" among data journalists in the USA, Belgium, Sweden and Norway, in terms of "their educational backgrounds, skills, tools and goals" although they faced "similar struggles, such as trying to define their roles within their organizations and managing scarce resources" (Fink and Anderson, 2016).

In a significant and helpful article published in *Digital Journalism* in 2015, journalism scholar Mark Coddington establishes a threefold typology, embracing **computer-assisted-journalism** and **computational journalism**, alongside data journalism, in order to try to clarify these distinctive components in what he terms "the quantitative turn in Journalism." The typology derived from a detailed reading of approximately 90 texts in professional and scholarly literatures (Coddington, 2015a: 331). After considering "points of overlap and divergence among their journalistic values and practice" he concludes that these journalistic forms are "related but distinct" (Coddington, 2015a: 331) and certainly not "mutually exclusive" (op cit: 333). He suggests that data journalism is the "term of choice" in the news industry where definitions tend to be broad. Citing Stray's formulation, data journalism involves "obtaining, reporting on, curating and publishing data in the public interest" (cited in Coddington, 2015a: 334).

Coddington then enumerates four dimensions that can be used to evaluate and compare the three identified strands in quantitative journalism. The first dimension stresses a commitment to openness and broad participation at one extreme with an emphasis on professional expertise and limited participation at the other end of the continuum. This dimension articulates "the difference between a production process limited to professionals ... and one open to a networked, loosely joined group" (Coddington, 2015a: 338). Data journalism favors openness and typically projects make data readily accessible.

The second dimension distinguishes between **transparency** and opacity. Data journalism is broadly committed to transparency in both its disclosure (openness concerning the news production processes) and participatory (opportunities for non-journalists to become involved in news production) dimensions (op cit: 340).

Coddington's brief description of the third dimension is "targeted sampling versus big data" (op cit: 341) which conveys the distinction between the classic social science approach of data sampling and the use of inference at one pole of the continuum, compared with the interrogation of large data sets aimed "at capturing the totality of a phenomenon" at the opposite pole (op cit: 341). Data journalists typically engage with substantive data sets and emphasize the scale of their data collection as "key to what is new about their practice" (op cit: 342).

Finally, data journalism may differ from the other two forms of data *driven* journalism by its perception of the **audience**/public as either active or passive. Data journalism (like CAR) is concerned to inform the public but wishes to make data accessible, thereby empowering the public to interrogate data for and by itself (Coddington, 2015a: 342–343). Coddington concludes that "data journalism is the closest we have to the melding of professional journalism and both open-source and computational principles" while data journalists' adoption of "narrative, storytelling and traditional reporting" ensures their work is "taken seriously by professional journalism" and that "they are seen as continuing its practices, rather than harming them" (Coddington, 2015a: 344).

Certainly data journalism has achieved remarkable successes in the early years of its reporting. In the UK, for example, the *Guardian* has pioneered the application of data journalism to break significant **global journalism** stories such as the Panama Papers; the *Guardian* data team also worked with Edward Snowden to report his leaking of the NSA papers and in that process won a Pulitzer Prize for public service journalism. The *Telegraph* has similarly developed its data journalism resources, perhaps most notably in its investigation and reporting of what came to be known in the UK as the "MPs' Expenses Scandal." In the USA, non-profit news organizations such as **ProPublica** and Gapminder have deployed the data journalism techniques of scraping, mining and analyzing data, in tandem with layout and presentation tools like interactive maps, to inform insightful reporting of topics such as the alarming and expansive rates of extinction of certain animals on a global scale and the diverse patterns of the health and wealth of nations (Bouchart, 2018).

Key Sources

Bouchart, M. 2018 "This Is What the Best of Data Journalism Looks Like" https://medium.com/data-journalism-awards/this-is-what-the-best-of-data-journalism-looks-like-6f1713d60479

Coddington, M.. 2015a "Clarifying Journalism's Quantitative Turn: A Typology for Evaluating Data Journalism, Computational Journalism, and Computer-Assisted Reporting" *Digital Journalism* 3(3): 331–348

Fink, K. and Anderson, C. W. 2016 "Data Journalism in the US: Beyond the 'Usual Suspects'" *Journalism Studies* 16(4): 467–481, doi:10.1080/1461670X.2014.939852.

Rogers, S. 2013a "What Is Data Journalism at the Guardian?" www.theguardian.com/news/datablog/video/2013/apr/04/what-is-data-journalism-video

Rogers, S. 2013b "The History of Data Journalism at the Guardian" www.theguardian.com/news/datablog/video/2013/apr/04/history-of-data-journalism-video

DATA VISUALIZATION *SEE* INFOGRAPHICS

DEADLINE

The date and time by which a story must be finished in readiness for publication or broadcast is referred to as a deadline. It is the absolute latest time for finishing before a newspaper goes to print or a program is broadcast. Curiously, the etymology of the word is more sinister, having originated from the idiom used to describe a boundary around a military prison. If a prisoner ventured across this "dead line" they were at risk of being shot dead by the guards. Although the repercussions are not deadly, there is immense pressure on journalists to meet deadlines and have their story ready for the next edition of the newspaper or program slot. Online news, with its continuous, rolling deadlines, has created additional demands as media organizations seek to be the first to break a piece of news, even if just by a few seconds.

Timeliness is inherent in the concept of **news**, although timeframes have shifted over the centuries from quarterly, to weekly, to daily, to every minute (Wheatley and O'Sullivan, 2017). On the one hand, online deadlines have accelerated and there is pressure to be continually producing and distributing news, while conversely there are no strictly enforced deadlines and news can be published at any time of day or night, at any frequency. This has led to an environment of **liquid news**, whereby the same story can appear in many different iterations as it is constantly updated and deadlines, in theory, are obsolete. The reality, however, is somewhat different, with evidence that the immediacy of news is a myth (Lim, 2012) and **newsroom** production remains centered around daily deadlines with journalists working in set shifts patterns which still largely follow a traditional routine (Wheatley and O'Sullivan, 2017).

One of the key challenges of the abbreviated news timeline and constant deadlines is that the internet is sacrificing accuracy for speed, a concern shared by more journalists than not in Europe (O'Sullivan and Heinonen, 2008). There is also the dilemma for legacy media organizations over which content to save for the print publication and which to publish immediately online, meaning journalists can often be simultaneously working to different print and online deadlines.

Key Sources

O'Sullivan, J. and Heinonen, A. 2008 "Old Values, New Media" *Journalism Practice* 2(3): 357–371

Wheatley, D. and O'Sullivan, J. 2017 "Pressure to Publish or Saving for Print?" *Digital Journalism* 5(8): 965–985

DEFAMATION

Any individual or company can sue for damage to their reputation caused by material broadcast to a third party, including material published online, as long as they are identifiable. Libel is a permanent defamatory publication or broadcast that can include written material in books, newspapers, magazines, websites and **social media** platforms, or allegations appearing in television or radio. Slander relates to the spoken word, which is more transient in nature, such as defamatory remarks made at a public event in front of an audience but not recorded in any manner. Under the new Defamation Act 2013, claimants need to demonstrate that the content would tend to lower them in the estimation of right-thinking people generally and cause serious harm to their reputation. Companies can only sue if they can prove serious financial loss. A defamation case can be brought against an author, **editor** or publishing company and even distributors of defamatory material such as website owners and internet service providers. There are four main defences available to a defendant in a libel or slander action, which are truth, honest opinion, publication on a matter of public interest and qualified or absolute privilege. British defamation law is regarded by journalists as the harshest in the Western world because of potentially massive legal costs and the high amounts awarded for damages, particularly since the loser of a trial pays both sides' costs. Many media organizations prefer to settle outside of court and offer damages to the claimant rather than risk an expensive trial, even if it believes what it published or broadcast was true. Trainee journalists in the UK are strongly advised to swot up and memorize the defamation chapter of *McNae's Essential Law for Journalists'* (2018) which, 60 years since the first edition, remains the definitive media law guide for journalists and students alike.

Despite extensive knowledge of the law and the employment of in-house legal teams, professional media still find themselves sued for defamation. In November 2018, Eurovision Song Contest winner Dana Rosemary Scallon received a six-figure settlement from the publishers of the *Sunday World* over false claims connected to her brother, John Brown, who was unanimously acquitted of child sex abuses charges in 2014. Scallon sued the publishers after an online report on sundayworld.com wrongly alleged she had covered up child abuse.

Reader comments on news websites have also come under scrutiny due to the potentially libelous content posted there by members of the public. Hungarian news portal Index.hu and an association for Hungarian internet firms were successfully sued for messages on its forum which included angry comments about a real-estate company. However, in 2016, the European Court of Human Rights ruled that news websites were not responsible for insulting and rude comments by readers and in this case judges in the Hungarian courts had failed to balance the need to prevent abuse with the right to free expression. Meanwhile, changes to defamation law in the UK mean that website operators no longer have to pre-moderate reader comments and instead should implement a report and remove system that people can use if they believe they have been defamed on a website message board.

The rise in self-publishing, **citizen journalism** and **blogging** has also led to prominent cases of non-journalists being sue for libel. In 2018, parish councillor Patrick Smith, who ran a community blog in Bedfordshire, was ordered to pay £37,500 libel damages to a property developer he falsely accused on a £10million fraud. In his judgment, Mr Justice Warby described the independent councillor, who published Caddington Village News online, as a "careless journalist who acted with a closed mind and in some respects irrationally" (BBC, 2018). The number of libel actions linked to posts on **Facebook** and **Twitter** has also risen in recent years, leading to the coining of the term "Twibel." One of the most famous UK cases was that of writer, cook and poverty campaigner Jack Monroe, who was awarded £24,000 in damages after suing MailOnline **columnist** Katie Hopkins for a series of tweets implying Monroe had defaced a war memorial. Hopkins was also ordered by the courts to pay £107,000 in legal costs, which led to her filing for insolvency. The result led to the UK's High Court publishing a bizarre 26-point Twitter "How-to" guide as an appendix to the 28-page ruling. Despite this pioneering defamation case, Twibel still continues, although now it is more likely to be at the hands of the public or politicians than journalists or news organizations. In February 2018, Mansfield MP Ben Bradley publicly apologized to Labour leader Jeremy Corby on Twitter: "On the 19th of February I made a defamatory statement about @jeremy-corbyn. I have apologised to Mr Corbyn and here is the complete text of my apology. Please retweet." Bradley also agreed to pay an undisclosed sum of money to charity after he falsely alleged that Corbyn had sold British secrets to communist spies.

Social media networks have also become host to a series of other legal breaches, due to a lack of media law knowledge by the public. Tommy Robinson, founder of the far-right English Defence League, was jailed for 13 months in 2018 for contempt of court. He broadcast an hour-long video via Facebook from outside Leeds Crown Court and made comments that risked causing a trial to collapse. Meanwhile, nine people were ordered to pay £624 to a woman who claimed she was raped by footballer Ched Evans, after they admitted naming her on Twitter and Facebook. Under the Sexual Offences Act 2003, victims and alleged victims of sex crimes are given lifelong anonymity. The Sheffield United and Wales striker was jailed for raping the 19-year-old but was later acquitted.

Key Sources
BBC. 2018 "Caddington Village News Blogger Sued for Libel over Fraud Claims" *BBC News* www.bbc.co.uk/news/amp/uk-england-beds-bucks-herts-46305141?__twitter_impression=true&fbclid=IwAROzqaocTp gir2qJS6BWMRWdj0NDIy8rdEs3ZAGLCyNrooYjkKFD8lrv-o
Dodd, M. and Hanna, M. 2018 *McNae's Essential Law for Journalists.* 24th edition. Oxford: Oxford University Press

DEMOCRATIC DEFICIT

The decline of local **journalism** via the closure of newspapers, staff redundancies and merger of newsrooms has left an information vacuum in communities known as a democratic deficit. Many regional publishers no longer have enough resources to cover court cases and council meetings and have abolished localized editions and cut beat reporters, once the bread and butter of printed content. This has left a democratic landscape where local authorities are not held accountable and justice is not seen to be done. However, the internet has enabled a number of solutions to spring forth to take up the challenge of filling the purported gap, including hyperlocal websites and blogs, not-for-profit **investigative journalism** sites, **BBC** local democracy reporters and journalists funded by global media platforms.

The loss of more than 200 **local newspapers** in the UK since 2005 has meant that sections of the country are unable to hold politicians and political processes to account. This has been particularly evident in Scotland, where Johnston Press is a leading local newspaper publisher and has reduced staff by almost 50 percent. To address this deficit, a cooperative of journalists set up The Ferret investigative journalism website to report on local democracy (Price, 2017). The site is funded by subscribers, who have a say in the content and direction of the organization. Similar non-commercial websites have emerged across the globe that are funded by a mixed business model of subscriptions, donations and patrons and are run by paid or volunteer journalists with considerable professional experience.

The internet, with its low entry barriers, has also created a space for non-professional journalists to report on their local communities and grassroots publishers have flourished online. Participatory journalism and **citizen journalism** have been heralded as having the potential to democratize journalism and foster greater civic engagement among citizens. Hyperlocal websites and blogs, often set up by retired individuals, have attempted to report on community matters and help to address the democratic deficit. These sites have met with mixed success but there is evidence that they are increasing public scrutiny of the powerful elite to some degree (Harcup, 2016).

Coordinated attempts to address the democratic deficit have also been made by public service broadcasters, governments and tech giants. In 2017, the BBC launched the UK Local Democracy Reporting Service and created 150 new journalism jobs as part of the BBC Charter commitment. These journalists are funded via the BBC license fee but employed by regional news organizations which range from radio stations to online media companies, although the bulk are established regional newspaper groups. These reporters cover top-tier local authorities and other public service organizations and their content is shared across 800 media outlets that have signed up to the Local News Partnership Scheme. The BBC is committed to investing up to £8 million a year until the end of 2026. Meanwhile, in 2013, the UK government launched the Local TV Network to counteract the decline in local newspapers. To date, 34 channels have been awarded licenses but the scheme has met with limited success due to low audience figures.

Further financial support to aid local reporting has been awarded to Bureau Local in the UK from the **Google** Digital News Initiative. Launched in 2017, the award-winning network of regional and national reporters, bloggers and technologists is part of the Bureau of Investigative Journalism, an independent, not-for-profit organization founded in 2010 by David and Elaine Potter. Bureau Local aims to hold power to account nationally and locally and "support, reinvigorate and innovate accountability reporting in the UK" (The Bureau of Investigative Journalism, 2018). In late 2018, **Facebook** also announced that it will be donating £4.5 million to fund 80 local newspaper jobs in the UK in a two-year pilot scheme.

See also **alternative journalism, hyperlocal journalism, local media, news beats, non-profit journalism.**

Key Sources
The Bureau of Investigative Journalism 2018 "About Bureau Local" *The Bureau of Investigative Journalism* www.thebureauinvestigates.com/explainers/about-the-project

Harcup, T. 2016 "Alternative Journalism as Monitorial Citizenship? A Case Study of a Local News Blog" *Digital Journalism* 4(5): 639–657

DIGITAL JOURNALISM

Much like **data journalism**, the various definitions and understandings of *digital* journalism occupy little common ground, are often used interchangeably and are typically conflated with cognate terms such as **online journalism**.

In *A Short History of Disruptive Technologies 1960 to 1990*, American historian Will Mari argues that some of the opacity surrounding definitions may be clarified by adopting an historical approach. He suggests, for example, that digital journalism has a considerably longer history than popular understanding appreciates by reminding readers that digital computers were increasingly common in US newsrooms from the late 1950s onwards, although their introduction and use for newswriting occurred in three phases, across more than 30 years and well ahead of the arrival of the internet, which triggered the major expansion of digital journalism. The mainframe computer era spanned the mid-1950s to the late 1960s; the minicomputer era from the 1970s to the 1980s and the microprocessor era from 1982–1992 (Mari, 2019). Then the pace of change from **legacy media** to digital media and digital journalism quickened with the arrival of the internet, increasingly sophisticated software packages, the **affordances** of **Web 2.0, (Live) blogs, smartphones, tablets, social media, algorithms, news bots, live streaming**, mobile news and the enhanced and varied uses of **artificial intelligence** (AI) in news journalism (Franklin, 2013b: 1–5).

Malik and Shapiro (2017) deal in turn with the etymology of the words "digital" and "journalism" in an effort to enhance clarity. They offer a stipulative definition of *journalism* that involves "the independent pursuit of, or commentary upon, accurate information about current or recent events and its original presentation for public edification" (Malik and Shapiro, 2017: 16). This initial account, however, identifies five conditions or "complementary tests" which must be satisfied for the definition to hold. First, the requirement for *independence* demands the absence of any connection between the economic interests of the author and journalistic content, rather than any confusion with impartiality. Second, *accuracy* is crucial and evidenced by rigor of verification. Third, content must focus on *recent and current work* while, fourth, the subject matter must be *original* and not a repurposing of others' work (See **creative cannibalism**). Finally, for work to constitute journalism, it must be offered for *public edification* – that is, accessible to a broad public rather than a limited group of specialists or experts. Work that meets these five conditions or specifications is journalism (Malik and Shapiro, 2017: 16–17).

Turning to "digital," Malik and Shapiro specify seven characteristics of contemporary journalism found in the digital realm (identified as **news** organizations' web sites/publications, social networks, comments on news stories, mobile and desktop applications) that distinguish digital journalism "from the journalism that existed up until the dawn of the internet."

First, digital journalism is *interactive*. The relationship between producers and consumers is two-way and, since readers/viewers contest or provide additional information for reports, news coverage constitutes co-production. Second, news stories are *unfinished* in the sense that they are rewritten as well as constantly and instantly updated as news stories unravel. Third, digital news and journalism is *long lasting*, if not eternal. The tweeting, retweeting and sharing of digital news facilitates such longevity. Removing information from the digital realm is near impossible, making the **right to be forgotten** an increasingly valued entitlement. Fourth, digital news is also *global*. Again, the sharing of even local stories on global networks ensures their potential for accessibility by anyone with a network connection. Fifth, digital journalism is *personal* or perhaps more conversational and informal in tone. Journalists increasingly combine their distant, authoritative, neutral approach to reporting with the "cultivation of a digital persona" (**personal branding**) allowing them to reveal more of their personality. Sixth, digital journalism is *unsiloed*. Journalism in the digital age links readers to other (even competitor) news sites and sources to create a "one-stop experience," while allowing readers autonomy in reading the story in their preferred order and denying journalists' their gatekeeping role. Finally, digital journalism involves what Malik and Shapiro term "*an evolutionary moment*" which can be helpful in the task of definition by asking "what happens at the moment at which analog work turns digital." The transition to digital journalism involves a number of such consequential moments. Digital journalism, they suggest, for example, "is born ... when the author–audience relationship becomes more interactive and engaged" (Malik and Shapiro, 2017: 16–21).

Malik and Shapiro concede that they have not delivered a precise and exclusive definition of digital journalism – a "genus defining line" which sets out a series of tests which journalism must meet in order to be "digital." But they conclude that "to present a series of characteristics that are commonly present in the genus is ... at least an important step towards definition" (Malik and Shapiro, 2017: 22).

See also **computational journalism, computer-assisted journalism, Digital Journalism Studies, journalism, mobile journalism; online journalism**.

Key Sources

Franklin, B. 2013b "Editorial" *Digital Journalism* 1(1): 1–5

Malik, A. and Shapiro, I. 2017 "What's Digital? What's Journalism" in Franklin, B. and Eldridge, II, S. (Eds) *The Routledge Companion to Digital Journalism Studies*. London: Routledge, 15–24

Mari, W. 2019 *A Short History of Disruptive Technologies 1960 to 1990; Introducing the Computer in the Newsroom*. London: Routledge

DIGITAL JOURNALISM EDUCATION

Former *Sun* newspaper **editor** Kelvin MacKenzie publicly decreed in 2011 that he would "shut all the journalism colleges down" and there was "no merit" in going to university if young people wanted to become a print **journalist** (MacKenzie, 2011). Instead, he advocated getting a job on a local newspaper and learning from first-hand experience. What the former tabloid editor failed to recognize was that the era of the singular print journalist was over. Today, trainee reporters must be accomplished in print, online and broadcast skills usually gained via a university course. During the past 40 years, **journalism** has progressed from a school-leaver occupation to a graduate job, making it extremely difficult – although not impossible – to enter the industry without an undergraduate or postgraduate degree. Training no longer occurs systematically on the job, as industry primarily relies upon higher education to provide this service. Advice to aspiring journalists given by the Society of Editors (2014) makes it abundantly clear that the vast majority of new entrants to the occupation have degrees and an approved journalism qualification. Data from the Journalists at Work report (Spilsbury, 2013) indicates that 82 percent of people working as journalists have a degree or higher level qualification compared to 38 percent of all employment in the UK, making journalism a highly qualified occupation. Yet, in 1968, less than 10 percent of UK journalists were graduates (Boyd-Barrett, 1970). A similar picture can be seen around the Western world, despite the fact that there is no set entry requirement into the occupation and modes of entry vary enormously. Journalism is invariably classified as a profession, craft, industry, literary genre, culture, social practice, community and ideology (Evans, 2014) and, as such, applicants can gain their first job in journalism via work experience, formal training schemes, freelancing or directly with no prior experience (Spilsbury, 2013).

The central conflict in journalism education is equipping students with a balance of practical skills and scholarly learning. Since **journalism** has largely become a graduate occupation, it is entrenched in academia, which is most concerned with research and yet education inside the academy is often criticized for being too vocational, technical and skills oriented (Creech and Mendelson, 2015) rather than theorizing the contextual role of journalism in society. Many scholars argue that journalism education should focus on the needs of citizens and communities (Carey, 2000) and should inform the industry rather than attempt to socialize students into existing **newsroom** norms (Mensing, 2010). However, critics of this approach argue that journalism education is too conceptual and does not spend enough time on the basics of writing, reporting and editing and responding to the needs of the profession (Creech and Mendelson, 2015). This dichotomy has been heightened further by digital technology, with university courses focusing even further on skills-based learning, in particular multimedia reporting, coding and **infographics**. Courses focusing on data visualization and **computational journalism** are on the rise, particularly in the US but these are mostly taught by non-academic staff, causing the field to lack strong academic underpinning (Heravi, 2018). Meanwhile, educators leading broader journalism degrees are preoccupied with filling their curriculum with digital storytelling techniques, alongside the traditional print and broadcast skills of information gathering, production and distribution, often at the expense of academic content. Mensing (2010) argues that adding multimedia and internet distribution to journalism school programs has essentially maintained the status quo of journalism education, where the role of the reporter is central. Students are still largely taught a correct way to report stories by former practitioners and are required to take part in industry internships as part of their training, reinforcing conceptions of what journalism is and how to practice it. Instead, Mensing advocates restoring the focus on journalism as an act of community with the goal of journalism education to be about building functioning communication structures within communities rather than simply working for a media organization.

In the UK, the focus on industry rather than community is strongly felt due to the influence of accreditation bodies that serve the interests of employers. Almost half of all working British journalists have a qualification from the National Council for the Training of Journalists (NCTJ), which accredits higher and further education courses (Spilsbury, 2013). Around 13 percent of all journalism Bachelor and Masters degrees in the UK are accredited by the NCTJ, with the Broadcast Journalism Training Council accrediting a further 17 percent of the 300 courses listed by UCAS, and the Professional Publishers Association accrediting another 7 percent (Canter, 2015b). In such a busy and expansive marketplace accreditation is an attractive "added value" for journalism degree applicants and, as such, is viewed by universities as a valuable marketing tool. As a result, currently a third of higher education journalism courses are accredited by at least one of the three bodies. But with the growth of interest in digital and broadcast media, higher education institutions are faced with the question of whether or not accreditation schemes are relevant to employability and career progression and if, indeed, there is any correlation between accreditation and graduate employment rates. Some journalism scholars and educators (Heseltine, 2010; McNair, 2010) argue that student employability is no longer dependent on accreditation in an era of rapid globalization and digitalization and these bodies are no longer providing the necessary skills that industry requires. Research by Canter (2015b), who interviewed employers involved in trainee recruitment across all types of media, found that accreditation was viewed as less valuable than a demonstration of skills via work experience and a productive digital profile. It also found that employers valued courses that taught a mixture of traditional skills and intermediate digital literacy rather than theoretical **journalism studies**.

Key Sources

Canter, L. 2015b "Chasing the Accreditation Dream: Do Employers Value Accredited Journalism Courses" *Journalism Education* 4(1): 40–52

Creech, B. and Mendelson, A. L. 2015 "Imagining the Journalist of the Future: Technological visions of Journalism Education and Newswork" *Communication Review* 18(2): 142–165

Evans, R. 2014 "Can Universities Make Good Journalists?" *Journalism Education* 3 (1): 66–87

Mensing, D. 2010 "Rethinking [again] the Future of Journalism Education" *Journalism Studies* 11(4): 511–523

Society of Editors 2014 "Advice for Aspiring Journalists" *Society of Editors* www.societyofeditors.co.uk

DIGITAL JOURNALISM AND THE ENVIRONMENT

The assumption that digital media is better for the environment than print because it does not involve deforestation or carbon intensive manufacturing processes is vehemently challenged by scholar Toby Miller (2015), who argues that **journalism** production is at the center of an ecological crisis. His startling message is that the technologies used by writers and publishers from print to the web have "drawn upon, created and emitted dangerous substances, generating multi-generational risks for ecosystems and employees alike" (Miller, 2015: 653). Historically, the raw materials required for print journalism involved deforestation, conflict mining and the use of poisonous solvents, inks, fumes and tainted wastewater. But today's manufacturing of electronic devices such as **smartphones**, tablets and laptops is equally, if not more, destructive as it involves an industry where battery workers are exposed to lead and pathogens that damage the lungs, skin and nervous system. Furthermore, the amount of electricity used to charge these mobile gadgets is astronomical, with most of it derived from fossil fuel power sources. Miller contends that communication devices are responsible for around 15 percent of the world's residential energy use, which will rise to 45 percent by 2030. Internet servers, the machines which support websites, are housed in data centers which are estimated to account for some two percent of all global greenhouse gases emissions – the same amount as aviation (Wood, Shabajee, Schien, Hodgson and Preist, 2014). Indeed, paper is more energy efficient to produce than electronic devices, with the average book using two kilowatt hours of fossil fuels compared to 100 kilowatts for an e-reader, which then uses more electricity when it is charged (Miller, 2015). And the waste produced by obsolete digital technologies, which are often discarded annually when the latest upgrade arrives on the market, can produce toxic chemical and noxious gases into the soil and water.

Despite growing evidence of the unsustainable nature of digital journalism, media organizations have been slow to respond, focusing instead on offsetting their carbon footprint from printing newspapers or reducing air travel. The *Guardian* has made a conscious effort to tackle the environmental damage caused by flying journalists around the world, particularly for travel writing "jollies" by offsetting flights with Climate Care, which funds sustainable energy products (Dodd, 2007). It also let researchers into its business to create a model of its estimated digital carbon footprint of www.theguardian.com, which was found to be 10,000 tonnes of carbon dioxide equivalent in 2012. This was comparable to the production of its newsprint which, unlike the digital product, is subject to environmental management (Wood, Shabajee, Schien, Hodgson and Preist, 2014).

However, the problem lies in how to reduce the overall carbon footprint when most of it is created by the consumer rather than the **news** producer. With newspapers, the bulk of energy is expended in paper production, which a publisher can directly influence, whereas digital news burns up most of its energy when it is consumed by its audience, which is outside the direct control of media organizations.

Key Sources

Dodd, C. 2007 "Carbon Copy" *Guardian* www.theguardian.com/environment/2007/apr/09/travelsenvironmentalimpact.mondaymediasection

Miller, T. 2015 "Unsustainable Journalism" *Digital Journalism* 3(5): 653–663

Wood, S., Shabajee, P., Schien, D., Hodgson, C. and Preist, C. 2014 "Energy use and Greenhouse Gas Emissions in Digital News Media: Ethical Implications for Journalists and Media Organisations" *Digital Journalism* 2(3): 284–295

DIGITAL JOURNALISM ETHICS

The rapid growth of online media has led to new complications in **journalism** ethics and practice as new kinds of interactions develop between **journalists** and **audiences** (Zion and Craig, 2015). Existing media ethics developed in the era of mass newspaper publication in the late 19th century when journalism was largely confined to the domain of the professional. This led to the creation of ethical norms of accuracy, objectivity and truth seeking supported by codes of conduct and regulation. But, as media ethics scholar Ward articulates (2010, 2015, 2018), the **news** ecology has moved to an environment where the amateur and professional are combined, which requires a new mixed media ethics, reinvented for the blogging, tweeting and photoshopping media of today. In *Radical Media Ethics*, Ward (2015) provides guiding principles and values for practising responsible global media ethics, including a code of conduct for a journalism that is global in reach and impact. He argues that this is necessary due to the prevailing tension between traditional journalism and online journalism.

> The culture of traditional journalism, with its values of accuracy, pre-publication verification, balance, impartiality, and gate-keeping, rubs up against the culture of online journalism which emphasizes immediacy, transparency, partiality, non-professional journalists and post-publication correction.
>
> (Ward, 2013)

The approach to digital media ethics, according to Ward, needs to be adjusted in light of seven key factors. The first is the existence of anonymity online, which is praised for allowing freedom of speech and exposing wrongdoing while conversely encouraging irresponsible and harmful comments. Ward accuses the mainstream media of hypocrisy in allowing anonymous comments on news content online but refusing anonymity to sources in newspapers and broadcast programs. He also argues that speed, rumor and corrections have altered the presentation of news, with newsrooms under pressure to publish and share stories immediately via **social media** before information is checked and verified, leading to the spread of rumors and **fake news**. Live blogging, reported at speed, also creates a product which is littered with poor spelling, punctuation and grammar and reliant on corrections to adjust errors at a later stage, sometimes not leaving a trace of the original mistake in what is called unpublishing. Next, Ward (2013) points to the growth in opinion, activism and partisan journalism online, which threatens impartiality and seemingly legitimizes conflicts of interest. This is even more prevalent on **blogging** platforms and social media, where journalists attempt to build a personal brand and express opinions which can be in direct contradiction to the impartial reporting expressed by their news organization. Then there is the question of entrepreneurial **non-profit journalism**, which can be reliant on funds from a limited number of donors and have benefactors and readers on management boards, which can influence the autonomy of the organization's journalists. The involvement of citizen content or **user-generated content** in a **newsroom** is another ethical grey area, since it is not clear whether **citizen journalism** content should be held to the same editorial standards as that of professional journalists. This is an issue addressed in detail in *Ethics for Digital Journalists* (Zion and Craig, 2015), which provides guidance on how to put digital ethics into practice using examples of the best emerging newsroom practices from across seven countries. Meanwhile, Ward (2013) raises the final issue surrounding the ethics of **photojournalism** and the use of images, particularly from the public, which can be easily manipulated and difficult to verify.

A further consideration, explored by Newton and Duncan (2012) is the ethics of death reporting in a digital age. There is now a ready supply of emotive quotes, personal details and pictures publicly available on social media networks which can often be published legally by journalists following a person's death without the family's consent. Yet, Newton and Duncan's research suggests that the death knock, the process whereby a journalist goes unsolicited to the home of the bereaved to obtain a human interest story about their deceased family member, remains an important journalistic activity. Indeed, this approach was deemed as more ethical than lifting information from digital sources. Interviews with journalists and bereaved families found that the offline death knock had therapeutic value to relatives in paying tribute to their loved one and enabled the community to be informed of events in their area (Newton and Duncan, 2012). Families also appreciated this approach more than journalists taking material directly from social media, which could be inaccurate, and in some cases has found publications scrutinized by regulation bodies for intrusion into grief.

Key Sources

Newton, J. and Duncan, S. 2012 "Hacking into Tragedy: Exploring the Ethics of Death Reporting in the Social Media Age" in Keeble, R. L. and Mair, J. (Eds) *The Phone Hacking Scandal: Journalism on Trial*. Bury St Edmunds: Abramis

Ward, S. J. A. 2010 *Global Journalism Ethics*. Montreal: McGill-Queen's University Press

Ward, S. J. A.. 2015 *Radical Media Ethics: A Global Approach*. Chichester: Wiley Blackwell.

Ward, S. J. A. 2018 *Disrupting Journalism Ethics: Radical Change on the Frontier of Digital Media*. London: Routledge

DIGITAL JOURNALISM STUDIES

Since the turn of the new millennium, **journalism** has experienced fundamental changes to its many and varied products, the (now digital)

technologies used to produce them, the prominent **business model** deployed to resource them, the number of journalists (and "robo-journalists") working in newsrooms to produce them, the emergence of **blogs, citizen journalism** and **social media** as expansive sources and drivers of news to inform them, along with radically shifting audience requirements for news, the emergence of **native advertising** to fund (and challenge the credibility of) media content and the development of mobile media (**smartphones** and **tablets**) which require a distinctive content and presentation of news (Franklin, 2015).

The collective impact of these developments has been dramatic and highly disruptive, "making definitional boundaries fluid" and prompting scholars of journalism to address once again, but in a radically modified context, all aspects of the professional practice of journalism, including even the most fundamental questions such as "Who is a **journalist**? and What is **journalism**?" (Franklin, 2013b). A further significant question queries the consequences of these changes for journalism scholarship and whether the theories, concepts and research methods of journalism studies remain adequate for analyzing the substantially revised journalism of the 21st century. If not, might such a task involve the establishment of a new disciplinary field of **Digital Journalism Studies**? Distinguished philosopher and ethicist Stephen J. Ward argues unequivocally that as a key element in Digital Journalism Studies, "journalism ethics needs radical conceptual reform – alternated conceptions of the role of journalism and fresh principles to evaluate practice ... brought together into a comprehensive perspective that explains what a responsible journalism means in a digital media world" (Ward, 2018).

A recent flurry of new journals such as *Digital Journalism* (https://www.tandfonline.com/loi/rdij20) and *Mobile Media and Communications* (http://journals.sagepub.com/home/mmc), along with a number of substantive edited book collections of research-based essays by distinguished scholars, teachers and practitioners, have echoed Ward's sentiments in their efforts to establish both the foundational methodological and theoretical elements of the new discipline of Digital Journalism Studies as well as charting and archiving its early intellectual and academic development (Eldridge and Franklin, 2019; Franklin, 2015; Franklin and Eldridge, 2017; Karlsson and Sjøvaag, 2016a; Steensen and Ahva, 2017; Witschge, Anderson, Domingo and Hermida, 2016).

In a special issue of *Digital Journalism* (Karlsson and Sjøvaag, 2016a), for example, devoted to "Rethinking Research Methods in an Age of Digital Journalism," guest editors Michael Karlsson and Helle Sjøvaag, argue that "research methods must be assessed, adjusted, redesigned and perhaps even invented" reflecting the "many challenges that follow from the characteristics of digital media and digital journalism" (Karlsson and Sjøvaag, 2016). Consequently, the various papers in the journal issue "offer new and updated methods on how to view and measure the production, content, distribution and consumption of news ... discuss problems and possibilities, but also provide examples and guides ... for the digital journalism novice" (Karlsson and Sjøvaag, 2016a). Digital Journalism Studies requires distinctive methodological approaches to research design to take account of the new affordances and academic challenges, problems and puzzles inherent in digital media and journalism.

Individual articles within the special issue explore innovative methodological approaches for conducting automated **content analyses**, analyses of **hyperlinks**, topic modeling in the analysis of journalistic texts, computational data gathering, the study of news events using **Google** Search, advances in news use studies, the effects of mixing web and mail modes in audience research and, finally, action research (Karlsson and Sjøvaag, 2016a).

It has been suggested, however, that Digital Journalism Studies requires not only a reconsideration of methodological approaches to research design, but a rigorous reassessment of extant theoretical approaches alongside the construction and consideration of innovative concepts such as news networks and the expansive role of technology in journalism (**actants, news bots**), necessary to analyze, explain and understand journalism in a digital setting.

In special issues of the journals *Digital Journalism* (Steensen and Ahva, 2015b) and *Journalism Practice* (Steensen and Ahva, 2015a), devoted to "Theories of Journalism in a Digital Age," guest editors Steen Steensen and Laura Ahva begin this task of conceptual review and reassessment with articles focused on the role of the "4 As" (Actors, **Actants, Audiences** and **Advertisers**) in news work, studies developing the actor-network perspective, journalism as cultures of circulation, socio-historical approaches to online journalism, the creation of spatial journalism, changing relations between journalists and politicians and the novel problems of comparative analyses in an article considering theoretical directions for examining African journalism in the age of digital media (Steensen and Ahva, 2015b).

Peter Bro (2017) explores particular case studies examining the history and current utility of **gatekeeping** and **agenda setting**, two of the most significant concepts to **journalism studies** across the 20th century, highlighting that "in the past decades the reach and relevance

DIGITAL JOURNALISM STUDIES

of the concepts" have been increasingly challenge by developments in digital journalism. Like Steensen and Ahva, Bro suggests these particular concepts must be "revisited" to assess "in what ways these concepts – and the theoretical, methodological and empirical foundations on which they were founded – still make sense and enjoy relevance" (Bro, 2017: 76). **Gatekeeping** and **agenda setting** have both received considerable critical attention, with Bruns arguing the former has been superseded by the concepts of **gatewatching** and **gatecrashing** (2005) while Bro notes that the enhanced plurality of news media and news providers in the digital age makes it "increasingly difficult for news organisations to set the agenda outside newsrooms," prompting some critics to call for the "retirement of these two classic concepts" (Bro, 2017: 78). Ultimately, however, Bro supports the argument of Vos and Heinderyckx (2015) favoring the continued relevance of such concepts, since "transition is not necessarily termination" (Vos and Heinderyckx, 2015: 11). There are, moreover, some "recurring features" in the ways in which gatekeeping takes place – not least "who the gatekeepers are" (Bro, 2017: 78).

In summary, Digital Journalism Studies is more than a simple description of the study of journalism in a digital age. Scholars and researchers are increasingly suggesting that the impact of digital technologies on the academic study of journalism constitutes a massive **disruption** that has challenged the theoretical and methodological foundations underpinning journalism studies. Consequently, Digital Journalism Studies employs new concepts and revised theoretical understandings, in tandem with innovative research designs, to explore and understand the processes of the production, content, dissemination and consumption of news. This prompts a final and highly provocative question. If Digital Journalism Studies does represent a distinctive field of inquiry, what is the nature, academic value and possible future utility of journalism studies?

See **journalism studies and digital journalism.**

Key Sources

Bro, P. 2018 "Gatekeeping and Agenda Setting: Extinct or Extant in a Digital Era?" in Franklin, B. and Eldridge, II, S. (Eds) *The Routledge Companion to Digital Journalism Studies.* London: Routledge, 75–84

Eldridge, II, S. A. and Franklin, B. 2019 *The Routledge Handbook of Developments in Digital Journalism Studies.* Abingdon: Routledge

Karlsson, M. and Sjøvaag, H. 2016 "Research Methods in an Age of Digital Journalism" *Digital Journalism* 4(1): 1–192

Steensen, S. and Ahva, L. 2015 "Theories of Journalism in a Digital Age" *Digital Journalism* 3(1): 1–131 and *Journalism Practice*, 9(1): 1–122

Vos, T. and Heinderyckx, F. 2015 *Gatekeeping in Transition*. New York: Routledge

DIGITAL WAR REPORTING

Advances in technology have profoundly impacted war reporting, affording audiences new ways in which to visualize conflict (Anderson, 2009). Satellites, **smartphones**, laptops and mobile broadband have enabled war reporters to communicate immediately and bring conflict live to air. But, as new technologies open up innovative ways for **journalists** to convey the horrors of warfare, they similarly create opportunities for propaganda, censorship and control (Matheson and Allan, 2009).

The reduction in size of video technology and integration of editing software onto laptops has meant that individual journalists can now report in the field as one-man operators rather than depend on their camera crew or sound recordists, enabling greater mobility. The war reporter thus has greater freedom, being able to file from anywhere, at any time, as a self-reliant correspondent. Having access to a vast array of frontline information online also affords journalists freedom from military control and gives them an insight into how the conflict is being reported elsewhere and what leads are not being followed (Callinan, in Anderson, 2009). However, the downside is that there is a constant demand for stories and interviews, making it harder to spend time in the field. There is also pressure on war correspondents to be on call 24/7 and always to be ready to file a report. The sheer volume of news that is demanded in a highly competitive digital market can lead to rushed picture-driven reports with little context or informed analysis, with editors failing to distinguish between spin, speculation and unverified content (Getlin and Jensen, 2003). Furthermore, journalists' use of **Twitter** to report conflict is blurring the boundaries between the personal and the professional in relation to images. A study of two Moscow-based correspondents during the 2014 Ukraine conflict examined how the pair created parallel conflict narratives on Twitter while reporting for legacy newspapers (Pantti, 2017). Their use of Twitter demonstrated a preponderance for personalized reporting that allowed for more opinion and display of emotion than is typically acceptable in mainstream media reporting.

The technological gains enjoyed by journalists are, conversely, counteracted by sophisticated government and military media management. The military continue to control media operations in war zones by holding live military briefings which are beamed to the world without any journalistic interpretation, effectively side-lining reporters. They also provide the media with combat footage from the nose cameras of precision guided munitions as they streak towards their targets (Anderson, 2009), thus controlling the images and messages reported to the public. Media access to troops and briefings is directly controlled by the military and only journalists embedded within a unit will receive protection in highly volatile zones.

The military may be losing some of their grasp, however, as the global spread of **social media** has opened previously closed doors to war reporters. The most defining moments in 21st century conflicts have been predominantly captured by civilians or by the soldiers perpetrating the very hostilities being documented (Ross, Tembeck and Tsentas, 2015). This has unlocked the rarely seen side of warfare which the military are unable to censor. Informed by the views of over 100 BBC staff, Bennett (2013) captures journalists' shifting attitudes towards blogs and internet sources used to cover wars and other conflicts in *Digital Media and Reporting Conflict*. The book explores the impact of new forms of online reporting on the BBC's coverage of war and terrorism and ongoing challenges such as maintaining impartiality in the face of calls for more open, personal journalism and ensuring accuracy when the power of the former audience allows **news** to break at speed. This **user-generated content (UGC)** most prevalent on social media platforms is a significant tool for war reporters, even enabling them to report from their home country when they cannot gain access to a conflict zone due to safety concerns or government restrictions. During the Syrian conflict of 2011, BBC and Western journalists were restricted from entering the country and many reports were filed by staff in London or neighboring countries such as Jordan and Lebanon, meaning UGC remained an important element of newsgathering (Johnston, 2016). This caused further complexities, as the volume of UGC coming from Syria was overwhelming and verification processes were lengthy. These volatile circumstances are also ripe for governments, terrorists and insurgents alike to spread misinformation and propaganda via online channels. As such, in the near future, insight into military and civil conflicts may become more reliant on unmanned systems, rather than human communications, as the use of aerial drones equipped with cameras becomes more prevalent in reporting.

Key Sources

Anderson, F. 2009 "Mosquitoes Dancing on the Surface of the Pond: Australian Conflict Reporting and Technology" *Journalism Practice* 3(4): 404–420

Bennett, D. 2013 *Digital Media and Reporting Conflict: Blogging and the BBC's Coverage of War and Terrorism.* London: Routledge

Matheson, D. and Allan, S. 2009 *Digital War Reporting.* Cambridge: Polity Press

DISRUPTION

The term disruption has come to refer to the radical changes triggered by the **affordances** of digital technologies, which occur at a pace and to a degree that disrupts established understandings and traditional ways of creating value, interacting and communicating both socially and professionally and, in the case of **digital journalism**, triggers changes in the **business models**, professional practices, roles, ethics, products and even the accepted definitions and understandings of **journalism**. For **Digital Journalism Studies**, the field of scholarly inquiry focused on the academic study of **digital journalism**, disruption results in paradigmatic and tectonic shifts in scholarly concerns and prompts reconsideration of research methods, theoretical considerations and responses (oppositional and consensual) to these changes in the world of digital journalism.

Conceived originally by economist Clayton M. Christensen to explain the processes whereby new entrants to a market achieve success and eventually displace existing market leading companies, the term disruption has been applied more generally beyond the economic sphere and has become shorthand for "disruptive innovation" (Christensen, Raynor and McDonald, 2015). Christensen's argument suggests that while established companies excel at developing technologies that serve their existing customers, they are limited by the very worldview that informs and explains their initial success. Worse, after a certain point, further technological change undermines their current corporate inter- ests. This "limitation" provides a facilitating space for companies deploying disruptive technologies to develop niche markets, customers and audiences (Christensen, 2013). Christensen stresses two features of

DIVERSITY

successful disruption. First, it must be understood as a process and not applied to a particular product rather than the evolution of that product. Second, enabled by technological change, disrupters typically build business models that differ markedly from those of incumbent competitors.

This theory of disruptive innovation can be readily applied to journalism (Christensen, Skok and Allworth, 2012; Pavlik, Dennis, Davis Mersey and Gengler, 2018) and informs explanations of the rapid decline and "crisis" of the print newspaper industry and its supersession by online news media, the availability of **news** on mobile phones and even the growth of **citizen journalism** with **Web 2.0** innovations (Chyi, Lewis and Zheng, 2012).

Key Sources

Christensen, C. M., Raynor, M. E. and McDonald, R. 2015 "What is Disruptive Innovation?" *Harvard Business Review* December 2015, 44–53 https://hbr.org/2015/12/what-is-disruptive-innovation

Christensen, C., Skok, D. and Allworth, J. 2012 "Breaking News: Mastering the Art of Disruptive Innovation in Journalism" *Neiman Reports*, 15th September http://neimanreports.org/articles/breaking-news

Chyi, I., Lewis, S. C. and Nan, Z. 2012 "A Matter of Life and Death? Examining How Newspapers Covered the Newspaper Crisis" *Journalism Studies* 13(3): 305–324

Pavlik, J., Dennis, E., Davis Mersey, R. and Gengler, J. 2018 *Mobile Disruptions in the Middle East: Lessons from Qatar and the Arabian Gulf Region in Mobile Media Content Innovation.* London: Routledge

DIVERSITY

Once an exclusively white, straight, male profession that sourced **news** from elite Caucasian, heterosexual men, **journalism** was anything but diverse. But the Civil Rights Movement of the 1960s, gradual acceptance of women into the workforce post the Second World War and the LGBTQ movement of recent years has seen a shift in the makeup of newsrooms, albeit at a slow rate. A 2018 report by the National Council for the Training of Journalists in the UK acknowledged that diversity remains a big issue, with 90 percent of journalists being white and 72 percent having at least one parent with a higher level occupation

DIVERSITY

compared with 41 percent of the workforce as a whole (Spilsbury, 2018). Gender equality is more evenly matched, with 55 percent of journalists being men, although there is evidence that women leave the profession more frequently than men due to its incompatibility with family life. In the US, the situation is less even, with only a third of the workforce comprising women, but minorities fare better, making up 17 percent of employees at daily newspapers and 24 percent at online-only sites (ASNE, 2017).

The greatest shakeup to diversity has been outside the mainstream media, due to the low cost and global reach of online publishing. **Web 2.0** saw the explosion of bloggers, fanzines and citizen journalists expressing a plurality of voices not seen since the **alternative media** movement of the 1960s in the UK and the public/civic journalism movement in the US during the early 1990s. Independent digital native news platforms have sprung up across the world, focusing on social and political niches with the aim of giving a voice to the voiceless. These range from far-right news and opinion website Breitbart to TransNews, a 100 percent positive transsexual and transgender news source. Larger online-only news media such as **BuzzFeed**, *HuffPost* and VICE Media – which sold a five percent share to 21st Century Fox in 2013 – have put a deliberate emphasis on diversity, choosing to cover the under reported stories of ethnic minorities, immigrants, trans people and those with mental health difficulties. Digital native websites have also embraced diverse **business models** to move beyond the reliance on traditional **advertising** and incorporate branded content and collaboration with **legacy media** companies.

The diversity of choice and ubiquity of news from myriad alternative sources has ultimately led to a fragmentation of the market. This raises concerns that, rather than expanding users' minds, diversity conversely leads to echo chambers and **filter bubbles** where consumers seek out ideas, beliefs and information that resonate with their own worldview rather than challenging it (Dubois and Blank, 2018).

Key Sources

ASNE 2017 "Newsroom Diversity Survey" *ASNE.* www.asne.org/diversity-survey-2017

Dubois, E. and Blank, G. 2018 "The Echo Chamber Is Overstated: The Moderating Effect of Political Interest and Diverse Media" *Information, Communication & Society* 21(5): 729–745

Spilsbury, M. 2013 "Journalists at Work www.nctj.com/downloadlibrary/jaw_final_higher_2.pdf

DOWNLOADS

The measurement of **news** consumption has a long history, with independent audits of newspaper and magazine circulation dating back over 100 years. In the US the Audit Bureaux of Circulations has been providing data since 1914 and in the UK the Audit Bureau of Circulations (ABC) has existed since 1931. These bureaus collect information on the number of copies of a particular edition of a print medium, be it a newspaper, magazine or book, which is sold or distributed for free. Radio and television audiences are also measured by other equivalent bodies. Auditors have recorded a significant, and steady, decline in newspaper circulation and broadcast news **audiences** since news first burst onto our computer screens. At the height of its success in the mid 1990s, the UK's most popular newspaper, the *Sun*, sold over 4.5 million copies. At the time of writing, this had been slashed to 1.4 million. There is now an acceptance in the industry that circulation will continue to fall and publishers are starting to close their printed products and move entirely online. This has created a new world of digital consumption measurements known as **web analytics** or web metrics. These data are far more complex to capture than circulation figures which, at their most basic, simply count the number of newspaper copies sold each day. In the murky world of web analytics, unique users, hits, page impressions (also known as page views), total sessions and time spent are fused together to measure the consumption of newspapers and magazines online via web browsers on static and mobile devices (Thurman, 2014). Muddying the water further is the measurement of downloads, which refers to the number of times a news organization's app has been downloaded but also the amount of pages viewed on said app. It is also used to refer to the pages viewed by non-app unique users via a web browser (Thurman, 2018).

In order to make sense of the complexity of digital news consumption and compare it more equitably with print circulation, a new measurement procedure was introduced to the UK in 2012. The National Readership Survey (NRS) launched Print and Digital Data, which amalgamates data on print audiences from the NRS and ABC with data about the online audience from comScore. This is not without its flaws, however, as the usage of some newspaper brands' iOS and Android **apps** are not tracked by comScore. Therefore, the data surrounding downloads remains incomplete, for the time being. Thurman (2018) also notes that it is a false economy for British newspapers to focus on online usage data, since audiences still spend 88.5 per cent of their time with the print product and just 11.5 per cent with the online brand.

Key Sources

Thurman, N. 2014 "Newspaper Consumption in the Digital Age: Measuring Multi-Channel Audience Attention and Brand Popularity" *Digital Journalism* 2 (2): 156–178

Thurman, N. 2018 "Newspaper Consumption in the Mobile Age: Re-Assessing Multi-Platform Performance and Market Share Using 'Time-Spent'" *Journalism Studies* 19(10): 1409–1429

DRONE JOURNALISM

The recent development and ready availability of drones, more formally referred to as unmanned aerial vehicles (UAVs), unmanned aerial systems (UAS) or remotely piloted aircraft (RPAs), have had an extraordinary impact on the day-to-day practices, principles, products and possibilities for **journalism** (Belair Gagnon, Owen and Holton, 2017; Gynnild, 2014; Gynnild and Uskali, 2018; Holton, Lawson and Love, 2015; Tremayne and Clark, 2014). Drones equipped with cameras deliver "unique visual perspectives and add new dimensions to storytelling and accountability in journalism" and can readily substitute for **photojournalists** in hazardous settings such as war and protest, fires, floods and other hazards, but also offer **journalists** new (literally) viewpoints on issues; drones are "cameras in the sky" (Tremayne and Clark, 2014). The use of drones for journalism, however, also generates a crop of new "legislative, ethical and transparency issues" mostly concerning privacy, accountability, transparency and issues arising from surveillance (Gynnild and Uskali, 2018). But as the closure of Gatwick airport at Christmas 2018 revealed, the extra-journalistic uses of drones can create considerable nuisance and illegality.

A key legal concern with using drones for journalism purposes is that in law there needs to be a way to distinguish the legitimate activities of what Goldberg calls the "Dronarazzi" and mere voyeurism (Goldberg, 2018: 37). Using drones for newsgathering, moreover, is unique among drone functions because "it is a constitutionally or rights protected activity" (Goldberg, 2018: 37). Drones also require legislation to resolve routine conflicts. For example, how low/high may a drone fly? How do these limits vary across countries and should they be unified? How are these upper and lower limits to be enforced and by whom? In the UK, complaints concerning snooping, burglary and mid-air collisions and near misses have risen sharply from 283 in 2014 to 3,456 in 2016 (Goldberg, 2018: 37). Journalists wishing to use drones for journalistic purposes will require practical and theoretical training, a brief which is increasingly being assumed by university level education resulting in the award of a licence to pilot drones (Nyre, Guribye and Gynnild, 2018: 71–84).

Gynnild and Uskali envisage three possible futures for the development of drones and drone journalism or "Dronalism": (1) "drones everywhere," (2) "total ban of camera drones," and (3) "drone mosaic." The first scenario suggests that drones will become ubiquitous "must have" tools for journalism, making a great impact on storytelling, especially on photojournalism and journalism education. For journalism, this means that "aerial imagery of everyday situations and events will be the new normal" (Gynnild and Uskali, 2018: 88). A second scenario contests this view and suggests that the potential (and real) dangers of flying drones near airfields, in heavily used flight paths and in war zones might trigger a complete ban on the use of camera drones for journalism purposes.

The third scenario adopts a "middle path" between the two and an app already exists which maps drone uses and possibilities in different countries, signalling this "mosaic" patterning. Since September 22nd 2017, 40 countries (the red zone) operate a total ban on camera drones, alongside 74 green countries, including United Arab Emirates and Puerto Rico, where "drone use is generally allowed," 40 Yellow countries, from Austria to Vietnam, where drone use is "limited or may require some cumbersome registration processes" and a final group of 85 grey countries (mostly in Africa, Asia and South America) where no data are available (Gynnild and Uskali, 2018: 91).

Key Sources

Belair Gagnon, V., Owen, T. and Holton, A. E. 2017 "Unmanned Aerial Vehicles and Journalistic Disruption" *Digital Journalism* published online 27 January, doi:10.1080/21670811.2017.1279019

Goldberg, D. 2018 "Dronalism, Newsgathering Protection and Day to Day Norms" in Gynnild, A. and Uskali, T. (Eds) *Responsible Drone Journalism*. London: Routledge, 36–46

Gynnild, A. 2014 "The Robot Eye Witness: Visual Journalism through Drone Surveillance" *Digital Journalism* 2(3): 334–343 www.tandfonline.com/doi/abs/10.1080/21670811.2014.883184

Holton, A. E., Lawson, S. and Love, C. 2015 "Unmanned Aerial Vehicles: Opportunities, Barriers, and the Future of 'Drone Journalism'" *Journalism Practice* 9(5): 634–650

Tremayne, M. and Clark, A. 2014 "New Perspectives from the Sky: Unmanned Aerial Vehicles and Journalism" *Digital Journalism* 2(2): 232–246

EDITOR

The editor is the senior managerial figure in a **news** organization with ultimate responsibility for the quality of the editorial content of the organization's journalistic products; additionally, she may be responsible for aspects of policy making. In reality, the editor manages, coordinates and appoints a hierarchy of editors with responsibility for specific areas of the organization's editorial content. So the editor will coordinate the work of the news editor, as well as the political, fashion, sport, culture and **lifestyle**, picture and financial editors, to name but a few. The word "edit" emerged in the mid-17th century (1649) deriving from the Latin infinitive *Edere*, which meant produced or to put out and eventually producer and exhibitor. It was not until 1712 that the term editor implied "One who edits a text, newspaper, etc" (*Shorter Oxford English Dictionary*, 1973: 630).

Editors of the large, **legacy media** newspapers such as *The Times* and *Wall Street Journal* enjoy high prestige and substantial salaries while simultaneously being members of the precariat with little more job security than managers of Premier League football clubs with flagging score lines (Franklin, 1997: 97–100)! Editors must also manage a number of potentially conflicting ambitions: the organization's editorial ambitions against the constraints imposed by sales and **advertising** revenues, the views of perhaps many millions of readers against the editorial concerns of the many hundreds of **journalists**, as well as pressures and, if editor's memoirs are accurate, downright interference from proprietors (Evans, 1994; Neil, 1997). Legendary editor and writer Harold Evans, the only journalist to edit *The Sunday Times* (1967–1981) and *The Times* (1981 until he was sacked by Murdoch in 1982), was voted the best newspaper editor "of all time" in a poll jointly organized by the *British Journalism Review* and the trade paper, the *Press Gazette*.

The history of journalism and media organizations reveals that developments in media technologies, whether the telegraph, telephone or the internet, have been influential in prompting rapid and far-reaching changes in **journalism** while also shaping changes to previously well-defined professional roles such as that of editor (Mari, 2017). A number of points are relevant here. First, while **digital journalism** has enhanced the status of some editors, for example graphics editors, who enjoy much greater status following the explosion of **data journalism** in mobile and online platforms, the prestige of picture editors has declined, reflecting the ready availability of **smartphones** incorporating digital cameras and the widespread use of images originating in **citizen journalism**, as well as the growth of **social media** platforms such as Instagram (Borges-Rey, 2015: 571–593). Second, the greatly enhanced use of contributions to news content by citizen and participatory journalists, as news has shifted to online and mobile platforms across the last two decades, has reallocated and reduced a major part of the editor's role. **Social media editors**, for example, have a specific brief to edit user-generated content. Similarly, readers' comments to conversation strings appended to journalists' articles do not fall within the editor's remit. Melissa Wall's paper on "Citizen Journalism" (Wall, 2015), offers fulsome testimony to the striking increase in the contribution of citizen journalism to the daily news agenda. Third, detailed ethnographic case studies of digitally native news organizations reveal that some operate with much reduced journalistic staffs; in some cases they may be a literal "one man (or woman) band." Tony Harcup's research, for example, about the online **hyperlocal** and **alternative** *Leeds Citizen*, reveals that while the single journalist/editor is busy as a reporter covering local political events, the editing activities of the paper are substantially reduced (Harcup, 2016).

Key Sources

Hagerty, B. 2002 "Announcing the Greatest Editor of all Time" *British Journalism Review* 13(4): 6–14

Harcup, T. 2016 "Alternative Journalism as Monitorial Citizenship? A Case Study of a Local News Blog" *Digital Journalism* 4(5): 639–657

Wall, M. 2015 "Citizen Journalism: A Retrospective on What We Know, an Agenda for What We Don't" *Digital Journalism* 3(6): 793–813

"What Exactly Is a Social Media Editor?" *Adweek* www.adweek.com/digital/what-exactly-is-social-media/

EMAIL

Email or e-mail are both short forms for electronic mail. Email has introduced nothing less than a revolution in personal and organizational communications, allowing individuals with access to the internet via personal computer, laptop, tablet or smartphone the possibility of connecting to global communication networks. Such access is relatively cheap, very recent and largely taken for granted, despite being a phenomenon which is barely two decades old. Email has rapidly become a central part of the everyday life of individuals, business organizations, governments and many occupations and professions, including **journalism** and other ways of working focused on communications.

More prosaically, many emails consist of little more than personal messages between individuals, text-based reminders of an appointment or a request for information or providing information about a social gathering or, more formally, a business or professional meeting. The email message may include "attachments" which may be additional text files, photographs, graphics, images or **hyperlinks** to further multimedia materials; perhaps a newspaper article, a research report, or a photograph from a **social media** site such as **Instagram**. Email can accommodate one-to-one or one-to-many communications where the same message and attachment can be "mailed" to a group of people by simply adding the name of a preformed group list into the address box.

Email embodies the two features that are central to, as well as defining of, communications based on digital media technologies: **Immediacy** and **interactivity** (Steensen, 2011). Immediacy refers to the near instantaneous speed with which email allows the distribution and receipt of messages between individuals and groups in the most far-flung and remote regions of the globe. This pace of communication means email fosters interactive communication that is dialogic. A **journalist**'s article, for example will not only include her byline but also her email address, so that readers, other journalists, or **editors** may contact her to discuss the article, to point up disagreement or to contest elements of argument or evidence presented.

Most notably, email has added impetus to journalism's transition to a desk-based job, with journalists spending less time out of the office directly observing news events. Email now provides a rapid contact with (and greater reliance on) news sources to exact "eye witness accounts." Email also facilitates the conduct of interviews, as well as access to copies of public records, press releases and official briefings, which all arrive via email to journalists at their desks. Some journalists and academics have been highly critical of the consequences of these changes to journalists' working practices for the quality and originality of news (Franklin, Lewis and Williams, 2010: 202).

Key Sources

Franklin, B., Lewis, J. and Williams, A. 2010 "Journalism, News Sources and Public Relations" in Allan, S. (Ed) *The Routledge Companion to News and Journalism.* Oxford: Routledge, 202–212

Mari, W. 2017 "Technology in the Newsroom; Adoption of the Telephone and Radio Car from c. 1920 to 1960" *Journalism Studies* 19(9): 1366–1389 doi:10.1080/1461670X.2016.1272432

Pavlik, J. 2001 *Journalism and New Media.* New York: Columbia University Press

Steensen, S. 2011 "Online Journalism and the Promise of New Technologies: A Critical Review and Look Ahead" *Journalism Studies* 12(3): 311–327

EMBARGO

Sources will sometimes release information to journalists under an embargo, which is a request to refrain from reporting the content until a particular time and date. The conditions are usually set by public relations practitioners in order to control the flow of information and is seen as a goodwill gesture to allow journalists time to research a topic and gather comment prior to publication or broadcast. The arrangement is more of a gentleman's agreement (Rubel, 2017), as the only repercussion for breaching an embargo is that it may damage relations between a **journalist** or media organization and a public relations firm.

However, with continuous breaking **news** online, the embargo is becoming increasingly obsolete as traditional boundaries of print deadlines and broadcast schedules are no longer relevant and the race to break a story first is stronger than ever. Furthermore, the growth of **social media** as a source of news means the rules of engagement have all but disappeared as public relation practitioners are unable to broker deals with millions of **Twitter** users.

Embargoed information and news releases are still currently sent to journalists but it may be that in the near future this practice will cease.

Key Sources
Rubel, G. 2017 "Making the Embargo Work in the Era of Real-Time Communications" *PR Week* www.prweek.com/article/1431571/making-embargo-work-era-real-time-communications

ENTREPRENEURIAL JOURNALISM

In his Introduction to a special issue of the journal *Journalism Practice* (March 2016), devoted to entrepreneurial **journalism**, Kevin Rafter argues that entrepreneurial journalism has become a "hot topic" in the 21st century for both the journalism industry and the academy (Rafter, 2016: 140). In the new millennium, academics have become increasingly preoccupied with including modules on entrepreneurial journalism in **Journalism Studies**' curricula, while also researching and writing about its causes and its consequences for journalism education and training (Baines and Kennedy, 2010).

But, while acknowledging that entrepreneurial journalism has achieved a new relevance for those seeking a career in journalism since "the contemporary 'crisis' in the journalism industry," Rafter also suggests that the recent history of journalism has been "marked by the entrepreneurial spirit" with these two aspects being closely intertwined (Rafter, 2016: 140). However, as the accepted **business model** for journalism, which required a strict separation between financial and editorial functions, rapidly eroded with the crisis of journalism post 2008, creating precarity in employment and uncertainty in journalism career paths, both industry and academy began to envisage a blurring of roles between content producers and managers which created conversations about entrepreneurial journalism. In Jarvis's more concrete formulation, "journalists must now take on the urgent responsibility of building the future of news" in "new entrepreneurial ventures" (Jarvis, 2012: xv).

In their three-nations study of entrepreneurial journalism (Germany, France and the Netherlands) Witschge and Harbers (2019) confirm Jarvis's view and argue that, in the modern digital ecosystem of **news**, journalists must assume a broader responsibility and can no longer

> "simply" produce the news but have to conduct part or all of the other aspects of the (economic) process as well, such as monetizing

content; identifying target audiences; defining niche markets; designing websites optimally; and maintaining networks of sources and funders.

(Witschge and Harbers, 2019: 65)

Consequently, Baines and Kennedy argue for a revised journalism curriculum to produce graduate journalists with the necessary skills and understandings for this changed working environment. Programs of journalism education must follow the lead of Schools of Business and Management by embracing and teaching entrepreneurial skills as a core element in curricula. Their central argument is that educators must "look beyond the demands of traditional employers of journalists and strive to give students the opportunity to become entrepreneurial self-employed agents, who might compete with, as well as serve, other media organisations" (Baines and Kennedy, 2010: 97). Critics suggested that the agenda of entrepreneurial journalism simply converts all journalists into **freelancers**, thereby "mopping up" and disguising the growing unemployment within the profession, while subjecting the new entrepreneurial journalists to the same precarity that characterized freelance status.

The shifting boundary disputes between who is an "entrepreneurial journalist" and who is a "freelance" underscore uncertain definitions here with the author of a key text book conceding that entrepreneurial journalism "can mean a number of things, and for many journalism students the meaning can change by the day" (Kelly, 2015: 94). Vos and Singer address definitional concerns in their study of "Media Discourse about Entrepreneurial Journalism," which reports journalists' own understandings of the phrase culled from an analysis of the content of journalists' trade publications across the period 2000 to 2014 (Vos and Singer, 2016: 149–150).

In the "everyday journalistic discourse" they analysed, entrepreneurial journalism was understood by journalists as a concept with which they were familiar but with a highly variable meaning that described and defined a wide variety of "practices and attitudes." Moreover, the phrase was used by some journalists with "messianic or apocalyptic" tones, with its "evangelists" using the phrase to signal a better style of journalism which they believed was urgently needed. Entrepreneurial journalism proposed a solution and offered salvation in troubled times. Other journalists, however, view entrepreneurial journalism as a "profound threat to fourth estate values." Worse, some articulations suggest a threat to "traditional journalism's existence" (Vos and Singer, 2016: 151).

But amid this diversity of understandings, "a rough picture" emerges of "what journalists seem to mean when they use the term." Entrepreneurial journalism is "an emerging field, a set of skills, a spirit, a drive and a serious act." The entrepreneurial journalist is conceived as "a founder, an innovator, a trailblazer, a business creator, and a freelancer"; one trade journal used the term "journopreneur" (Vos and Singer, 2016: 151). Vos and Singer conclude that they were slightly surprised by the openness of journalists to accepting both the idea and the prospect of working in a distinctive form of journalistic enterprise. Indeed, many of the articles they analyzed suggested that journalists believed that entrepreneurialism "was not only acceptable but even 'vital' for survival in a digital age" (Vos and Singer, 2016: 155).

See also **freelance**.

Key Sources

Baines, D. and Kennedy, C. 2010 "An Education for Independence: Should Entrepreneurial Skills be an Essential Part of the Journalist's Toolbox?" *Journalism Practice* 4(1): 97–113

Jarvis, J. 2012 "Foreword" in Briggs, M. (Ed) *Entrepreneurial Journalism: How to Build What's Next for News*. Thousand Oaks, CA: Sage

Rafter, K. 2016 "Introduction: Understanding Where Entrepreneurial Journalism Fits in" *Journalism Practice* 10(2): 140–142

Vos, T. and Singer, J. 2016 "Media Discourse about Entrepreneurial Journalism: Implications for Journalistic Capital" *Journalism Practice* 10(2): 143–159

Witschge, T. and Harbers, F. 2019 "The Entrepreneurial Journalist" in Eldridge, II, S. and Franklin, B. (Eds) *The Routledge Handbook of Developments in Digital Journalism Studies*. London: Routledge, 64–76

ETHNOGRAPHY

The systematic study of people and cultures is a growing research method within the social sciences and humanities and is used to investigate professional sub cultures such as **journalism**. The researcher observes society from the point of view of the subject of the study and immerses themselves in their lifestyle and work routines. It entails the examination of the behavior of participants in a specific social situation, such as a **newsroom**. It usually involves the detailed examination of a limited number of case studies and emphasizes exploring social phenomena rather than testing hypotheses. Data collection involves observation and interviews carried out in extensive fieldwork and analysis focuses on the interpretation of human actions. The researcher will look for patterns in the group's ideas and beliefs expressed through language or other activities (Dewan, 2018). Within the field of journalism, it allows researchers to gain access into the inner sanctum of newsrooms and explore complex structures from the inside out.

Researchers have utilized ethnography to understand how the digital revolution is impacting upon **journalists** within the newsroom setting. Canter (2013a, 2014b) spent a total of five weeks embedded within two UK regional newspapers, the *Leicester Mercury* and the Bournemouth *Daily Echo*, as an observer-as-participant. In this role, she interacted with subjects but did not take an established role within the group (Sapsford and Jupp, 1996). During the observation period, Canter shadowed reporters on assignments, attended **news** conferences and observed different editorial desks at varying times of day, including early and late shifts, 7am through to 10pm, Monday to Saturday. During her ethnographic study, she also interviewed 28 journalists individually to gain an understanding of how they interpreted their relationship with their growing online, participatory audience. Canter also conducted a digital ethnography, via a content analysis of journalists' **Twitter** profiles. She captured tweets from each profile over a month-long period and from this was able to map their behavior and interactions online. This approach was further developed when Canter returned to the Bournemouth *Daily Echo* (2014b) two years later to carry out comparative ethnographic research focusing on journalists' evolving use of Twitter.

Using a similar method, Johnston (2016) conducted a newsroom ethnography at **BBC** World News TV to investigate how eyewitness video, known as **user-generated content (UGC)**, was being integrated into the public sector broadcaster's coverage of conflicts, with Syria as the main case study. Johnston spent two periods of observation at the UGC hub in London for two weeks each. This involved sitting with staff on shift observing their work and writing notes while also asking questions where appropriate. This was complemented with interviews with eighteen journalists working within BBC World News, BBC Arabic and the UGC hub. The ethnographic approach was then triangulated with a content analysis of news reports.

Key Sources
Dewan, M. 2018 "Understanding Ethnography: An 'Exotic' Ethnographer's Perspective" in Mura, P. and Khoo-Lattimore, C. (Eds) *Asian Qualitative Research in Tourism: Perspectives on Asian Tourism*. Singapore: Springer
Sapsford, R. and Jupp, V. 1996 *Data Collection and Analysis*. London: Sage

FACEBOOK (WHATSAPP, INSTAGRAM)

What started as a misogynistic college game in 2004 matured into a $442 billion company, with more followers than the Catholic church in less than 14 years. Founded by Harvard University students Mark Zuckerberg and Eduardo Saverin, global social networking service Facebook now has 2.2 billion users and is celebrated as the "most successful firm in history" (Denning, 2018). It can be accessed from a large range of internet-enabled devices and **apps** and allows users to create a customized profile to share messages, photos, video and links with other users known as "friends." Users may also join common interest groups centered around a workplace, school, hobby or any other topic which can be open, closed or hidden from the public. People use the website seemingly for free but in return Facebook reaps immense profits from their data. Five million advertisers on Facebook target users by promoting products on their news feeds which directly relate to their demographic information and lifestyle interests. The global reach of Facebook has enabled it to provide unrivalled marketing scale and targeting, which has secured its place as one of the five largest firms on the planet and the world's biggest seller of display **advertising**.

As a journalistic tool, Facebook is a newsgathering resource for stories, case studies, sources and **user-generated content** as well as a platform for promoting and disseminating **news** using tools such as Facebook Live, which enables live video streaming. Journalists can also interact with their audiences and gauge reaction to, and engagement with, stories by monitoring comments, likes and shares. A content analysis of the way in which journalists use Facebook by Paulussen and Harder (2014) suggests that the platform turns the elite source pyramid upside down. Although newspaper journalists use Facebook to retrieve information from politicians, official institutions and experts, they primarily use the **social media** platform in relation to ordinary citizens, celebrities and sports people. Meanwhile Canter (2013a) identified that individual journalists were engaging with their readers in a more informal, personal and reciprocal manner on Facebook in a bid to build loyalty to their brand and themselves. The public also utilize Facebook as a platform for global dissemination and its use has been particularly prevalent during political uprisings. In February 2008, a Facebook group called One Million Voices Against FARC organized a protest march against the Revolutionary Armed Forces of Columbia (known as FARC) which was attended by hundreds of thousands of Columbians. During the Arab Spring of 2011, Facebook was a vital source of newsgathering and played a major role in galvanizing protestors in Tunisia, Egypt and Bahrain.

However, the tech giant has come under increasing political and financial pressure in recent years to improve its business conduct in both the US and Europe. It has been accused of tax avoidance, censorship, promoting hate speech, permitting depictions of violence, supporting government **surveillance** and having a negative impact on users' mental health. Studies have shown that Facebook causes negative effects on self-esteem and the longer people spend time on the site the worse they feel about their own lives. The platform has also been blamed for taking away the advertising revenue of traditional publishers particularly **local newspapers**. This is compounded by Facebook's refusal to acknowledge that it acts as a publisher rather than just a platform, handing the company a get-out-of-jail-free card to avoid regulation. However, despite its negative impact on advertising, Facebook together with search engine **Google**, sends substantial traffic to mainstream media websites and publishers have become increasingly reliant on them for readers. This backfired in 2018 when Facebook changed its newsfeed algorithm, which had a detrimental impact on local publishers. Facebook claimed the change was introduced to prioritize posts from high quality news **sources** and local news so users could see topics having a direct impact on them and their community (Hardiman and Brown, 2018). But in reality, local papers found that their traffic dramatically declined. Research by the Tow Center for Digital Journalism found that 11 out of the 13 regional newspapers participating in Facebook's Local News Subscription Accelerator scheme actually experienced fewer interactions per post in the two months following the algorithm change than in the two years before (Owen, 2018). Meanwhile, British digital publisher Little Things was forced to close after the change to Facebook's news algorithm decimated its business. The lifestyle site, which attracted 12 million followers on Facebook, claimed that it lost 75 percent of its organic traffic due to the "catastrophic" change. In a bid to address its critics, Facebook announced in late 2018 that it would be donating £4.5 million to fund 80 local newspaper jobs in the UK in a two-year pilot scheme. The aim of these posts was to fill the lost **news beats** and to help tackle the **democratic deficit** in many local communities that have lost court and council reporters.

At a global level, Facebook has been under fire for failing to handle misinformation and **fake news** circulating on its platform. This has also spread to the Facebook owned smartphone messaging service **WhatsApp**, which is particularly prevalent in Brazil and India. During the 2018 Brazilian elections, 120 million WhatsApp users in the country were deluged with political messages featuring disinformation. A study found that of 100,000 WhatsApp images shared in Brazil, more than half contained misleading or false information. An international committee formed to investigate Facebook's role in spreading fake news now features policy makers from the UK, Argentina, Brazil, Canada, Ireland, Latvia and Singapore. Moreover, the international community is putting further pressure on Facebook following the Cambridge Analytica scandal, which revealed a giant data breach for political gain. The data analytics firm that worked with Donald Trump's election team and the winning Brexit campaign harvested millions of Facebook profiles of American voters to build a software program to target users with personalized political ads. During the 2016 US Presidential campaign, the electorate were also targeted by 120 fake, Russian-backed Facebook pages that created 80,000 posts and reached 126 million Americans.

Yet, despite a mounting assembly of criticisms and scandals, Facebook has remained relatively silent, with chief executive Mark Zuckerberg taking his time to apologize over the Cambridge Analytica data breach, making only vague promises to improve the use of users' data in the future. The billionaire has also sent representatives to a number of global committee hearings rather than appear himself, saying he is unable to attend. But he has acknowledged that the worldwide shift towards private messenging, new European privacy laws and lower user numbers are creating serious financial challenges for the business, which had falling share prices in 2018. Zuckerberg warned investors that Facebook's audience in North America is now close to saturation and that future growth would come from developing countries. Recognizing the growth of private messenging and photo sharing apps, Facebook acquired WhatsApp in 2014, following its purchase of Instagram in 2012. WhatsApp is a free smartphone application that allows the sending of encrypted text messages and multimedia together with voice and video calls across the internet. The acquisition, for $19billion, was the most ever paid for a venture-capital backed start-up. The European Commission subsequently fined Facebook 110 million Euros for misleading it in the takeover of WhatsApp by falsely claiming it was technically impossible to automatically combine user information from Facebook and WhatsApp. The companies started sharing information in 2016, such as phone numbers from WhatsApp that could be used for targeted Facebook advertisements.

WhatsApp, which was founded in 2009 by former Yahoo! employees Brian Acton and Jan Koum, is particularly popular in Brazil, India, the UK and France. It has more than 1.2 billion monthly active users worldwide and handles more than 1.6 billion photos and messages per day. At the time of writing, the firm was developing a business platform to enable companies to provide customer service to users at scale. News organizations have been keen to tap into WhatsApp's extensive user base to deliver stories and to news gather among established sources. Although the platform is closed, users can subscribe to news alerts which then link through to **legacy media** websites and the public can securely leak tips and footage to journalists from stories on the ground as they break. In Mexico and Israel, police footage is often leaked to the press via the messaging app before any official release.

Similarly, photo and video sharing network Instagram has proved a great source of content for journalists. Unlike WhatsApp, the content can be shared publicly and tagged with geolocation information. The service was launched by Kevin Systrom and Mike Krieger in 2010 and was bought by Facebook for $1 billion just two years later. By June 2018, Instagram had amassed one billion active users worldwide and daily active users stood at 500 million. The platform has over a million advertisers who promote content on the news feed. However, the popularity of ephemeral messaging app **Snapchat**, where images disappear shortly after being posted, has led Facebook to imitate their format by introducing short term Stories on Facebook and Instagram. This demonstrates Facebook's shift away from its traditional newsfeed product, in a bid to rival Snapchat and its younger demographic. However, these young people are being adversely affected by social media platforms, with a study by the Royal Society for Public Health revealing that Instagram was the worst platform for the mental health of 14 to 24-year-olds. This has not stopped journalists from taking the opportunity to promote their visual content on Instagram while also harvesting content and story ideas from the platform. During Hurricane Sandy in 2012, users of Instagram posted ten photographs per second of the devastation (Laird, 2012), which were an invaluable source to journalists although many admit they still require help with verification. The *Guardian* publisher, which has more than 1.3 million followers on Instagram to date, has introduced Stories to keep readers interested and encourage them to their website and apps. One weekly story is called Fake or For Real? and features a *Guardian* journalist explaining and debunking fake news of the week.

Key Sources

Canter, L. 2013 "The Interactive Spectrum: The Use of Social Media in UK Regional Newspapers" *Convergence: The International Journal of Research into New Media Technologies* 19(4): 472–495

Owen, L. 2018 "Facebook's News Feed Changes Appear to be Hurting – Not Helping – Local News" *NiemanLab* www.niemanlab.org/2018/04/face books-news-feed-changes-appear-to-be-hurting-not-helping-local-news/

Paulussen, S. and Harder, R. 2014 "Social Media References in Newspapers: Facebook, Twitter and YouTube as Sources in Newspaper Journalism" *Journalism Practice* 8(5): 542–551

FACT CHECKING

News organizations and the general public increasingly use **social media** such as **Facebook, Instagram, Twitter** and **YouTube** as sources of information but, perhaps paradoxically, also report concern with the problems arising from their growth. Two out of three American adults, for example, report experiencing **fake news** as a problematic source of confusion (Brantzaeg, Folstad and Chaperro-Dominguez, 2017: 1113). Worse, the "share" and "like" facilities provided by social media encourage a previously unattainable virality for all information carried by social media, whether accurate or "fake."

In response to this challenge, a number of online sites devoted to identifying and checking "facts" provided by social media and other **sources** have grown to maintain trust and credibility in news organizations and reliable sources of credible information, to enable the media's traditional fourth estate functions (Graves, 2016: 324). An international survey in 2016 identified 96 fact checking organizations, which marked a substantial increase above the previous year, doubtless informed by growing concerns about a "post truth society" (Stenchel, 2016).

Consequently, fact checking organizations have come to be defined as individuals or organizations that analyze and establish the accuracy and claims of content in the public domain (but especially in news organizations and social media) and inform news readers about the reliability and credibility of information (especially online information). Fact checking organizations such as Factcheck.org (http://www.factcheck.org), Stopfake (http://stopfake.org) and Snopes (http://snopes) are becoming increasingly well known and used (Brantzaeg, Folstad and Chaperro-Dominguez, 2017).

Allied to fact checking services, but distinct from them, are verification services which follow a more limited remit. Verification services may support the authenticating of online information detailed above, but focus on text, videos and images and deploy algorithms to expedite and make verification of information more accurate. Tineye (http://tineye.com), for example, conducts searches for images similar to those appearing in news items to establish historical uses of similar or the same image/text.

The efficacy of such fact checking services in denying credibility to wide spread myths and misrepresentations is uncertain. In 2017, for example, the claim of the newly elected President Donald Trump that his phone had been hacked by GCHQ at the request of his predecessor Barak Obama retains credence in some quarters despite denials by Obama, the British Government on behalf of its information services, along with Trump's unwillingness to offer any evidence to support his originally Tweeted claims.

Key Sources

Brantzaeg, P., Folstad, A. and Chaperro-Dominguez, M. A. 2018 "How Journalists and Social Media Users Perceive Online Fact-Checking and Verification Services" *Journalism Practice* 12(9): 1109–1129

Graves, L. 2016 *Deciding What's True; The Rise of Political Fact-Checking in American Journalism*. New York: Columbia University Press

Stenchel, M. 2016 "Global Fact Checking Up 50% in Last Year" http://reporterslab.org/globsal-fact-checking-up-50-percent

FAKE NEWS

Public concern about fake news – an evident paradox since one of the paradigmatic concerns of journalistic culture is that reported news should be factual, objective and connect to events in the real world – reached previously unprecedented levels in the run up to, and immediately following, the American Presidential Election in November 2016. Losing Democratic Presidential candidate Hillary Clinton claimed that fake news had become "an epidemic" (*Guardian*, Brinkhurst-Cuff, 2017: 10). Public anxiety focused not only on the implications of fake news for the quality and integrity of political journalism in the US, but also stressed the implications of fake news – especially fake news reported on **social media** such as **YouTube** and **Facebook** – for the democratic character of the election itself (Allcott and Gentzkow, 2017; Tandoc, Lim and Ling, 2018; Graves, 2016; McNair, 2017).

Such significant concerns created widespread calls for new forms of regulation, requiring internet based companies such as **Google, Twitter** and Facebook to assume greater responsibility for the veracity of news by deploying new technologies and devising novel protocols to secure the integrity of **news. Audiences** and consumers of news also demanded new ways to identify the **sources** and credibility of news carried by social media (*Guardian*, Brinkhurst-Cuff, 2017: 10). One fact checking site advised readers to check the cited sources of news, to look closely at the author and date of publication and to consider the article's headline very carefully; Factcheck.org also "encouraged readers to be sceptical of viral claims and make good use of the delete key" (Kiely and Robinson, 2016). Shortly after Trump's inauguration as President, Channel 4 announced a week of programmes on fake news (*Guardian*, Jackson, 2017).

This recent preoccupation with fake news, however, in the sense of news that is not necessarily factual or true, has been an element in what might be termed the *legitimate* news industry for a good while. The fake news of the internet era has at least two predecessors which require brief discussion.

The first source of fake news is exemplified by the UK tabloid newspaper the *Sunday Sport*, launched in 1986. Even by tabloid standards, the paper's mix of "soft" pornography, celebrity news, free gifts and offers as well as regionalized advertisements for sexual services, marked a nadir for journalistic professional standards. But the paper's use of bizarre headlines announcing preposterous and unbelievable stories became cult, attracting both readers and advertisers. The **editor** claimed that such headlines were not misleading since no one believed them. Moreover, the purpose of the paper was less to inform than to entertain, thereby exemplifying the mission of tabloid journalism, while maximizing profits. Headlines including "Booted out of ISIS for wearing ALDI Trainers," the rather perplexing "Gordon Ramsey sex Dwarf eaten by Badger," "Elvis Alive and Living on the Moon" and, continuing the obsession with lunar concerns, "World War Two Bomber Found on the Moon" were typical (www.buzzfeed.com/alex finnis/boiled-mangled-orange-burst-bellends?utm_term=.xfvz38gRb#. ag1O5lxLV).

A second journalistic group of purveyors of false news, ranging from the self-conscious parody of a newspaper the *Onion* (Dikkers, 1999), to the *Daily Show* hosted by Jon Stewart, were motivated less by profit than a commitment to satire and a mission to critique mainstream journalism. The *Onion* launched in 1988, moved online in 2007 and began uploading satirical videos in 2011. With headlines such as "CNN Deploys Troops to Iraq" (18 January 1991), "Rodney King video Cameraman Signs $1.2mn Deal for Upcoming Mexican Beating" (30th April 1992) and "Killer Robots storm Home of Bill Gates' Childhood Bully" (10 January 1998), The *Onion* delights in describing its mission as "misinforming half a million readers a week with one-of-a-kind satire both in print and online" (Dikkers, 1999; cover note).

The *Daily Show*, launched in July 1996, is a late-night talk show with an emphasis on satire. Jon Stewart joined as anchor in January 1999 and from the outset made politics and the media the central focus of his satirical wit. The show was immensely popular, especially with young audiences and won 23 Emmy Awards. Stewart who described the *Daily Show* as the "fake news show," not only came to personify what critical journalism should be, but also illustrated the importance of undertaking research and investigation. On the day he resigned, a *Guardian* assessment of Stewart and the *Daily Show* claimed "he skewered the powerful and pushed US satire forward" (Moylan, 2017).

In its most recent guise, fake news is essentially a phenomenon of the internet and especially social media. Fake news flourishes on social media, where news reporting is not subject to the rigours of traditional news organizations where standard journalism practice checks the accuracy and veracity of facts and verifies sources. Social media, moreover, fall prey to **clickbait** (sensational stories) intended to serve as a magnet for **audiences** with advertisers trailing closely behind.

Unlike its "predecessors" discussed briefly above, contemporary fake news is consciously fabricated and contrived content, deliberately published lies and misinformation, designed to mislead readers (and for political and ideological purpose) rather than for entertainment or profit and subsequently achieving widespread (sometimes viral) reach via the internet and social media, where it is shared and retweeted many times. It is this potential to "go viral" and mislead which makes "fake news" so problematic; it has – to repeat Clinton's phrase – become "an epidemic."

Research by scholars at Stanford and New York Universities into the allegation that fake news had favored Trump's 2016 campaign and shaped the electoral outcome studied news coverage for the last three months of the campaign, but while they denied any such determining effect, they concluded that "fake news was both widely shared and tilted in favour of Trump." The researchers also revealed that in their sample of election coverage, fake news stories which favored Trump were shared 30 million times on Facebook while those supporting Clinton were shared only 8 million times (Allcott and Gentzkow, 2017). Research by Buzzfeed recorded a substantial increase in likelihood of readers' use of fake news compared with news offered by mainstream media such as the *New York Times* and *Washington Post* (Brinkhurst-Cuff, 2017).

This dramatic emergence of fake news, with its alleged consequences for democratic politics and decision making, has triggered political and journalistic responses. In the UK in January 2017, the House of Commons Select Committee on Media, Culture and Sport announced an inquiry into the nature and definition of the phenomenon of "fake news," along with its causes. The inquiry also intended to outline the responsibilities of social media such as Google and Facebook concerning the spread and impact of fake news and will require them to monitor news providers and guide users concerning the integrity of news carried on their sites.

Editorially, while journalists have always rigorously checked the facts and sources informing particular stories (Borel, 2016), in recent times new organizations such as Factcheck.org, Politifact and the *Washington Post*'s Fact Checker have begun to hold public figures accountable for what they claim (Graves, 2016: 324). Fact checking has progressed from an individual journalistic act to a movement which seeks to sustain the quality of journalism and improve the integrity of public life.

Key Sources

Allcott, H. and Gentzkow, M. 2017 *Social Media and Fake News in the 2016 Election* http://web.stanford.edu/~gentzkow/research/fakenews.pdf

Graves, L. 2016 *Deciding What's True; The Rise of Political Fact-Checking in American Journalism.* New York: Columbia University Press

McNair, B. 2017 *Fake News: Falsehood, Fabrication and Fantasy in Journalism.* London: Routledge

Moylan, B. 2017 "Jon Stewart's Daily Show Skewered the Powerful and Pushed US Satire Forward" *Guardian* www.theguardian.com/tv-and-radio/2015/aug/05/jon-stewart-daily-show-pushed-american-satire-forward

Tandoc, E., Lim, Z. W. and Ling, R. 2018 "Defining Fake News: A Typology of Scholarly Definitions" *Digital Journalism* 6(2): 137–153

FILTER BUBBLE

A term coined by internet activist Eli Pariser, who also co-founded Upworthy, a website for "meaningful" viral content. In his 2011 book *The Filter Bubble: What the Internet is Hiding from You*, Pariser argues that website algorithms are causing intellectual isolation because users get less exposure to conflicting viewpoints. Instead, personalized searches select information based on past behavior and previous searches giving a person more of the same rather than challenging their cultural or ideological bubble. Pariser claims that the filter bubble effect, most prominent in **Google** personalized search results and Facebook's personalized news-stream, may have a negative impact for civic discourse. The circulation of **fake news** without questioning, particularly during the 2016 US Presidential Election, has spurred new interest in the filter bubble phenomenon and its impact on democracy. The concern was echoed by Barack Obama in his farewell address (*New York Times*, 2017) when he spoke about the danger of retreating into

> our own bubbles ... our social media feeds, surrounded by people who look like us and share the same political outlook and never challenge our assumptions ... we start accepting only information, whether it's true or not, that fits our opinions, instead of basing our opinions on the evidence that is out there.

A similar idea is that of the echo chamber, a setting where only certain ideas, information and beliefs are shared – or echoed back and forth – among people inside the particular chamber. According to Dubois and Black, anyone who disagrees in these echo chambers is "misinformed at best and wilfully ignorant at worst" (2018: 729). Furthermore, as a high choice environment where people can select their information sources, the internet may foster a space where echo chambers are more common and dangerous. Indeed, personalized searches curated by **algorithms** can create a further filter bubble within these echo chambers.

However, there is plenty of counterargument to the alarmist view of filter bubbles and echo chambers, with tech giants taking strides to remove **personalization**. Google claims that it has algorithms in place designed to limit personalization and promote variety in the results page (Weisberg, 2011) and Facebook is testing new technology to give "people more ways to see a more complete picture of a story or topic" (Vanian, 2017). Data analyzed by Dubois and Blank (2018) found that those interested in politics, with diverse media diets, tended to avoid echo chambers and overall the existence of echo chambers was overstated. Exploratory studies by Haim, Graefe and Brosius (2018) found no support for the filter bubble hypothesis and suggested that concerns about algorithmic filter bubbles in the context of online **news** might be exaggerated. Analyzing 1,000 Danish Facebook News Feeds, Bechmann and Nielbo (2018) concluded that less than 10 percent of participants were in a filter bubble. Meanwhile, Weisberg, editor-in-chief of online current affairs magazine *Slate*, who conducted his own preliminary research on filter bubbles, proclaimed that Pariser is "dead wrong in assuming that personalization narrows our perspectives rather than broadening them" (2011).

Key Sources

Bechmann, A. and Nielbo, K. L. 2018 "Are We Exposed to the Same 'News' in the News Feed?" *Digital Journalism*, doi:10.1080/21670811.2018.1510741

Dubois, E. and Blank, G. 2018 "The Echo Chamber Is Overstated: The Moderating Effect of Political Interest and Diverse Media" *Information, Communication & Society* 21(5): 729–745

Haim, M., Graefe, A. and Brosius, H. 2018 "Burst of the Filter Bubble? Effects of Personalization on the Diversity of Google News" *Digital Journalism* 6(3): 330–343

New York Times 2017 "President Obama's Farewell Address" *New York Times* www. nytimes.com/2017/01/10/us/politics/obama-farewell-address-speech.html

Pariser, E. 2011 *The Filter Bubble: What the Internet Is Hiding from You*. New York: Penguin Press

FLAT EARTH NEWS

Refers to the non-fiction book *Flat Earth News: An Award-winning Reporter Exposes Falsehood, Distortion and Propaganda in the Global Media* by award-winning *Guardian* journalist Nick Davies. The title of the book is an analogy for the falsehoods circulated by the global media today, which have similar characteristics to the pseudoscience belief perpetuated by Flat Earth societies that the earth is flat rather than spherical.

In his damning book, Davies (2008b) argues that mass news production has turned newsrooms into news factories where journalists, chained to desks, churn out copy rather than fact checking, finding stories and making contacts. In the most extreme cases newsrooms have become **content farms** where freelancers, part-timers and amateurs produce articles that are expected to end up high in web searches, often for very little pay (Bakker, 2012).

Journalism is reduced to "mere churnalism" (Davies, 2008a) and once active news gatherers have become passive processors of second-hand material feeding off the falsities provided by the public relations industry and a handful of wire agencies. Research by Cardiff University (Lewis, Williams and Franklin, 2008) revealed that half of the **news** stories published in the UK quality press were wholly or mainly dependent on materials produced and distributed by wire services, in particular the Press Association. A further fifth of domestic news reports derived from public relations sources.

Furthermore, in the digital world, where journalists are under pressure to provide quantity over quality, it becomes easy and more efficient to copy and repurpose content from existing sources than to research and create original stories. This creative cannibalization of content is not new in journalism but it has been exacerbated by the internet, as journalists now lift exclusive material such as quotes and case histories within minutes of its publication (Phillips, 2010a). Davies, rather optimistically, prophesized that the internet could liberate the mass media from **churnalism** but instead it has facilitated it and put mass scale aggregation into the hands of tech giants such as **Google** and **Facebook**. Journalism online now "insidiously feeds off itself and swallows up rivals; consumes and regurgitates, or to put it more politely: recycles, recontextualises and repurposes" (Johnson and Forde, 2017: 943).

Key Sources

Davies, N. 2009 *Flat Earth News: An Award Winning Reporter Exposes Falsehood, Distortion and Propaganda in Global Media.* London: Vintage Books, 420

Johnson, J. and Forde, S. 2017 "Churnalism, Revised and Revisited" An Introduction to a Special issue of the journal *Digital Journalism* 5(8): 943–946. The special issue examined the impact and implications of churnalism in an age of digital media and journalism

Lewis, J., Williams, A. and Franklin, B. 2008 "Four Rumours and an Explanation" *Journalism Practice* 2(1): 27–45

FLICKR

A vast image and video hosting service created by Ludicorp in 2004 where users can manage and share content. It is largely used by individuals to store photographs publicly and privately, with more than 3.5 million new images uploaded daily. It has changed ownership several times and was most recently taken over by SmugMug in April 2018. It has grown to a membership of 87 million registered members and hosts more than six billion images.

Users can release images on the site under a range of licences, including creative commons attribution-based, which enables others to use their work for free without infringing **copyright** laws. Journalists use the service primarily as a source for **user-generated content**. The use of Flickr became particularly prevalent during the Arab Spring of 2010 as activists and citizens used it to share images of civil unrest which journalists then "cherry-picked" to retell the protests story to audiences across the globe (Russell, 2011: 1242). At this time users could not directly upload photos to **Twitter** so Flickr played a key role in visualizing the revolution across the Middle East and North Africa.

In more recent years, its popularity has waned as billions of photos are shared on **Facebook, Instagram** and Twitter each day, but it has a core following with around 13 million unique visitors a month (Terdiman, 2018) and has become the home of quality photography online.

Key Sources
Flickr 2018 "About" www.flickr.com/about
Russell, A. 2011 "Extra-National Information Flows, Social Media, and the 2011 Egyptian Uprising" *International Journal of Communication* 5: 1238–1247

FREELANCE

Freelance journalists, also known as freelances or freelancers, are self-employed journalists who work for a range of **news** organizations. They pitch ideas to editors or are allocated particular briefs for which they are paid a set fee. Once considered an atypical form of work, the practice has flourished as home broadband speeds and smartphone technology have enabled journalists to work remotely. In many countries, the majority of journalists are now freelance (International Federation of Journalists, 2018) either through choice or circumstance. From 2000 to 2015, the numbers of freelance journalists in the UK increased from 15,000 to 25,000 – an increase of 67 percent (Spilsbury, 2016), while between 2002 and 2012 the proportion of new journalists who entered the profession through freelancing increased from five percent to 12 percent (Spilsbury, 2013). Meanwhile, a report from the European Federation of Journalists found the number of freelance journalists has been steadily rising in recent years, with around 20 percent or more of journalists on freelance contracts (Nies and Pedersini, 2003).

Those who elect to become freelance – often following a period of employment at a news organization – are happier working for themselves and satisfied with their working hours, earnings and life–work balance (Edstrom and Ladendorf, 2012; Massey and Elmore, 2011; Turvill, 2016). The freedom and flexibility that working from home brings is one of the main reasons freelances enjoy their work more than staffers, with some even revealing that it allows them to work naked (Turvill, 2016).

However, there remains a proportion of journalists who would prefer traditional employment but have been forced into "fake freelance" positions by employers who "break local rules on employment by using freelances to fill full-time posts while avoiding state welfare and social charges" (International Federation of Journalists, 2018). Furthermore, economic cutbacks in the media sector have diminished the chances of employment for journalists (Edstrom and Ladendorf, 2012) and, consequently, freelances are growing worldwide, reflecting current trends in Western labor markets as a whole. Brown's (2010) qualitative research interviewing formerly well-paid UK columnists concludes that life is tougher than it has ever been for today's freelances due to stiff competition from former Fleet Street specialists and reduced fees. But there is growing evidence that for many, freelancing is a lifestyle choice that is not dependent on earnings. A longitudinal quantitative survey of Swedish freelances (Edstrom and Ladendorf, 2012) affirms that participants seem to be more content with life than other journalists, despite the apparent paradox of lower levels of security and income. With a lifelong career with one employer less likely, self-employment transfers the decision about changes and transformations to the individual rather than the organizations, in turn giving greater "individualization and flexibilization" (Edstrom and Ladendorf, 2012: 719).

Nevertheless, journalists' unions around the world have a growing challenge to address the issues of contracts and fees, benefits and authors' rights for the freelance community. Cohen (2016) highlights the paradoxes of freelancing, which can be simultaneously precarious and satisfying, risky and rewarding. She documents the transformation of freelancing from a way for journalists to resist salaried labour in pursuit of autonomy into a strategy for media firms to intensify exploitation of freelance writers' labor power. One of the biggest issues facing freelances the world over is payment on publication whereby a freelance is not paid for their submission until it is published, which can be several weeks or even months after the work is completed (Costello, 2018).

Key Sources

Cohen, N. 2016 *Writers' Rights: Freelance Journalism in a Digital Age.* Montreal: Queens University Press

Edstrom, M. and Ladendorf, M. 2012 "Freelance Journalists as a Flexible Workforce in Media Industries" *Journalism Practice* 6(5–6): 711–721

International Federation of Journalists 2018 "Freelances' Rights" www.ifj.org/issues/freelances-rights/

Massey, B. and Elmore, C. 2011 "Happier Working for Themselves?" *Journalism Practice* 5(6): 672–686

FREEMIUM PAYWALL

Paywalls generate resources for news organizations by charging for access to news content (Carson, 2015). But a "freemium" wall is distinguished from a **metered paywall**, or simply a paywall, because, while much editorial content is "free," there is a charge for premium content and hence the neologism, "freemium" paywall. In part, this differential pricing of content reflects the relative costs of newsgathering and reporting in different areas; for example, economic and political **news** coverage is especially costly. But it also reflects editors' assessments of readers' willingness to pay for certain types of editorial.

In an early study of UK online newspapers, Thurman and Herbert (2007) discovered, in interviews with editors and managers of online sites, that while advertising remained the main source of revenues for online sites, all UK newspapers were charging for certain kinds of content. They discovered, for example, that "columnist content [especially the then distinguished middle eastern correspondent Robert Fisk] is a major selling point of the *Independent* newspaper" and such content was not available for free but was ensconced "behind a subscription barrier" so that "our [the *Independent*'s] margins are damaged as little as possible by our move into digital" (Thurman and Herbert, 2007). Many newspapers placed their unique brand (USP) editorial behind such barriers. The *Financial Times*, for example, charged for the majority of its financial news and coverage while *The Times* charged for access to its legendary crossword.

See also **metered paywall** and **paywall**.

Key Sources

Carson, A. 2015 "Behind the Newspaper Paywall and Lessons in Charging for Online Content: A Comparative Analysis of Why Australian Newspapers Are Stuck in the Purgatorial Space between Digital and Print" *Media, Culture and Society* 37(7): 1–20

Thurman, N. and Herbert, J. 2007 "Paid Content Strategies for News Websites: An Empirical Study of British Newspapers' Online Business Models" *Journalism Practice* 1(2): 208–226

FUTURE OF JOURNALISM CONFERENCE

The Future of Journalism Conference is convened biennially and hosted by the School of Journalism, Media and Cultural Studies at Cardiff University, Wales. Routledge, Taylor and Francis, who publish the journals *Digital Journalism, Journalism Practice* and *Journalism Studies*, co-sponsor the Conference. A selection of conference papers has always been published as a special issue in each of the journals but also combined in a single edited volume (Allan, Carter, Cushion, Dencik, Garcia-Blanco, Harris, Sambrook, Wahl-Jorgensen and Williams, 2019; Franklin, 2009, 2011, 2013a; 2016). The Conference typically attracts 250 leading and distinguished academic scholars and researchers from around the globe.

The Conference, initially launched in 2007 as "The Future of Newspapers," subsequently changed its name and broadened its focus to "The Future of Journalism" in 2009, with the specific focus of subsequent conferences being signaled by the subtitle following the heading: *The Future of Journalism: Developments and Debates* (2011); *In An Age of Digital Media and Economic Uncertainty* (2013): *Risk, Threats and Opportunities* in (2015): *Journalism in a Post Truth Age* (2017) www.cardiff.ac.uk/confer ences/future-of-journalism-conference-2017

This development of theme and title seemed appropriate, since what was becoming evident in 2007, but is in much sharper focus a decade or more later, is that journalism has been experiencing a period of far-reaching, sustained and significant change in all aspects of day-to-day **journalism** practice; the organization, staffing and resourcing of the journalism industry and, significantly, scholarly research in the field of **journalism studies**. A key driver for these changes has been the development of digital, especially mobile, media technologies with their far-reaching consequences for the conduct of journalism. In turn, these changes have impacted on the academic study of journalism and have involved changes to the dominant research agenda, the need to reconsider basic concepts and theoretical frameworks, as well as the need to rethink and develop new methods for conducting journalism research. In short, the emergence of **Digital Journalism Studies** as a new field of inquiry, rather than Journalism Studies conducted in an age of digital media. The Future of Journalism Conferences have tried to monitor, track and explore these radical changes, but also to set an agenda for scholarly research in the immanent but developing field of Digital Journalism Studies.

Key Sources

Allan, S., Carter, C., Cushion, S., Dencik, L., Garcia-Blanco, I., Harris, J., Sambrook, R., Wahl-Jorgensen, K. and Williams, A. 2019 *The Future of Journalism: Risks, Threats and Opportunities*. London: Routledge

Franklin, B. 2009 *The Future of Newspapers*. Oxford: Routledge

Franklin, B. (Ed) 2011 *The Future of Journalism*. Oxford: Routledge

Franklin, B. (Ed) 2013 *The Future of Journalism: Developments and Debates*. Oxford: Routledge

Franklin, B. 2016 *The Future of Journalism: In an Age of Digital Media and Economic Uncertainty* Oxford: Routledge

GATECRASHING

In everyday usage, the word **gatecrashing** implies that someone has attended a party or other social event without being formally invited (https://dictionary.cambridge.org/dictionary/english/gatecrash). In the context of **digital journalism**, however, gatecrashing concerns the ways in which **citizen journalists** and **bloggers** report and cover news events (uninvited by professional **journalists** or anyone else): In the setting of news reporting, gatecrashing involves crashing **news** gates.

Their reports typically focus on crisis related events such as floods, hurricanes or mass shootings in schools, bars or churches. But in the process of news gathering via gatecrashing, citizen journalists typically become curators of news and morph into **gatewatchers**. Their reports, for example, may require them to extract elements of stories taken from traditional online news media coverage, or police scanner information, as well as a range of **social media** and **blogs**, and to meld them into a single **news** item. In sum, gatecrashing represents one of the innovative newsroom practices increasingly evident in online and digital newsrooms (Toff, 2017).

Morgan Denver's blow-by-blow account of the mass shooting at the Aurora Theatre in Denver in 2014, posted on his **Reddit** account, offers an archetypal example of gatecrashing. Professional journalists from around the globe began to cite his reports even though Jones was not a journalist but "a gatecrasher ... who chose NOT to have his voice heard through traditional mainstream media channels, but rather via his own profile on *Reddit*" (Wordpress, 2014)

Key Sources

Cambridge English Dictionary online https://dictionary.cambridge.org/diction ary/english/gatecrash

The Power of Citizen Journalism, 2014 Blog #3 Wordpress https:// mfjs2210win2014.wordpress.com/tag/media-gatekeeping-gatewatching-gate crashing-citizen-journalism/

Toff, B. 2017 "The 'Nate Silver Effect' on Political Journalism: Gatecrashers, Gatekeepers and Changing Newsroom Practices around Coverage of Public Opinion Polls" *Journalism*, doi:10.1177/1464884917731655

GATEKEEPING

Gatekeeping has been one of the most popular and significant concepts in **journalism studies**, provoking discussion and informing scholarly research within the academic community which studies **journalism**, but also more broadly among the general public (Vos and Heinderyckx, 2015). In his recent appraisal of the gatekeeping concept, Peter Bro suggests that since David Manning White's initial research paper, published some 70 years ago (1950), gatekeeping has achieved the status of a "classic," a "household name" and a "milestone in mass communications research" (Bro, 2018).

Applying social psychologist Kurt Lewin's work on consumer choice to explain the presence or absence of **news** stories from newspapers, White deployed the relatively simple metaphor of a gate to illustrate the work of news **editors** who, by their editorial choices, decided which items should be included or excluded from the columns of the press. In his case study of a wire editor in a regional newspaper, White declared that "Mr. Gates" – as he referred to him – was a gatekeeper controlling the information flow through the gate by his selection of news items judged to be worthy of publication and his rejection of the great majority of what he considered to be less important and uninteresting stories. White's study showed that Mr. Gates was indeed a highly interventionist and restrictive gatekeeper with only 1,297 column inches of the 12,400 column inches (slightly more than 10 percent) of potential news across the week-long sample period of his study being allowed to pass through the gate (White, 1997: 65). White concluded from this case study and an extensive interview with Mr. Gates that his editorial choices were personalized and "highly selective", reflecting the gatekeeper's own "experiences, attitudes and expectations" (White, 1997: 65). In this sense, criticism of the concept of gatekeeping has been endemic from its initial inception. More was to follow.

First, critics have suggested that White's account of gatekeeping offered a highly individualized and psychologistic account of news selection. Second, the metaphor of the gate lacked precision concerning the different types of story which successfully transit through the gate and that which do not, the criteria employed by the gatekeeper to decide what is newsworthy and what is not and, significantly, how and why such considerations might change over time. Third, gatekeeping was envisaged as a process of deciding how news stories were accepted or rejected, – "decisions about what's in or out" (Bro, 2018: 77) – but the reality is that news is constructed rather than selected: and by a complex range of actors (editors, **journalists, sources**, readers and even **advertisers**) in a wide range of news organizations.

But what has mostly called the usefulness of the gatekeeper concept into question has been the development of digital media technologies and their deployment in digital newsrooms. Bro cites scholars of **Digital Journalism Studies** who suggest that the concept of gatekeeping has been "'undermined', has 'collapsed', has been 'busted', is 'dead' and 'even gone'" (Bro, 2018: 78). These pessimistic assessments reflect the

affordances of **digital journalism**, but especially the explosion of newsrooms and the provision of an infinite digital space for news. The scarcity of editorial space for news that characterized legacy media and required contemporary gatekeepers to select a relative handful of stories for publication while consigning the remainder to the dust heap of history has been eradicated. Bruns (2005) suggests that the innovative concepts of **gatewatching** and **gatecrashing** more accurately reflect the circumstances of journalism in an age of digital media; gatekeeping has been superseded. It seems that Mr. Gates may have been given his cards!

Key Sources

Bro, P. 2018 "Gatekeeping and Agenda Setting: Extinct or Extant in a Digital Era?" in Franklin, B. and Eldridge, II, S. (Eds) *The Routledge Companion to Digital Journalism Studies*. London: Routledge, 75–84

Bruns, A. 2005 *Gatewatching: Collaborative Online News Production*. New York: Peter Lang

Vos, T. and Heinderyckx, F. 2015 *Gatekeeping in Transition*. New York: Routledge

White, D. M. 1950 "The 'Gate Keeper': A Study in the Selection of News" *Journalism Quarterly* 27(3): 383–390

GATEWATCHING

Until recently, a traditional but significant role for **journalists** has been their position as gatekeepers. The limited number of **legacy media** and provision of news spaces meant journalists selected stories they considered to be significant or of likely interest to the public and rejected the remainder. Journalists were believed to possess the appropriate specialist and professional knowledge and skills to make these selections and were motivated by a desire to promote the public interest (Vos and Heinderyckx, 2015). Critics such as Rosen (2006), however, interpreted journalists' gatekeeping activities as elitist, patronizing and undemocratic (Rosen, 2006).

Axel Bruns has argued that **gatekeeping** as traditionally understood has become unsustainable in the context of an online digital news ecology, where the number of news gates has multiplied exponentially as citizen journalists, **bloggers** and commentators have become "interlopers" (Eldridge, 2015) in what previously had been the exclusive domain of professional journalists (Bruns, 2005). The recent growth of citizen journalism, he suggests, has given rise to the new practice of **gatewatching**, which Bruns defines as

> observing the many gates through which a steady stream of information passes from these sources, and of highlighting from this stream that information which is of most relevance to one's own personal interests or to the interests of one's wider community.
>
> (Bruns, 2005)

Burns (2014) similarly argues that in this sense gatewatching is essentially the opposite of gatekeeping, since "rather than controlling what is considered news and distributing it as they please, gatewatchers serve as **produsers**. They produce news, by accessing other news media, and deciding and sharing what material is relevant to other users" (Burns, 2014). In this way, **social media** have provided **citizen journalists** with the ability to produce and distribute almost unlimited information, when and how they wish, to other citizen journalists and gatewatchers. Burns concludes that "the power of gatewatchers is immeasurable [since] citizen journalism ... has completely transformed the way in which we receive information and the credibility we place in the media" (Burns, 2014).

Key Sources

Bruns, A. 2005 *Gatewatching: Collaborative Online News Production.* New York: Peter Lang

Burns, L. K. 2014 "Wikipedia, Wikinews and Gatewatching" https://mfjs2210win2014.wordpress.com/2014/02/13/wikipedia-wikinews-and-gatewatching/

Eldridge, II, S. A. 2015 "Boundary Maintenance and Interloper Media Reaction: Differentiating between Journalism's Discursive Enforcement Processes" *Journalism Studies* 15(1): 1–16

Rosen, J. 2006 "The People Formerly Known as the Audience *PRESSthink*, 27th June http://archive.pressthink.org/2006/06/27/ppl_frmr.html

Vos, T. and Heinderyckx, F. 2015 *Gatekeeping in Transition.* New York: Routledge

GEO-SOCIAL NEWS

Small commercial newspapers that serve a geographic territory are commonly referred to by a range of definitions, including community media, country newspapers, regional newspapers and the local press. Examples of these titles are the *Ballyclare Gazette, Hebden Bridge Times* and the *Pocklington Post* in the UK, the *Whistler Question* in Canada and the *Maitland Mercury, Warrnambool Standard* and *Wimmera Mail Times* in Australia (Hess, 2013). However, Hess argues that the global nature of online **news** means that these definitions are no longer accurate or particularly useful. In the digital age the term community media often refers to alternative, **not-for-profit** news outlets united by a particular issue or viewpoint rather than a geographic location. Similarly, the term local is problematic, as readers of a small newspaper may be dispersed and access the newspaper online from any part of the world.

Hess (2013: 49) proposes "geo-social news" as an alternative way to conceptualize news outlets which have a solid link to a geographic territory, while "acknowledging the wider social space in which these publications play a role, both in holding an influential position in certain social flows and movements and as a node to the wider global news media network." She argues that geography remains an important characteristic of small commercial newspapers, particularly in terms of news values and the location of people and events in stories, but it must also be recognized that these organizations now operate in a boundless social space. These small news outlets act as mediators and interpreters of global networks as journalists localize national and global news, making it relevant to their own readers (Hutchins, 2004). In this sense, they operate as wider social spaces through which individuals see the world while retaining a geographic link and sense of place.

Key Sources
Hess, K. 2013 "Breaking Boundaries: Recasting the 'Local' Newspaper as 'Geo-Social' News in a Digital Landscape" *Digital Journalism* 1(1): 48–63

GLOBAL JOURNALISM

Berglez argues that, in an increasingly global world, it is inappropriate to categorize **news** stories by employing the dichotomous terms and understandings of "domestic news" or "foreign correspondence" (2008, 2011). The global reach of online and digital media, in tandem with the emergence of transnational issues such as the Ebola epidemic, a raft of environmental concerns, as well as protracted wars which hemorrhage across national borders with the subsequent problems of mass migration, suggest that news is "more and more deterritorialised involving complex relations and flows across national borders" (Berglez, 2008: 845). Politics and environmental news represent two broad editorial beats that are increasingly assuming a global outlook and a global reach: features previously restricted to financial news.

Given these events, scholars claim an urgent need for elaborating a correspondingly "global journalism," which academics in the field of **Digital Journalism Studies** must develop (Berglez, 2008; Slavtcheva-Petkova and Bromley, 2018). Berglez also suggests that global journalism must assume the form of "a *news style* which makes it into an everyday routine to investigate how people and their actions, practices, problems, life conditions etc., in different parts of the world are interrelated" (Berglez, 2011: 143). The task of global journalism is not simply to increase reportage of neglected "distant events" in "remote" parts of the world: it "must actively interconnect the local with the global" (Van Leuven and Berglez, 2016: 667).

Research exploring the extent to which the practice of global journalism has been incorporated into the newsroom practices of three substantive mainstream media organizations – *The Times, Le Monde* and *De Standaard* – which analyzed 850 items of news coverage across the three titles between January and June 2013, revealed that one quarter of all articles incorporated at least one tenet of global journalism practice with a fifth of articles being focused on a global event and/or presenting "a global outlook on the reported matter." Researchers concluded that *Le Monde* "is the most global newspaper" although *The Times* and *De Standaard* "embed global outlooks in their domestic news sections" (Van Leuven and Berglez, 2016).

By contrast, Miki Tanikawa in her quantitative study of news content across thirty years, found that certain key words judged to be incompatible with global journalism were increasingly evident in publications of major international news organizations (Tanikawa, 2018).

Key Sources

Berglez, P. 2011 "Global Journalism: An Emerging News Style and an Outline for a Training Program" in Franklin, B. and Mensing, D. (Eds) *Journalism Education, Training and Employment.* London: Routledge, 143–154

Tanikawa, M. 2018 "Is 'Global Journalism' Truly Global? Conceptual and Empirical Examination of the Global, Cosmopolitan and Parochial Conceptions of Journalism" *Journalism Studies* https://doin.org/10.1080/1461670X.2018.1520610

Slavtcheva-Petkova, V. and Bromley, M. 2018 *Global Journalism: An Introduction*. London: Macmillan

Van Leuven, S. and Berglez, P. "Global Journalism Between Dream and Reality: A Comparative Study of *The Times, Le Monde* and *De Standaard*" *Journalism Studies* 17(6): 667–683

GOOGLE

A googol is the number one followed by 100 zeros, an infinite mathematical concept appropriated by the founders of the most visited website in the world to reflect its mission to organize the limitless amount of information on the web. Launched in 1998 by Stanford University PhD students Larry Page and Sergey Brin, the technology company rapidly grew into the most valuable brand in the world. Google Search generates most of its revenue from advertisements associated with search keywords which are text-based to avoid page cluttering. By 2018 Google was generating $34 billion in annual revenue (Statista, 2018c) via **advertising**, app sales, licencing and service fees. Although it began as a search engine, Google now specializes in a range of internet related services and products, including online advertising technologies, cloud computing, software and hardware, under the conglomerate Alphabet Inc. The company's services include Google Doc, Google Sheets, Google Slides, Gmail, Google Calendar, Google Drive, Google+, Google Translate, Google Maps, Google Earth and it acquired video sharing website **YouTube** in 2006. It is also the lead developer of the Android smartphone operating system, which is based on the Google Chrome browser. Hardware devices under the Google brand include the Nexus electronic devices, Google Pixel smartphone, Google Home smart speaker, Google Wifi wireless router and Google Daydream virtual reality headset.

Google's mission statement is to is "to organize the world's information and make it universally accessible and useful" (Google, 2018) but its unofficial slogan for many years was "Don't be evil." The company has attempted to brand itself as socially conscious but this has not prevented it from receiving staunch criticism over privacy concerns, tax avoidance, **censorship**, search neutrality and **surveillance**. It is one of the nine major tech giants embroiled in the PRISM program, which allowed the US National Security Agency to capture and store data from online users. It has also been blamed for poaching advertising from the mainstream media and being central to the collapse of **local newspapers**, alongside **Facebook**. The way in which Google News aggregates content from other news sources without payment, and personalizes news based on its own **algorithms**, is also viewed as immensely damaging to traditional **business models** and highly detrimental to the democratization of news (Haim, Graefe and Brosius, 2018; Pariser, 2011). In order to alleviate some of these claims, and to protect its reputation, Google formed the Google News Lab in 2015 to support and drive innovation in newsrooms. In 2018, the lab was folded into the Google News Initiative, which purports to focus on improving the situation around misinformation and **fake news**, local news networks, inclusive journalism and emerging technologies. The scheme helps news organizations learn how to use Google tools but also provides grants via the £150 million Innovation Fund. In 2018, grants were issued to 461 projects at news organizations across Europe.

See also **personalization of news, filter bubble**.

Key Sources
Google 2018. "About" Google www.google.co.uk/about/
Haim, M., Graefe, A. and Brosius, H. 2018 "Burst of the Filter Bubble? Effects of Personalization on the Diversity of Google News" *Digital Journalism* 6(3): 330–343
Statista 2018 "Revenue of Google from 1st Quarter 2008 to 3rd Quarter 2018 (in Million U.S. Dollars)" *Statista* www.statista.com/statistics/267606/quarterly-revenue-of-google/

HACKS

The image of a bolshie, Fedora-wearing newspaper reporter, emerging from a smoky **newsroom** shouting "hold the front page!" is a classic visualization of the self-deprecating hack. But this 1940s image, made all the more famous by screwball comedies like *His Girl Friday*, is far removed from the reality of today's journalists.

The word hack, shortened from the East London borough Hackney, derives from 1700, when it described a horse that was easy to ride and available for hire. It soon became associated with prostitutes and, by 1734, was used as a metaphor for a writer hired on a short-term basis or writing speculatively for payment. In order to earn a living, hacks were driven to digging up dirt on the powerful and indulging in a compromising lifestyle (Conboy and Tang, 2016). Viewed as mercenaries paid to write low-quality, often scandalous articles, hacks are a peculiarly British, even English, phenomenon, according to Conboy and Tang.

The pejorative term has survived until the present day and remains closely aligned with UK tabloid **journalism**. The *News of the World* phone-hacking scandal, which saw tabloid reporters hack into the mobile phone voicemail of celebrities and citizens, gave unsolicited *double entendre* to the word hack.

However, as the power and reach of the tabloid press diminishes under the shadow of tech giants and digital native news sites gain more traction among young audiences, the tsunami of bloggers, activists, citizen witnesses and commentators who jostle alongside "professional" journalists may soon drown out the anti-heroic hack all together.

It is also worth noting that a further derivative of the word is "hackademic," which is used to describe a journalist-turned-journalism-educator, by combining the words hack and academic (Engel, 2003).

Key Sources

Conboy, M. and Tang, M. 2016 "Core Blighty? How Journalists Define Themselves through Metaphor *British Journalism Review* 2011–2014" *Journalism Studies* 17(7): 881–892

HACKS/HACKERS

Finding a common language between journalists who seek to portray complex human issues in an accessible manner, and technologists who live and breathe algorithms and acronyms, is far from easy. The two communities are seemingly worlds apart – one situated in the field of liberal arts and communication, the other in computer science and technology. But the rapid growth of technology in the production and presentation of digital **news** has forced the clashing cultures to come together more frequently than in the past. **Computer assisted reporting** has been a feature of newsrooms for several decades but it is only more recently that individuals who know how to write software code have begun to assume a more prominent role in journalism (Lewis and Usher, 2014). Specialized **newsroom** teams now consist of developers, data scientists and programmer–journalists who work alongside everyday **hacks** to build news applications, **infographics** and interactive features. On the back of this shift in newsroom personnel, the transnational grassroots organization Hacks/Hackers was founded in 2009. Its mission is to bridge the two worlds between journalists (the hacks) and technologists (the hackers) to rethink the future of news and information. It believes that these two distinct professions are working to help people make sense of the world and by bringing them together it can enable hackers exploring technologies "to filter and visualize information" and journalists "to find and tell stories" using technology (Hacks/Hackers, 2018). The global organization has more than 75 city-based chapters with more than 23,000 members connected via Meetup.com. These members meet for discussions, talks, hack days and social events with the aim of potentially collaborating on projects and new ventures. In the US it receives support from journalism institutions, including the Online News Association, the National Institute for Computer-Assisted Reporting, Columbia and Northwestern University and the *New York Times*.

See also **computational journalism, data journalism**.

Key Sources
Hacks/Hackers 2018 "About" Hacks/Hackers. https://hackshackers.com/about/
Lewis, S. and Usher, N. 2014 "Code, Collaboration, and The Future of Journalism: A Case Study of the Hacks/Hackers Global Network" *Digital Journalism* 2(3): 383–393

HAMSTERIZATION

Hamsterization is a neologism that refers to the growing list of professional skills that **journalists** must possess to complete the expansive requirements of day-to-day professional practice in the digital newsroom. Journalists must continue to file **news** stories and features, but additionally the job of the digital **journalist** involves tweeting, podcasting, selecting and posting pictures to accompany stories, posting on **Facebook** and using it as a news **source, blogging** and video blogging, as well as meeting rolling **deadlines** and constantly updating stories already posted. Additionally, all this multi-skilling is required in a much reduced news industry that (in many newsrooms) employs radically reduced editorial staffs, while maintaining story counts. In short, journalists seem to be busier than ever and the image of a hamster frenetically charging around and chasing its own tail in a wheel seems to capture the recent dilemma of the modern journalist.

Some observers argue that reflective editorial and journalistic quality will be the inevitable victims as the wheel spins ever faster; as it gathers pace it will empower the role of PR and reduce journalists **agenda setting** potential (Waldman, 2011: 53). In an article in the *Columbia Journalism Review* (2010), Starkman described the Hamster Wheel as

> volume without thought. It is news panic, a lack of discipline, an inability to say no. It is copy produced to meet arbitrary productivity metrics … It's a recalibration of … the factors that affect the reporting of news … How much time versus how much impact? … Journalists will tell you that where once newsroom incentives rewarded more deeply reported stories, now incentives skew toward work that can be turned around quickly and generate a bump in Web traffic.

Starkman concludes on a bleak note "The Hamster Wheel, really, is the mainstream media's undoing, in real time, and they're doing it to themselves … The Hamster Wheel, then, is investigations you will never see, good work left undone, public service not performed" (Starkman, 2010).

Key Sources

Sehgal, U. 2011 "'Hamsterization': The Official Term for What the Internet Has Done to Journalism" *Adweek*, 13 June www.adweek.com/fishbowlny/journal ism-hamsterization/38631

Starkman, D. 2010 "The Hamster Wheel: Why Running as Fast as We Can Is Getting Us Nowhere" *Columbia Journalism Review* Sept/Oct 2010 www.cjr. org/cover_story/the_hamster_wheel.php?page=all

Waldman, S. 2011 "The Information Needs of Communities: The Changing Media Landscape in a Broadband Age, Federal Communications Commission" July 2011 http://transition.fcc.gov/osp/inc-report/The_Information_ Needs_of_Communities.pdf

THE *HUFFINGTON POST (HUFFPOST)*

Describing itself as the "original internet newspaper" the *Huffington Post*, founded in 2005, fully encompasses the contrary world of exploitative, progressive and liberating new media. It has been at the center of numerous debates surrounding aggregation, unpaid labor and **native advertising** while simultaneously embracing **diversity**, campaigning for women's rights and serving unheard voices. In 2012, the left-leaning **news** and opinion website was the first commercially run American digital media enterprise to win a Pulitzer Prize and in 2015 it was nominated for a Responsible Media of the Year award at the British Muslim Awards. Its contradictory reputation is less surprising when placed in the context of its founders, who were the eclectic foursome Andrew Breitbart (who went on to found right-wing opinion website Breitbart), conservative commentator Adrianna Huffington plus Kenneth Lerer and Jonah Peretti, chairman and CEO of **Buzzfeed**, respectively. The site, which originated in the US, now has editions in 15 countries, including Australia, Canada and the UK. It is largely funded via its Partner Studio, which creates native advertising campaigns. Following its acquisition by AOL for $315million in 2011, the *Huffington Post* now sits within the Oath subsidiary of Verizon Communications alongside blogging platform **Tumblr**.

The biggest controversy faced by the *Huffington Post*, which was rebranded *HuffPost* in 2017, has been its use of aggregated content from elsewhere on the web and its bank of 9,000 unpaid bloggers. In its early years, the site was a mixture of third-party content with links, blog posts and some original content, much of it opinion (Lee and Chyi, 2015). It encouraged writers to provide content for free, driving down the price of quality journalism in the process and taking advantage of bloggers keen to reach a wider audience. However, by 2018 the newly launched *HuffPost* (also known as HuffPo) had altered its publishing approach, removing its blogging platform in the US and paying **freelance** writers for the first time. Despite continual criticism, the global brand has grown audience traffic significantly in the past 13 years, with the American site huffingtonpost.com receiving more than 130 million visits per month in 2018, on average. *HuffPost* is also celebrated for its diversity agenda and its ability to approach stories inclusively and create a diverse newsroom. Its journalists seek to use non-traditional sources and give non-officials a strong voice. This is evident in its use of **Twitter** as a news source, with less than half of the Twitter quotes it uses in reporting originating from official **sources** compared to 74 percent in traditional print organizations (Bane, 2017).

See also **aggregators, huffinization, news values**.

Key Sources

Bane, K. 2017 "Tweeting the Agenda: How Print and Alternative Web-Only News Organizations Use Twitter as a Source" *Journalism Practice*, doi:10.1080/17512786.2017.1413587

Lee, A. and Chyi, I. 2015 "The Rise of Online News Aggregators: Consumption and Competition" *International Journal on Media Management* 17(1): 3–24

HUFFINIZATION

An expression conceived by Bakker (2012) in his paper discussing the alternative **business models** of digital **platforms**, which also includes **aggregators** and **content farms**. Huffinization refers directly to the digital native **news** website *HuffPost* (formerly **the *Huffington Post***) which, until 2018, relied heavily on the content of around 9000 unpaid bloggers. This no-pay model of **journalism** was widely criticized, as professional journalists and bloggers alike were not compensated for their work. Much of the content of the site was from well-known authors, celebrities and politicians who were invited to blog and use the website as a "podium for their opinions" (Bakker, 2012: 634). Criticism rose further when the company was sold to AOL for $315 million in 2011 and thousands of unpaid bloggers unsuccessfully sued the *Huffington Post*.

In January 2018, *HuffPost* announced it would be changing its approach to publishing after 13 years of taking a vast amount of content for free. In the US it closed down its blogging platform and in the UK it decided to control the type of blog posts on its site to improve the quality. It also started to pay **freelance** columnists for content, separate to the blogging platform (Curtis, 2018) for the first time. But critics have claimed that the damage has already been done, as the "The *Huffington Post* Effect" has driven down the price paid for quality journalism and encouraged writers to give away their content for free (Hays, 2018).

Key Sources

Bakker, P. 2012 "Aggregation, Content Farms and Huffinization: The Rise of Low Pay and No-Pay Journalism" *Journalism Practice* 6(5–6): 627–637

HYPERLOCAL BUSINESS MODELS

The funding of **hyperlocal journalism** remains a precarious and diverse business which relies heavily on voluntary labor and grants or donations, together with traditional **advertising** models. In the UK, there has been a strategic move to invest in innovative community projects and fund hyperlocal journalism as part of the Destination Local program. In 2012, business innovation charity Nesta offered organizations up to £50,000 to develop the next generation of hyperlocal media services that would make the most of mobile technologies to deliver geographically relevant local media. Jon Kingsbury, program director, said the aim of the program was to understand whether these new technologies and **platforms** could deliver sustainable, scalable models that served local communities and delivered economic benefit (Nesta, 2012). Similarly, in the US around the same time, the argument was being made that the future of **news** was "more likely to happen in new entrepreneurial ventures than through continuing to try to right the unwieldy old ships of media" (Briggs, 2012: xv).

Reflecting on their investment program, in 2015 Nesta produced the *Where Are We Now?* community **journalism** report, which presented the wide range of business and service models being utilized across the sector. Somewhat ironically, the report acknowledged that many of these business models were unique to a given locality and not necessarily replicable or scalable as originally intended. However, despite the strong current of volunteerism, the sector also has a growing cohort of entrepreneurs who work full-time in hyperlocal media. On the whole, only modest amounts of money are made from hyperlocal endeavours, with only 13 percent of participants in the Nesta research stating that they generated more than £500 per month (Radcliffe, 2015). Furthermore, just one in six publishers made enough money to return a profit to pay themselves or others or reinvest in the site. Income came from a range of diverse sources, including print products, secondary consulting/training services, sponsored features, grants, subscriptions and digital advertising, which constituted 77 percent of overall revenue.

A similar picture is emerging in the Netherlands, where independent hyperlocal initiatives, with a focus on campaigning journalism, are springing up. Sites that are predominantly commercially driven are few and far between, but there is a range of models from fully staffed operations to home-operated websites (Kerkhoven and Bakker, 2014). Banner advertising, the mainstay of traditional media, is also the dominant revenue source for Dutch hyperlocals. The biggest challenge for these sites is not offering local content, but running and sustaining the business in the long term.

Key Sources

Kerkhoven, V. M. and Bakker, P. 2014 "The Hyperlocal in Practice: Innovation, Creativity and Diversity" *Digital Journalism* 2(3): 296–309

Nesta 2012 "Million Pound Boost to Develop UK Hyperlocal Media Sector" *Nesta* www.nesta.org.uk/news_and_features/assets/features/1million_boost_to_develop_uk_hyperlocal_media_sector

Radcliffe, D. 2015 "Where Are We Now? UK Hyperlocal Media and Community Journalism in 2015" *Nesta* www.communityjournalism.co.uk/wp-content/uploads/2015/09/C4CJ-Report-for-Screen.pdf

HYPERLOCAL JOURNALISM

First used in the 1980s by American cable television operators to describe local **news**, the term hyperlocal has come to represent digital websites whose coverage focuses within specific geographic boundaries. Hyperlocal journalism, also known as hyperlocal media, community media or **citizen journalism**, can also incorporate non-professional **local newspapers** and magazines and even television stations, such as the UK Local TV Network. Metzgar, Kurpuis and Rowley (2011: 744) helpfully define hyperlocal journalism as "geographically-based, community-oriented, original-news-reporting organizations indigenous to the web and intended to fill perceived gaps in coverage of an issue or region and to promote civic engagement," while Radcliffe (2012: 6) defines hyperlocal media sites in the UK as "online news or content services pertaining to a town, village, single postcode or other small, geographically defined community."

These websites have emerged rapidly in the UK, the US and across Europe over the past two decades as publishing barriers have been removed. Harte, Howells and Williams (2018) give a comprehensive account of how the sector is developing in the UK in *Hyperlocal Journalism*, painting a vivid picture of citizens creating their own news services via **social media** and **blogs**. On these **platforms** volunteers and semi-professionals hold power to account, redress negative reputational geographies and tell everyday stories of community life. A large-scale study of hyperlocal news content in the UK, including interviews with producers, a content analysis of 313 sites and a survey of community news practitioners found that these sites produce a healthy sum of news about community activity, local politics, civic life and local business (Williams, Harte and Turner, 2015). On these hyperlocal sites, official news **sources** get a strong platform but local citizens and community groups get more of a say than in mainstream local news. Coverage does not tend to be traditionally balanced but there still remains a plurality of debate around contentious local issues and hyperlocal news producers are able to cover community campaigns and public-interest investigations effectively. However, the future sustainability of these ventures remains unclear, even in the face of optimism from commentators and policy makers.

Meanwhile, in the US, there is some evidence that smaller local news publishers, which are often non-profit, are faring better than their mainstream counterparts. The biggest component of the US digital news sector is now hyperlocal digital organizations (Jurkowitz, 2014). However, these sites tend to follow journalistic behaviors and gatekeeping practices (Chadha, 2016), showing skepticism towards **user-generated content** and unsupervised contributors. Nonetheless, there is acknowledgment that these kinds of news outlets are a "form of bridge media, linking traditional forms of journalism with classic civic participation" (Schaffer, 2007: 7) and have a role to play in sustaining US democracy (Downie and Schudson, 2009). The hope, or assumption, that hyperlocal journalism will treat the malaise of declining **local newspapers** is echoed in the UK, where falling revenues, reduced staff and increased workloads in mainstream local news has led to a reliance on public relations and elite sources at the expense of investigations and holding power to account. This has raised increasing concerns about the industry's ability to play its democracy-enabling roles (Williams, Harte and Turner, 2015). Communications regulator Ofcom has identified hyperlocal websites as having "the potential to support and broaden the range of local media content available to citizens and consumers at a time when traditional local media providers continue to find themselves under financial pressure" (Ofcom, 2012: 103). Innovation foundation Nesta also believes hyperlocal media can address the **democratic deficit** facing local communities (2015) by providing valuable content to non-typical local media consumers. But hyperlocal media face many challenges and, like the mainstream media, are under financial and time pressures. Around seven percent of adults in the UK currently access these sites once a week or more, and 14 percent at least monthly, limiting the reach of hyperlocal media and the potential **advertising** revenue they can generate. Access and accreditation is another stumbling block, with hyperlocal outlets restricted from covering public bodies or speaking to politicians, because they are not recognized as professional media outlets. Whether hyperlocal journalism is plugging the democratic deficit remains to be seen but there is evidence of pockets of significant public reporting.

See also **hyperlocal business models**.

Key Sources

Harte, D., Howell, R. and Williams, A. 2018 *Hyperlocal Journalism: The Decline of the Local Newspapers and the Rise of Online Community News*. Oxford: Abingdon

Harte, D., Howell, R. and Williams, A. 2018 *Hyperlocal Journalism: The Decline of the Local Newspaper and the Rise of Online Community Newspaper*. London: Routledge.

Metzgar, E., Kurpius, D. and Rowley, K. 2011 "Defining Hyperlocal Media: Proposing a Framework for Discussion" *New Media & Society* 13(5): 772–787

Ofcom 2012 *The Communications Market Report: United Kingdom*. London: Ofcom

Williams, A., Harte, D. and Turner, J. 2015 "The Value of UK Hyperlocal Community News" *Digital Journalism* 3(5): 680–703

HYPERTEXT

Hypertext systems, which date as far back as 1945 (Nielsen, 1995), cross-reference information in a non-linear way. Hypertexuality is one of the key underlying concepts of the World Wide Web, which consists of nodes of information connected by links, known as hyperlinks. In this web of nodes, users can browse at will (Berners-Lee and Cailliau, 1990) by the simple click of a mouse or touch of a screen. Hyperlinks are represented by a word, phrase, image or other object and, once selected on a web page or electronic document, can take the user to another internal, or external, page or image. Author and designer Theodore Nelson, who coined the term hypertext in the mid-1960s, first defined it as "a body of written or pictorial material interconnected in such a complex way that it could not conveniently be presented or represented on paper" (1965: 96). Later, Landow surmised that hypertext "denotes text composed of blocks of text ... and the electronic links that join them" (2006: 3) while hypermedia extended this notion across to multimedia rather than simply text. The word hyper in the use of hypertext is applied in the mathematical sense of "extension," such as in hyperspace rather than in the medical sense of "excessive," for example hyperactivity.

In the field of **online journalism**, hypertext can be used to add background to a story by connecting to related articles and sources of information, making for a "much richer historical, political and cultural context" (Pavlik, 2001: 16). It can, therefore, facilitate "greater depth in reporting and allow stories to be told from multiple perspectives" (Doherty, 2014: 124), deepening the relationship with the audience and keeping them engaged for longer. It is considered to be one of the three essential characteristics of online journalism, along with multimedia and interactivity, as it provides greater credibility, transparency and diversity (De Maeyer, 2012). The process of hyperlinking demands that the reader think "about the text in a way that print or broadcast texts do not" (Hall, 2001: 68). In a discourse analysis, De Maeyer (2012) found that hyperlinks were considered by educators and practitioners alike to be a fundamental part of the web and added depth to reporting; however, on the ground they were not commonly used by journalists. Moreover, multiple empirical studies show that there is limited use of hyperlinks in online journalism, with the majority of links leading to pages on the same website and not to primary sources or related background information. This has the effect of "diluting the potential for the depth in reporting that hypertext affords" (Doherty, 2014: 126).

Key Sources

De Maeyer, J. 2012 "The Journalistic Hyperlink: Prescriptive Discourses about Linking in Online News" *Journalism Practice* 6(5–6): 692–701

Doherty, S. 2014 "Hypertext and Journalism: Paths for Future Research" *Digital Journalism* 2(2): 124–139

IMMEDIACY

Early in the emergence of digital news and journalism, academics and researchers identified what some colloquially dubbed the "two Is theory," which identified two **affordances** of digital media technologies which became the signature characteristics of **digital journalism**, distinguishing it from its analogue predecessor; namely, immediacy and **interactivity** (Steensen, 2011; Zamith, 2019: 93).

The term immediacy refers to the ability of consumers to view content immediately following its production (usually by **journalists**) and readers' expectation that content will be updated when it is reopened. Expressed slightly differently, immediacy refers to the radical shortening of the news cycle; that is, the gap between a news organization's initial awareness of a newsworthy event and the time it takes a journalist to research, draft and publish a story about that occurrence. In the context of digital journalism, however, what Cushion and Lewis called the "thirst to be first" by publishing ahead of competitors becomes an even more widespread and treasured ambition among journalists. But the difficulties involved in contacting **sources**, gathering comments and verifying information to inform journalists' copy prompted initial scholarly research about immediacy to assume "an 'accuracy-problem' perspective" concerned with "how online news lives up to traditional journalistic standards" (Karlsson and Strömbäck, 2010).

Journalism scholars such as Jeongsub Lim remain skeptical about the extent to which news is being constantly revised and updated. Drawing on evidence from his study of news sites in South Korea, he argues that the "immediacy of online news is a myth" which reflects the "beliefs of researchers, journalists and users" rather than any reality concerning the immediacy of news (Lim, 2012: 71).

Key Sources

Cushion, S. and Lewis, J. 2009 "The Thirst to be First: An Analysis of Breaking News Stories and Their Impact on the Quality of 24 Hour News Coverage in the UK" *Journalism Practice* 3(3): 304–318

Karlsson, M. and Strömbäck, J. 2010 "Freezing the Flow of Online News: Exploring Approaches to the Study of the Liquidity of Online News" *Journalism Studies* 11(1): 2–19

Lim, J. 2012 "The Mythological Status of the Immediacy of the Most Important Online News: An Analysis of Top News Flows in Diverse Online Media" *Journalism Studies* 13(1): 71–89

Steensen, S. 2011 "Online Journalism and the Promise of New Technologies: A Critical Review and Look Ahead" *Journalism Studies* 12(3): 311–327

IMMERSIVE JOURNALISM

Immersive journalism uses 3D gaming, immersive technologies and virtual reality headsets to allow audiences a first-hand, "being there" experience of the events occurring in a particular news event by creating a virtual location ("place illusion") to replicate the circumstances where the events in the **news** story actually took place in the real world. The pioneering research in immersive **journalism** has been conducted by Nonny de la Peña and her colleagues at Annenberg in 2010 (de la Peña, Weil, Llobera, Giannopoulos, Pomés, Spanlang, Friedman, Sanchez-Vives and Slater, 2010).

The overall effect of immersive journalism is to create in the **audience** member the sense of being a participant in the actual news event, allowing them to gain insights, understandings, engagement and even empathies with the position of particular actors in the original real news event (Sánchez Laws, 2017). The *Guardian*, for example, in one of its immersive journalism reports (the "6 x 9" project), created the experience of virtual incarceration in a prison cell for audiences and journalists, to assess their empathy with the prisoner in the news story (Sánchez Laws, 2017). Sánchez Laws concludes that immersive journalism technologies are beginning to approximate formats that may enhance empathy (Sánchez Laws, 2017).

A major ambition for the news organization, alongside its editorial goal of enhancing audience engagement and appreciation of news storytelling, is to win access to new, probably younger, audiences (Jones, 2017: 171).

Key Sources
de la Peña, N., Weil, P., Llobera, J., Giannopoulos, E., Pomés, A., Spanlang, B., Friedman, D., Sanchez-Vives, M. V. and Slater, M. 2010 "Immersive Journalism: Immersive Virtual Reality for the First Person Experience of News" *Presence: Teleoperators and Virtual Environments* 19(4): 291–301
Jones, S. 2017 "Disrupting the Narrative: Immersive Journalism in Virtual Reality" *Journal of Media Practice* 18(2–3): 171–185
Sánchez Laws, A. L. 2017 "Can Immersive Journalism Enhance Empathy?" *Digital Journalism*, doi:10.1080/21670811.2017.1389286

IMPARTIALITY *SEE* TRANSPARENCY

IN-BETWEENERS

In her article "How is Participation Practiced by 'In-Betweeners' of Journalism," Laura Ahva argues that **journalism** should be conceptualized as a structure of public communication that involves the practices of a variety of actors (**journalists, audiences**, citizen actors, **freelances**, artists, academics, students and local residents, for example) who operate in a range of settings beyond – as well as within – the newsroom (Ahva, 2017: 142). What she calls the "In-Betweeners of journalism" are "citizens who are not professional journalists, yet play a greater role in the journalistic process than mere receivers" (Ahva, 2017: 143). To explore the nature and style of their engagement with journalism, in-betweeners were interviewed at three journalistic organizations: *Voima*, an alternative monthly magazine in Finland; *Cafébabel*, an online magazine in France and *Södra Sidan*, a public journalism local newspaper in Stockholm.

Interviews revealed fundamental misunderstandings in some scholarly accounts of participation in journalistic work. In-betweeners, for example, were sometimes incorrectly styled as "amateurs" or "**citizen journalists**," which fails to capture accurately the reality of some people (working at *Voima*, for example) who were highly experienced freelance journalists but who were choosing to work for very modest honorariums. Such one size fits all labels are inaccurate and inappropriate. Ahva argues that her more "inclusive view" of in-betweeners and their varied participatory engagement with journalism allows the possibility "to see how a continuum of varying participant positions is created between the roles of 'journalists' and 'audiences'" (Ahva, 2017: 145). Melissa Wall suggests that Ahva's in-betweeners are "performing in a liminal state that exists between fulltime professionals and clueless amateurs committing one-off acts of journalism" (Wall, 2019).

Drawing on the work of Nico Carpentier (2011), Ahva identifies a number of possible "orientations of practice" articulated by in-betweeners which were evident at each of the three news sites in the study, although to varying degrees; she labels them participation *through* journalism, participation *in* journalism, participation *with* journalism, participation *around* journalism and participation *for* journalism.

Participation *through* journalism involves engagement with journalism to win access to public discussion via an alternative platform and to help shape or influence that public conversation. Consequently, this orientation to participation is "political in the broad sense of the term." Participation *in* journalism concerns editorial content where participation allows opportunities to "co-decide" the agenda and the themes, topics and angles of reporting of particular stories (Ahva, 2017). In this sense, the participants were adopting the position of collaborators (Canter, 2013b: 1098). Participation *with* journalism was oriented towards what Ahva terms "the community of practice" which journalists and participants formed around the news organization with its ambitions, traditions and shared history. Participation *around* journalism reflects in-betweeners' involvement in cultural life, such as social debate, education and neighbourhood projects that may form the bases of stories. Finally, participation *for* journalism is where "actors adopt their position between salaried journalists and audience members because they aspire towards journalism as a career" (Ahva, 2017).

Ahva concludes by offering a "shorthand" to illustrate that participation by in-betweeners may be defined by opportunities and possibilities to:

(1)   be able to get one's ideas through to the public sphere;
(2)   take part in the news making process;
(3)   work together with like-minded people;
(4)   engage in activities that are loosely organised around media work, and
(5)   do this for the sake of gaining better placement in the job market.

(Ahva, 2017)

See also **citizen journalism**.

Key Sources

Ahva, L. 2017 "How is Participation Practiced by 'In-Betweeners' of Journalism" *Journalism Practice* 11(2–3): 142–159

Canter, L. 2013 "The Source, the Resource and the Collaborator: The Role of Citizen Journalism in Local UK Newspapers" *Journalism* 14(8): 1091–1109

Carpentier, N. 2011 *Media and Participation: A Site of Ideological-Democratic Struggle.* Bristol: Intellect Press

Wall, M. 2019 *Citizen Journalism: Practices, Propaganda, Pedagogy.* London: Routledge

(THE) *INDEPENDENT*

The UK national newspaper the *Independent* was launched on October 7th 1986 by three ex-*Telegraph* **journalists**, Andreas Whittam Smith, Stephen Glover and Matthew Symonds. It adopted the bold advertising claim "It is, are you?" (i.e., independent), articulating its ambition to produce a high quality national newspaper while

(THE) *INDEPENDENT*

positioning itself editorially on the center ground at a time when the national press confronted increasing allegations of partisanship exemplified by the *Sun* under Kelvin McKenzie's editorship (Chippindale and Horrie, 1990). The *Independent* challenged the *Guardian* on the left and *The Times* on the right (Franklin, 1997: 83–87; Glover, 1993). The paper achieved considerable initial success in terms of circulation (in excess of 400K by 1989), **advertising** revenues, innovative page design and the quality and even-handedness of its editorial commitments.

A casualty of Murdoch's declaration and sustained prosecution of a price war, the *Independent* was bought in 1997 by Tony O'Reilly's Independent News and Media and Newspaper group and in 2010 joined the corporate portfolio of Russian oligarch Alexander Lebedev. But the *Independent* failed to flourish under both new corporate owners and on March 26th 2015 the *Independent* announced that it was moving to an online edition only to save the costs involved in the daily print run. At the time of its closure, the *Independent's* circulation had plummeted to 58,000 copies daily, a striking 85 percent down on its 1990 high (Franklin, 2008).

The closure of the print edition acknowledged the harsh realities of the UK national *newspaper* market where newspapers were operating in a hyper-competitive market in an age of digital and online newspapers. Its rival, the *Guardian*, spoke generously of its late rival. "Especially in its early years," the Editorial argued, "the *Independent* was a really rather wonderful newspaper. But all news journalism is being turned upside down by the digital revolution" (Editorial, *Guardian* March 25th 2016b). The *Independent* remains the first, and so far only, example of national newspaper closure as a result of the failure to adapt the title's business model to the disrupted circumstances of **digital journalism** in the UK.

Key Sources

Chippindale, P. and Horrie, C. 1990 *Stick It Up Your Punter! The Rise and Fall of the Sun*. London: Heinemann

Franklin, B. (Ed) 2008 *Pulling Newspapers Apart: Analysing Print Journalism*. London: Routledge

Glover, S. 1993 *Paper Dreams*. London: Jonathan Cape

Guardian 2016 "Editorial: the Guardian View on the End of the Independent: All News Journalism Being Turned Upside Down by the Digital Revolution" 25 Marchwww.theguardian.com/commentisfree/2016/mar/25/guardian-view-end-independent-in-print

INFOGRAPHICS

Infographics is a neologism built around the root words "information" and "graphics" and means the visual and graphical presentation of complex information, knowledge and/or data to promote accessibility and understanding of editorial messages better than words alone can achieve. In brief, infographics offer comprehension at a glance. As well as simplifying complexity, infographics tend to offer a more entertaining and engaging articulation of information than a textual account, since quality infographics are 30 times more likely to be read than text statements (So, 2012). Classic infographic formats include bar charts, pie charts, histograms and diagrams of every kind and stripe, but in the age of data, **digital journalism** and data visualization, when the infographic has enjoyed a "meteoric rise in popularity," pictograms are probably equally, if not most, likely (Ritchie, 2017: 2). Infographics have become ubiquitous as editorial content in "national and regional papers around the world ... across quality, mid-market and tabloid formats and are routinely found in our television **news**" (Dick, 2017: 498).

Recent research illustrates that infographics are popular with news consumers across a range of media platforms (print newspaper, e-newspaper, on **tablet** and on news websites) and are valued as an element in the news mix but only if they are well contextualized into the news story (De Haan, Kruikemeier, Lecheler, Smit and van der Nat, 2018). Infographics, however, have become an especially popular design feature of news online and consequently news organizations in the second decade of the new millennium, for example the *Guardian* and the **BBC**, have markedly increased their infographic output and the numbers of people employed to generate them (Reid, 2014).

Murray Dick identifies three broad areas of scholarly research focused on infographics in **Digital Journalism Studies**. First, research which explores users' reactions and interactions with infographics in news, which includes studies examining why audiences prefer particular infographics above others. Second, there are research studies which involve conducting content analyses of infographics in news, including, for example, case studies of infographics in news reporting in particular countries or regions, while the final category of research reflects scholarly interest in organizational studies about the activities of the visual journalist in the digital newsroom (Dick, 2018: 499–500).

While a key function of infographics is to render highly complex ideas and data sets immediately accessible, Dick's study of their routine use at the *Daily Express* (quickly dubbed "Expressographs") suggested that the interpretation of infographics was compromised by ideological values embedded in the newspaper's editorial. Dick argues that infographics were routinely "used not as a means of conveying data accurately and objectively, but in order to propagate the paper's editorial line, and to further Lord Beaverbrook's political interests" (Dick, 2015: 152). He concludes a later study with a warning that infographics in "contemporary, networked media pose a serious civic challenge" especially to our "democratic engagement" because of the way they mediate our lived experience to a degree where it becomes uncertain whether audiences have the critical facility to "interpret and critically appraise them" (Dick, 2018: 505). Such a development may have resonance with arguments about **fake news**.

Key Sources

De Haan, Y., Kruikemeier, S., Lecheler, S., Smit, G. and van der Nat, R. 2018 "When Does an Infographic Say More Than a Thousand Words? Audience Evaluations of News Visualizations" *Journalism Studies* 19(9): 1293–1312

Dick, M. 2015 "Just Fancy That: An Analysis of Infographic Propaganda in the *Daily Express* 1956–1959" *Journalism Studies* 16(2): 152–174

Dick, M. 2018 "Developments in Infographics" in Franklin, B. and Eldridge, II, S. (Eds) *The Routledge Companion to Digital Journalism Studies*. London: Routledge, 498–508

So, A. 2012 "You Suck at Infographics" *Wired*, 23 July www.wire.com/2012/07/you-suck-at-infographics/

INFORMATION SUBSIDIES

The significant and widely used concept of information subsidies has its origins in the path-breaking analysis of **agenda setting** and agenda building by **journalism** scholar Oscar Gandy in his classic text *Beyond Agenda Setting: Information Subsidies and Public Policy* (Gandy, 1982). Gandy argued that information subsidies offered literally a "free gift or subsidy" of pre-packaged **news** to **journalists** looking for content to inform their **news** coverage, or seeking source materials or quotations from senior politicians or corporate leaders to help them "stand up" their reports; the price to be paid, he argued, was journalists' editorial autonomy and independence of judgment.

These subsidies, Gandy suggests, are distributed by a growing band of information specialists, public relations professionals and other communications specialists working in government and significant economic and cultural organizations. They typically assume the form of press releases, press conferences, freely distributed official statements, as well as conversations (directly or by telephone) with journalists. In this way, information subsidies offer an important subsidy to journalists who, in their day-to-day professional practice, have become increasingly reliant on them to meet news editors' growing demand for stories, especially in times of increasing competition between news organizations for readers and advertising revenues.

In more recent times, journalists' reliance on these subsidies has grown apace while their implications for editorial autonomy, accuracy and veracity have been very critically assessed by *Guardian* journalist Nick Davies, who argued that "**journalism**" had been replaced by "**churnalism**," in which the journalist's daily task had been reduced to simply choosing between the plethora of press releases flooding into newsrooms, rewriting them and adding their own byline to the prepackaged copy written by public relations professionals and distributed via the web (Davies, 2008b). Curiously, Davies saw the internet as a kind of "liberator" detached from churnalism, offering an escape route from this passive process of (re)producing news. He says in his epilogue: "And, of course, there is the Internet ... The real promise of the Internet ... [is] that it could liberate the mass media from churnalism" (Davies, 2008b; Johnson and Forde, 2017).

The recent "crisis in journalism" (Chyi, Lewis and Nan, 2012), triggered by rapid and fundamental changes in journalism in a digital age, has further exacerbated journalism's reliance on information subsidies (Franklin, 2013: 3). The collapse of traditional **business models** at **legacy media**, the increasing competition for **advertising** revenues from online news organizations, as well as the emergence of **social media** platforms such as **Twitter** and **Facebook**, which serve both as sources and drivers of the news (Franklin, 2016), create a greater financial and editorial dependency on these subsidies for news organizations. The drafting of information subsidies is, moreover, massively facilitated by the use of "machine written news" (Van Dalen, 2013) "robot news" (Clerwall, 2014) and the employment of **news bots** (Lokot and Diakopoulos, 2016), while their distribution is speedy and widespread within digitally networked communities.

Key Sources

Davies, N. 2008b *Flat Earth News: An Award Winning Journalist Exposes Falsehood, Distortion and Propaganda in the Global Media* London: Chatto and Windus

Franklin, B., (Ed) 2016 *The Future of Journalism: In an Age of Digital Media and Economic Uncertainty* Oxford: Routledge, 1–22

Gandy, Jr., O. H. 1982 *Beyond Agenda-Setting: Information Subsidies and Public Policy.* Norwood, NJ: Ablex

Johnson, J. and Forde, S. 2017 "Churnalism, Revised and Revisited" An Introduction to a Special Issue of the Journal *Digital Journalism* 5(8): 943–946. The special issue examined the impact and implications of churnalism in an age of digital media and journalism

Lokot, T. and Diakopoulos, N. 2016 "Newsbots: Automating News and Information Dissemination on Twitter" *Digital Journalism* 4(6): 682–699

INFOTAINMENT

The term "infotainment" combines the two words "information" and "entertainment" to describe **news** and current affairs articles and programs (and factual programming more generally) in which the content mixes these two elements to make factual programming and reportage more accessible to audiences while enhancing audience size and reach (Fallows,1997),; a process sometimes referred to as "dumbing down." Increasingly competitive markets for readers and advertisers, as well as **audience** demand, are usually cited as the driving forces behind the growth of infotainment, although such an analysis rests on the unproven assumption that moving editorially downmarket will "automatically" increase audience appreciation and size.

The advent of **digital journalism** has witnessed a rapid growth in the popularity of **listicles** – short and pithy articles structured in the format of a list – that is, articles which are high on entertainment and factual elements, that attract high downloads/readerships and are easy for **journalists** to write (Poole, 2013). Legacy tabloid newspapers, along with digital-native start-ups such as **BuzzFeed**, show a strong commitment to listicles while even the Pulitzer Prize winning UK newspaper, the *Guardian*, publishes at least one listicle most days on the inside cover of its G2 Section (Davis, 2019: 6).

See also **listicles**.

Key Sources
Davis, N. 2019 "Seven Ways to Prevent Colds, or Get Over Them" *Guardian G2*, 7 January 2019, 6
Fallows, J. 1997 *Breaking the News: How the Media Undermine American Democracy.* New York: Vintage Books
Poole, S. 2013 "The Top Nine Things you Need To Know About Lists" *Guardian* www.theguardian.com/books/2013/nov/12/listicles-articles-written-lists-steven-poole

INSTAGRAM *SEE* FACEBOOK

INTERACTIVITY

Journalism scholar Mark Deuze, writing in the early days of online media, identified interactivity, along with **immediacy**, as essential and defining features of **digital journalism**; central **affordances** of digital media distinguishing them from their analog predecessors (Deuze, 1999).

Interactivity offered individuals new possibilities, including an empowered engagement with digital journalism, a newly achieved ability to shape, influence and even contribute to editorial content (beyond the "letters page"), but also the capacity to contact and establish interactive channels of communication with **journalists**, reinforcing their ability to discuss, negotiate and co-create editorial content. A widely held belief was that such interactivity would prove empowering, giving those **"people formerly known as the audience"** an enhanced voice with beneficial consequences for democratic conversation and decision making (Rosen, 2006).

The vehicles for achieving interactivity have subsequently become commonplace: Journalists' provision of email address alongside their byline; the provision and encouragement of **user comment threads**; news organizations' enthusiasm for **user-generated content** and, more broadly, the growth of **citizen journalism**. Some of these mechanisms enabling interactivity, however, have proved problematic. The growth of incivility in readers' comment threads, for example, has prompted some news organizations to close these interactive spaces, at least temporarily (Greenslade, 2018).

Key Sources
Deuze, M. 1999 "Journalism and the Web's Analysis of the Skills and Standards in an Online environment" *International Communications Gazette* 61(5): 373–390

Greenslade, R. 2018 "Digital Revolution: Opinion Is Valued More than Fact as We Turn Full Circle" *Guardian* 30th July, 25

Rosen, J. 2006 The People Formerly Known as the Audience *PRESSthink*, 27th June http://archive.pressthink.org/2006/06/27/ppl_frmr.html

Santana, A. D. 2013 "Virtuous or Vitriolic: The Effect of Anonymity on Civility in Online Newspapers' Readers' Comment Boards" *Journalism Practice* 8(1): 18–33

INTERVIEW

At the heart of **journalism** is the interview which has been the dominant method of news-gathering among journalists since the 19th century. It is a conversational-like interaction between two people that requires a notable amount of techniques on the part of the interviewer (Ryan, Coughlan and Cronin, 2009). Interviewees are asked questions by a **journalist** and provide facts or opinions in response, which are then recorded either in writing (sometimes using shorthand) or more frequently via a recording device such as a dictaphone or smartphone. Interviews can be conducted face to face, on the telephone, via email, or on **Skype**, FaceTime, WhatsApp, you name it, and are the stable tool of all reporters and feature writers. Despite the growth in **data journalism** and the use of statistics to tell stories, interviews are still at the heart of all reporting and always will be according to Lee-Potter.

> Virtually all news stories and features depend on an interview of some kind. It could be an interview with a police officer appealing for witnesses to a crime, an interview with a minister seeking to explain a new government policy or an interview with an author on a mission to promote their latest book – whatever the rationale, interviews give journalists the opportunity to assemble the facts, details and quotes that will inform, inspire and entertain their readers.
>
> (Lee-Potter, 2017: 1)

The interview can be a brief informal chat on the phone, a lengthy conversation over a meal, a live talk or a surprise encounter on a person's doorstep. Whatever the location and situation, the art of journalistic interviewing is complex and involves a range of competencies. Carpenter, Cepak and Peng (2018) suggests ten key skills that expert journalism interviewers possess: Listening, interaction management, research, empathy, articulation, self-presentation, verification, news judgment, observation, and open-mindedness.

As part of their skill set, journalists are expected to plan carefully for interviews, preparing questions in advance and establishing a rapport with their interviewee. They will generally ask open questions to illicit a more expansive response, and potentially juicy quotes, unless a yes or no answer is specifically required (Boyd, 2001). In broadcast interviews there is a strong element of performance on behalf of the interviewer and interviewee, while in print and online much of what is said in the interview will not be directly quoted and may become part of reported speech, which raises ethical issues in terms of what is selected (Harcup, 2002). Increasingly, journalists will resort to lifting quotes or sound bites from **social media** to present public feedback or a comment from a specific individual that in turn can be used to craft an entire **news** story. What a celebrity or public figure tweeted or blogged can become a news story in itself, without the necessity of interviewing. However, the act of interviewing is still seen as sacred among reporters and remains central to hard news and **investigative journalism**, with reporters preferring to speak directly to a source than send questions on email via a public relations agent. There are concerns, nonetheless, that an increased reliance on interviewing via the telephone or email makes it more difficult to verify **sources** or information (Pavlik, 2000).

Key Sources
Carpenter, S., Cepak, A. and Peng, Z. 2018 "An Exploration of the Complexity of Journalistic Interviewing Competencies" *Journalism Studies* 19(15): 2283–2303
Harcup, T. 2002 *Journalism: Principles and Practice*. London: Sage
Lee-Potter, E. 2017 *Interviewing for Journalists*. London: Routledge

INVERTED PYRAMID

The inverted pyramid is the name given to the standardized editorial format that **journalists** employ for writing hard **news** stories. The inverted pyramid places the most significant information about the story in the opening paragraph and addresses the "five W questions": Who? What? Why? Where? and When? and sometimes How? Subsequent paragraphs "fill out" the lesser details of the story in a declining order of significance to enable any necessary editing to be achieved by simply "cutting" paragraphs from the bottom of the text until the required word length is achieved (Broersma, 2007; Johnston and Graham, 2012). This style of writing was pioneered by American **journalists** in the late 19th century and superseded the older narrative style which reported events according to their chronology rather than the presumed significance of their various composite elements, reflecting the oral tradition which, in parodied form, proceeds with the phrase, "To begin at the beginning ...".

In his magisterial study of the adoption of the inverted pyramid, Horst Pottker identifies four explanations accounting for its emergence as a professional format at the time of the American Civil War (1861–1865) which reflected: the unreliability of the (then) new technology of the telegraph (technological factors); the information policy of the Union (political factors); the increasing competition between publishers (economic factors); and finally, publishers' and editors' increasing enthusiasm for including illustrations, graphics, headlines and other editorial devices intended to increase the comprehensibility of their products; in Pottker's words, "the professional effort to strengthen the communicative quality of news" (Pottker, 2003: 501).

Pottker's conclusions about the timing of the transition from a narrative editorial style to the inverted pyramid format were based on the findings of a content analysis of news articles published in the *New York Herald* and the *New York Times* between 1855 and 1920. His research revealed that the inverted pyramid did not appear as a standard news format until the 1880s, more than two decades later than previous research had indicated (Pottker, 2003: 507–510).

Since new technologies have always proved influential factors in reshaping editorial design (Broersma, 2007; Pavlik, 2001), it is perhaps unsurprising that scholars of **Digital Journalism Studies** are already noting the impact of digital media technologies on editorial preferences for storytelling. Johnston and Graham (2012) suggest that "analysis of news during the first decade of the 2000s indicated narrative story telling techniques were increasingly used within the news pages of metropolitan dailies, challenging the more traditional style of the inverted pyramid," while Hartsock suggests that the journalistic move away from the inverted pyramid is "simply a return to a style which has been marginalised for nearly a century" (Hartsock, 2007: 258). Erik Neveu argues forcefully for a return to a narrative style in **journalism** (Neveu, 2014: 533).

How is this reversion to narrative news and the declining presence of the inverted pyramid to be explained? First, in a digital age characterized by increased competition between news organizations, narrative storytelling is simply "more compelling to read than the information model of the inverted pyramid and this approach may help to retain newspaper readers who are being lost to other media" (Johnston and Graham, 2012: 517). This led Neveu, for example, to favor not only narrative formats but a journalistic engagement with "Slow News" (Neveu, 2014: 533). Second, digital and online presentation of news ends the scarcity of space that was so important in shaping (literally) the format of news into an inverted pyramid. Online news luxuriates in almost unlimited editorial space that journalists can use to tell stories in different ways and at greater length with an expansive narrative or by using affordances such as **hyperlinks**.

Key Sources

Broersma, M. (Ed) 2007 *Form and Style in Journalism: European Newspapers and the Representation of News, 1880–2005.* Leuven: Paris and Dudley

Johnston, J. and Graham, C. 2012 "The New, Old Journalism: Narrative Writing in Contemporary Newspapers" *Journalism Studies* 13(4): 517–533

Neveu, E. 2014 "Revisiting Narrative Journalism As One of the Futures of Journalism" *Journalism Studies* 15(5): 533–542

Pottker, H. 2003 "News and Its Communicative Quality: The Inverted Pyramid – When and Why Did It Appear?" *Journalism Studies* 4(4): 501–511

INVESTIGATIVE JOURNALISM

Although all **journalism** investigates subjects to a certain degree, the work of investigative journalists is held on a pedestal as the pinnacle of watchdog reporting for the public good. Investigative journalism involves deep reporting into a single topic and often leads to the exposure of criminal, political or corporate wrongdoing – and in some cases all three. A **journalist** may spend months or even years investigating a single topic, doggedly hunting down new leads and wading through thousands of dense legal and governmental documents in an indomitable bid to uncover the truth.

Campaigning journalism and the exposure of crooks began in the 19th century but investigative journalism did not take off in its own right until the 1960s. It became a popular form of exposing politicians and public role models, particularly within the British tabloid press but also on national television. In its print heyday, investigative journalism, often involving undercover stings on celebrities and politicians, exposed criminal activity and in some cases led to prison sentences, such as that of former deputy chairman of the Conservative Party, Jeffrey Archer, jailed for perjury following a *News of the World* investigation. In the US, the Watergate Scandal of the 1970s is held aloft as the height of investigative journalism after reporters Bob Woodward and Carl Bernstein of the *Washington Post* uncovered the illegal activity of the Nixon administration, which ultimately led to the President's resignation and the trial of many of his top officials.

Due to the amount of time involved in investigative reporting, which can potentially lead to nowhere, it is an expensive form of journalism. As media companies have sought higher profits, they have made cost cuts in newsrooms, dismantling many investigative teams. This has been compounded by greater competition and fragmented **audiences** online since the turn of the century. In television, the ratings-driven environment has put pressure on program budgets, particularly investigative reports that are costly to make but may not attract high audience figures. Meanwhile, the closure of regional and national newspapers and the streamlining of staff mean there are now fewer reporters, and those that remain have less time to carry out investigative work. But although legacy media bemoans the loss of investigative journalism, online **platforms** to a certain extent have risen in their place, with investigative centers worldwide more than doubling between 2000 and 2012 (Carvajal, García-Avilés and González, 2012) in part due to start-ups across Europe, the US and Australia (Price, 2017). Most of these organizations are based on **non-profit journalism** models which are supported by **crowdfunding, subscriptions**, grants, training and benefactors such as award-winning website *ProPublica* in America.

In Scotland, The Ferret was launched online in 2015, offering to "nose up the trousers" of those in power. It is run as a not-for-profit, independent, public-interest platform and has readers sitting on its board. Its three main purposes are to fill a democratic, economic and ethical deficit. The loss of local newspapers in Scotland, including a reduction by Johnston Press of 49 percent of its editorial and photographic staff between 2009 and 2014, has led to a **democratic deficit** with "journalists no longer able to effectively hold politicians and power to account" (Price, 2017: 1339). The Ferret is also trying to find a sustainable economic model for doing time-consuming journalism and address the financial crisis in the traditional media. Third, it aspires to improve the ethical standards of journalism by restoring public trust in journalists through being accountable and transparent in everything they do.

Although the revival of investigative journalism is largely attributed to digital native platforms, such as the **BuzzFeed** global investigations team, **computational journalism** in **legacy media** firms has also driven much of the recent interest and investment in investigative journalism. The practice of **data journalism** has enabled mainstream journalists to investigate otherwise impenetrable documents, often working in collaboration with other media organizations or relying on the public for crowdsourcing. The *Guardian* newspaper opened up documents to the public to help them decipher the MPs' expenses scandal. Meanwhile, The International Consortium of Investigative Journalists, an independent organization of more than 100 journalists and 100 media organizations in over 70 countries, came together to release the Panama Papers. These were 11.5 million confidential documents originally leaked to German newspaper *Süddeutsche Zeitung* that contained information on more than 214,000 offshore companies, including various heads of governments. More than 107 media organizations participated in analyzing the documents, including BBC *Panorama* and the *Guardian*, with the leak leading to the resignation of the Prime Minister of Iceland. Without the use of computers to organize and analyze the data, and the provision of **data visualization** to present the information with clarity to the public, the global exposé would not have been possible.

That being said, traditional methods of investigative reporting still have a role to play. *The Times* reporter Andrew Norfolk spent over a year uncovering the Rotherham child exploitation scandal, mostly via sensitive face-to-face interviews. Furthermore, research shows that the use of **social media** by television investigative reporters does not translate into increased productivity and traditional newsgathering methods still prevail (Abdenour, 2017).

See also **slow journalism, long form narrative**.

Key Sources

Carvajal, M., García-Avilés, J. A. and González, J. L. 2012 "Crowdfunding and Non-Profit Media: The Emergence of New Models for Public Interest Journalism" *Journalism Practice* 6(5–6): 638–647

Price, J. 2017 "Can the Ferret be a Watchdog? Understanding the Launch, Growth and Prospects of a Digital, Investigative Journalism Start-Up" *Digital Journalism* 5(10): 1336–1350

JOURNALISM

Answers to the question, "What is journalism?" have proved notoriously elusive, not least to **journalists** themselves. Perhaps this is because journalism is not always highly valued, even by its most distinguished practitioners. American **journalist** and editor, H. L. Mencken, for example, described journalism as "a craft to be mastered in 4 days and abandoned at the first sign of a better job" (Delano, 2001: 261). Similarly Ernest Hemingway, who worked as a reporter for the Kansas City Star in the 1920s, dismissed his newspaper work as "just journalism" – a second order, lesser form of writing than scholarship or creative writing – even though his journalism informed much of his later creative writing (cited in Zelizer, 2004: 1).

Academic responses to the question typically evoke three options. First, journalism may constitute an arena of professional activity. Expressed simply, if not almost tautologically, it is what journalists do. Journalism is the activity by which journalists produce content for media formats which stretch from magazines such as *Drummer, Asian Babes* and *Women's Weekly* to encompass *Al Jazeera*, the *Wall Street Journal*, the *Sheffield Telegraph, Panorama*, BBC Radios 1 to 6, as well as myriad blogs, online newspapers and hyperlocal community papers.

Second, journalism is an expansive industry with a global reach with economic, political, but also cultural significance: McNair describes journalism as "the preeminent cultural form of our era" (McNair, 2005: 25). Third, journalism, or, more accurately, **journalism studies**, is a field of intellectual inquiry based on the reflective and scholarly study of the practice of journalism.

It is the first response that has been the most fruitful for academic research and study. Schudson, for example, identifies three requirements for journalism: The provision of information, which is current rather than historical, and which has public consequence. In his own words, journalism involves "information or commentary on contemporary affairs taken to be publicly important" (Schudson, 2003: 11). Note that these requirements do not exclude the efforts of "citizen" or "participatory" journalists from inclusion within journalism.

McNair complements Schudson's brief definition by identifying three ambitions for journalism. First, it must supply information that is necessary for the **audience**/readership to monitor their environment. The information must be detached, impartial and objective since, for McNair, journalism is always information for sale in a market and, consequently, anything less than accurate and objective information will have little market value. Second, journalism has close connections to democracy, which reflects its requirement to facilitate and participate in political debate. Journalism must be a central component in what Habermas called the "public sphere." Consequently, the history of journalism has been, at the same time, a history of censorship and attempts to control journalists and news media by the state, governments, the church, businesses and others who objected to journalism's political role.

Finally, McNair claims journalism has "recreational" or "cultural" functions which oblige it to deliver "education, enlightenment and entertainment," a trilogy of ambitions reminiscent of Lord Reith's public service declaration that the BBC must "educate, inform and entertain."

This complexity and uncertainty about the nature of journalism is, however, complicated further by the emergence of innovative digital media with their implications for all aspects of journalism, which oblige reconsideration of even the most fundamental issues such as what is journalism? And has journalism been replaced by **digital journalism**? Even when the qualifying adjective is occasionally silent, it is always assumed (Malik and Shapiro, 2017). Some journalism scholars argue that the meaning of journalism has expanded and changed as digital technologies have facilitated the growth of online **news**, digital newspapers, social media, **blogs** and **citizen journalism**, which in turn raise "boundary disputes" between journalism and seemingly cognate activities (Carlson and Lewis, 2015).

Such a development was foreseen in John Pavlik's early, portentous and classic study *Journalism and New Media* (2001), which argued that digital media technology was influencing the role of the journalist in at least four ways: How journalists do their work, the content of news, the structure or organization of the newsroom, and the "realignment of the relationships between or among news organizations, journalists and their many publics, including **audiences, sources**, competitors, **advertisers** and governments" (Pavlik, 2001: xiii). First, it influences how journalists do their work, by making sources and digital data bases accessible without leaving the newsroom, ultimately converting journalism into a "desk based job." Second, the **immediacy, interactivity** and global reach of digital technology has exerted an influence on the content of news and the pace at which news travels. Third, digital technology has created many new online news sites, along with online outlets for established news organizations and, in the process, has impacted on the structure and organization of newsrooms. Finally, digital media technology offers much greater opportunities for interactivity between journalists and readers and thereby changes the fundamental relationship between news organizations, journalists and their audience. Digital interactivity triggers a shift from the "broadcast model" of "one to many" to the more dialogic and interactive communication of the digital age that facilitates "many to many" conversations.

See also **digital journalism**.

Key Sources

Malik, A. and Shapiro, I. 2017 "What's Digital? What's Journalism" in Franklin, B. and Eldridge, II, S. (Eds) *The Routledge Companion to Digital Journalism Studies*. London: Routledge, 15–24

McNair, B. 2005 "What is Journalism?" in de Burgh, H. (Ed) *Making Journalists: Diverse Models, Global Issues*. London: Routledge, 25–47

McQuail, D. 2000 *Mass Communication Theory* 4th edition. London: Sage

Pavlik, J. 2001 *Journalism and New Media*. New York: Columbia University Press

Schudson, M. 2003 *The Sociology of News*. New York: W. W. Norton

JOURNALISM STUDIES

Journalism studies is the multidisciplinary study of **journalism** as an arena of professional practice and a subject of scholarly inquiry. America pioneered the institutionalizing of the academic study and teaching of journalism by establishing major schools of journalism in universities such as Columbia, Iowa and Missouri in the mid-19th century. Almost a century later, the first school of journalism in the UK was established at Cardiff University in 1970 and a year later the first Diploma program in Journalism was launched under the leadership of Sir Tom Hopkinson, who had been the distinguished **editor** of *Picture Post*. Intellectually and organizationally, the newly established study of journalism was located under the broader heading of Communication Studies (Wahl-Jorgensen and Franklin, 2008).

Traditions of teaching and research varied widely across different national settings although, in most universities and colleges, early courses relied heavily on the involvement of professional journalists to design curricula which were essentially practice based "how to do it" programs with more academic elements such as journalism history, ethics, law and public administration being incorporated later. In the US, leadership roles in the new schools of journalism were typically assigned to senior ex-journalists, a tradition widely adopted in the UK when university departments began to grow rapidly during the mid-1990s. There are currently more than 50 UK universities offering undergraduate and postgraduate provision in journalism studies.

As a field of inquiry, journalism studies is necessarily engaged with conceptual and methodological concerns as well as the conduct of research inquiries generating empirical evidence exploring the professional activities of **journalists**. More specifically, it involves the analysis and critique of the various processes involved in gathering, assessing, interpreting, researching, writing, editing and distributing information (factual) and comment (opinion) on a wide range of subjects (including business, education, fashion, health, lifestyle, news, politics, sport and travel) that are disseminated via an expansive range of media platforms (including the internet, **magazines, tablets, smartphones, newspapers**, radio, **social media**, television and wearables – watches and glasses), to diverse **audiences** and communities (distinguished by culture, identity and intellectual interests), and resident in local, regional, national and global settings.

It follows that journalism studies adopts an international and interdisciplinary approach which explores academic and professional issues and attempts to meld theoretical with practical and professional concerns, using a wide range of qualitative and quantitative methods typical of the social sciences and humanities, including content analysis, critical textual analysis, documentary and archival analysis, ethnographic and participant observation studies, focus groups, interviews and questionnaire based surveys. The subject area explores the full range of journalistic beats, including sport, crime, fashion and politics, as well as lifestyle concerns such as health, travel and personal finance, alongside news journalism, **photojournalism**, cartoons and agony aunts and uncles. Journalism studies considers the divergent media contexts in which journalism is conducted, as well as the distinctive and varied patterns of media ownership, organization, finance and journalistic cultures which characterize the different media platforms. The concerns of journalism studies are global in focus but also address local and national media, as well as concerns arising from the global market for journalism and its products.

The eponymously titled journal *Journalism Studies*, published by Routledge, Taylor and Francis and launched in 2000, illustrates the intellectual ambitions and outputs of this academic subject (www.tandfonline.com/toc/rjos20/current). The launch of the journal coincided with the development of undergraduate programs in Journalism and Journalism Studies at a growing number of UK universities at the turn of the millennium that facilitated, but also reflected, the development of a lively research culture for journalism studies (Wahl-Jorgensen and Franklin, 2008: 172–184).

A recent article in *Journal of Communication* (Carlson, Robinson, Lewis and Berkovitz, 2018) defines journalism studies as a scholarly discipline which "examines the realm of informative, public texts involving news and the people, organizations, professions, institutions, and material artifacts and technologies that produce those texts as well as the individuals and multivariate forces shaping their circulation and consumption." More significantly, the authors argue that academic disciplines such as journalism studies, which are typically grouped within the broader scholarly "umbrella" of Communication or Communication Studies, can be unpicked and identified by isolating their specific *commitments*, which they define as "particular normative assumptions and identity practices" which "animate journalism studies as a distinct and fruitful scholarly project." These commitments not only identify the essential dimensions of journalism studies, but erect fences which demarcate the boundaries of the field with cognate areas of inquiry. They suggest journalism studies embodies six such conceptual commitments that "define its core ontological and epistemological premises" (Carlson, Robinson, Lewis and Berkowitz, 2018).

Contextual sensitivity, for example, stresses the importance of placing the subject matter of the discipline (news) in its economic, social, political and organizational context, while *holistic relationality* acknowledges that journalism is "co-created" and must be understood as being shaped by a complex "system of interacting actors, artifacts and activities." Deriving from its emphasis on context, journalism studies' commitment to *comparative inclination* avoids all attempts to universalize the particularities of the cultural norms and practices and cultures of journalism. *Normative awareness* acknowledges that journalism practices are connected to normative commitments and these norms – such as a reliance on officials and experts as authoritative sources – are important objects of study within journalism studies. *Embedded communicative power* focuses on journalism's location among the wider range of communicative power where journalism enjoys a special place because it generates "representations of the real" which give "shape and meaning to the world." Finally, journalism studies is *methodologically pluralistic* and draws upon interdisciplinary sources for its conceptual and methodological approaches.

Recent and rapid developments in digital media, however, with their consequences for virtually every aspect of journalism, have prompted some scholars to argue that journalism studies is experiencing a growing *sociotechnical* emphasis, with researchers focusing on the overlapping social and technological aspects of journalism's transformation in the digital age (Carlson, Robinson, Lewis and Berkowitz, 2018).

Significantly, these radical changes in the professional practice of what has become *digital* journalism require, in turn, it is argued, a new subject area of **Digital Journalism Studies** characterized by innovative conceptual and theoretical frameworks and methodological approaches to explore and analyze the unravelling world of digital journalism (Steensen and Ahva, 2015; Franklin and Eldridge, 2017; Karlsson and Sjøvaag, 2016a).

A new academic journal, *Digital Journalism* (www.tandfonline.com/toc/rdij20/current), was launched in 2013 to "document and record these significant changes to journalism practice" but also to provide "a place of intellectual companionship" where "common academic interests can be discussed" which is "what journals have always offered readers and contributors" (Franklin, 2013b: 1)

See also **Digital Journalism Studies**.

Key Sources

Carlson, M., Robinson, S., Lewis, S. C. and Berkowitz, D. 2018 "Journalism Studies and Its Core Commitments: The Making of a Communication Field" *Journal of Communication* 68(1): 6–25

Dick, M. 2018 "Developments in Infographics" in Franklin, B. and Eldridge, II, S. (Eds) *The Routledge Companion to Digital Journalism Studies*. London: Routledge, 498–508

Karlsson, M. and Sjøvaag, H. 2016a "Research Methods in an Age of Digital Journalism" *Digital Journalism* 4(1): 1–192

Wahl-Jorgensen, K. and Franklin, B. 2008 "Journalism Research in the UK: From Isolated Efforts to an Established Discipline" in Löffelholz, M. and Weaver, D. (Eds) *Global Journalism Research: Theories, Methods, Findings, Future*. Oxford: Blackwell

JOURNALIST

The meaning of the word "journalist" has changed radically in recent times, reflecting developments in media technologies. But public understandings have always been characterized by diversity if not contestation. Initially, the word **journalist** was used to describe anyone who wrote in a journal. But from the 18th century, one view of journalists suggested they were more significant figures, central actors in a democratic polity that kept a watchful eye on the activities of economically and politically powerful elites, articulating and defending the public interest and thereby exercising what came to be termed "watchdog" or "fourth estate" functions (Franklin, 1997: 27–29).

There is, however, a second, more populist, much bleaker and negative perception of the journalist as an unprincipled muckraking tabloid hack who is guided less by any noble commitment to the professional ethics of journalism than the need to file a "good story." *In extremis*, some journalists may even engage in illegal, as well as unethical, activities, as exemplified by the phone hacking scandal which resulted in the closure of the *News of the World*, the imprisonment of journalists and the establishment of the **Leveson** Inquiry (http:// webarchive.nationalarchives.gov.uk/20140122145147/http:/www.leve soninquiry.org.uk).

Somewhere between these two diverse understandings, a journalist is someone who gathers information, which must be verified in professionally agreed ways, about events of public consequence and human interest, who presents it in written or spoken form in news stories, features and documentaries and across all media platforms (See **Journalism**). Peters and Tandoc, for example, define journalists by their activities, outputs and social roles and, consequently, posit a journalist as "someone employed to regularly engage in gathering, processing and disseminating (activities) news and information (outputs) to serve the public interest (social role)" (Peters and Tandoc, 2013: 6). But the American Press Institute (API) claims that "Asking *who* is a journalist is the wrong question, because journalism can be produced by anyone" (www.americanpressinstitute.org/journalism-essentials/what-is-journal ism/journalist/).

Recent changes in digital technologies which have enabled the growth of online **news**, digital newspapers, **social media, blogs** and **citizen journalism** trigger "boundary disputes" between professional journalists and others who produce and distribute news and other information on a part time or "amateur" basis (Carlson and Lewis, 2015; Johnston and Wallace, 2019*)*. The availability of **Web 2.0** technology, for example, means that anyone who owns a computer terminal with a web connection can produce information for presentation and distribution to a potentially global **audience**. Journalism, moreover, unlike law, for example, is not a profession that requires any stipulated qualifications to become a practitioner; in this sense anyone can become a **citizen journalist**. However research studies reveal notable differences between journalists and citizen journalists: citizen journalists use different and fewer sources than their professional counterparts; the information in citizen journalist reports may not be able to sustain claims to impartiality and objectivity in the same way; and citizen journalists cannot usually match the experience and may lack the formal training which professional journalists can claim. As distinguished journalism scholar Jane Singer reminds us, "while all journalists publish information, not all publishers of information are journalists" (Singer, 2006: 5).

Some journalists, like Andrew Marr, for example, denounce citizen journalism as merely the "spewings and rantings of very drunk people late at night" Moreover, "most citizen journalism," he claims, "strikes me as nothing to do with journalism at all. It is fantastic at times but it is not going to replace journalism." (www.theguardian.com/media/2010/oct/11/andrew-marr-bloggers). But others are more open to change in journalism to the point where they believe it is important to discuss whether news written by **algorithm** (Robot news), without the involvement of any human agency, should be allocated a Byline which reflects the name of the algorithm or its designer, or a human journalist (Montal and Reich, 2016: 1).

Given these technological developments in **digital journalism** and **artificial intelligence**, Johnston and Wallace conclude that,

> the past decade has seen unprecedented attention given to the questions of "Who is a journalist" and "What is the news media?" Far from being … taken for granted as they may have been in the past, these questions have become challenging and vexing [not least] for courts, legislators, policymakers, and media organizations.
>
> (Johnston and Wallace, 2019: 24)

The most recent study of journalists, who they are and their perceptions of their working conditions, routines, social roles, trust in institutions and ethics, was published by the Reuters Institute at Oxford University and based on 700 survey responses from a representative sample of UK journalists (Thurman, Cornia and Kunert, 2016). The report's Executive Summary claims that women constitute a slight majority of journalists in the UK but remain less well paid and less likely than men to occupy senior positions; 98 percent have a degree and 36 percent a Master's degree; journalism has a "significant diversity problem" with black journalists scarce and underrepresented; pay remains low with 20 percent of journalists earning less than a living wage (£19,200) and with a further 27 percent involved with other paid work (Thurman, Cornia and Kunert, 2016: 7).

Key Sources

Johnston, J. and Wallace, A. 2019 "Law Defining Journalists: Who's Who in the Age of Digital Media" in Eldridge, II, S. and Franklin, B. (Eds) *The Routledge Handbook of Developments in Digital Journalism Studies*. Abingdon: Routledge, 15–27

Montal, T. and Reich, Z. 2016 "I Robot, You Journalist: Who Is the Author?" *Digital Journalism* 5(7): 829–849, doi:10.1080/21670811.2016.1209083

Peters, J. and Tandoc, E. 2013 "'People Who Aren't Really Reporters at All, Who Have No Professional Qualifications'; Defining a Journalist and Deciding Who May Claim the Privileges" *New York Journal of Public Policy Quorum* 34: 34–63

Singer, J. 2006 "The Socially Responsible Existentialist: A Normative Emphasis for Journalists in A New Media Environment" *Journalism Studies* 7(1): 2–18

Thurman, N., Cornia, A. and Kunert, J. 2016 *Journalists in the UK*. Oxford: Reuters Institute for the Study of Journalism

JOURNALISTIC CULTURES

Defined as "a particular set of ideas and practices by which journalists legitimate their role in society and render their work meaningful" (Hanitzsch, 2007: 369) journalism cultures differ between nations and media institutions. Even within Western countries there is substantial **diversity** in the professional role perception among journalists, particularly in the perceived importance of analysis, partisanship, entertainment and a critical attitude towards the powerful. There can also be cultural and professional variation within a country between different territorial contexts. In Australia, local newspaper journalists exhibit much stronger support for the community forum and advocacy role of their job than their metropolitan counterparts (Hanusch, 2015). Yet, at the same time, and contrary to expectation, local journalists support the watchdog role to the same extent as metropolitan newspaper journalists.

Across international boundaries similarities can be found in journalists' professional role conceptions, ethical views, editorial procedures and socialization processes in countries as diverse as Brazil, Germany, Tanzania, Uganda and the US. A comparative study of 1800 journalists across 18 countries shows that detachment, non-involvement, providing political information and monitoring the government are considered essential journalistic functions around the globe. Impartiality, the reliability and factualness of information, as well as adherence to universal ethical principles, are also valued worldwide, though their perceived importance varies across countries (Hanitzsch, Hanusch, Mellado, Anikina, Berganza, Cangoz, Coman, Hamada, Hernández, Karadjov, Moreira, Mwesige, Plaisance, Reich, Seethaler, Skewes, Noor and Yuen, 2011). The cultural differences are more pronounced in the realms of interventionism, objectivism and the importance of separating facts from opinion. Journalists from non-Western contexts, particularly those in politically less free countries, are more likely to embrace interventionism to influence public opinion and advocate for social change than Western journalists (Hanitzsch, Hanusch and Lauerer, 2016). Despite living in societies that grant them more freedom, Western journalists are less supportive of any active promotion of particular values, ideas and social change. Furthermore, journalists in previously communist countries have struggled to adapt to liberal, democratic models of journalism (Lauk, 2009; Xin, 2008) as, despite the global nature of digital journalism, there does not exist one pattern for these countries to follow. Instead, each of these nationals creates their nationally coloured journalism culture based on their historical and cultural traditions (Lauk, 2009).

Key Sources
Hanitzsch, T. 2007 "Deconstructing Journalism Culture: Towards a Universal Theory" *Communication Theory* 17(4): 367–385
Hanitzsch, T., Hanusch, F., Mellado, C., Anikina, M., Berganza, R., Cangoz, I., Coman, M., Hamada, B., Hernández, M., Karadjov, C., Moreira, S., Mwesige, P., Plaisance, P., Reich, Z., Seethaler, J., Skewes, E., Noor, D. and Yuen, E. 2011 "Mapping Journalism Cultures across Nations" *Journalism Studies* 12 (3): 273–293

JOURNALISTS' IDENTITY

What makes a **journalist** and how they identify themselves as professionals has been the subject of much scholarly scrutiny since there is no entry requirement into the industry. Unlike disciplines such as law, medicine or engineering, anyone can become a journalist within a mainstream media organization via work experience, formal training schemes or directly with no prior experience. Similarly, anyone can promote or identify themselves as a journalist without any legal repercussions. However, there is an understanding among journalists and academics alike that **journalism** is a profession with a special body of knowledge, skills and expertise (Örnebring, 2010) that brings with it a set of professional values. These values, which influence and shape journalists' identity, are largely centered upon autonomy and a code of ethics. Furthermore, Deuze (2005) identifies professional journalism ideology as being made up of the five ideal traits of public service, objectivity, autonomy, **immediacy** and ethics. Journalists fulfil these traits by observing and informing, commenting, and providing a platform for outsider voices (Heinonen, 2011). This is amid economic pressures which drive journalists to reach the widest audiences and shift their values from social to market driven (Donsbach, 2010). As Bourdieu's influential work on the journalistic field conveys, journalists exist in a state of constant friction between economic and cultural capital (2005).

The arrival of the World Wide Web and digitization of the media has further muddied the water, resulting in "a partial dissolution of previously taken-for-granted boundaries and distinctions, blurring the line between professional journalists and other types of information brokers" (Olausson, 2017: 61). As Deuze suggests, "journalists are thus increasingly forced to give meaning to their work and thus construct their own professional identity in the context of rapidly changing and often overlapping work contexts" (2008: 111). Within this shifting open-access world, journalists maintain diametrically opposed viewpoints on the amount of control they are willing to hand over to the public. This has left journalists' identity divided into three camps: The conventional journalist, dialogical journalist and ambivalent journalist (Heinonen, 2011). Conventional journalists see a clear demarcation between journalists writing facts and readers writing opinion and argue that the public want journalists to remain in this traditional, professional role. The dialogical journalists see a blurring of boundaries between users and journalists that can result in better journalistic performance when users are viewed as companions rather than competitors. The ambivalent journalists, who make up the majority, view a mixture of the conventional and dialogical roles as necessary. Research of traditional local newspaper reporters in the UK (Canter, 2014c) revealed that although journalists in theory were accepting of the changing nature of their gatekeeping role, in practice they tended to hold onto traditional claims of authority even while acknowledging that their role had adapted from disseminators of news to verifiers and amplifiers. This position was based on the belief that the role of the journalist contained professional traits, skills and standards that were not adhered to by the public acting as citizen journalists. The eight professional traits were training, media law knowledge, quality, objectivity, trust, accountability, accuracy and access.

Further examination of exclusively digital journalists suggests that journalistic identity varies between online-only and traditional journalists. Objectivity, as a focal point of journalistic practices and principles, is less significant for online journalists who favor ethical transparency (Agarwal and Barthel, 2015). Furthermore, interviews with 53 full-time digital journalists from 49 diverse organizations (Ferrucci and Vos, 2017) found that they distinguished themselves from traditional journalists by their willingness to take the side of their readership. The journalists interviewed strongly suggested that objectivity was no longer applied to the field and dispassionate reporting was not within the realm of the digital journalist. Studies of journalists' identity on Twitter have also revealed a break from the norm with j-tweeters oscillating between traditional positions as watchdogs and news disseminators to emerging discourses of self-promotion and subjectivity (Canter and Brookes, 2016; Olausson, 2017). The only thing that does remain clear is that "the reinvention of journalistic identity is an ongoing and largely unpredictable process" (Olausson, 2017: 81).

Key Sources

Deuze, M. 2008 "The Professional Identity of Journalists in the Context of Convergence Culture" *Observatorio* 2(4): 103–117

Ferrucci, P. and Vos, T. 2017 "Who's In, Who's Out? Constructing the Identity of Digital Journalists" *Digital Journalism* 5(7): 868–883

Olausson, U. 2017 "The Reinvented Journalist: The Discursive Construction of Professional Identity on Twitter" *Digital Journalism* 5(1): 61–81

Örnebring, H. 2010 "Reassessing Journalism as a Profession" in Allan, S. (Ed) *The Routledge Companion to News and Journalism*. Abingdon: Routledge, 568–577

LEGACY MEDIA

Since the first decade of the new millennium, legacy media is the name widely given to the large and previously highly successful news media organizations (newspapers, radio, television and magazines), such as the *New York Times*, the BBC and *El Pais*, as they began to struggle with the financial **disruptions** and consequences of the arrival of new digital and online **media**. Academic and industry commentators have typically couched this recent decline of legacy media fortunes in apocalyptic terms that usually reference the "slow death" or "crisis" of legacy media (Desjardins, 2016). Even Paul Dacre, for example, the long serving (but now retired) **editor** of the *Daily Mail*, which is considered to be the UK's most successful national newspaper (at least in terms of sales and profits), shares this apocalyptic view of the future for legacy media. "It is an ineluctable truth," he argued, "that many provincial papers and some nationals, are now in a near terminal condition." Moreover,

> if our critics spent as much zeal trying to help reverse this tragic situation and work out how good **journalism** – which is, by its nature expensive – is going to survive financially in an internet age, then democracy and the public's right to know would be much better served.
>
> (Dacre, 2010)

The reasons informing these doom-laden predictions include legacy media's sustained downturn in sales and market share, the collapse in **advertising** revenues and the substantial reduction in the number of **journalists** they employ. In brief, legacy media have come to be identified by their failure to manage the disruption of their **business model** triggered by the arrival of digital news and **social media**. Unlike digitally native news organizations, the problem which legacy media must resolve to restore their fortunes is how to "survive" on their subscription and advertising revenues while also developing their online products; a task which has been described as being akin to "fixing the plane while you're flying it" (Desjardins, 2016).

In a series of studies based on the *New York Times*, however, Chyi and Tenenboim argue that revenues from print and advertising sales have persistently outrun their online equivalents. Worse, by precociously reducing their print operations and investing in online products, which have yet to show any sustained profitability, legacy media may have taken a wrong turn in their business strategy (Chyi and Tenenboim, 2018).

Key Sources

Chyi, I. and Tenenboim, O. 2018 "What if the Future Is Not All Digital? Trends in US Newspapers' Multiplatform Readership" in Eldridge, II, S. and Franklin, B. (Eds) *The Routledge Handbook on Developments in Digital Journalism.* London: Routledge, 157–171

Dacre, P. 2010 "Killing the Myths" www.editorscode.org.uk/downloads/reports/webLH_Report_2009.html

Desjardins, J. 2016 "The Slow Death of Legacy Media" *Business Insider* www.businessinsider.com/the-slow-death-of-legacy-media-2016-10?IR=T

LEVESON INQUIRY

A lengthy and costly judicial review into the culture, practices and ethics of the UK press following the News International phone hacking scandal. Lord Justice Leveson chaired the Inquiry, which held a series of public hearings throughout 2011 and 2012, to the tune of £5.6 million. In November 2012, a 2,000-page Inquiry report was published which found the existing press regulatory body, the Press Complaints Commission, to be insufficient and recommended the establishment of a new independent body, able to sanction newspapers more effectively. At the heart of the Inquiry was the conduct of journalists at tabloid newspaper the *News of the World*, who extensively hacked into the mobile phone voicemails of the rich and famous to intercept messages and gain exclusive stories. Although the mercenary behaviour and underhand tactics of tabloid **hacks** was somewhat expected, and to a certain extent tolerated, by the celebrity-obsessed sensation-seeking public, the hacking of the voicemail of murder victim Milly Dowler was deemed abhorrent and beyond reproach. Public opinion turned against the populist tabloid and in 2011, just days before Lord Justice was appointed to the Inquiry, the *News of the World* closed down after 168 years.

The Leveson Inquiry, alongside a series of civil and criminal prosecutions, led to the imprisonment of journalists and millions of pounds being paid out in compensation to victims of phone hacking. The Press Complaints Commission was closed and a Royal Charter was drawn up, stating that newspapers that refused to sign up to a regulator recognized by the Press Recognition Panel (PRP) would be penalized. However, at the time of writing, the government and the press continue to be locked in a stalemate with no major newspaper signing up to a recognized regulator. The *Daily Mail*, the *Sun* and the *Daily Telegraph* are members of the Independent Press Standards Organisation (IPSO), which has refused to apply for state-backed sanction under the PRP. Meanwhile, the *Guardian* and the *Financial Times* are independently regulated. Max Mosley, the former president of the Formula One governing body, who was exposed by the tabloids for sadomasochistic sex orgies, has backed small regulator Impress, but its members to date only consist of small websites and **blogs**, including **investigative journalism** site The Ferret. Much like the media landscape today, press regulation in the UK post-Leveson is more fragmented than ever before.

Journalists' own views about the hacking affair, Leveson and regulation have undergone some scholarly scrutiny, with Thomas and Finneman (2014) seeking to understand the press's long-standing resistance to accountability. Their study pointed to an institutional ideology which was quick to assert rights but reluctant to accept any reciprocal responsibilities. Furthermore, Tong (2018) asserts that the Leveson Inquiry and subsequent skepticism about journalism's capacity for self-regulation in the UK has impaired the legitimacy of journalism in the Anglo-American news world, despite various **news** organizations trying to distinguish and distance themselves from the *News of the World*.

The impact of the Inquiry on journalism is much disputed, but journalists and academics have raised concerns over the continued freedom of the press, in particular severed relationships with the police (Colbran, 2016), the rising influence of public relations and the negative impact on investigative journalism. However, the ethical concerns raised in the Inquiry have now largely been superseded by urgent economic threats, hence the government's decision not to proceed with Leveson Part Two. The first part of the Inquiry looked at culture, practices and ethics of the press and the second part was intended to investigate the relationship between journalists and the police. However, former Culture Secretary Matt Hancock argued in 2018 (Sweney, 2018a) that there had been extensive reforms to press regulation and practice and the world had changed since Leveson Part One. The closure of more than 200 **local newspapers**, the rapid loss of print revenue, the control of **Google** and **Facebook** over the UK digital advertisement market and the largely unregulated **social media** world should now be the focus of journalistic reform, according to Hancock.

See also **defamation, news beats, sources**.

Key Sources

Thomas, R. and Finneman, T. 2014 "Who Watches the Watchdogs? British Newspaper Metadiscourse on the Leveson Inquiry" *Journalism Studies* 15(2): 172–186

Tong, J. 2018 "Journalistic Legitimacy Revisited: Collapse or Revival in the Digital Age" *Digital Journalism* 6(2): 256–273

LIFESTYLE JOURNALISM

Lifestyle journalism is a distinct journalistic field that primarily addresses its **audiences** as consumers rather than as citizens. Folker Hanusch describes lifestyle journalism as providing audiences "with factual information and advice, often in entertaining ways, about goods and services they can use in their daily lives" (Hanusch, 2013: xiii). The editorial concerns of lifestyle journalism are remarkably wide and include gardening, cookery, health and fitness, music, leisure, DIY, food, clothing and fashion, the arts, personal finance and travel (McGurr, 2010: 50–67).

Lifestyle journalism has its origins in the 1950s and 1960s, coinciding with the emergence of consumer culture in the global north, although academic and **journalist** Peter Cole suggests the prolific growth in this broadly conceived journalistic beat reflected developments in print technologies which allowed newspapers to increase pagination dramatically, which created a substantial news hole that conventional news journalism was unable to fill (Cole, 2005: 21).

Hanusch argues that lifestyle or "service" journalism has suffered a curious academic neglect, if not opprobrium; it is often considered "a frivolous pursuit" or even "a guilty pleasure" (Hanusch, 2013: 4), perhaps reflecting its emphasis on "soft news" and proximity to "market driven news" and "**infotainment**" (Franklin, 1997). In contrast, Fursiche suggests considerable public service and democratic roles for lifestyle journalism (Fursiche, 2013: 11–24), while Cocking argues it is the cultural and economic context in which travel news is produced – that is, its close alliance to the world's largest industry, tourism – which makes it worthy of study (Cocking, 2017).

If Cole was correct to identify technological change as the driver of the prolific expansion of lifestyle journalism in the 1950s and 1960s, it seems probable that the advent of **online journalism**, with the expansive editorial space and opportunities that it offers, will similarly promote the profile and popularity of lifestyle journalism with audiences.

Key Sources

Cocking, B. 2017 "News Values Go on Holiday: The Ideological Values of Travel Journalism" *Journalism Studies* 27th January ahead of print www.tandfon line.com/doi/full/10.1080/1461670X.2016.1272066

Cole, P. 2005 "The Structure of the Press Industry" in Keeble, R. (Ed) *Print Journalism: A Critical Introduction*. Abingdon: Routledge, 21–38

Fursiche, E. 2013 "Lifestyle Journalism as Popular Journalism: Strategies for Evaluating Its Public Role" *Journalism Practice* 6(1): 11–24

Hanusch, F. 2013 "Broadening the Focus: The Case for Lifestyle Journalism as a Field of Scholarly Inquiry" *Journalism Practice* 6(1): 1–10

McGurr, L. 2010 "The Devil May Care: Travel Journalism, Cosmopolitan Concern, Politics and the Brand" *Journalism Practice* 6(1): 41–57

LIKE

Users of **news** websites, **blogs** or **social media** platforms such as **Twitter** or **Facebook** can register their approval or enjoyment of a particular message or content by "liking" that content by clicking the "like button." On Facebook, the "like" button is represented by the graphic symbol of a hand making a "thumbs up" sign. In this way, "liking" offers users a shorthand means of expressing the user's pleasure and/or support for particular content rather than obliging them to draft a bespoke message. In aggregate, the site may deliver a quantitative measure of the balance of "likes" to "dislikes" which users can deploy to assess whether material may be worth reading.

In May 2016, Facebook offered users the opportunity to respond to posts by identifying one among a range of emotional reactions to the particular post which included "Love," "HaHa," "Wow," "Sad" and "Angry." In a study of the influences of these reactions to content on sharing and what types of materials users shared, Anders Olaf Larsson found that reactions such as "Love," "Haha," "Wow," "Sad" and "Angry" seemed relatively unpopular compared to the original "Like" functionality (Larsson, 2017)

Twitter's "like" button is heart shaped, but users can also use the retweet (RT) function provided by the platform to express their support, approval or enjoyment of a particular **Tweet**. This function also allows users to add a bespoke written comment, allowing a more extensive and nuanced response to content. News users' willingness to "share" content may also articulate a degree of approval or liking of materials.

Key Sources

Larsson, A. O. 2017 "Diversifying Likes: Relating Reactions to Commenting and Sharing on Newspaper Facebook Pages" *Journalism Practice* 12(3): 326–343, doi: 10.1080/17512786.2017.1285244

LIQUID NEWS

Traditionally, **journalism** production was a linear process of static texts determined by print deadlines and broadcasting schedules. Other than via live broadcasts, there was no opportunity to amend or update the **news** until the next printing or broadcasting slot became available. However, as production platforms have migrated from offline to online, contemporary practices have become non-linear, characterized by flexible and elastic deadlines (Widholm, 2016). Today, news is continually updated online and is subject to constant alteration, meaning it is no longer a static product. Instead, it has become liquid news characterized by **immediacy** and **interactivity** (Karlsson and Strömbäck, 2010). This liquidity, a term described by Deuze (2005) more than a decade ago, enables users to add information to the news content or context via interactivity without the control of the news organization. Similarly, journalists work on a continual deadline, tweaking and erasing content online at any given time (Karlsson and Strömbäck, 2010). Widholm (2016) argues that this changes the very nature of journalism as while accuracy may still be the central goal in news production, liquid news creates an increasingly open process in which journalists walk a long way in order to achieve this.

Karlsson and Sjøvaag (2016b: 186) refer to the "flowing river" of online news, an analogy that supports the idea of news as an intangible liquid. But the assertion that immediacy, and thus liquidity, is a fundamental trait of online news has been challenged by Lim (2012), who describes it as a mythology. A study tracking news websites in South Korea demonstrated that media institutions have established routines and rules for updating content (Lim, 2012) and there is only a low level of immediacy. This is also supported by Saltzis (2012), who concludes that news stories do not change much after the initial hours of publication.

Although there is debate over the exact fluidity and pressure flow of online news, it is evident that news is no longer a static entity. This causes challenges for researchers who wish to capture constantly (or regularly or sporadically) updating content. Methodologies for capturing online news are rapidly developing, with content analysis remaining a firm favourite for analyzing the ephemeral web (Hurwitz, Alvarez, Lauricella, Rousse, Montague and Wartella, 2016; Karlsson and Sjøvaag, 2016b; Karlsson and Strömbäck, 2010; Karpf, 2012). This often involves computer-assisted approaches using automatic techniques to data gather, collect and store different versions of web pages at given intervals. Researchers use variables such as positioning, time and duration to assess the liquidity of a news topic or news story (Widholm, 2016).

Key Sources

Karlsson, M. and Strömbäck, J. 2010 "Freezing the Flow of Online News: Exploring Approaches to the Study of the Liquidity of Online News" *Journalism Studies* 11(1): 2–19

Lim, J. 2012 "The Mythological Status of the Immediacy of the Most Important Online News: An Analysis of Top News Flows in Diverse Online Media" *Journalism Studies* 13(1): 71–89

Widholm, A. 2016 "Tracing Online News in Motion: Time and Duration in the Study of Liquid Journalism" *Digital Journalism* 4(1): 24–40

LISTICLES

Many of the articles written for the internet adopt the stylistic form of a numbered or bullet pointed list which provides the article's thematic structure; "Listicles" are popular with readers and writers. A **BuzzFeed** listicle titled "21 Pictures that Will Restore Your Faith in Humanity," for example, has enjoyed 8,810,383 views (accessed 16 June 2016), while *Guardian* **journalist** Steven Poole confesses, "I'll let you into a secret. A listicle is much easier to write than a regular article" (Poole, 2013). There are even websites such as Listverse, where the entire content is devoted to listicles, grouped under headings such as Bizarre, Mystery, Creepy and Crime (Listverse).

For readers, the listicle is "seductive" because it promises to reduce any topic, no matter how wide ranging and complex, into a finite number of "facts" which are typically rank ordered in terms of relevance and consequence. Thus the passions and complexities of the European referendum in the UK in 2016 were reduced, by the *Daily Telegraph* to the simple and dispassionate certainties promised by their article, "10 Reasons Why David Cameron Will Enjoy the EU Referendum Campaign" (A. Bennett, 2016). Other listicles explore themes with a more historical bent: "10 Ancient Prophecies Which Helped Shape the World" (Listverse).

While listicles have become more commonplace in the internet age, perhaps reflecting a general "dumbing down" of online editorial content, the literary use of the list was not invented by "internet content farmers and media corporations hungry for cheap **click bait**" (Poole, 2013). With tongue planted firmly in cheek, Poole cites the Ten Commandments as an early religious listicle and also reminds readers that Umberto Eco has published a book length listicle titled *The Infinity of Lists*. Classical scholar Mary Beard also recalls the section of Homer's *Iliad*, known as the "Catalogue of Ships," which is dominated by a 350-line list of the various Greek forces that made up the "coalition of the willing" in the invasion of Troy (Beard, 2009).

Key Sources

Beard, M. 2009 "Is There Still Life in the List?" *Guardian* 12 December, www.theguardian.com/books/2009/dec/12/umberto-eco-lists-book-review

Bennett, A. 2016a "10 Reasons Why David Cameron Will Enjoy the EU Referendum Campaign" *Daily Telegraph* 26th February www.telegraph.co.uk/news/newstopics/eureferendum/12173413/10-reasons-David-Cameron-will-enjoy-the-EU-referendum-campaign.html

BuzzFeed www.buzzfeed.com/expresident/pictures-that-will-restore-your-faith-in-humanity?utm_term=.uqGzOA0QAQ#.tuVgYoQrorListverselistverse.com/ Accessed 16 June 2016

Poole, S. 2013 "The Top Nine Things You Need to Know about Lists" *Guardian* www.theguardian.com/books/2013/nov/12/listicles-articles-written-lists-steven-poole

LIVE BLOGGING

Blogs and **blogging** provided early opportunities for people who were formally outside **journalism** to contribute information, comment and opinion about issues of current **news** concern to public debate. Bloggers typically addressed controversial subjects, employing emotive and partisan content. Blogs were dated, listed in reverse chronological order and seen as discrete, rather than open-ended contributions to debate. Individual blogs were rarely updated.

The arrival of "live blogging" since 2007 has revitalized the format, as well as the content, of the "traditional" blog. Live blogging has been a feature of *Guardian* journalism since 1999, although for the first eight years it was used almost exclusively to report on live football or cricket (Thurman and Walters, 2013: 83). As the name suggests, the blog is live, written in real time and (typically) involves a professional journalist offering a précis of a breaking news story such as the London Bombings in July 2005, a key sporting event or a significant parliamentary debate, in real time. It offers readers **immediacy** in the reporting of events. Thurman and Walters (2013) offer the most comprehensive research based account of live blogging to date in their case study of these blogs convened at the UK *Guardian* website. They define live blogging as "a single blog post on a specific topic to which time-stamped content is progressively added for a finite period – anywhere between half an hour and 24 hours" (2013: 83). In a more recent study of the BBC's live blogging of "terror attacks," D. Bennett (2016) suggests the "live page" has become a significant source of breaking news. Moreover, the inclusion of eyewitness material has increased the uses of "non official **sources**" making online **news** more "multiperpectival."

In his seminal essay "Why I Blog," American **journalist** Andrew Sullivan, an early convert to blogging, identified the huge potential of blogs and suggested that "the interaction it enables between the writer and reader is unprecedented, visceral and sometimes brutal. And make no mistake: it heralds a golden era of journalism" (Sullivan, 2008). He claims a number of advantages for live blogs above traditional legacy journalism. First, the blog format changes the journalist's editorial ambition. The purpose becomes to establish an open-ended, interactive and continuing conversation with the reader rather than a limited and finite (in time and content) article for the audience to read. Second, that conversation takes place in real time, although the structure of the blog may generate unusual sensations for the readers who, as they read the blog, have "the curious sense of moving backwards in time as [they] move forward in pages" (Sullivan, 2008: 2). The same blog logistics create a distinctive sense of immediacy for the journalist, since blogging "is not so much daily writing as hourly writing … for bloggers the deadline is always now." Consequently, blogging is always more "free form, accident prone, less formal, more alive. It is … writing out loud" (Sullivan, op cit: 3). Third, blogs can liberate journalists of a liberal disposition from the "ideological straitjacket" of a newspaper's partisan commitments. Fourth, blogging offers liberation from other organizational constraints. When writing for the *New Republic*, Sullivan often

> Chafed … at the endless delays, revisions, office politics, editorial fights and last minute cuts for space that dead-tree publishing entails. Blogging … was intoxicatingly free in comparison. Like taking a

narcotic ... With one push of the Publish Now button, all these troubles evaporate.

(Sullivan, 2008: 5)

Fifth, blogs generate reader feedback which can be "instant, personal and brutal" but preferable to writing columns which "were essentially monologues published to applause, muffled murmurs, silence or a distant heckle" (Sullivan, 2008: 6); writing a blog is a learning experience. Sixth, journalists incorporate **hyperlinks** into blogs that connect the reader with vast data sets and offer the blogger much greater editorial depth than print **journalism** can achieve, and at the "click of a mouse." Moreover, hyperlinks mean the reader is no longer reliant on the journalist's interpretation of a particular survey or report, but can explore the report for themselves. Seventh, blogs develop a distinctive relationship with the **audience** that is corrosive of deference. Sullivan notes that "when readers of my blog bump into me in person, they invariably address me as Andrew. Print readers don't do that. It's Mr. Sullivan to them" (Sullivan, 2008: 10). Writing a blog in real time is impossible "without revealing a huge amount about yourself" (Sullivan, ibid.). Finally, journalists learn from readers' comments. Readers inform the journalist about breaking news, counter perspectives and offer advice, tips and comments – "a good blog is your own private **Wikipedia**" (Sullivan, op cit: 11). Sparrow argues that although feedback can be negative, it ultimately improves his reporting. In short, readers offer the sorts of scrutiny of the journalist's work which improves the journalism.

Journalist Andrew Sparrow convenes and writes the live blog of the proceedings in the Houses of Parliament which is hosted by the *Guardian* (www.theguardian.com/politics/blog/live/2016/may/25/eu-referendum-vote-leave-calls-ifs-biased-after-it-warns-brexit-would-pro long-austerity-politics-live). The blog follows the parliamentary agenda by carrying a live audio visual feed of events in both chambers of the House. Given journalistic news values, there is a particular focus on major debates (for example, following the Chancellor's Budget Speech), high profile parliamentary occasions such as the twice-weekly Prime Minister's Questions (PMQs) or set piece occasions such as the Queen's Speech to formally outline the government's legislative program and to open the new parliamentary session.

Sparrow's commentary logs the time of politicians' contributions and the responses to them by other politicians, so that readers and participants in the blog can see the debate unravel in real time; their comments often exceed more than 1,000 at PMQs.

Additionally, the blog contains archive materials of previous, relevant debates and/or parliamentary occasions, as well as still images and hypertext links to allow readers to follow through those aspects of the issues which most interest them.

Live blogs are popular and an expansive web native news format. Thurman and Walters' findings reveal that unique visitor numbers at the *Guardian* were 230 percent higher than for conventional articles, and in page view counts, exceeded articles by 300 percent (Thurman and Walters, 2013: 8).

See also **blogs**.

Key Sources

Bennett, D. 2016 "Sourcing the BBC's Live Online Coverage of Terror Attacks" *Digital Journalism* 5(7): 861–874.

Thurman, N. and Walters, A. 2013 "Live Blogging – Digital Journalism's Pivotal Platform? A Case Study of the Production, Consumption and Form of Live Blogs at Guardian.Co.Uk" *Digital Journalism* 1(1): 82–101

Sparrow, A. "Politics Live with Andrew Sparrow" *Guardian* www.theguardian.com/politics/blog/live/2016/may/25/eu-referendum-vote-leave-calls-ifs-biased-after-it-warns-brexit-would-prolong-austerity-politics-live

Sullivan, A. 2008 "Why I Blog" *Atlantic Monthly* 302(4). www.theatlantic.com/magazine/archive/2008/11/why-i-blog/307060/

LOCAL MEDIA

Often seen as interchangeable with **local newspapers**, local media goes beyond the printed press and incorporates radio, television and hyperlocal websites. Although newspapers dominate the local news industry, most towns or regions have a dedicated commercial and/or public service radio station and television news program. In 1967, the BBC launched local radio stations across the UK, which aired locally made programs aimed at local people on a daily basis. The commercial sector followed suit, broadcasting programs with a higher proportion of music content over speech (Chantler and Harris, 1997). Today, there are also a handful of community radio stations in the UK serving a small area, run by local volunteers on a not-for-profit basis. There are 39 BBC local radio stations which take nearly seven percent of audience share, according to the latest Radio Joint Audience Research. This is compared to 111 local commercial stations with a 27 percent audience share and a further 198 national commercial groups which include many city and regional stations such as Smooth Radio Devon and Heart Solent.

By contrast, local television in the UK is largely served by **public service** broadcasters rather than commercial enterprises. The BBC has 15 regional **news** programs while ITV is required to provide local news as part of its franchise agreement and fulfills this across 14 regions. In 2011, the then Culture Secretary, Jeremy Hunt, laid out plans for a local TV network across the country in a bid to plug the **democratic deficit** compounded by the closure of local newspapers. The Local TV Network was launched in November 2013 and, to date, 34 channels have been awarded licences. However, the scheme has an uncertain future after media regulator Ofcom proposed scrapping any further roll-out due to concerns over economic viability. Many of the existing channels have faced financial difficulties and struggled to attract an audience, in part due to the low quality of their output, often produced by volunteers or low-paid amateurs. The business model of local television is successful in the US, but local stations there are usually affiliated with a larger television networks such as Fox or NBC.

Local broadcast media have faced similar challenges to newspapers, with falling audience numbers and a loss of advertising revenue. Competition from on demand podcasts and digital streaming services mean younger audiences are harder than ever to reach. Furthermore, although television has managed to successfully switch over from analog to digital, radio is still lagging behind because half of the audience still receives audio programs via an analog platform. Meanwhile, local broadcast journalists are continuing to feel the pressure of cuts in newsrooms and the shift to **MOJO Journalism** and reporting on **social media** mean they have had to become tech-savvy jacks-of-all-trades rather than rely on production crew. Against this backdrop, audiences still expect their local media to provide objective information, foster social integration, provide inspiration, ensure representation, increase local understanding, create civic memory and contribute to a sense of belonging (Meijer, 2010).

See also **hyperlocal journalism**.

Key Sources

Meijer, C. 2010 "Democratizing Journalism? Realizing the Citizen's Agenda for Local News Media" *Journalism Studies* 11(3): 327–342

Chantler, P. and Harris, S. 1997 *Local Radio Journalism*. Oxford: Focal Press

LOCAL NEWSPAPERS

Emerging in the late 17th century, local newspapers have long been the lifeblood of communities, feeding them **news**, information and entertainment while providing "answers to questions of direct and immediate concern to readers" (Freer, 2007: 89). There are many variations in terminology surrounding non-national newspapers, with small weekly titles in rural areas also referred to as provincial or country newspapers and larger, county-wide titles known as regional newspapers. Meanwhile, urban areas can be home to a city or metropolitan newspaper, usually published daily and in the past printed as a morning and evening edition. Some of these local newspapers were distributed as free newspapers or "freesheets," posted through letterboxes or made available in public spaces. The common denominator between all these titles is that their coverage and availability is centered around a specific geographic location, rather than being purchasable anywhere in the country. As a result, these publications have a "closer connection to community" than their national counterparts (Aldridge, 2007: 57) and often champion local issues on behalf of their readers. One of their key roles is to articulate the concerns of the local community and be central to local democracy by "providing a forum for public debate" (Franklin, 1997: 114). As the UK Culture, Media and Sport Committee report (Franklin, 2009) suggests, local newspapers are fundamental to the underpinning of all **journalism**, owing to their unique position at the bottom layer of the news pyramid. Thousands of local newspaper journalists generate stories every day that are then picked up by those further up the pyramid, such as national newspapers and BBC News.

Although concerned with politics and public affairs, local newspapers have always walked a fine line between the civic and the commercial. The growth of local newspapers during the industrial revolution led to the publication of almost 1,000 separate titles in the UK during the 19th century. As the cover price of newspapers dropped, the market was opened up to a mass audience, particularly the working classes. Proprietors started to pursue commercial interests more vigorously and, by the turn of the 20th century, local newspapers were turning to more sport, crime and human interest stories in order to compete with the rising popular national tabloid press. Globalization in the second half of the 20th century saw small family newspaper businesses swallowed up by multi-national conglomerates via widespread acquisitions and mergers, leaving local newspapers in the hands of a few major profit-driven corporations. The focus on empire expansion meant these publishing giants failed to act quickly enough to develop online **business models** and relied too heavily on their legacy print stock. Johnston Press, the UK's fourth largest regional publisher and owner of 200 local newspapers, went into administration in 2018 after failing to pay back £220 million of debt built up during aggressive expansion in the 1990s and early 2000s.

Dramatic changes in consumption has caused local newspaper circulation to crash as young **audiences** seek news via their **smartphones** from **social media**, digital native news websites and news **aggregators**. Simultaneously, **advertising** revenue, the most important source of finance for many local newspapers, has shifted from print to online and is largely dominated by large American **platforms** such as **Google** and **Facebook**, which offer "low prices, precise targeting and unduplicated reach" (Jenkins and Nielsen, 2018). Furthermore, classified advertising has been swallowed up by online sellers such as Ebay, Gumtree and Craigslist, and property, motoring and recruitment have also moved to specialist websites. Local newspapers, many of which are owned by debt-ridden corporations, now find themselves desperately trying to implement online strategies to arrest financial decline. But while they invest in online infrastructure and train reporters to become multimedia journalists, they are having to cut costs with widespread redundancies, newspaper closures and moving offices out of the community to cheaper, publicly inaccessible out-of-town units.

Across Europe, local news organizations are still generating 80–90 percent of their revenues from legacy print operations while building digital offerings across their websites, **apps** and social media accounts. A range of strategies is being executed online, including **paywalls**, subscriptions and charging for premium content. Independent titles and those in smaller ownership companies are focusing on local depth, whereas those that are part of larger parent companies such as Reach, Keskisuomailainen, and Funke Mediengruppe are pursuing regional breadth or national scale, which involves corporate traffic targets. Parent companies in Germany and the UK have launched initiatives to "better understand and monitor audiences' web-usage patterns and respond with personalised content and advertising" (Jenkins and Nielsen, 2018). The concern is that target-driven journalism will lead to further **clickbait** and widen the **democratic deficit** as reporters no longer report on local courts and councils.

See also **geo-social news**.

Key Sources

Aldridge, M. 2007 *Understanding the Local Media*. Maidenhead: Open University Press

Freer, J. 2007 "UK Regional and Local Newspapers" in Anderson, P. and Ward, G. (Eds) *The Future of Journalism in the Advanced Democracies*. Aldershot: Ashgate, 89–104

Jenkins, J. and Nielsen, R. 2018 "The Digital Transition of Local News" *Reuters Digital News Report* www.digitalnewsreport.org/publications/2018/digital-transition-local-news/

LONG FORM NARRATIVE

This is the type of storytelling which appears in the growing **slow journalism** movement (Le Masurier, 2015) and shares some traits with **investigative journalism**. The antithesis to sound bites, breaking **news** tweets and **live blogging**, long form narrative involves taking time to enable a story to unfold, often via multimedia outputs or extended text. Since 2014, the *Guardian* newspaper has been publishing the Long Read thrice weekly to enable readers to immerse themselves in a 5,000-word feature spread across three pages. Topics range from the rise of the British sandwich through to political corruption in Brazil and often take months to research and write (Shainin, 2018). News websites specializing in long form digital storytelling have sprung up across the globe, using the infinite space of the web to tell powerful stories with text, imagery and graphics, including *Longreads, Epic Magazine* and *Atavist Magazine*.

Digital journalism, in particular native online media companies, have given a fresh lease of life to long form narrative, which first developed in the 1960s under the moniker New Journalism. The form was made famous by Tom Wolfe and Hunter S. Thompson, who wrote long form journalism enhanced with literary and artistic flair. Today, these flourishes often come in the guise of interactive graphics or even web comics with 360-video experience, such as the groundbreaking work of Marc Ellison. The photo and data journalist created the House Without Windows, exploring conflict in the Central African Republic via the eyes of children for the *HuffPost* (2017).

Key Sources
Shainin, J. 2018 "How We Make the Long Read: From the Rise of the Sandwich to the Meaning of Neoliberalism" *Guardian* www.theguardian.com/member ship/2018/apr/07/long-read-how-we-make-it-guardian-shainin
HuffPost 2017 "The House without Windows" https://housewithoutwindows. huffpost.com/#1

MAGAZINE JOURNALISM

Similar to print newspapers, contemporary magazines have been confronted with the challenges of digitalization, participatory media and splintering audiences. Most publishers have seen "consistently declining revenues as both audiences and advertisers migrate to free, immediate and interactive platforms" (Duffy, 2013: 4). Just seven percent of UK magazines saw any readership growth in 2016 and many glossy women's mags (*Bliss, Sugar, More*) and once behemoth lads' mags (*FHM, Zoo, Nuts*) have closed, including the tenth biggest selling magazine, *Glamour*, which went digital-only in 2017 (Carey, 2017). Publishers are using a wide range of tactics to desperately attract readers, including dropping their cover price and giving out free copies. *Cosmopolitan* magazine slashed its price from £3.80 to £1 in 2015 and gave away 100,000 free copies, helping it to increase circulation by 57 percent. It also set up a cheap housing initiative in London under its Home, Made campaign and rehoused women as property guardians.

The biggest shift for magazine journalism has been its identity crisis as content has spilled from the printed page onto the internet, accessible via tablets, **smartphones**, computers and many more emerging devices. Magazines are having to evolve from static objects into transmogrified brands and rethink, repackage and redistribute multimedia content, whether it be an interactive feature for an iPad subscription, a reader poll on a website or an image and links on the magazines' **Facebook** feed (Duffy, 2013). As a result, magazines have launched **subscription**-based digital versions for tablets, **apps** for smartphones and paywall websites in a bid to survive flagging print sales.

Some of the most successful brands have been born online, which has enabled them to adopt new business models such as **native advertising**, brand sponsorship, masterclasses and crowdfunding. For example *Pink News* has recently partnered with **SnapChat** to become the first

LGBT+ publisher to launch on their Discover **news** section. This enables them to share **advertising** revenue with the messaging app via their Story Ads. Magazines are also experimenting with reader participation, such as the established women's magazine *Olivia* in Finland, which launched a co-creation platform, MyOwnOlivia, in 2011. Via the websites, readers and journalists collaborated to identify story topic, angle and interviewees before the journalists then wrote the stories based on readers' choices and wishes. This negotiated the conventional "we write, you read" dogma of journalism to a new order of "we ask, you respond, we listen, we write, you read" (Aitamurto, 2013).

Other forms of sustainable magazine journalism have arisen via not-for-profit organizations which have embraced the **slow journalism** movement, creating **long form narrative** and **investigative journalism** online.

Key Sources

Aitamurto, T. 2013 "Balancing between Open and Closed: Co-Creation in Magazine Journalism" *Digital Journalism* 1(2): 229–251

Duffy, B. 2013 *Remake, Remodel: Women's Magazines in the Digital Age*. Chicago: University of Illinois Press

MASHUP

A mashup combines unrelated pre-existing material to create a new piece of derivative work. Digital technology, in particular open source software, has enabled mashup culture to flourish in the arenas of music and video as tech savvy individuals have sought to remix content to create something new for artistic, humorous or political means. These mashups, which are popular on **YouTube** channels, have found their way into entertainment journalism, appearing on digital native **news** sites such as **Buzzfeed**, *HuffPost* and VICE News. *HuffPost* has a whole page dedicated to mashups such as "Great Scott! Someone Mashed Up 'Back To The Future' And 'Westworld'" (McDonald, 2016) which hosts a video created from edited clips of 1990 film *Back to the Future Part III* and 2016 television adaptation *Westworld* – both Western genres. This type of content is often viewed as having social lift and virality, meaning it is likely to be shared on **social media** and reach a wide, global audience.

Edwards and Tyron (2009) argue that political video mashups, which became popular during the 2008 American presidential election, are a prime example of citizen generated content and act as allegories of empowerment. The mashups allow the creator to form new meaning by juxtaposing two pieces of original source material, such as a politician's speech and footage from a popular reality television show. In doing so, citizens create new meaning and immerse themselves in media literacy, reading through the media rather than against it.

In the UK, it is now legal for people to use a limited amount of copyright material for the purposes of parody, caricature or pastiche without the consent of the copyright holder. Ironically, this amendment to the Copyright, Design and Patents Act 1988, introduced by former Prime Minister David Cameron in 2014, made it legal for mashup duo Cassetteboy to remix Cameron's speeches (Perraudin, 2014). Their blistering rap parody of David Cameron has now been viewed more than 6.7 million times on YouTube.

Key Sources

Edwards, R. and Tyron, C. 2009 "Political Video Mashups as Allegories of Citizen Empowerment" *First Monday* 14(10) http://journals.uic.edu/ojs/index.php/fm/article/view/2617/2305

METASOURCES

In their 2013 article "Metasources: Authorizing The **News** of Gaddafi's Death," Norgaard Kristensen and Mortensen argue that the emergence of a globalized, digitized and convergent media ecology, with the resultant inclusion of **bloggers, citizen journalists** and members of the general public as active contributors to news making and dissemination, has created distinctive patterns and arrangements for news **sourcing**, which they term "Metasourcing."

These innovative arrangements are especially evident in war **journalism** and involve what might be termed a "staged," multi-level, or upstairs–downstairs relationship between elite and non-elite sources, reflecting both their proximity and access to the unravelling news events as well as the chronological ordering of their involvement in journalistic reports of the event.

In the initial phase, non-elite sources are likely to be prominent and Norgaard Kristensen and Morten argue that these amateur sources are increasingly likely to break the news in war zones. The quality, veracity and credibility of their input to news making, however, is limited, since it typically derives from unsupported first-person witnessing of an event or a photograph or video shot without any convincing or substantiating evidence. "Amateur sources," the authors suggest, offer crucial triggering information but remain little more than "raw and fragmented bits of visual and verbal information" (Norgaard Kristensen and Mortenson, 2013).

By contrast, elite sources can rarely achieve such ready proximity to events but journalists use them subsequent to the initial feed to "comment on, validate and grant legitimacy to amateur sources" (ibid.). In this way, the elite and non-elite sources function in a complementary fashion. Amateur sources break stories, or at least deliver information and access at great speed, which is crucial for digital journalism, while elite sources confirm, contextualize and offer credibility and transparency to the often disconnected but informative citizen witnessing.

Zvi Reich's (2006) study of the role of sources and journalists in news making identifies a similar shifting balance between two news-making communities and suggests that *sources* are often dominant in news reporting at the early stages of the development of a story while *journalists* are prominent at the news writing and dissemination phase of coverage. In the case of metasourcing, it is sources (elite and non-elite) that play distinctive and variable roles in unravelling news stories.

See also **sources**.

Key Sources

Norgaard Kristensen, N. and Mortensen, M. 2013 "Metasources Authorizing the News of Gaddafi's Death; New Patterns of Journalistic Information Gathering and Dissemination in the Digital Age" *Digital Journalism* 1(3): 352–367

Reich, Z. 2006 "The Process Model of News Initiative: Sources Lead First, Reporters Thereafter" *Journalism Studies* 7(4): 497–514

METERED PAYWALLS

A paywall is a revenue raising strategy employed by media corporations which charges readers for access to previously free online **news** content. A metered paywall is a "mixed" model which offers readers the opportunity to read a limited number of articles (usually ten) for free, but then charges for any subsequent access to content (Franklin, 2016). The ability of **paywalls** to provide sufficient revenue to replace newspapers' previous income from copy sales and advertising revenues has been contested (Myllylahti, 2014). To attract more subscribers to buy content, some newspapers have limited their offer of free access to news. In August 2013, for example, the *New York Times'* metered paywall reduced its offer of free content from 20 stories to ten. The metered mixed model nonetheless remains the most popular form of paywall.

See also **paywalls** and **freemium paywalls**.

Key Sources

Myllylahti, M. 2014 "Newspaper Paywalls – The Hype and the Reality; A Study of How Paid News Content Impacts on Media Corporation Revenues" *Digital Journalism* 2(2): 179–194

Franklin, B. 2016 "The Future of Journalism in an Age of Digital Media and Economic uncertainty" in Franklin, B (Ed) *The Future of Journalism in an Age of Digital Media and Economic Uncertainty*. London: Routledge, 2016

METRO

Launched in 1999, the British *Metro* newspaper has bucked the publishing trend and created a profitable printed product with stable circulation. Published Monday to Friday and targeted at commuters, the tabloid format newspaper is distributed for free on public transport across urban areas of England, Scotland and Wales. Copying the free newspaper concept originating in Sweden, the newspaper was initially launched on the London Underground with a print run of 85,000. Gradually, the product was rolled out to towns and cities across the country and by 2018 had become the country's most read newspaper, overtaking the *Sun* (Tobitt, 2018). Its daily readership of 1.4 million people has an average age of 39, which is significantly younger than its printed competitors (Martinson, 2018). The newspaper is owned by the Daily Mail General Trust, but despite being a sister paper to the conservative *Daily Mail*, it retains a neutral political stance. Nonetheless, *Metro* has not avoided digitalization altogether, as it is available via an app and web browser through metro.news. There is also a separate website, metro.co.uk, launched in 2001 which has operated independently from the newspaper since 2014, although it shares the same owner.

During the 2012 London Olympics and Paralympics, the *Metro* published seven days a week and provided free copies to spectators at the games. This was particularly lucrative for the newspaper, due to a reported £2.25 million deal with sportswear company Adidas, which ran cover wrap adverts on each of the 17 days of the Olympics.

Key Sources
Martinson, J. 2018 "How Metro Became the Most Read Paper in Britain" *Prospect* www.prospectmagazine.co.uk/magazine/how-metro-became-the-most-read-paper-in-britain

MOBILE NEWS

News on the go is now available to most people at any time, in any location, from a variety of mobile internet-enabled devices. Globally, 62 percent of online users consume their news from a smartphone at least weekly, with rates as high as 79 percent in some European countries (Newman, Fletcher, Kalogeropoulos, Levy and Nielsen, 2018). In the UK, the smartphone has become the most used device for news, overtaking the computer and laptop. Increasingly, citizens are diverting their attention away from **legacy media** such as newspapers and rolling television news, fuelling the decline in newspaper readership and scheduled television audiences (Sambrook and McGuire, 2014). In their place a plethora of mobile news **platforms** have emerged, which reach **audiences** through multiple means of distribution from customized news alerts by SMS or MMS to mobile news sites and mobile **apps** (Westlund, 2013). Users receive this news on a range of touchscreen devices, including **smartphones,** tablets, phablets, e-readers and notebooks. The use of mobile news apps peaks during consumers' commute to and from work, although many people also consume news on a smartphone in bed, during the morning and in the evening. Rather than sitting down to read extensively on their smartphones, users fill gaps in their day with "sporadic news consumption," grabbing bits of news here and there (Molyneux, 2018: 643). These are shorter sessions than on other platforms – less than twelve minutes at a time – but happen more frequently. This has led to an environment where audiences flit between different devices and platforms throughout the day to consume news from a number of mobile and static sources.

To capture this snacking mobile audience, news publishers have developed tailored content via niche apps. The *Guardian* focuses on live and breaking news summaries while the *San Francisco Chronicle* prioritizes opinion articles and blogs. Furthermore, the *New York Times* has developed an election app while the *Chicago Tribune* has an app specifically for the basketball team, the Chicago Bulls. Other news outlets have focused on utility services such as restaurant guides by *Göteborgs-Posten* and sudoku games by *Svenska Dagbladet* in Sweden (Westlund, 2013). The disadvantage with native apps is that they currently have more restraints regarding hyperlinks and sharing via social media, meaning it is more difficult for companies to generate user traffic, measure **web analytics** or redirect users to other sites through advertisements.

This trend for accessible mobile news will only increase further in the future as the internet-of-things infiltrates a greater number of electronic devices and news organizations seek diverse opportunities to reach fragmented audiences.

See also **MOJO journalism**.

Key Sources

Molyneux, L. 2018 "Mobile News Consumption: A Habit of Snacking" *Digital Journalism* 6(5): 634–650

Newman, N., Fletcher, R., Kalogeropoulos, A., Levy, D. A. and Nielsen, R. K. 2018 *Reuters Institute Digital News Report 2018*. Oxford, UK: Reuters Institute for the Study of Journalism

Westlund, O. 2013 "Mobile News: A Review and Model of Journalism in an Age of Mobile Media" *Digital Journalism* 1(1): 6–26

MOJO JOURNALISM

The use of **smartphones** by reporters to take photographs, shoot video, record audio, edit packages and upload multimedia content to websites and **social media** is known as MOJO journalism. It has grown in prevalence alongside the expansion of touchscreen enabled mobile devices and faster broadband network coverage. New recruits entering the profession are now expected to be skilled in multimedia **journalism** rather than specializing in print, web or broadcast media, as was commonplace prior to the 21st century. Digital technology has created economic challenges for legacy **news** organizations, meaning there is now pressure to produce more content in a greater variety of formats with fewer staff. The smartphone enables journalists to become jacks-of all-trades and perform reporting tasks that previously would have been undertaken by numerous staff with a range of equipment. MOJO journalists are also known as video journalists, multimedia journalists, solo journalists, backpack journalists or simply as one-man bands. The MOJO – or mobile journalist – has redefined the field of journalism from the print **newsroom** of the *Hindustan Times* (Kumar and Shuaib Mohamed Haneef, 2017) to television studios in the south eastern corner of the United States (Blankenship, 2016). The requirement of single reporters to write, report, shoot and edit their own stories for local television news organizations in the US and around the world is a rapidly growing trend, a job that traditionally has been done by multi-person crews.

There are concerns over the widespread practice of mobile **journalism** and the way in which it is altering journalistic practice. Although journalists are being enskilled with techniques in multimedia production, they are suffering due to a lack of time to learn and produce quality MOJO stories (Kumar and Shuaib Mohamed Haneef, 2017), which ultimately deskills and demotivates staff. There is also evidence that mobile journalists have less specialized expert knowledge because they are being spread so thinly and they are relying more on public relation practitioners to accomplish their work tasks within specified deadlines with limited time and resources (Blankenship, 2016). There are also considerable concerns over the lack of checks and balances as reporters publish straight to the web while on the road without their work being edited by another staff member (Canter, 2015a).

Key Sources

Blankenship, J. 2016 "Losing Their Mojo? Mobile Journalism and the Deprofessionalization of Television News Work" *Journalism Practice* 10(8): 1055–1071

Kumar, A. and Shuaib Mohamed Haneef, M. 2017 "Is Mojo (En)De-Skilling? Unfolding the Practices of Mobile Journalism in an Indian Newsroom" *Journalism Practice*, 1–19, doi:10.1080/17512786.2017.1389291

NATIVE ADVERTISING

At first glance native advertising seems to represent merely the transition of the advantages and practices that created **advertorial** into the age of digital media and **journalism**. It also generates many of the same antagonisms. Like advertorial, for example, native journalism signals a paid advertisement disguised as editorial content which closely emulates the editorial style and format of a **news** article. In his article "Camouflaging Church as State," Ferrer Conill defines native advertising as "a form of paid media where the commercial content is delivered within the design and form of editorial content, as an attempt to recreate the user experience of reading **news** instead of advertising content" (Ferrer Conill, 2016: 904). Similarly, Couldry and Turow (2014: 1716) suggest native advertisements are "textual, pictorial, and/or audio-visual material that supports the aims of an advertiser (and is paid for by the advertiser) while it mimics the format and editorial style of the publisher that carries it."

But, like advertorial, native advertising tends to undermine the important distinction between editorial (factually based news coverage produced by **journalists**) and **advertising** (commercial text designed to sell goods and ideas and produced by advertising staffs). However, the boundaries between advertising and editorial, often separated by what was typically described as an "unbreachable firewall" in the age of **legacy media**, blur more readily in the digital media age when digitally native organizations mix news and entertainment with alacrity under pressure of the economic imperative to grow advertising revenues to fund their publishing operations (Carlson, 2014; Coddington, 2015b).

A key development which has broken down this "unbreachable wall" has been the growing trend across the last decade for news organizations to create their own "**Brand Studios** such as T.Brand at the *New York Times* and to employ advertising creatives (often redeployed journalists) to write the actual advertising copy on advertisers" behalf and present them in an editorial style for publication in the newspaper (Lynch, 2018: Chapter 2). In this way, the arrival of native advertising means that journalists have not so much been tempted to ignore this "unbreachable wall" as to pick up an editorial hammer and demolish it. Between 2014 and 2016,

> legacy outlets rushed to create in-house content studios, and by the end of 2016 the presence of a brand or content studio seemed to be

de rigeur at both online-only and legacy publications, whether that studio was effectively a two-person team mining a stable of free-lancers or (as in the case of the [*sic*] *Times*) a global company with scores of employees.

(Lynch, 2018: Ch 2)

In his recent study of 12 news websites in four countries (Sweden, Spain, the UK and the US), Ferrer Conill explores and analyzes to what degree the digital editions of traditional news media have introduced native advertising in their websites. He identifies observable distinctions between countries such as the US and the UK, the most market oriented media systems which display a stronger preference for native advertising than the more public service driven Swedish papers which did not reveal any native advertising across the study period. But nearly three out of four online publishers in the US now offer native advertising opportunities. The US leads in native advertising expenditures but the practice is gaining global momentum with significant spending occurring worldwide, particularly in China, Japan and the UK (AdYou-Like, 2015).

Given the journalism industry's continuing failure to develop a coherent business plan to generate sufficient resources to fund high quality journalism, it seems likely that the expansion of native advertising and the growing revenues it generates will continue. Ferrer Conill concludes on a somber note for the veracity and quality of news: "The long-standing divide between editorial and commercial content has started to be questioned by powerful actors within the industry" (2016).

See also **advertising**.

Key Sources

AdYouLike 2015 "Native Advertising Set to Double by 2018" PRNewswire, 18 December www.prnewswire.com/news-releases/native-advertising-set-to-double-by-2018-562919861.html

Coddington, M. 2015b "The Wall Becomes a Curtain: Revisiting Journalism's News Business Boundary" in Carlson, M. and Lewis, S. C. (Eds) *Boundaries of Journalism: Professionalism, Practices and Participation*. New York: Routledge, 67–82

Ferrer Conill, R. 2016 "Camouflaging Church as State: An Exploratory Study of Journalism's Native Advertising" *Journalism Studies* 17(7): 904–914, doi:10.1080/1461670.2016.1165138

Lynch, L. and Sirrah, A. 2018 *Native Advertising: Advertorial Disruption in the 21st Century News Feed*. London: Routledge

NETWORK JOURNALISM

This concept developed from the social, political, economic and cultural theory defined by Jan van Dijk in *The Network Society* and Manuel Castells in *The Rise of the Network Society* in the 1990s, during the height of the emerging information age. American professor Jeff Jarvis, an advocate of living life more publicly on the web, was one of the first media academics to apply the concept of the network society to **journalism** in a commentary on his acclaimed blog BuzzMachine. In his 2008 post, he described network journalism as a linked ecology of the internet where the professional and amateur, **journalist** and citizen, could now work together to gather and share news in more ways to more people than ever before. Networked journalism according to Jarvis, is founded on the truth that "we can do more together than we can apart" (2008).

Heinrich (2012) emphasizes the global nature of network journalism arguing that digitalization has created a new form of journalism characterized by an increasingly global flow of **news** and growing number of news deliverers. Within this transformed news sphere, the roles of journalistic outlets change and they become nodes, arranged in a dense net of information gatherers, producers, and disseminators. The interactive connections among these news providers constitute what Heinrich calls the sphere of network journalism. Furthermore, the development and reach of social media now enables individuals, rather than just news outlets, to become integrative information nodes that can potentially contribute to a complex global news map within the sphere of network journalism (Heinrich, 2012).

See also **crowdsourcing**.

Key Sources

Heinrich, A. 2008 *Network Journalism: Journalistic Practice in Interactive Spheres*. New York: Routledge

Jarvis, J. 2008 "Supermedia" BuzzMachine. www.buzzmachine.com/2008/06/06/supermedia/

NEWS

Deriving from the Latin word *nova*, meaning new things, news is information of public interest but also of interest to the public. The distinction is important because it underpins the dichotomy at the heart of **journalism**, which is centered around "hard" versus "soft" news. Current affairs and matters which help citizens make informed democratic choices are considered hard news, whereas entertainment, celebrity gossip and sport may interest the audience, but are not fundamental to the public sphere and are, therefore, considered soft news. Items of information are considered newsworthy to journalists based on a set of intrinsic, yet ambiguous, judgments which are highly subjective and based on a set of experiences, attitudes and expectations (White, 1997). Generally speaking, news is about people, events and quirky moments that are based on fact rather than fiction, delivered in a timely manner to an audience. The receiver is an important factor, as this further highlights the subjectivity of news. If an individual's sister becomes engaged, this is news to their friends and family. However, if a celebrity becomes engaged, this is softer news which will warrant coverage in entertainment-based media such as tabloid newspapers. And if a high-profile public figure such as an heir to the British throne becomes engaged, this will be deemed of interest to an international audience and as such will be covered by a wide range of serious and lighter news outlets. News is completely dependent on the audience, so a local newspaper will cover a car accident in their patch but a national newspaper or television news bulletin would not. News is also about the unusual and not about things running smoothly, and most people would say it is something new that has happened, something they did not know before, something that affects their life or something they are interested in (Harcup, 2002). It is about the big and the small, from a stolen purse to a nuclear power plant meltdown.

How journalists decide what is news and which items have "newsworthiness" has been subject to much empirical scrutiny, particularly in the study of **news values**. These are the criteria or set of unwritten rules that guide journalists when deciding whether information or events are newsworthy. There are also professional norms which journalists seek to fulfill, such as objectivity, impartiality, balance and fairness (Tuchman, 1972) although some media sociologists argue that all journalism is "fundamentally interpretative" (McNair, 2001: 51). There is also the claim that news is controlled by media owners (Curran, 1990) who have political affiliations and commercial imperatives that drive the news agenda.

Prior to the internet, journalists were the gatekeepers of such news, deciding which information the public should know. But since these publishing boundaries have been broken online there is now a wealth of information readily available for the public to consume via blogs and

social media. But what makes a tweet a news item? Does it only become news when it is covered by a recognized media organization? And what constitutes this recognition? The concept of news is in a state of flux with **liquid news**, breaking live, tweet-by-tweet, every second. Mainstream media are often reporting on information that is previously known and is not necessarily "new" but they verify it, amplify it and add context, creating a news package. News values are also shifting, with opinion often taking precedence over fact. A tweet by President Donald Trump is considered newsworthy even if it is just another barrage of insults or an opinion based on falsehoods. The rise of **clickbait**, where an intriguing headline draws a reader into a story presenting no new or valuable information is also shifting the definition of news. Is news any new piece of information the audience read or click on? The spread of viral content, particularly photos and video, have introduced the notion of shareability as a news value (Harcup and O'Neill, 2016) and such content tends to be more positive in nature but has been criticized for being unsubstantial and leaning towards soft news. The growth of digital native news websites such as **BuzzFeed** and the *Huffington Post* is also impacting upon news values (Canter, 2018) with an emphasis on opinion, **listicles**, "funny cat videos" (Bednarek, 2016: 232) but also more diverse stories from unheard voices.

Ultimately, in the digital world readers choose which stories to click on and which sources to trust. Rather than be fed whatever the mainstream media reports, the public decide what is news from a wider pool of information. News, it seems, is no longer just what the news editor says it is.

Key Sources
Harcup, T. 2002 *Journalism: Principles and Practice*. London: Sage
McNair, B. 2001 *News and Journalism in the UK*. New York: Routledge
White, D. M. 1950 "The 'Gate Keeper': A Case Study in the Selection of News" *Journalism Quarterly* 27: 383–390

NEWS AGENCY

Wire copy underpins much of the content created by journalists and is often repurposed without any further checks. News agencies are the source of such copy and are also known as a wire service or newswire.

This alternative name dates back to the use of wires on telegraph machines, which became the common method of long distance communication in the 19th century when news agencies began to emerge. News agencies gather **news** reports and sell them to subscribing news organizations such as newspapers, magazines, broadcasters and online **platforms**. There are three global news agencies: Agence France-Presse in France, Associated Press in the US and Reuters in the UK, which have offices in most countries and produce wide ranging multimedia news content. The philosophy of these news services is to provide a single objective news feed to all subscribers – meaning they all receive exactly the same material. Such is the power and influence of news agencies that reporters rely on them for national and international news, particularly in newsrooms that have seen staff cutbacks and the reduction of foreign correspondents. Research by Lewis, Williams and Franklin (2008) found that almost half of news stories published in the quality UK press were wholly or mainly dependent on materials supplied by news agencies. The pressure to churn out more copy with fewer staff has increased the reliance on agency copy, which is often repurposed without further verification or acknowledgment of the original author. Although this could be considered similar to **creative cannibalism**, the subscription service means that journalists are permitted to copy and paste news agency copy since their employers have paid for it.

More recent research on news agency **journalism** in Brussels (Lorenz, 2017) reveals that agency reporters themselves rely heavily on material supplied by political institutions within the European Union due to time pressure and poorly staffed newsrooms. Agency correspondents are, therefore, at the whim of public relations staff and there is a question over their ability to uphold journalistic autonomy. Competition from the public has also meant that news agencies no longer have privileged access to global events and news outlets are less reliant on them for eyewitness accounts, as they can turn directly to **citizen journalism** and **user-generated content** widely available online. The national wire service Press Association in the UK has made several rounds of redundancies in recent years due to a fall in revenue from regional newspapers, which are cutting subscriptions to stave off their own economic difficulties.

However, in other parts of the world, news agencies are booming, particularly the Xinhua News Agency in China, which has become the largest of its kind among developing countries and has ambitious plans to become the leading world news service. The agency has been the mouthpiece of the Chinese Communist Party since its establishment in 1931 but has sought to transform its business since China adopted the market economy in the late 1970s. By 2008, it had a total of 33 domestic bureaus and 123 overseas bureaus covering 190 countries and producing 300 news stories and 1,500 news photos per day in seven languages. Reflecting the hybrid nature of the country, which has an economic capitalist system but is politically communist, Xinhua has evolved from a solely propaganda machine to a multi-purposed service providing news, information, entertainment, and expression of public opinions, serving as a forum for criticizing the wrongdoing of officials (Hong, 2011). And yet, no matter how market oriented their content and practice may be, Xinhua still remains a tool of the communist party to serve its political and ideological interests, while simultaneously making profits as a commercial corporation. Furthermore, all Chinese news media are required to use Xinhua as the only official news source, ensuring that it has a tight monopoly on information. The structural changes within the organization have not transferred Chinese journalism from party journalism to watchdog journalism as a consequence of marketization (Xin, 2008). Indeed, some argue that the one-way communication released from the state-sponsored Xinhua has met with limited success in resonating with international news media and setting the news agenda abroad (Cheng, Golan and Kiousis, 2016).

See also **propaganda model**.

Key Sources

Hong, J. 2011 "From the World's Largest Propaganda Machine to a Multi-purposed Global News Agency: Factors in and Implications of Xinhua's Transformation since 1978" *Political Communication* 28(3): 377–393

Lewis, J., Williams, A. and Franklin, B. 2008 "Four Rumours and an Explanation" *Journalism Practice* 2(1): 27–45

NEWS BEATS

A beat is a topical or geographical area that a specific reporter covers. In local **journalism** it is often referred to as patch reporting, with a **journalist** covering a designated postcode or region of a city known as a patch. Popular news beats which cover a specific topic, rather than location, include crime, politics, health, business, foreign affairs and so on. Beat reporters build up knowledge and expertise of a particular topic by fostering a rapport with sources whom they routinely contact. This often enables them to provide insight and commentary in addition to reporting straight facts, and to distinguish themselves from general news reporters who may occasionally cover similar stories (Iszard, Culbertson and Lambert, 1990). Beat reporters have greater autonomy over the stories they cover (Weaver, Beam, Brownlee, Voakes and Wilhoit, 2007) due to their exclusive **sources**, which they build and nurture over time (Scanlan, 2002). The term "beat" refers to the act of following a regular routine by contacting the same sources at regular intervals to obtain new information.

Social media has eroded some relationships between beat reporters and sources as official organizations such as the police bypass the media to communicate with the public. Empirical research by the London School of Economics, exploring relations between the Metropolitan Police Service and the national press four years on from the **Leveson Inquiry**, found that serving officers were no longer communicating off the record with beat journalists and their contact with the press was heavily controlled and restricted. This, together with the rise of social media and cuts in newsroom staff, means the police are more in control of the flow of information to the public than ever before and police corruption is left unexposed (Colbran, 2016). As a result, crime news beats are more reliant on unverifiable information and speculative online rumours. In the past, the crime reporter would have had regular informal chats with the local desk sergeant but instead is having to rely increasingly on the police press office, which withholds information. Beat reporters are now more likely to be scouring social media for sources of information or developing virtual contacts online than cultivating face-to-face sources.

Social media, in particular **Twitter**, is also a convenient and cheap beat for political journalism with millions of tweets readily available to transform into quotes. Broersma and Graham (2012) were correct when they predicted that in the future the reporter who attends events, gathers information face-to-face, and asks critical questions would instead operate as an aggregator of information, altering the balance of power between journalists and sources. Indeed, many **news** organizations continue to cull beat reporters in favour of general reporters, who can cover a range of beats, often while metaphorically chained to their desks. This has led to a **democratic deficit**, particularly within the regional press, as there are no court reporters or political reporters to cover these particular news beats. In the UK, this has led to the creation of the BBC funded Local Democracy Reporting Service to help fill the gap in the reporting of local democracy issues in regional news organizations. These reporters spend much of their time in local government meetings, reporting on the decisions of committees, a luxury which many newspaper groups could not afford without the BBC's finances.

Key Sources

Broersma, M. and Graham, T. 2012 "Social Media as Beat: Tweets as a News Source during the 2010 British and Dutch Elections" *Journalism Practice* 6(3): 403–419

Colbran, M. 2016 "Leveson's Lasting Effect on Press Police Relations" *Media Policy Project Blog*, London School of Economics http://blogs.lse.ac.uk/media policyproject/2016/11/14/levesons-lasting-effect-on-press-police-relations/

NEWS BOTS

These refer to the use of automated accounts on **social media** that participate in the dissemination of news and information. **Twitter** estimates that almost 9 percent of accounts on the platform are automated in some way. News bots are an extension of **robot journalism**, which is the broader application of automation in journalistic tasks such as **news** writing, curation and data analysis. Sometimes known as social bots, or simply bots, news bots are not to be confused with cyborgs, which combine automation with human input.

Lokot and Diakopoulos (2016) studied 238 news bots on Twitter to understand how they are being used and how **algorithms** may change the modern media environment. They surmised that news bots present an intriguing opportunity for news organizations, particularly in the sphere of niche and hyperlocal news, where they can service the information needs of micro **audiences**. But there are still questions about the limits of automation in the journalistic workflow and the need for transparency and accountability. Lokot's and Diakopoulos''s (2016) findings indicate that not all news bots are transparent about their sources, the algorithms behind their outputs or the fact that they are bots. There also remains the challenge of who is accountable in the case of a legal breach.

BBC News Labs is currently experimenting with a series of Twitter, **Facebook** and Telegram news bots in collaboration with the BBC's Visual Journalism and World Service Team. The bots, which often have conversational interfaces, allowed the public service broadcaster to automate their coverage of the 2016 EU Referendum and 2016 US Election on Twitter by automatically tweeting graphics showing voting results. The BBC also claims that the bots enable them to reach audiences where BBC World Service websites are blocked (BBC News Labs, 2018).

Key Sources
BBC News Labs 2018 "Bots" http://bbcnewslabs.co.uk/projects/bots/
Lokot, T. and Diakopoulos, N. 2016 "Newsbots: Automating News and Information Dissemination on Twitter" *Digital Journalism* 4(6): 682–699

NEWSROOM

Once a noisy hub of phone calls, coffee machines and frantic typing, the newsroom was a hive of activity in the heart of a town or city. This was the office where newspapers, radio shows and television broadcasts were formulated by a team of journalists, working in an open plan environment sharing ideas and arguing over the lead story of the day. It was not uncommon for members of the public to drop by on a daily basis to bring in tip-offs or complain about coverage of a recent story.

Newsrooms still remain the focal point of most **news** organizations and are awash with computers and equipped with meeting rooms for the daily conference briefing between news editors. However, many newsrooms have shrunk considerably in size due to staff cost cutting and newspapers in particular have lost, or significantly reduced, staff numbers on their features, subbing and pictures desks. In many cases this has led to office relocation to a smaller, cheaper, out of town building that has no physical or social connection to the local community. At their most extreme, these news outlets have become closed to the public and there is no reception staff at all (Canter, 2014a). Content is no longer printed in an adjacent press, but in another part of the country and in some cases subbing (copy proofing, editing and page layout) is conducted in a sub hub abroad.

Remote working, **MOJO journalism** and increased reliance on **freelance** journalists operating from home mean that newsrooms are now far quieter and less well populated than in the past. Interestingly, newsrooms didn't exist as a place to write and discuss news until the mid-19th century (Hoyer, 2003; Wilke, 2003) despite newspapers existing since the 17th century. In the 21st century, some small and alternative news organizations are now returning to the non-newsroom model as software tools such as DropBox, Slack and Trello enable staff to communicate, manage and share content online.

Key Sources
Hoyer, S. 2003 "Newspapers without Journalists" *Journalism Studies* 4(4): 451–463

NEWS UPDATING *SEE* DEADLINE; LIQUID NEWS

NEWS VALUES

These are the criteria or set of rules which guide journalists when deciding whether information or events are newsworthy. **News** that contains a range of factors, or news values, will appeal to the audience and the more a story satisfies multiple factors the more likely it is to be selected as news. These ground rules are unwritten, instinctive and somewhat vague and journalists often describe them as a gut feeling, or as having a nose for a story. However, despite their lack of codified form – they are not written down in a manual, for example – they "exist in daily practice and in knowledge gained on the job" (Harcup and O'Neill, 2001: 261).

The criteria by which journalists select events or information to become news stories, has a century of rich scholarship spanning the globe. In 1922, political commentator Walter Lipmann argued in his influential tome, *Public Opinion,* that the public was not fit to make decisions about newsworthiness and it was the job of the newsman to shape the public's view of the world (Lippmann, 1997). His thinking was further developed in the 1950s (Staab, 1990) and 1960s (Ostgaard, 1965) when a seminal, but flawed, paper was published by Galtung and Ruge (1965). The duo used a systematic content analysis to explore the international reporting of conflict in the Congo, Cyprus and Cuba and devised 12 news values (frequency, threshold, unambiguity, meaningfulness/relevance, consonance, unexpectedness, continuity, composition, elite nations, elite people, personification, negativity). The limitations of Galtung and Ruge's study were most vehemently critiqued by Harcup and O'Neill in their equally significant 2001 paper which argued that "despite the way it has been so widely cited, Galtung and Ruge's taxonomy of news factors appears to ignore the majority of news stories" (276). The authors conducted their own content analysis of 1,276 news articles published in three British national newspapers, testing and modifying Galtung and Ruge's taxonomy to develop ten contemporary news values. They subsequently updated this list in 2016 to 15 news values, following a wider analysis of ten newspapers together with a preliminary examination of stories with high sharing metrics on **Facebook** and **Twitter** (Harcup and O'Neill, 2016). Their 2016 list included exclusivity, bad news, conflict, surprise, audio-visuals, shareability, entertainment, drama, follow-up, power elite, relevance, magnitude, celebrity, good news and news organization's agenda.

Shareability, which journalists acknowledge is a slippery and often unpredictable factor to determine, has become a significant news value for online media. Stories which become viral due to being shared hundreds of thousands of times on **social media** are the "Holy Grail" for many news organizations due to the global impact and reach that they have. Digital native news website **Buzzfeed** measures "social lift," which is the multiple of traffic that a story gets from sharing, to track and predict a post's overall success. Buzzfeed maintains that their content is popular on social media due to five key factors: Identity, emotion, conversation, aspirational and global (Jones, 2015).

Although news values research to date has analyzed a range of media **platforms** including online, these studies have concentrated on **legacy media** and all but ignored digital native news websites (Canter, 2018). These are news outlets that originated online and are not born out of legacy offline media such as *HuffPost*, Buzzfeed News, LADbible, Breitbart and The Canary. One unsubstantiated justification for the lack of investigation into news values on digital native sites is the assumption or misconception that these websites contain soft news and are pervaded with "funny cat videos" (Bednarek, 2016: 232). This is despite evidence that journalists working for traditional news organizations positively welcome Buzzfeed's entry into the journalistic field and see it as reinforcing existing professional norms (Tandoc and Jenkins, 2017: 495).

Key Sources

Canter, L. 2018 "It's Not All Cat Videos: Moving beyond Legacy Media and Tackling the Challenges of Mapping News Values on Digital Native Websites" *Digital Journalism* 6(8): 1101–1112, doi:10.1080/21670811.2018.1503058

Galtung, J. and Ruge, M. 1965 "The Structure of Foreign News: The Presentation of the Congo, Cuba and Cyprus Crises in Four Norwegian Newspapers" *Journal of International Peace Research* 2: 64–90

Harcup, T. and O'Neill, D. 2016 "What Is News? News Values Revisited (Again)" *Journalism Studies* 18(12): 1470–1488

NEWSZAK

The neologism *newszak* was coined to capture the changing **news values** and **news** formats evident in **legacy media** news reports from the 1980s. The suggestion was that such changes signalled a deterioration in the quality of news much as the term *muzak* had implied for music (Franklin, 1997). Newszak implied a retreat from hard news to softer stories typified by **life style journalism**; a focus on entertainment rather than reporting factual information; an emphasis on human interest stories above the public interest; news presented in a sensational rather than measured way; an editorial preference for the trivial above the weighty; a neglect of the international news agenda in favor of domestic concerns. News was judged to be dumbing down by substituting factually informed reporting with **infotainment** (Sampson, 1996). "Stories which interested the public" replaced "stories in the public interest" (Franklin, 1997: 4).

The triggers for such shifting editorial priorities included the increasingly competitive market for **audiences**, readers and **advertising** revenues, as well as the development of digital media technologies which prompted de-skilling, multi-skilling, casualization, job cuts, newspaper closures and takeovers which resulted in a growing press concentration in local and national markets. A similar ambition to attract large audiences with low cost, popular editorial formats gives rise to **listicles** and **clickbait** in contemporary **digital journalism**.

Key Sources
Franklin, B. 1997 *Newszak and News Media.* London: Arnold
Sampson, A. 1996 "The Crisis at the Heart of Our Media" *British Journalism Review* 7(3): 42–56

NON-PROFIT JOURNALISM

Non-profit or not-for-profit journalism does exactly what it says on the tin and is the practice of **journalism** to serve the public good rather than to make a profit. Organizations that run on a non-profit business model tend to rely on private donations and crowdfunding as well as grants and revenue created from hosting training and events. Some non-profit media do sell **advertising** to help cover the costs of overheads and staff wages but any additional money is invested straight back into the company. Many of these organizations focus on **investigative journalism** but they also cover niches such as hyperlocal news, health or crime. Journalism non-profits have been operating since newspapers began and the international news agency Associated Press, which was founded by five New York newspapers in 1846, remains a non-profit cooperative today. *News Internationalist* magazine, published since 1973 in the UK, is one of the world's longest running non-profit publications while the Center for Investigative Reporting, founded in 1977, is American's oldest non-profit investigative news organization.

Non-profits have rapidly flourished in the digital era due to the relatively low production costs of setting up and running a news website compared to a printed publication. Since 2000, the number of non-profit investigative centers across the globe has risen from 15 to nearly 40 (Carvajal, García-Avilés and González, 2012) including multi award-winning website *ProPublica*. There are also many organizations supported by philanthropists that focus on local journalism, such as *California Watch* and university-based centers such as the New England Center for Investigative Reporting. Some of these organizations, such as The Overtake in the UK, rely heavily on volunteers and shy away from sponsored content.

Key Sources
Carvajal, M., García-Avilés, J. A. and González, J. L. 2012a "Crowdfunding and Non-Profit Media: The Emergence of New Models for Public Interest Journalism" *Journalism Practice* 6(5–6): 638–647

ONLINE FIRESTORMS

An online firestorm is a phenomenon involving a "sudden discharge of large quantities of messages containing negative word-of-mouth and complaint behaviour against a person, company or group in social networks" (Pfeffer, Zorbach and Carley, 2014: 118). The concept has its origins in studies of online public relations, marketing and reputation management. When any such explosion of online criticism is noticed by mainstream media/**journalists** it can escalate into a full-blown scandal. Online firestorms tend to deal in opinion rather than unequivocal facts and consequently share some features with "hate speech" and "flaming," which tends to deploy insulting, profane or offensive language. This last tendency perhaps derives from the fact that in the German language press the same feature is known as a "shitstorm." Coined by net activist and journalist Sascha Lobo in 2010, it officially became part of the German language in 2013 when it appeared in the German Dictionary *Duden* (Einwiller, Viererbl and Himmkelreich, 2017: 1178–1197).

Key Sources

Einwiller, S., Viererbl, B. and Himmkelreich, S. 2017 "Journalists' Coverage of Online Firestorms in German Language News Media" *Journalism Practice* 11(7): 1178–1197

Pfeffer, J., Zorbach, T. and Carley, K. 2014 "Understanding Online Firestorms: Negative Word of Mouth Dynamics in Social Media Networks" *Journal of Marketing Communications* 20(1–2): 117–128

ONLINE JOURNALISM

The beginning of the end of what French novelist Proust delighted in describing as

> that abominable and sensual act called reading the newspaper, thanks to which all the misfortunes and cataclysms in the universe over the last twenty-four hours ... are transformed for us, who don't even care, into a morning treat, blending in wonderfully, in a particularly exciting and tonic way, with the recommended ingestion of a few sips of cafe au lait.

Online journalism was the new form of **journalism** of the mid 1990s, which became a mass communication medium in its own right as **news** began to be posted on the World Wide Web. This was the start of the eradication of the printed press, which has seen sales and revenues decline rapidly ever since new media technology enabled content to be presented in a rich, multimedia, interactive and personalized format via the internet. Online journalism was the precursor to what scholars, journalists and the public refer to as digital journalism today and, indeed, almost all forms of journalism, whether print, broadcast or online now embody some element of digitization. One of the early academic texts on the emerging news media was *Online Journalism: A*

Critical Primer (Hall, 2001), which introduced readers to how "cyber-journalism" worked and the limitations of the medium at the time. Now viewed as a largely anachronistic term, online journalism conjures up memories of static web pages with slow, clunky multimedia, limited searchability and communication via one-to-many rather than the post **Web 2.0** many-to-many conversation via multiple mobile devices to which we are accustomed today. Meanwhile, online **sources** referred to the shift from offline contacts, which largely included officials and institutions, to a world where every reader was a potential source of information and **user-generated content**.

Going online created more opportunities for newspapers, giving them the ability to compete with broadcast news and break stories in a timely manner. To begin with, online newspapers tended to be an exact replica of their printed counterpart and exclusive stories were saved for the newspaper. However, over time, media organizations began to separate their printed and online products to create separate identities, content and brands, before recognizing the need to break news first online. The *Daily Telegraph* launched Britain's first daily web-based newspaper in 1994 under the name Electronic Telegraph (Richmond, 2009). At the time there were as few as 10,000 websites on the internet and only one percent of the British population had internet access at home. Newspapers and broadcasters followed suit, with the BBC launching BBC News Online in 1997. The **public service broadcaster** had previously created special websites marking the 1995 Budget and the 1996 Olympic Games, but had no permanent online presence.

Advertisers were slow to follow the online trend, with many companies initially stopping advertising in online media by 1999 and using traditional media to draw customers to their websites instead (Hall, 2001). However, online **advertising** began to recover following the dot-com bubble of the early 2000s and news organizations began expanding their digital advertising offer. Almost two decades later and problems still persist with formats such as traditional banner ads proving unpopular with users and ad blockers being utilized by consumers. **Web analytics** have enabled online newspapers to demonstrate their traffic to advertisers but online revenues are still far below their print equivalent.

Key Sources

Hall, J. 2001 *Online Journalism: A Critical Primer*. London: Pluto Press

PAYWALLS

A paywall is a very specific kind of subscription to a **news** organization that requires potential readers to pay an agreed sum of money to access the content of the news site. The prohibited access may apply to all news content or just specific items. Paywalls are being erected at a rapid rate to provide a substitute revenue source for the decimated **advertising** revenues and income from copy sales in the new millennium, especially since the global recession in 2007–2008. A survey by the American Press Institute (2016) revealed that 77 of the most widely circulating 98 newspapers (above 50,000 copies) in the US now employ some form of paywall (Myllylahti, 2016). They come in all shapes and sizes. A **metered paywall**, for example, offers readers access to a finite number of articles (typically 10) to read for free, with payment required to read beyond that free allocation. A **"freemium"** wall provides readers with selected items of content for free, but places premium, and popular content, such as specialist columnists, behind the wall.

News organizations' new-found enthusiasm for paywalls represents a U-turn on their earlier commitment, inspired by Rupert and James Murdoch, that "news must remain free" (Murdoch, MacTaggart Lecture, 2009). But the success of paywalls in generating new revenues is patchy, leading companies to "demolish" them as promptly as they are erected (Gorman, 2015: 135–145). An eight-country survey of paywalls (Myllylahti, 2014) found that they deliver only ten percent of media companies' revenues and, moreover, while the average print subscriber generates $1,100 a year, the equivalent figure for a digital subscriber is a mere $175. Myllylahti concludes that paywalls are "not a viable business model" (Myllylahti, 2014). Moreover, in their study of paywalls at *Die Welt's* online edition before and after the erection of the paywall, Brandsetter and Schmalhofer (2014) found no discernible improvement in the quality or uniqueness of published news stories above that which was available elsewhere on the internet for free. A similar but later study of three Norwegian papers found that content behind the paywall related closely to the most costly, "resource demanding" topics of newspaper coverage and was, therefore, a rational response by the news sites to protect their costly investment in editorial (Sjøvaag, 2016. See also Carson, 2015).

Paywalls also contribute to a democratic deficit. The closure of regional newspapers has reduced the capacity of those remaining papers, supported by online and **hyperlocal** news sites, to exercise any effective fourth estate role, thereby making local power holders accountable (Pickard and Williams, 2014). By using the "ability to pay" to gatekeep exclusion from high quality local news, paywalls constitute a modern version of the enclosure movement in which the common pastures of high quality, wide ranging news reporting – which were open and accessible to everyone – are suddenly fenced off to allow access only to a privileged few. The future of paywalls and their role as resource generators in news organizations' business plans and financial strategies seems moot (Picard, 2016).

See also **business model**.

Key Sources

Brandsetter, B. and Schmalhofer, J. 2014 "Paid Content: A Successful Revenue Model for Publishing Houses in Germany?" *Journalism Practice* 8(5): 499–507

Carson, A. 2015 "Behind the Newspaper Paywall and Lessons in Charging for Online Content: A Comparative Analysis of Why Australian Newspapers are Stuck in the Purgatorial Space between Digital and Print" *Media, Culture and Society* 37(7): 1–20

Myllylahti, M. 2016 "What Content Is Worth Locking behind a Paywall? Digital News Commodification in Leading Australian Financial Newspapers" *Digital Journalism* 5(4): 460–471, doi:10.1080/2167081.2016.1178074

Pickard, V. and Williams, A. T. 2014 "Salvation of Folly? the Promise and Perils of Digital Paywalls" *Digital Journalism* 2(2): 195–213

Sjøvaag, H. 2016 "Introducing the Paywall: A Case Study of Content Changes in Three Online Newspapers" *Journalism Practice* 10(3): 304–322

THE PEOPLE FORMERLY KNOWN AS THE AUDIENCE

The phrase, "the people formerly known as the **audience**" was coined by, and remains firmly associated with, Jay Rosen, a media scholar based at New York University. He uses the phrase to convey the revolution in communications that occurred with the development of digital media and **Web 2.0**, which facilitated the more pluralistic participation of a wider range of people in gathering, selecting, writing and distributing the **news**. In this way, people who previously and passively had constituted the "audience," simply receiving "news" handed down to them by **journalists** who claimed authority for their views, became active participants in the production of news and even contested journalistic accounts; a process Bruns describes as a shift from news "production" to "**produsage**" (Bruns, 2008). In this sense, this move from audience to **citizen journalist** is essentially a transition in power relationships between press and the public with significant implications for the openness of democratic debate.

In his PRESSthink manifesto, Rosen (2006) expressed the transition as follows; it is worth quoting at some length.

> The people formerly known as the audience are those who *were* on the receiving end of a media system that ran one way, in a broadcasting pattern, with high entry fees and a few firms competing to speak very loudly while the rest of the population listened in isolation from one another – and who *today* are not in a situation like that *at all*.

Expressed in this way and with the consequences he lists, Rosen understands the shift from mere audience to "the people formerly known as the audience" to be substantial, significant and revolutionary.

Key Sources

Bruns, A. 2008 *Blogs, Wikipedia, Second Life and Beyond: From Production to Produsage*. London: Peter Lang

Rosen, J. 2006 The People Formerly Known as the Audience PRESSthink 27th June http://archive.pressthink.org/2006/06/27/ppl_frmr.html

THE PEOPLE PREVIOUSLY KNOWN AS THE EMPLOYERS

The growth of co-creation in **news** work during the early years of the new millennium, especially the emergence of individual and independent **bloggers** and **citizen journalists**, prompted Rosen's classic observation concerning the rise of **the people formerly known as the audience** (Rosen, 2006). His phrase has subsequently been usefully complemented by a second phrase coined by Mark Deuze that commented on the changing role of "the people formerly known as the employers" (Deuze, 2009).

What Rosen was highlighting with his phrase concerning the growing contribution and influence of citizen journalists and other communities of non-professional journalists was the dramatic and inclusive shift in power which allowed individuals with previously only a passive or highly marginal role in news production to become more active in creating the public conversation via their growing access to the tools and digital technologies of **news journalism**.

Deuze concedes the significance of Rosen's observation so far as **audiences** are concerned, but argues that it risks ignoring or understating a similar, if not more significant, redistribution of power in the news ecosystem; namely "a sapping of economic and cultural power away from professional **journalists** by what [Deuze] likes to call **the people formerly known as the employers**" (Deuze, 2009). Deuze is concerned here with the extent to which employers in the journalism and media industries have increasingly retreated, "from taking responsibility for their creative workforce – instead giving them the feeling that they are just assets that cost money" (Deuze, 2009).

The **disruptions** of **digital journalism** have prompted dramatically changing roles for journalists and employees, but also for the people formally known as the employers. The list is lengthy but includes the substantial losses of journalism jobs, the decline in the number of journalists employed on permanent or temporary contracts, the ever worsening conditions of service, including the loss of holiday pay and sickness benefits, the growing competition for fewer jobs, the expansion of freelance working, the increased use of **news bots** and **churnalism**. These industry restructuring and radical changes to the professional identity of journalists and a host of other factors have radically shifted the role, but not always the perception of the employer, while also enhancing the precarity of the journalism profession (Cohen, 2016; Sherwood and O'Donnell, 2018)

In summary, Deuze's phrase has been a useful reminder concerning the changing role of the "people formerly known as the employers" in the news ecology.

Key Sources

Cohen, N. 2016 *Writers' Rights: Freelance Journalism in A Digital Age.* Montreal: Queens University Press

Deuze, M. 2009 "The People Formerly Known as the Employers" *Journalism* 10 (3): 315–318

Sherwood, M. and O'Donnell, P. 2018 "Once A Journalist, Always A Journalist: Industry Restructure, Job Losses and Professional Identity" *Journalism Studies* 19(7): 1021–1038

PERSONALIZATION OF NEWS

The use of "machine-learning technology" to tailor **news** to individual tastes is referred to as personalization (Powers, 2017: 1315). **Algorithms** select which news content to prioritize and present before a user, guided by their past consumption behavior. **Facebook** and **Google** are among the most "voracious extraction engines into which we pour the most intimate details of our lives" and in return get personalized news (Pariser, 2011: 4). The prioritization of news is determined by a complex set of signals such as how often and in what way a person interacts with a friend, page or post and how long they spend viewing content (Powers, 2017). Millennials identify Facebook as their top gateway to news, followed by Google, affording these tech giants huge influence as algorithmic gatekeepers of personalized news. News publishers are also experimenting with personalized news, including Reuters, the *New York Times*, the *Washington Post* and the BBC. Indeed, three years before the launch of Facebook, the *Washington Post* was allowing audiences to customize their own personal page at MyWashingtonPost.com (Thurman, Moeller, Helberger and Trilling, 2018). News brands are continuing to develop personalization, particularly on their mobile **apps**, allowing users to decide what types of news to receive. The approach of BBC News is to blend technologies that outsource gatekeeping functions to **audiences** and algorithms with human editors so that audiences can still receive a common set of top stories.

The advantage of personalization is that it can "serve the worthwhile purpose of lessening information overload by winnowing down news options (Powers, 2017: 1315) for consumers. Collectively, audiences believe algorithmic selection guided by a user's past consumption behavior is a better way to get news than editorial curation, particularly the young and those that use **smartphones** to access news (Thurman, Moeller, Helberger and Trilling, 2018). But there is concern that personalization may lead to exclusion from important information that has wide general appeal but is not specifically relevant to the user. Consumers also worry that news personalization technology collects personal data and breaches their privacy. Furthermore, research by Haim, Graefe and Brosius (2018) indicates that bias is involved in Google News personalization, with smaller, more conservative news outlets over-represented and highly frequented news websites under-represented. The lack of transparency or awareness surrounding personalization algorithms has created an environment where consumers lack knowledge about the types of actions and criteria that affect news selection and prioritization on Facebook, Google, and other news sources (Powers, 2017). Further alarmist discourse has been raised by academics, who state that personalization may lead to a reduction in exposure to challenging viewpoints, otherwise known as a **filter bubble** (Pariser, 2011) although the evidence for this is largely unsubstantiated.

Key Sources

Powers, E. 2017 "My News Feed Is Filtered? Awareness of News Personalization among College Students" *Digital Journalism* 5(10): 1315–1335

Thurman, N., Moeller, J., Helberger, N. and Trilling, D. 2018 "My Friends, Editors, Algorithms, and I: Examining Audience Attitudes to News Selection" *Digital Journalism*, doi:10.1080/21670811.2018.1493936

PHOTOJOURNALISM

The English-language idiom, "a picture is worth a thousand words," is the perfect verbalization of the power of the **news** photograph, which can capture the essence and emotion of an entire story in a single frozen moment. Since their introduction to the press more than 160 years ago, photographs have recorded dramatic events throughout modern history, such as a little girl running away screaming from a napalm bomb attack during the Vietnam War to the chilling image of a policeman moments after he shot and killed the Russian ambassador to Turkey in an art gallery in December 2016. Even on **local newspapers** it is common for reporters to be told by their editors to write a story around a picture, such is the value of the image. This is due to photography's "uniqueness as a contribution to understanding the world we cannot see ourselves" (Evans, 1979: 6). But things are not always as they seem in photographs as, like words, they are open to manipulation because a scene may be managed or "set up." In 2004, *Daily Mirror* **editor** Piers Morgan was sacked after the newspaper published fake photographs purporting to show British soldiers abusing an Iraqi prisoner. An investigation later concluded that the photos had been staged. Following his departure from the tabloid newspaper, Piers Morgan revealed in his book *The Insider* how press photographers regularly worked with celebrities to capture photos that gave the impression that they were snapped surreptitiously when in fact they were agreed by both parties in advance.

This murky realm of celebrity photography is a niche within photojournalism and is most closely associated with the paparazzi. "Paps" suffer from a poor reputation owing to the tactics they employ to snap pictures of high profile people going about their usual daily routines. Paparazzi tend to be **freelance** and make their living selling photographs to tabloid newspapers and magazines, often for several thousand pounds an image. They track down celebrities and follow them with their long lens cameras in a behavior akin to stalking and harassment. Some stars have successfully achieved restraining orders against paparazzi or won damages for invasion of privacy. The most tragic case of paparazzi harassment was the deaths in 1997 of Princess Diana and Dodi Fayed, who were killed in a car crash as they were being pursued by photographers. The paparazzi were blamed for the death of the "People's Princess" and as a result the Press Complaints Commission – the regulatory body at the time – updated its code of practice to include the use of long-lens photography in private spaces and put regulation in place to protect children of celebrities. Meanwhile, in 2017, Kate Middleton and Prince William received €100,000 in damages after topless photos of the Duchess of Cambridge were published in French *Closer* magazine after being rejected by British tabloids. They were taken with a long-range lens camera half a mile away as Middleton sunbathed in a 640-acre estate in Provence. Photos such as these are potentially gold dust to paparazzi in a world where celebrity selfies and fan-snapped shots on the internet have cut the prices snappers can charge for photos. Veteran American paparazzi Cesar Pena told the *New York Post* that before Instagram a picture that now costs $400 would be worth up to $20,000. However, he uses social media to his advantage to track down celebrities from clues hidden in their selfies, such as the décor of their hotel room.

Digital advancements have also had a major impact on the production of photos that were previously processed from film in a darkroom. The development of editing software has enabled digital photos to be adjusted with additions, subtractions and modifications in post production. The most common industry software is Photoshop, which has led to its use as a verb and the practice of "photoshopping" images. This is prevalent in advertising and lifestyle magazines, where images of models are manipulated to change body shapes, skin tones and to remove blemishes. Manipulated images are also prevalent in **fake news**, creating verification challenges for news organizations that are constantly having to create additional measures to verify **user-generated content** before sharing it.

Indeed, the biggest impact on photojournalism has been the emergence of compact, accessible digital technology, which can be shared instantly and globally via social media by any non-professional. The audience has transformed into producers with "new technologies, new platforms and new methods of visual storytelling ... exerting a range of pressures and influences that require photojournalists to adapt and respond in different ways" (Haynes, Hadland and Lambert, 2017: 820). Every major political or natural event is captured with smartphones by citizen image-makers on the scene performing acts of accidental journalism (Allan, 2013) or, indeed, deliberating risking their lives to gather photographic testimony in an act of civic martyrdom (Andén-Papadopoulos, 2013). These content creators not only capture the images, but they also share them, edit them, mash them and mix them with other media (Hadland, Lambert and Campbell, 2016). As a result, billions of images are uploaded to the internet every day, to sites such as **Flickr, Twitter, Facebook**, Pinterest and **SnapChat**, making the field of photography crowded. This massification of image production has coincided with media company cutbacks and photographers have often been the first to go (Haynes, Hadland and Lambert, 2017). The content once provided by photojournalists is now scooped up online, largely for free, as the mainstream media blend user-generated content with their own words and imagery. Female photojournalists have been hit the hardest and continue to be underrepresented in the profession, leading to a further decline of the female gaze (Hadland and Barnett, 2018). Furthermore, photojournalists who continue to be employed by news organizations feel more at risk of physical harm or death in the digital era. Less than one in ten photographers say they are never exposed to risk at work and 92 percent acknowledge they are exposed to physical risk at some point (Hadland, Lambert and Campbell, 2016). One way of overcoming such risk, particularly when photographing war zones or natural disasters, is the use of remote controlled camera drones, which can take high quality aerial photographs with the operator being a safe distance away. However, although this lessens physical risks, there are potential legal pitfalls as this practice is still in its infancy and is banned in many countries.

See also **drone journalism**.

Key Sources

Evans, H. 1979 *Pictures on a Page: Photo-Journalism, Graphics and Picture Editing.* London: Book Club Associates

Hadland, A. and Barnett, C. 2018 "The Gender Crisis in Professional Photojournalism: Demise of the Female Gaze?" *Journalism Studies* 19(13): 2011–2020

Hadland, A., Lambert, P. and Campbell, D. 2016 "The Future of Professional Photojournalism: Perceptions of Risk" *Journalism Practice* 10(7): 820–832

PLATFORMS

More than just a website, a digital platform is a business model that allows producers and consumers to connect to it, interact with each other and create and exchange value (Castellani, 2016). Platforms have open connectivity enabling third party developers to create new services via **application programming interface** (API) and they are also easy to use independently, without any training needs. The aim of a platform is to address millions of consumers without performance degradation. O'Reilly and Battelle, the originators of the term **Web 2.0**, contend that digital platforms offer more than software as a service because they utilize collective intelligence networks to not only acquire users, but learn from them and build on their contributions. Platforms such as **YouTube, Facebook** and **Twitter** "depend on managing, understanding, and responding to massive amounts of user-generated data in real time" (O'Reilly and Battelle, 2009: 1). These colossal platforms have changed the way the public interact online, directly impacting upon the way in which journalists gather, produce, present and disseminate **news**.

Key Sources
Castellani, S. 2016 "Everything You Need to Know about Digital Platforms" *Stephane Castellani* http://stephane-castellani.com/everything-you-need-to-know-about-digital-platforms/

PODCAST, PODCASTING

A podcast is an audio or video file that can be downloaded to computers, laptops and portable devices such as MP3 players, tablets and **smartphones**. The expansive use of these latter devices has accelerated the recent growth in podcasts with US audiences almost doubling between 2008 and 2015. In 2014, podcasting achieved a significant audience milestone when the podcast Serial – which reinvestigated the 1999 murder of Maryland high school student Hae Min Lee – became the fastest podcast to reach five million streams or downloads in iTunes history (Vogt, 2015).

Podcasters include a great number of professional **journalists**, for example those who work at the BBC making programs which air as conventional, if digital, broadcasts but which are later available (sometimes with additional content) as podcasts (Starkey, 2017). But podcasts are also the terrain for academics, politicians, community groups and amateur enthusiasts of every stripe who are eager to podcast about their particular enthusiasms, political causes or current obsessions. Consequently, perhaps the most striking, if predictable, trend is the bourgeoning use of podcasts for **citizen journalism** (Park, 2016; Pew Research Center, 2013). Public perceptions of podcasting characterize it as an amateur/enthusiast activity, conducted outside formal news organizations and media institutions and, in that sense, somewhat akin to **blogging** (Pew Research Center, 2013).

But a recent comparative research, drawing on journalistic role conceptions of citizen podcasts in South Korea and the US, highlighted two significant findings. First, Americans view citizen podcasts as performing predominantly the role of *interpreters* of social and political issues, whereas Koreans favor the view of podcasters as *adversarial* and critical commentators on government. Second, Koreans trust citizen podcasts to a much greater degree than Americans. Consequently, Park (2016) concludes that citizen podcasts perform, "an alternative role in Korean journalism, while they complement professional journalism in the United States."

Key Sources

Park, C. S. 2016 "Citizen News Podcasts and Journalistic Role Conceptions in the United States and South Korea" *Journalism Practice* 11(9): 1158–1177

Pew Research Center 2013 "Over a Quarter of Internet Users Download or Listen to Podcasts" 27 December www.pewresearch.org/fact-tank/2013/12/27/over-aquarter-of-internet-users-download-or-listen-to-podcasts/

Vogt, N. 2015 *Podcasting: Fact Sheet.* Pew Research Center. www.journalism.org/2015/04/29/podcasting-fact-sheet

Starkey, G. 2017 "The New Kids on the Block: The Pictures, Text, Time-Shifted Audio and Podcasts of Digital Radio Journalism Online" in Eldridge, II, S. and Franklin, B. (Eds) *The Routledge Companion to Digital Journalism Studies* London: Routledge, 469–478

PRECISION JOURNALISM

The precursor to **computer assisted reporting**, precision journalism is a term that was coined by "the de facto godfather" (Coddington, 2015a: 333) Philip Meyer in his classic 1973 book (Meyer, 1973) where he encouraged journalists to use social science research techniques to increase the depth and accuracy of stories. At the time, this involved using methods such as surveys, sampling and content analysis to enable journalists to make their own definitive conclusions rather than relying on sources to give anecdotal evidence. The *Detroit Free Press* worked with Meyer to investigate the underlying causes of the 1967 summer riots via a quantitative survey and won a Pulitzer Prize for their subsequent coverage.

As technology progressed, these research methods became more heavily integrated with computer software, and developed into computer assisted reporting in the 1990s before evolving into the **computational journalism** and **data journalism** we see today.

Key Sources
Coddington, M. 2015a "Clarifying Journalism's Quantitative Turn: A Typology for Evaluating Data Journalism, Computational Journalism, and Computer-Assisted Reporting" *Digital Journalism* 3(3): 331–348
Meyer, P. 1973 *Precision Journalism*. Bloomington: Indiana University Press

PRODUSAGE

A theory developed by Axel Bruns in the 2000s, produsage recognizes how the internet has disrupted the traditional boundaries between users and producers of information. Bruns (2008) argues that the role of the consumer and end user have long disappeared due to the rise of collaborative creation in online media spaces such as blogs, **Wikipedia** and virtual world Second Life, where users lead content creation. In respect of **news** output specifically, Bruns and Highfield (2012) depict a shared space of news produsage that is most prevalent in **social media**, particularly **Twitter**, as participants who engage in random acts of journalism are neither simply users nor fully producers of news coverage, but placed in a hybrid role as "produser."

This merger of audience and journalist creates prosumers or produsers of us all, as online users participate in the production of news via creation and dissemination (Bowman and Willis, 2003) of content. The active involvement of users in **news** production has moved far beyond the traditional role of passive audience members; however, there is still much debate over where the control lies. The more open a news production system is to citizen participation the more produsers are able to influence the entire process of news production and distribution. But traditional news outlets are still tightly controlled by journalists, and "offer opportunities for citizen contribution only when they can filter the contribution, or where the contribution is clearly separated from the work of journalists" (Scott, Millard and Leonard, 2015).

Key Sources
Bruns, A. 2008 *Blogs, Wikipedia, Second Life and Beyond: From Production to Produsage.* London: Peter Lang
Bruns, A. and Highfield, T. 2012 "Blogs, Twitter and Breaking News: The Produsage of Citizen Journalism" in Lind, R. (Ed) *Produsing Theory in a Digital World 2.0: The Intersection of Audiences and Production in Contemporary Theory.* New York: Peter Lang, 15–32

PROPAGANDA MODEL

In their 1988 book, *Manufacturing Consent: The Political Economy of Mass Media*, Herman and Chomsky presented the propaganda model as an explanation for the reliance of news media on corporate and elite **sources**. The model views private media as businesses interested in the sale of a product – readers and **audiences** – to other businesses – advertisers – rather than to produce **news** to serve the public good. Herman and Chomsky argue that the news media serve political and/or economic elites, promoting their agenda and protecting their interests to the exclusion of democratic views. In that respect, the model is concerned with the relationship between government, corporation and commercial media and how this influences media content. Rather than explicitly conspire with elite forces, journalists behave and perform in a particular manner due to structural and financial factors.

Central to the propaganda model are the five filters on the production of news which influence the emphasis, tone and fullness of treatment which the media grants to different individuals, social groups and ideological perspectives. The five filters are:

- The size, ownership and profit orientation of the mass media;
- Advertising as the primary source of media income;
- Journalists' reliance on government, corporate and military sources;
- Flak as a method of controlling media dissidence;
- Anti-communism as a control ideology, framing media representation.

But the media landscape has dramatically altered since Herman and Chomsky set out their model 30 years ago, with the field of modern information and communication demonstrating the difficulty of reconciling propaganda (vertical and controlled communication) with social networking (horizontal and interactive communication) according to Papa (2012). Journalists now regularly incorporate non-elite sources into the reporting of breaking news by scouring **social media** for eyewitness content. Meanwhile, digital native websites that operate commercially are taking conscientious steps to include a **diversity** of voices and not rely on elite sources. Some even seem to welcome flak as a way of distinguishing themselves from mainstream media. Traditional **business models** are also adapting and moving away from reliance on **advertising** as a means to ensuring future sustainability and **non-profit journalism** is flourishing online, weakening the power of the five filters.

But while some factions of the news media are less influenced by the propaganda model, others are reinforcing the status quo. Goss (2013) argues that digitization has strengthened the ownership, advertising and sourcing filters and refutes the claim that the advent of new media has effectively rendered the propaganda model redundant. Instead, he argues the neo-liberal economy has encouraged the consolidation of media ownership and the creation of tech giants, leading to greater homogeny, a concentration of power and a news ecology obsessed with profit margins that poses a great risk to democracy. Furthermore, the exponential growth of the public relations industry and the pressure on journalists within a multimedia, 24/7 work environment has combined to create a system where **churnalism** rules at the expense of corroboration, fact checking and **investigative journalism**.

Key Sources
Goss, B. 2013 *Rebooting the Herman and Chomsky Propaganda Model in the 21st Century*. New York: Peter Lang Publishing
Herman, E. and Chomsky, N. 1988 *Manufacturing Consent: The Political Economy of the Mass Media*. New York: Pantheon

PROPUBLICA

Founded in 2008 by billionaires Herbert and Marion Sandler, former chief executives of the mortgage lender Golden West Financial Corporation, *ProPublica* is an award-winning non-profit **newsroom**. It became the first online news **source** to win a Pulitzer Prize for **investigative journalism** in 2010 for its examination of exhausted doctors working in a hospital cut off by the floodwaters of Hurricane Katrina. The American organization is largely funded by donations, including $10 million a year from the Sandler Foundation, and works closely with print news publications including the *New York Times* and the *New York Daily News*.

ProPublica's mission statement is to "expose abuses of power and betrayals of the public trust by government, business, and other institutions, using the moral force of investigative journalism to spur reform through the sustained spotlighting of wrongdoing" (*ProPublica*, 2018). It has a team of more than 75 journalists, many of whom are paid generous salaries of over $170,000.

ProPublica is one of the many non-profit **news** organizations that have sprung up online since the turn of the century (Konieczna, 2018). These platforms, funded by donations from the community or wealthy benefactors, have relatively low set up costs and promote audience involvement in the pursuit of public interest **journalism** (Carvajal, García-Avilés and González, 2012). They include The Ferret in Scotland, a registered co-operative that has both journalists and subscribers on its board.

See also **non-profit journalism**.

Key Sources
Konieczna, M. 2018 *Journalism without Profits: Making News When the Market Fails*. Oxford: Oxford University Press
ProPublica 2018 "About" www.propublica.org/about/

PUBLIC SERVICE

Public service **journalism**, public service broadcasting and public broadcasting is the production of content for the primary mission of public service. This involves speaking to, engaging with, and representing citizens either locally or nationally for public benefit rather than commercial gain. Funding usually comes from the government, via fees, or from foundations, public donation and not-for-profit corporations. In some countries, public broadcasting is run by a single organization whereas others have multiple operators in different regions and languages.

The British Broadcasting Corporation (**BBC**), launched in 1927, was the first of its kind and its model was emulated and adapted by countries around the world. The BBC principles include universal geographic accessibility, attention to minorities, direct funding and universality of payment, universal appeal and high quality programming. In some countries, public broadcasters are controlled by the government but in places such as the UK the BBC is completely independent and has its own editorial board. The UK also has public service embedded in Channel 4, a publicly owned, commercially funded public service broadcaster, and commercial broadcasters ITV and Channel 5 also have public service obligations they must meet.

Cultural polices are often addressed by public service broadcasters which ensure that content is provided in multiple national languages and represents a diverse cultural heritage. For example the Canadian Broadcasting Corporation is committed to bilingualism and employs journalists who speak both English and French. And in New Zealand, the public broadcasting system provides support to Maori broadcasting. Trust in public service broadcasters tends to be high and in the UK, Germany, Denmark, Italy, and Japan, they are the most trusted type of brand. In Greece, Hungary, and Spain, however, trust in public broadcasting is compromised by perceived government interference in editorial decisions or appointments (Newman, Fletcher, Kalogeropoulos, Levy and Nielsen, 2018).

Funding problems in the digital era have not hit public sector broadcasters as hard as their commercial counterparts since they do not rely on **advertising** revenue. However they face fiercer competition than ever before due to dispersed audiences online and a loss of television and radio audience share which began with the emergence of market-driven multi-channel broadcasting in the 1990s (Barnett and Seymour, 1999). The rise in popularity of podcasts available online has shifted audiences away from traditional public broadcasters, and similarly on demand subscription services Netflix and Amazon Prime are gaining the lion's share of young television audiences, along with video sharing website **YouTube**. In the UK, there has been continuous debate over whether the BBC licence fee should be scrapped and the corporation has made considerable cutbacks to its online offering as it tries to redirect money into developing its on demand service, the iPlayer (Moore, 2018).

Key Sources

Barnett, S. and Seymour, E. 1999 *A Shrinking Iceberg Travelling South: Changing Trends in British Television – A Case Study of Drama and Current Affairs*. London: Campaign for Quality Television

Newman, N., Fletcher, R., Kalogeropoulos, A., Levy, D. A. and Nielsen, R. K. 2018 *Reuters Institute Digital News Report 2018*. Oxford, UK: Reuters Institute for the Study of Journalism

RECIPROCAL JOURNALISM

An idea conceptualized by Lewis, Holton and Coddington (2014) which frames the way in which journalists might develop more mutually beneficial relationships with **audiences** in order to build trust, connectedness and social capital in online settings. They argue that community journalism is the key conduit for a more reciprocal form of **journalism** that "goes beyond mere engagement and participation in the service of news organizations" (2014: 232). With reciprocal journalism, the end goal is mutual benefit with citizens' concerns at its heart rather than encouraging participation to suit a news organization's own interests or bottom line. Lewis, Holton and Coddington (2014: 237) surmise that by more readily acknowledging and reciprocating the input of audiences and fostering spaces for audiences to reciprocate with each other, "journalists can begin to fulfil their normative purpose as stewards of the communities they serve."

Their formula for effective reciprocal journalism is divided into three levels: Direct reciprocity such as one-to-one exchanges between journalists and audiences, indirect reciprocity, which encompasses one-to-many exchanges and is intended for community benefit, and sustained reciprocity through continuous exchanges that lead to longer-term relationships (Coddington, Lewis and Holton, 2018).

In practice, reciprocal journalism is still in its infancy and there is a continued reluctance among journalist to develop reciprocally oriented relationships with audiences. A survey of American journalists (Holton, Lewis and Coddington, 2016) revealed that journalists tended to put higher value on engagement and reciprocity in offline settings than interactions online. Although journalists were open to building relationships with audiences this was "mostly on their own terms and not necessarily for the long term" (Holton, Lewis and Coddington, 2016: 856). However, some inroads are being made in hyperlocal media in the UK with a study by Harte, Williams and Turner (2017) indicating that reciprocal exchange offline and online successfully underpins the work of many hyperlocal publishers.

See also **geo-social news, hyperlocal journalism**.

Key Sources

Coddington, M., Lewis, S. C. and Holton, A. E. 2018 "Measuring and Evaluating Reciprocal Journalism as a Concept" *Journalism Practice* 12(8): 1039–1050

Harte, D., Williams, A. and Turner, J. 2017 "Reciprocity and the Hyperlocal Journalist" *Journalism Practice* 11(2–3): 160–176.

Holton, A. E., Lewis, S. C. and Coddington, M. 2016 "Interacting with Audiences: Journalistic Role Conceptions, Reciprocity, and Perceptions about Participation" *Journalism Studies* 17(7): 849–859

Lewis, S. C., Holton, A. E. and Coddington, M. 2014 "Reciprocal Journalism: A Concept of Mutual Exchange between Journalists and Audiences" *Journalism Practice* 8(2): 229–241

REDDIT

Launched on June 23rd 2005 and based in Medford, Massachusetts, Reddit (https://www.reddit.com/) is a **social news** site employing **citizen journalism** to facilitate a public conversation around a wide range of topics, although its content focuses on news more than is typical for cognate sites. Its content is listed in a drop-down menu of 49 Subreddits that embrace Announcements, Arts, Books and History, moving via Space to World News and Writing Prompts (https://www.reddit.com/). Its proud boast is captured in the slogan that Reddit is "The Front Page of the Internet."

The quality of its news reporting is enhanced by the lack of any restriction on word or character counts (unlike the initial 140 character limit which restricts **Twitter** conversations, which was doubled in November 2017). Consequently, Reddit is popular with people seeking news, seeking to post news but also seeking to comment on news. The site is the tenth most visited in the US, ranked 32nd globally and has 45 percent of users living outside the USA (Suran and Kilgo, 2015). Reddit is global in reach and expansive in numbers of users, influence and reputation (Chen, 2012).

A recent research study focused on media reporting of the Boston Marathon bombing concluded that Reddit's reputation was boosted by the quality of its coverage of the Boston events and mainstream media's reliance on that reporting. Posts to the site included "a comprehensive, streaming timeline of occurrences, information that the mainstream media did not immediately cover, such as eye witness and personal accounts; pertinent news links; attempts to identify the bombers; and additional material that users considered important information" (Kilgo, 2015). Moreover, Reddit's discussions of public affairs typically draw on a wide range of sources (legacy and digitally native) including "government sources [the largest source type cited], blogs, commercial sites, original images and video, non-profit websites including campaign sites, alternative news media, and peer produced sites" (Straub-Cook, 2018), which adds to Reddit's authority as a new source.

This prominence is acknowledged in a Pew Research Center Study which found that Reddit topped all other social networking sites which were visited to find news even though the sample included very popular and well regarded sites such as **Facebook**, Google Plus, MySpace and **Twitter** (Holcomb, Gottfried and Mitchell, 2013). Suran and Kilgo claim that the posting of news content on Reddit makes its users important "information gatekeepers" (Suran and Kilgo, 2015).

Key Sources

Chen, B. 2012 "How Reddit Scooped the Press on the Aurora Shootings" Bits Blog *New York Times*, July 23. http://bits.blogs.nytimes.com/2012/07/23/reddit-aurora-shooter-aff/

Straub-Cook, P. 2018 "Source Please? A Content Analysis of Links Posted in Discussions of Public Affairs on Reddit" *Digital Journalism* 6(10):1314–1332

Suran, M. and Kilgo, D. 2015 "Freedom from the Press: How Anonymous Gatekeepers on Reddit Covered the Boston Marathon Bombing" *Journalism Studies* 18(8): 1035–1051, doi:10.1080/1461670X.2015.1111160

REVENUE STREAMS *SEE* ADVERTISING; BUSINESS MODELS; CROWDSOURCING; PAYWALLS

RIGHT TO BE FORGOTTEN

The rather unflattering but innovative ethical and legal claim that citizens should enjoy the right to be forgotten has assumed an unprecedented significance for **digital journalism** and **digital journalism ethics** (Shapiro and MacLeod Rogers, 2019). Asserting the right to be removed from online public accounts of particular events is also referred to as "unpublishing decisions" (McNealy and Alexander, 2018), the "right to erasure" or even the "right to oblivion." Possession of this entitlement is growing. An individual citizen's claim to enjoy some element of control over information published about them is now recognized in the European Union (Shapiro and MacLeod Rogers, 2019: 324).

The substantive claim made here is that citizens should enjoy a human right and legal entitlement to be "forgotten" by being removed from published accounts of a particular news item, not because the report is necessarily inaccurate or untrue (although that may be the case in some instances), but because news coverage may be proving personally damaging for those individuals. In this sense, the concern with the right to be forgotten has connections with society's long-standing legal, ethical and regulatory concern to protect the privacy of individuals.

There are many circumstances in which such reputational damage could arise. People may have made indiscreet personal disclosures of information in their youth, or committed minor misdemeanours, for example, which they now regret and wish to remove from the "digital public record." The issues here are complex for **journalists** as well as lawyers and ethicists. Paradoxically, for example, sexually explicit photographs published by one party to a relationship following the conclusion of that relationship, often referred to in press reports as "revenge porn," may, in turn, become the basis for a new **journalism** story even if it is about how "victims" of such photographs are seeking legal redress and remedy.

Such problematic reporting and burgeoning claims to the right to be forgotten become more acute in the context of **digital journalism** because enhanced and ready accessibility to **news** stories, especially via search engines such as **Google**, means that specific news content can be read by more people (not least because of the ability to "share" news items) and, consequently, enjoys a greater potential to cause harm to individuals who appear in news items. And all this at a time when the **affordances** of digital media technologies mean alterations to the historical record can be more readily achieved.

Shapiro and MacLeod Rogers identify "six ethical principles" involved in the "unpublishing debate" with three tending to "foster continuity of publication even of potentially harmful material" and a further three tending "in the opposite direction." Those favoring continuity of publication include the requirement to defend freedom of expression, the need to protect (in its original form) the historical record and, finally, accountability. Principles which favor restricting publication include the reduction of harm to individuals, a respect for privacy and the notion of redemption, which involves cognate notions of individuals deserving a second chance and the opportunity to place previous and distant misdemeanours behind them (Shapiro and MacLeod Rogers, 2019: 329–330).

See also **digital journalism ethics**.

Key Sources

Shapiro, I. and MacLeod Rogers, B. 2019 "Who Owns the News? The 'Right to Be Forgotten' and Journalists' Conflicting Principles" in Eldridge, II, S. and Franklin, B. (Eds) *The Routledge Handbook of Developments in Digital Journalism Studies*. London: Routledge, 324–336

McNealy, J. E. and Alexander, L. B. 2018 "A Framework for Unpublishing Decisions" *Digital Journalism* 6(3): 389–405

ROBOT JOURNALISM *SEE* ALGORITHMIC JOURNALISM; ARTIFICIAL INTELLIGENCE; NEWS BOTS

RSS FEEDS

Developed at the turn of the century, an RSS feed is a Rich Site Summary, more commonly known as a Really Simple Syndication. The web feed allows users to access updates from online content in a standardized, computer-readable format via a feed reader. **News** feeds allow users to see when websites such as BBC News have added new content. Rather than revisiting the news website, a user can open their news reader application and see all of the latest headlines and videos in one place, from multiple sources, as soon as they are published. The most popular RSS feeds on BBC News are Top Stories, World and UK (BBC, 2011).

RSS Feeds were once a popular way of organizing online content to enable users to view news updates all in one place. News organizations had multiple feeds for different types of content and the orange RSS Feed button could be easily spotted at the top of web stories. In the early 2000s, RSS was everywhere, every website masthead had an RSS feed icon and every blog category and news topic had its own independent feed that a user could subscribe to (MH Themes, 2018). These feeds consisted of a list of news that the user had subscribed to and had limited images and no sharing capability.

Although RSS readers such as Feedly, NewsBlur and Feed Wrangler still exist today, their inevitable demise was strongly signaled by the closure of Google Reader in 2013. In their place, **social media** platforms and news **apps** have flourished, enabling users to customize feeds, share content and access high quality multimedia aesthetics.

Key Sources

BBC 2011 "News Feeds from the BBC" BBC News www.bbc.co.uk/news/10628494

MH Themes 2018 "Is RSS Dead? The Uses and Benefits of RSS Feeds for Websites Today and Beyond" MH Themes www.mhthemes.com/blog/uses-and-benefits-of-rss-feeds/

SCARECROW JOURNALISM

A central function of **news journalism** has been to maintain oversight and scrutiny of the activities of powerful economic and political institutions to make them accountable in the public interest. But since the **disruption** of many traditional **local** and regional **newspapers** and their replacement with **hyperlocal** or online community papers, with reduced journalistic staffs complemented by **citizen journalists**, academic observers have begun to query whether these replacements have sufficient economic and editorial resources to maintain this democratic, watchdog function effectively. A study of the local government content in 48 citizen journalism sites, 86 weekly newspapers and 138 daily newspapers found that it differed sufficiently for the researchers to conclude that, "citizen journalism sites are, at best, imperfect information substitutes for most newspapers" (Fico, Lacy, Wildman, Baldwin, Began and Zube, 2013: 152).

But, more recently, Anderson, Bell and Shirky (2014) have suggested that in the age of **digital journalism**, the metaphorical press watchdog is complemented by the less evident but effective journalism "scarecrow." The latter discourages malpractice by the possible threat of exposure resulting from the routine and regular coverage of issues (including the constant surveillance which is achieved by investigative **data journalism** activities), while the watchdog delivers episodic, but deeper and investigative, reporting that uncovers misdemeanours (Howells, 2015: 70–71). The press watchdog will still bark periodically, while scarecrow journalism exercises a more furtive constraint; the mere presence of the scarecrow, the fact that potential transgressors know the scarecrow is out there watching, provides sufficient disincentive often enough to constrain bad behaviour on the part of powerful institutions (Anderson, Bell and Shirky, 2014).

Key Sources

Anderson, C. W., Bell, E. and Shirky, C. 2014 *Post Industrial Journalism: Adapting to the Present.* Retrieved from http://towcenter.org/research/post-industrial-journalism-adapting-to-the-present-2/

Chua, R. 2013 "The Scarecrow and the Watchdog" http://gijn.org/2013/03/28/the-scarecrow-and-the-watchdog/ (28th March)

Fico, F., Lacy, S., Wildman, S., Baldwin, T., Bergan, D. and Zube, P. 2013 "Citizen Journalism Sites as Information Substitutes and Complements for United States Newspaper Coverage of Local Government" *Digital Journalism* 1 (1): 152–168

Howells, R. 2015 "Journey to the Centre of a News Black Hole: Examining the Democratic Deficit in a Town with No Newspaper" PhD Thesis, Cardiff University

SHOVELWARE

A mostly derogatory term used to describe content taken from one communication medium to another with little or no change. The practice of shoveling content from print to online was common in the early years of online news (Pavlik, 2001) when the words from the previous day's newspaper were uploaded to the web verbatim. Most **news** providers quickly abandoned the practice of shovelware (Hall, 2001) because the content did not appeal to users due to its lack of originality, **interactivity** or **hypertext** presentation.

According to Hermida (2013) the initial approach to **Twitter** by media organizations a decade later was also one of shovelware. Material was shoveled onto Twitter by journalists who tweeted headlines and a link back the news website rather than posting original content. In many organizations, this was an automatic feed generated by the news website every time an item was published. However, over time, as with print shovelware, there was a shift away from automated Twitter accounts as the **social media** platform became a place to develop brand identity.

Contemporary echoes of shovelware are the repurposing of traditional print and broadcast content for online audiences. Video packages from television news may be placed online with additional written context, or a print story may be uploaded to a newspaper website with a different headline, extra images and embedded hyperlinks. There are also links with **churnalism**, as journalists repurpose the text from press releases to the web without any fact checking, in a frantic bid to churn out copy.

See also *Flat Earth News*.

Key Sources
Pavlik, J. 2001 *Journalism and New Media*. New York: Columbia University Press

SKYPE

As a telecommunication application software, Skype enables users to conduct free video and voice calls via the internet between computers, tablets, **smartphones**, games consoles and even smart watches, using microphones and webcams. Users can now also transmit and exchange video and text content and make calls to landline and mobile phones over traditional networks for a fee. The name Skype derives from the concept "sky peer-to-peer." Far from being a product of Silicon Valley, the application was collaboratively developed in Europe and was first released in 2003 by Swede Niklas Zennström and Dane Janus Friis, in cooperation with Estonians Ahti Heinla, Priit Kasesalu, and Jaan Tallinn who created the software. At the end of 2010, Skype had obtained over

SKYPE

660 million worldwide users and by July 2018 it had over 300 million active users per month (Statistica, 2018). The Luxemborg-based Skype Technologies was acquired by eBay in 2005 before being sold to private equity firm, Silver Lake, venture capitalists Andreessen Horowitz, and the Canada Pension Plan Investment Board in 2009. It was then snapped up by Microsoft for $8.5billion in 2011, with the software giant keeping the development team in Estonia.

The encrypted internet phone service enables journalists to replace telephone interviews with video interviews, allowing them to read body language and build up a rapport with interviewees. Since calls are free at both ends, it means mobile and **freelance** journalists can avoid huge telephone bills (Gahran, 2008) and talk to sources for indefinite periods of time. The software has also become a powerful tool for journalists and citizen journalists alike, as it enables communication through multiple internet enabled devices and does not rely on tethered landlines or induce expensive charges. Via Skype, journalists are able to conduct video interviews with citizens in war-torn countries and broadcast live on mainstream television, empowering **citizen witnessing**.

However, Skype is not without its dangers, particularly from government intervention. In 2008, the Electronic Frontier Foundation asked the Federal Bureau of Investigation whether it had the capability to hack into Skype communications, after news broke that the German government had commissioned a program to hack into Skype calls there (Kirchner, 2014). The same year, researchers revealed that the Chinese version of Skype was being monitored by the government and a malicious spyware was being circulated on the software to target Syrian activists. In July 2012, nine months after Microsoft bought Skype, the National Security Agency in the US tripled the amount of Skype calls being collected through **surveillance** program Prism to share with intelligence agencies (Greenwald, 2013). Grégoire Pouget, an information security expert at Reporters Without Borders, told the *Guardian* in 2013: "If you are a journalist working on issues that could interest the US government or some of their allies, you should not use Skype" (Gallagher, 2013).

Key Sources

Gallagher, R. 2013 "Skype under Investigation in Luxembourg over Link to NSA" *Guardian* www.theguardian.com/technology/2013/oct/11/skype-ten-microsoft-nsa

Kirchner, L. 2014 "Why Skype Isn't Safe for Journalists" *Columbia Journalism Review* https://archives.cjr.org/behind_the_news/skype_alternatives.php

Statistica 2018 "Most Famous Social Network Sites Worldwide as of July 2018, Ranked by Number of Active Users (In Millions)" *Statistica* www.statista.com/statistics/272014/global-social-networks-ranked-by-number-of-users/

SLOW JOURNALISM

The antidote to the contemporary journalistic environment which places emphasis on speed and production over quality and ethics. The slow journalism movement, which has been gaining momentum over the past decade, is not prescriptive but acts as a counterbalance to the limitations of contemporary **journalism** practice (Le Masurier, 2015). Neveu (2016) argues that the term has many possible meanings, including journalism that takes time, is investigative, longer form narrative, fair, transparent, ethical, serves a community, participatory or tells untold stories. Much of this slow journalism comes from a perceived crisis of quality journalism under pressure, and has emerged from alternative spaces away from the mainstream media. Start-ups include *De Correspondent* in the Netherlands, *Delayed Gratification* in the UK and *Slow News* in Italy. These alternative news organizations have created a range of **business models** that often avoid **advertising** and utilize **crowd funding**, brand sponsorship, subscriptions and high cover prices as publishers believe readers are willing to pay for stories written to a higher journalistic standard (Dowling, 2016).

Slow journalism also embraces multimedia, not just the printed or digital word, and for photojournalist David Burnett it is a means to create a significantly different aesthetic in an age of instant digital images. His acts of slow journalism have permanently captured Hurricane Katrina, the Sochi Winter Olympic Games and the survivors of the Pinochet regime in Chile, forcing viewers to mindfully question and think about the subject matter (Mendelson and Creech, 2016). Even more ambitious is the multimedia project Out of Eden Walk by Paul Salopek, which saw him travel the world on foot from Ethiopia to South America tracing the pathway of human migration out of Africa. He reported the journey via **long form narrative** magazine articles, videos, photographs, audio files and social media posts. This became the basis of a course at Virginia Commonwealth University, where students have developed their own slow journalism walk (Belt and South, 2015).

Key Sources

Belt, D. and South, J. 2015 "Slow Journalism and the Out of Eden Walk" *Digital Journalism* 4(4): 547–562

Le Masurier, M. 2015 "What Is Slow Journalism?" *Journalism Practice* 9(2): 138–152

Mendelson, A. and Creech, B. 2016 "'Make Every Frame Count': the Practice of Slow Photojournalism in the Work of David Burnett" *Digital Journalism* 4(4): 512–529

Neveu, E. 2016 "On Not Going Too Fast with Slow Journalism" *Journalism Practice* 10(4): 448–460

SMARTPHONES

The rapid expansion of mobile technology in the past two decades has led to the truism that the majority of the world's population now own a mobile phone. By 2019, the number of mobile phone users in the world was expected to pass the five billion mark, an estimated 65 percent of the earth's population. The increasing popularity of smartphones, led by vendors Samsung and Apple, has created such a vast market that, by 2021, 40 percent of the world will own one (Statista, 2018b). It is not an overstatement to say that this immense reach is dramatically changing the way in which people consume **news** and how it is produced by journalists and distributed by news organizations.

Prior to smartphones, users largely accessed the internet via a physical connection from a phone wall jack to a computer, and later, via wireless routers. But the development of compact, touchscreen smartphones with a decent battery life and mobile access to the internet has transformed communication, making it truly mobile. Smartphones are effectively a multi-purpose mobile computing device with the ability to connect to the internet and facilitate software, web browsing, multimedia playback and, once in a while, make an offline telephone call. Rather than having a QWERTY keyboard like the BlackBerrys of the 2000s, the latest smartphones support multi-touch gestures, offer the ability to download or purchase additional applications from a centralized store and use cloud storage as well as mobile payment services. The first smartphone was the iPhone, launched in 2007 by Steve Jobs, the deceased CEO of Apple.

The most significant development in smartphones has been the introduction of software applications, known as **apps**. It is possible for anyone with the technological know-how to develop an app and make it available to the world. Apps make it easier for users to access niche content without the need to browse and navigate the web. In 2010, app was listed as the Word of the Year by the American Dialect Society. **News** organizations have leapt upon the opportunity to create their own personalized apps to reach and engage busy, distracted and dispersed audiences. This race to develop smartphone-friendly news products has introduced a new actor into the field of **online journalism**, that of the app developer. Their role is to create mobile news apps that generate "novel news experiences that live in between news content production and consumption" (Ananny and Crawford, 2015: 193). These developers do not source original content but instead, through a set of interface and algorithm design decisions, create the conditions under which audiences encounter and circulate personalized content. Ananny and Crawford define these designers as an emerging "liminal press," who do not self-identify as journalists but nonetheless define the conditions under which news is created and circulated (2015: 193). In the new transitionary world of app-led **journalism** there is a focus on personalized information, consumers and audience size over the normative function of public service.

See also **mobile news, MOJO journalism, tablet**.

Key Sources

Ananny, M. and Crawford, K. 2015 "A Liminal Press: Situating News App Designers within A Field of Networked News Production" *Digital Journalism* 3(2): 192–208

Statista 2018b "Number of Mobile Phone Users Worldwide from 2015 to 2020 (In Billions)" *Statista* www.statista.com/statistics/274774/forecast-of-mobile-phone-users-worldwide/

SNAPCHAT

Originally launched in July 2011 under the name Picaboo, the multimedia messaging app was relaunched as Snapchat two months later and is today owned by technology and camera company Snap Inc. Cofounder Evan Spiegel, who created Snapchat with fellow Stanford University students Bobby Murphy and Reggie Brown, was named the youngest billionaire in the world in 2015.

Live life in the moment is the ethos of the popular platform, which only allows pictures, videos and messages to be available for a short time. Instead of placing an emphasis on capturing the perfect picture, Snapchat presents itself as a fun photo sharing tool to express the full range of human emotions while avoiding the stress caused by the longevity of personal information on social media (Spiegel, 2012). Users are able to overlay quirky virtual stickers and augmented reality objects onto videos and photos – known as snaps. At the time of writing, the app had amassed 188 million daily active users worldwide, creating three billion snaps daily. More than 70 percent of Snapchat users are under 35 and in the US 78 percent are aged 18 to 24.

In order to monetize content, Snapchat launched Discover in 2015, an area containing channels of short form content from media brands including **Buzzfeed, BBC** One, CNN, ESPN, VICE and the *New York Post*. These include advertisements, text and videos plus interactive features such as polls. Media organizations continue to experiment with content for Snapchat Discover, particularly vertical video in a bid to capture the hard to reach younger audience. And as the use of **Facebook** as a source of news declines, Snapchat has seen slight growth in the number of consumers using it for **news** (Newman, Fletcher, Kalogeropoulos, Levy and Nielsen, 2018).

Discover also features a number of original shows, including NBC News' *Stay Tuned*, a twice-daily broadcast that reaches five million people a day and a version of ESPN's *SportsCenter* which reaches 17 million people a month. In an effort to find new avenues for growth following falling user accounts, Snapchat launched Snap Originals in October 2018, a slate of self-produced programs. The shows are all shot vertically, with episodes an average of five minutes in length interspersed by adverts lasting a few seconds (Newton, 2018).

Key Sources

Newton, C. 2018 "Snapchat Announces a Slate of Original Programming for Discover" *The Verge* www.theverge.com/2018/10/10/17955916/snap-origi nals-snapchat-programming-endless-summer

SOCIAL INFLUENCE

Individuals on **social media** who possess the power to affect the purchase decisions of others due to their authority, knowledge, position or relationship with their audience are said to have social influence. These influencers build a reputation for their knowledge and expertise on a particular niche topic and make regular posts on their preferred social media channels, in particular **YouTube** and **Instagram**, generating a large following of "enthusiastic engaged people who pay close attention to their views" (Influencer Marketing Hub, 2018). Most social influencers are either celebrities, industry experts, bloggers or micro influencers, defined as everyday people who have become known for a specialist niche, such as UK fashion and beauty blogger Zoella. Although the number of followers is important, it is not the only indicator of clout, as an influencer's relationship and interaction with their followers is also highly valued. Brands court social media influencers, paying them sponsorship or giving them free products in return for positive coverage which will encourage their followers to buy the products they promote. This can be as straightforward as posting a photograph wearing a particular brand on a regular basis, also known as product placement. Some influencers have risen from obscurity to earn several million dollars a year.

This type of insidious **advertising**, which feeds off anxiety and low self-esteem, is having a damaging impact on **journalism** as brands move away from traditional television and print advertisement to contracts with social media influencers (Noor, 2018). There is also competition over audience share, as young people's time and attention is drawn away from traditional media outlets towards following social media vloggers and bloggers. Lifestyle journalists face increasing competition with influencers over access to events, products and **sources**. Brands increasingly prefer to engage with sycophantic "cheerleading media" over quality, impartial reviewers who may criticize their product (Lethlean, 2016). This has created an environment where businesses expect supportive, positive coverage rather than the honestly held opinion of a specialist **journalist** and **audiences** are not always aware whether a post is genuine or not.

See also **vlogs**.

Key Sources

Influencer Marketing Hub 2018 "What Is an Influencer?" https://influencermar ketinghub.com/what-is-an-influencer/

Lethlean, J. 2016 "Restaurant Reviews: Bloggers Don't Cut the Mustard" *The Weekend Australian* www.theaustralian.com.au/life/food-wine/restaurant-

reviews-bloggers-dont-cut-the-mustard/news-story/480db526e3ff92c9264
cebe7efbdd2a3

Noor, P. 2018 "Brands are Cashing in on Social Media Envy, and Using Influencers to Sell It" *Guardian* www.theguardian.com/commentisfree/ 2018/nov/05/brands-cashing-in-social-media-envy-influencers

SOCIAL MEDIA

The collective term for interactive **Web 2.0** internet-based applications that enable the creation and sharing of multimedia information via many-to-many communication. Prior to Web 2.0, websites only enabled one-to-many communication, limiting the networked capacity of virtual communities (O'Reilly, 2005). Popular social media networks include **Facebook, Twitter, YouTube, Reddit** and **Instagram**. These are not to be confused with multimedia messaging apps such as **WhatsApp** and **Snapchat**, which enable users to share content within a more secure environment with encryption and time controls.

Social media has grown exponentially over the past decade and it is estimated that in 2019 there will be around 2.77 billion social network users across the globe, with 71 percent of internet users on social networks (Statista, 2018a). Like the trashy "penny dreadfuls" of the 19th century or the British tabloid press that preceded the internet, social media has been castigated for perpetuating the ills of society and blamed for the loss of social conscience. And yet, like all of the internet, it simply reflects the world in which we live and enables people to connect and communicate for better or worse. Within the field of journalism it is an effective tool for reaching mass audiences, empowering users via **citizen journalism, citizen witnessing** and **user-generated content** and sourcing global data. But it is also home to cyber bullying, trolling and incitement of violence, with journalists often on the receiving end.

Key Sources

O'Reilly, T. 2005 "What Is Web 2.0" *O'Reilly* www.oreilly.com/pub/a//web2/ archive/what-is-web-20.html

Statista 2018a "Number of Social Network Users Worldwide from 2010 to 2021 (In Billions)" *Statista* www.statista.com/statistics/278414/number-of-world wide-social-network-users/

SOCIAL MEDIA EDITOR

While some functions of the **editor** in a **news** organization are reducing, reflecting the development of **digital journalism** technologies, innovative editorial roles are emerging; one such role is that of the social media editor. This role is expanding rapidly with the LinkedIn website offering 647 posts for Social Media Editors in 2018 (LinkedIn, 2018). The tasks involved in being a social media editor reflect the needs of the particular organization and are, consequently, highly variable.

In general terms, social media editors manage a news organization's social media image, create engaging content for their users and try to reach new readers and to create the public brand of the company on **social media**. More specifically, social media editors may: "handle **Twitter** accounts for my newspaper"; establish accounts for reporters who wish to **tweet**; handle "all things **Facebook**"; coordinate "all the **blogging** that we do both internally and externally" and; experiment with harnessing "tools like **Twitter**." Social media editors also contribute to the organizations' revenues and "make money." Another social media editor explained their role as being

> the chief strategist for our newsroom's use of new social media tools. I work with our staff members to more effectively engage our community, I write a weekly in-house newsletter on best practices and give brown bag-style seminars on new and effective techniques. I also spend a fair amount of time reading up on the latest on the intersection of journalism and social media so we can continue to innovate. I'm also the editor of our college football fan site, which is an aggregator that is heavy on social media.
>
> (*Adweek*, 2010)

As **journalists** have increasingly come to view **social media** as a potential site and **source** for **journalism**, most news organizations have now agreed and adopted a set of **social media guidelines** with which journalists must comply in their professional practice (Opgenhaffen and Scheerlink, 2014).

See also **editor**.

Key Sources

Ad week 2010 "What Exactly Is a Social Media Editor/Manager?" *Adweek* www.adweek.com/digital/what-exactly-is-social-media/

LinkedIn JOBS 2018 https://uk.linkedin.com/jobs/social-media-editor-jobs

Opgenhaffen, M. and Scheerlink, H. 2014 "Social Media Guidelines for Journalists: An Investigation into the Sense and Nonsense among Flemish Journalists" *Journalism Practice* 8(6): 726–741

SOCIAL MEDIA GUIDELINES

The emergence of the new editorial role of **social media editor**, to encourage and guide **journalists'** expansive uses of **social media** as both **source** and **audience** for their **news** stories, has prompted news organizations to compile and distribute Social Media Guidelines to regulate, with differing degrees of required compliance, journalists' professional practice concerning **social media** such as **Facebook, Instagram** and **Twitter** and their contributions to sourcing, breaking, diffusing and reporting news stories (Opgenhaffen and Sheerlink, 2014).

Michael Opgenhaffen and Harald Sheerlink, in their research based on interviews with Flemish journalists about their journalistic work with **Twitter**, reported that the majority believed that the development of rules and protocols to govern their professional behavior and contacts with social media were mostly unnecessary. Journalists suggested that their education, training, working experience and professional commitments to such values as **transparency**, accuracy and truth telling offered sufficient guidance to manage their relationships with social media (Opgenhaffen and Scheerlink, 2014: 726). Some journalists believe that the enforcement of such guidelines, moreover, may imply wholly unacceptable consequences, either because they restrict journalists' professional autonomy and freedom of speech or, worse, because such requirements constitute little more than an attempt to promote the news organization and its corporate brand. Journalists' ambivalence is recorded in other interview-based studies (Brantzaeg, Folstad and Chappero-Dominguez, 2017).

Given the concerns of politicians, the public and journalists concerning **fake news**, however, the expansion of such guidelines to contain, if not reduce, fake news via journalistic practices such as **fact checking** seems likely (Graves, 2016).

Key Sources

Brantzaeg, P., Folstad, A. and Chaperro-Dominguez, M. A. 2017 "Usefulness and Trust in Online Fact-Checking and Verification Services" *Journalism Practice*, doi:10.1080/17512786.2017.1363657

Graves, L. 2016 *Deciding What's True: The Rise of Political Fact-Checking in American Journalism*. New York: Columbia University Press

Opgenhaffen, M. and Scheerlink, H. 2014 "Social Media Guidelines for Journalists: An Investigation into the Sense and Nonsense among Flemish Journalists" *Journalism Practice* 8(6): 726–741, doi:10.1080/17512786.2013.869421

SOURCES

The **news** production process relies on sources, which are the people, places and organizations that supply journalists with information and ideas for potential stories. Often referred to as "contacts," journalists' human sources can vary from anonymous tip-offs to regular briefings with public sector bodies. Sources can also be material such as news cuttings, archive footage, documents or information found on websites. A reporter will need to build up trust with regular contacts (Randall, 2000), who may be the key to an investigation or the source of ready-made content in the form of press releases or access to government spokespeople. Journalists sometimes receive information off the record, meaning it is not for public release or to be directly attributed to an individual.

The protection of sources is a fundamental principle in journalism but many fear it is being undermined by government legislation. *Guardian* editor Katherine Viner, who has backed a report on Protecting Sources and Whistleblowers in a Digital Age, has urged for more journalism training on the practicalities and limitations of protecting sources in an age of increased government **surveillance**. Viner heavily criticizes the Investigatory Powers Act, which she claims "enables law enforcement and agencies to access journalists' data without the journalist ever knowing" (Mayhew, 2017).

The information age has drastically changed the way in which journalists source information, with a shift away from face-to-face and telephone interviews in favor of emails, encrypted WhatsApp messages and **Skype** chats. Gone are the days of digging through thousands of pages of documents in a library basement, as reporters can now search through public data online or submit a freedom of information request. Journalists now consult websites, blogs, search engines, **social media** networks and collaborative platforms such as **Wikipedia** and **Wikileaks** to gather and check information from a variety of actors (Lecheler and

Kruikemeier, 2016). In the world of minute-by-minute news cycles, online sources are a quick, effective and cheap way for journalists to gather information on developing stories (Van Leuven, Kruikemeier, Lecheler and Hermans, 2018). From these multiple online sources, journalists gather background research behind the scenes such as monitoring **Twitter** for story inspiration and breaking news (Johnson, Paulussen and Van Aelst, 2018). When a major news story or crisis does break, journalists turn to the internet for information and to search for **user-generated content** shot on **smartphones** or embed posts from social media in live blogs. This speed of reporting has led to legitimate concerns surrounding verification of sources and the spread of misinformation and **fake news**.

The use of online sourcing practices has frequently been associated with the democratization of **news** because it potentially enables journalists to access non-elite actors and represent more diverse voices. Yet, research demonstrates that journalists continue to rely upon elite sources within the digital environment (Deprez and Van Leuven, 2018). Indeed, the pressure of the 24/7 multimedia news cycle and subsequent increased workloads lends itself to journalists sticking to old sourcing routines and relying on public relations (Von Nordheim, Boczek and Koppers, 2018) as a quick source of information. Content analysis of UK news websites also indicates that most news domains are still dominated by elite actors, with the exception of sports live blogs (Thorsen and Jackson, 2018). Studies, therefore, repeatedly demonstrate that journalists continue to rely on a limited number of elite sources (Van Leuven, Kruikemeier, Lecheler and Hermans, 2018).

See also *Flat Earth News*.

Key Sources

Lecheler, S. and Kruikemeier, S. 2016 "Re-Evaluating Journalistic Routines in a Digital Age: A Review of Research on the Use of Online Sources" *New Media & Society* 18(1): 156–171

Van Leuven, S., Kruikemeier, S., Lecheler, S. and Hermans, L. 2018 "Online and Newsworthy: Have Online Sources Changed Journalism?" *Digital Journalism* 6 (7): 798–806

Von Nordheim, G., Boczek, K. and Koppers, L. 2018 "Sourcing the Sources: An Analysis of the Use of Twitter and Facebook as a Journalistic Source over 10 Years in the *New York Times*, the *Guardian* and *Süddeutsche Zeitung*" *Digital Journalism* 6(7): 807–828, doi:10.1080/21670811.2018.1490658

STYLE GUIDE

The use of language is at the forefront of **journalism**, where a hack's reputation can be ruined with a misspelt name, grammatical error or errant punctuation mark. The reason why the media is so concerned with language usage is that it is fundamentally tied to journalistic credibility (Ebner, 2016). In the eyes of the public, if a reporter cannot correctly place an apostrophe or pronounce a source's name then how can they be trusted to provide accurate information? It is also crucial that journalese is clear and uses vocabulary that is commonplace and up to date. In order to ensure that all journalists working for the same media organization follow a consistent word usage and style, guides are created for reference. These style guides, as they are known, contain reminders and clarifications over the correct use of English, the use of active rather than passive prose and how to refer to political and occupational titles. Each **news** organization will create its own unique style guide, which is often in alphabetical order and explains how various words and phrases should be presented and which jargon to avoid. Some organizations have detailed and prescriptive guidelines whereas others, such as *HuffPost*, which relies heavily on user content, use their style guide to broadly outline the preferred presentation of stories (*HuffPost*, 2018).

With the advent of **online journalism**, more news organizations have made their style guides transparent, publishing them to the web and indicating when they were last updated. The *Guardian* and *Observer* style guide (*Guardian*, 2015) has an accompanying **Twitter** account, @guardianstyle, where sticklers can posit questions regarding the correct style of specific words and phrases; for example, Big Data or big data. And since digital journalism has brought with it a wealth of new words and meanings, creating a world where tweeting is no longer limited to birds, style guides have to be updated more frequently in response to changes in language and common, casual usage. Digital native news websites such as **BuzzFeed** pride themselves on publishing news and entertainment "in the language of the web" (Favilla and Paolone, 2018) and rely on their style guide to govern everything from hard-hitting journalism (spelt with a hyphen) to fun quizzes. Their style guide also acts as a social political tool which goes to great lengths to avoid negative representations or victimization of subjects of a story and has detailed guidance on appropriate language when describing mental health, LGBT and disability matters.

Key Sources

Ebner, C. 2016 "Language Guardian BBC? Investigating the BBC's Language Advice in Its 2003 News Styleguide" *Journal of Multilingual and Multicultural Development* 37(3): 308–320

Favilla, E. and Paolone, M. 2018 "BuzzFeed Style Guide" www.buzzfeed.com/emmyf/buzzfeed-style-guide

Guardian 2015 "The Guardian and Observer Style Guide" www.theguardian.com/guardian-observer-style-guide-a

SUBEDITOR

Once a key role in the newspaper **newsroom**, the subeditor was the last line of defence against factual and legal errors safeguarding the publication against law suits. Also known as a copy editor their job was to "sub" copy to make sure it fitted the printed page and to check it for the correct use of spelling, grammar, syntax and tone. They were also responsible for writing headlines and ensuring that an article's themes were "consistent with the vision and style of the media outlet they represent" (Vandendaele, 2018: 270). Fundamentally a final **gatekeeping** role, the subeditor's duties developed with technological change to encompass page design and layout.

Swingeing job cuts in newspapers since the turn of the century have hit sub editors hard, leaving US newsrooms some 30 percent smaller (Rosenstiel and Mitchell, 2011). The move to newspaper templates and fixed content management systems for **news** websites has lessened the need for page designers, a large part of the contemporary subeditor role. Furthermore, posting software with built-in spelling and grammar checks has shifted the duties of subeditors onto reporters. Subeditors whose duties do not include the production of measurable amounts of textual or visual content (Vultee, 2015) have been subjected to large scale redundancies due to the misguided view by senior managers that it does not require a subeditor to throw copy online with a photo (Greenslade, 2014).

This has resulted in an "unnerving practice of reporters writing straight to the web with not many checks and balances" (Canter,

2015a). The impact of the loss of skilled subeditors is a reduction in quality in textual news, with spelling, grammar and even legal errors littering newspaper pages and website posts. This has not been lost on the audience, who believe that editing improves perceptions of news articles' professionalism, organization, and quality of writing, as well as a sense of whether the article is worth paying for (Vultee, 2015).

Key Sources

Canter, L. 2015a "Weeklies Cutting Corners in Rush to Publish on Web" *Hold the Front Page* www.holdthefrontpage.co.uk/2014/news/weeklies-cutting-corners-in-rush-to-publish-on-web/

Vandendaele, A. 2018 "Trust Me, I'm a Sub-Editor" *Journalism Practice* 12(3): 268–289

Vultee, F. 2015 "Audience Perceptions of Editing Quality" *Digital Journalism* 3(6): 832–849

SUBSCRIPTION

Prior to digitization, subscription was a method of gaining loyal customers who pay in advance for the receipt of a regular product, be it a printed newspaper, magazine or television service such as Sky. However, subscription models have radically altered in the past two decades in response to the move to online news. Between 2013 and 2017, the use of tablets for online **news** consumption steadily rose and, with it, subscriptions to digital versions of printed magazines and newspapers boomed.

These electronic products emulated their printed counterparts with front covers/pages and tactile features such as the ability to turn a page and browse through a hyperlinked contents page. But consumers have now shifted to **smartphones** for their news consumption with just 16 percent of users accessing news via a **tablet** in 2018 compared to 44 percent, and rising, consuming news on smartphones (Newman, Fletcher, Kalogeropoulos, Levy and Nielsen, 2018). The design of digital subscriptions, downloaded via an app store, are now more akin to legacy websites and have mobile-friendly navigation.

For some publishers, subscriptions have also become synonymous with **paywalls** and online content can only be viewed for a regular fee via a web browser or app. This has proved successful for many newspapers, including the *New York Times*, which now has more than 1.6m digital news subscribers and the *Wall Street Journal*, which says its one million total digital subscribers account for more than half of its overall subscriber base. In the UK, the digital subscriptions of *The Times* and *Sunday Times* outnumbered print for the first time in June 2018, rising to 255,000. Deloitte (2018) estimated that by the end of 2018, news and magazine media would have more than 20 million digital-only subscribers and predicted that the proportion of subscription **advertising** revenue for publishers would be a 50–50 split between print and digital by 2020. TV subscriptions also continue to rise, with young people in the UK foregoing the payment of the **BBC** television licence and opting instead to pay for a live-streaming Netflix subscription. The on demand video service now has more than three million subscribers in the UK and 137 million worldwide.

An alternative form of subscription implemented by Guardian Media Group has been the contribution and membership scheme. Readers can donate money as a one-off payment or regular contribution or become a supporter, partner or patron and gain access to special events and ad-free content. This has helped the *Guardian* to secure its future and, from 2018, it began earning more money from its digital operation than from its print newspapers for the first time in its history. It now has more than 570,000 members who give regular financial support and its income is boosted further by 370,000 one-off contributions per annum (Waterson, 2018b). Digital revenues, which include reader contributions and online advertising, rose to more than £108 million in 2018 as income from the print newspaper and events business fell to £105 million.

Key Sources

Deloitte 2018 "Digital Media: The Subscription Prescription" *Deloitte* www.deloitte.co.uk/tmtpredictions/predictions/digital-only-media-subscriptions/

Waterson, J. 2018b "Guardian Media Group Digital Revenues Outstrip Print for First Time" *Guardian* www.theguardian.com/media/2018/jul/24/guardian-media-group-digital-revenues-outstrip-print-for-first-time

SURVEILLANCE

State surveillance of suspected criminals and political enemies has always formed the backbone of intelligence agencies and been largely accepted by the public as a necessary evil. However, the 2013 revelation that governments were also spying on the general population in cahoots with other nations and leading technology companies was a major blow to public trust across the Western world. In May 2013, the Associated Press declared that the United States Department of Justice had secretly subpoenaed phone records from their telephone lines over a two-month period in early 2012 (Johnson, 2017). A few days later, the *Washington Post* revealed the same government department had been tracking the activities of Fox News' chief Washington correspondent James Rosen. In the UK a month later, the *Guardian* journalist Glenn Greenwald published a story exposing the United States National Security Agency (NSA) for collecting and analyzing millions of telephone records of American users. The source of the leaked information was Edward Snowden, a contractor for the NSA who also passed thousands of classified documents onto journalists Ewen MacAskill and Laura Poitras. Snowden's disclosures revealed the existence of a project code-named PRISM which allowed the NSA to capture and store emails, audio and video chat, documents and other data retrieved from nine internet companies, including **Google**, Apple, Microsoft, **Facebook, YouTube**, AOL, **Skype**, Yahoo! and Paltalk. The documents also uncovered details of upstream collection, whereby the NSA intercepted telephone and internet traffic from major domestic and foreign internet cables. These operations were part of a global surveillance program exposed by Snowden, including the Five Eyes Intelligence Alliance, also known as ECHELON, comprising Australia, Canada, New Zealand, the UK and the US. Snowden, who faces spying and government theft charges in the US, escaped to Russia with the help of **WikiLeaks** in June 2013. He remains there under his right of asylum and has subsequently become president of the Freedom of the Press Foundation, which aims to protect journalists from hacking and government surveillance. Snowden has since publicly criticized WikiLeaks for its indiscriminate approach to releasing data without redaction, something he claims he went to great lengths to employ himself.

The fallout of the Snowden disclosures on **journalism** has been considerable, with reporters having to adopt security technologies for safe, private communication online (Waters, 2017). Journalists have reported that mass surveillance has the potential to silence whistleblowers and make **investigative journalism** increasingly difficult, potentially damaging their communications with sources. For example, in the wake of Snowden's revelations, the partner of journalist Glenn

Greenwald was apprehended under terrorism laws and the *Guardian* was forced to destroy hard drives containing the classified materials under the watchful eye of the British intelligence agency GCHQ. This and other measures, such as fortifying security laws and redoubling control and penalties, has put profound obstacles in the path of journalists trying to report on the world of intelligence gathering (Ruby, Goggin and Keane, 2017). Furthermore, research suggests that although journalists are highly aware of the problems of surveillance, they are inhibited from articulating their critiques due to their reliance upon official government sources (Wahl-Jorgensen, Bennett and Cable, 2017).

Key Sources

Johnson, C. 2017 "Massive and Unprecedented Intrusion: A Comparative Analysis of American Journalistic Discourse Surrounding Three Government Surveillance Scandals" *Digital Journalism* 5(3): 318–333

Ruby, F., Goggin, G. and Keane, J. 2017 "Comparative Silence Still? Journalism, Academia, and the Five Eyes of Edward Snowden" *Digital Journalism* 5(3): 353–367

Wahl-Jorgensen, K., Bennett, L. and Cable, J. 2017 "Surveillance Normalization and Critique: News Coverage and Journalists' Discourses around the Snowden Revelations" *Digital Journalism* 5(3): 386–403

Waters, S. 2017 "The Effects of Mass Surveillance on Journalists' Relations with Confidential Sources. A Constant Comparative Study" *Digital Journalism* 6 (10): 1294–1313, doi:10.1080/21670811.2017.1365616

SYNDICATION

In order to maximize the potential profit of their content, commercial **news** organizations often syndicate their stories to other media outlets. In effect, they licence content for publication or broadcast elsewhere in return for a fee. This is something of a gripe for trainee reporters and freelancers in particular, who previously could make additional money on the side from selling their stories to other news organizations once their original story was published. This was a useful revenue stream for low paid local newspaper reporters, who would often sell unseen stories to national publications. But, as debt-riddled publishers try to make ends meet, by any means, to stave off the onslaught of digital competition, they have established syndication deals making a few additional pounds every time a story is sold to another company.

Syndication deals also exist within online news platforms and are a standard part of a freelancer's contract. For example, it is not uncommon for a **freelance** journalist to be commissioned by the *Guardian* website and to find their content on the *Irish Times, Sydney Morning Herald, South China Morning Post* website or newspaper a day later, as these are syndication partners with Guardian News & Media. These outlets pay a regular syndication **subscription** to receive all of the *Guardian* and/or *Observer* news and feature feeds in their territory. The journalist will receive no remuneration for this syndication because their commission fee is an all-inclusive one, covering syndication rights as set out in the Freelance Charter (*Guardian*, 2017). A freelancer will only receive additional payment if the story is a spot sale syndication, which is an *ad hoc* selling of an individual article. However, by maintaining the rights to their content, freelance journalists can syndicate it to other publications in several countries for little or no additional work (Marshall, 2011).

The rapid repurposing of content online can make it difficult for news organizations to enforce **copyright** permission and syndication deals as reporters lift and rewrite content from other media websites on a daily basis. This **creative cannibalism** again has a negative impact on freelance journalists and their ability to earn money for their work.

Key Sources

Guardian 2017 "Freelance Charter" *Guardian* www.theguardian.com/info/guardian-news-media-freelance-charter

Marshall, S. 2011 "How to Syndicate Freelance Articles Abroad" Journalism.co.uk www.journalism.co.uk/skills/how-to-syndicate-freelance-articles-abroad/s7/a545852/

TABLET

The tablet computer, commonly shortened to tablet, is a lightweight mobile device with a touchscreen, largely used for browsing the internet and installing **apps**. The device became mainstream with the launch of the iPad in 2010, which sold 100 million units in the first six months. Other tablets followed, including those with Android operating systems and the Kindle Fire and the Nook. By 2014, 44 percent of American online consumers owned a tablet and by 2017 worldwide sales had surpassed desktop computers. However, the market has begun to stagnate more recently, due to the popularity and technological sophistication of **smartphones**. This is also reflected in online news consumption habits, with the Reuters Digital News Report (Newman, Fletcher, Kalogeropoulos, Levy and Nielsen, 2018) revealing that the smartphone has become the most used device for news, overtaking the computer/laptop. Tablet use for online news consumption, which rose steadily worldwide from 2013, started to decline in 2017 and is now just 16 percent compared to 44 percent for smartphones, which continues to rise.

At the height of the tablet consumer boom, news organizations were scrambling to build their brands and compete for market share of the growing number of users (Dowling and Vogan, 2015). The *New York Times'* 2012 publication of "Snow Fall: The Avalanche at Tunnel Creek" inspired other media outlets to create similar long form digital storytelling products for the tablet audience. The harrowing story of skiers caught in an avalanche was told by John Branch with interactive graphics, animations and aerial video, winning a 2013 Pulitzer prize in feature writing. It coined the industry verb "to snow fall" as other publications desperately tried to replicate its success.

Similarly, the initial popularity of tablets led to many publications launching digital editions which were designed to be viewed on a tablet computer much like a printed magazine, via a paid for **subscription**. However, as smartphones have become more powerful and versatile, users have begun to turn away from tablets, creating a new challenge for publishers. Smaller mobile screens affect the type of **news** content produced and pictures and videos are being reformatted using vertical aspect ratios, often annotated with text so they can be viewed without sound. The flashy graphics of "Snow Fall" and the high quality design of digital subscriptions are now in direct competition with a device that can be held in one hand by a user with a possibly short attention span.

Key Sources
Dowling, D. and Vogan, T. 2015 "Can We 'Snowfall' This? Digital Longform and the Race for the Tablet Market" *Digital Journalism* 3(2): 209–224

TRANSPARENCY

Transparency is a "new journalistic norm" (Koliska and Chadha, 2017), an ethical principle which challenges journalism's traditional ideas concerning objectivity while also providing ways for **journalists** to connect with citizens to nurture credibility and trust; for simplicity's sake it can perhaps "generally be understood as openness" (Karlsson and Clerwall, 2018).

The notion of transparency arises in the context of the enhanced number of actors, (especially **citizen journalists**, who may lack any formal **journalism** training) and the greater plurality of cited **sources** in **online journalism** and the problems of opacity, which both can create credibility for the public and news users (Phillips, 2010b).

Karlsson (2010) distinguishes between what he terms *disclosure* and *participatory* transparency. The former concerns the varying degrees of openness that journalists and **editors** adopt in explaining and "laying bare" for readers the complex processes and practices involved in news making and how these are organized and conducted within their particular news organization. The latter involves a different way of "opening up" the organization of the news making processes by encouraging participation and inviting the public to engage with, and become part of, those processes.

Consequently, *disclosure* transparency encourages a watchdog or surveillance attitude among the public (which will encourage media workers to explain their **news** selection processes and decisions, develop a willingness among editorial staff to acknowledge and correct editorial errors, while also institutionalizing mechanisms for the public to criticize journalistic processes), while *participatory* transparency encourages engagement and involvement (and at all levels of the journalistic news making process).

Transparency has become a burgeoning focus for research studies, with specific foci on the impact of transparency on source and message credibility (Karlsson, Clerwall and Nord, 2014), as well as journalists' (Koliska and Chadha, 2017) and public (Karlsson and Clerwall, 2018) perceptions and acceptance of transparency.

Karlsson, Clerwall and Nord's (2014) findings revealed an "almost total absence of transparency effect" on the credibility of either sources or message in their study of 1,320 news users' reactions to the impact of transparency on news reports (Karlsson, Clerwall and Nord, 2014: 668). In their study of transparency as a journalistic innovation in leading German news organizations, Koliska and Chadha concluded that while certain forms of openness have been adopted, "transparency is far from being embraced as an innovation" nor, in contrast to newsrooms in the US, "institutionally implemented" (Koliska and Chadha, 2017). Karlsson and Clerwall turn their research attention to "public views on transparency" using data from a public survey and focus groups conducted in Sweden between 2013 and 2015. Results suggest that public knowledge about transparency is modest, prompting little discussion in focus groups, although the provision of "hyperlinks, explaining news selection and framing, and correcting errors, are viewed positively" (Karlsson and Clerwall, 2018).

Key Sources

Karlsson, M. 2010 "Rituals of Transparency: Evaluating Online News Outlets' Uses of Transparency Rituals in the United States, United Kingdom and Sweden" *Journalism Studies* 11(4): 535–545

Karlsson, M. and Clerwall, C. 2018 "Transparency to the Rescue? Evaluating Citizens' Views on Transparency Tools in Journalism" *Journalism Studies* 19 (13): 1923–1933, doi:10.1080/1461670X.2088.1492882

Karlsson, M., Clerwall, C. and Nord, L. 2014 "You Ain't Seen Nothing Yet: Transparency's (Lack of) Effect on Source and Message Credibility" *Journalism Studies* 15(5): 668–678

Koliska, M. and Chadha, K. 2017 "Transparency in German Newsrooms: Diffusion of a New Journalistic Norm" *Journalism Studies* 19(16): 2400–2416, doi:10.1080/1461670X.2017.1349549

Phillips, A. 2010b "Transparency and the New Ethics of Journalism" *Journalism Practice* 4(3): 373–382

TUMBLR

Founded by David Karp in 2007, Tumblr is a micro-blogging and social networking platform that allows users to post multimedia content and short blog posts. It now sits within the Oath subsidiary of Verizon Communications alongside digital brands Yahoo!, TechCrunch and *HuffPost*. The website, which hosts 435 million blogs and 164 billion posts (Tumblr, 2018), features functions that enable users to create individual profiles and connect with others through journal-like entries (Kilgo, 2015).

Like all social networks, Tumblr has received its fair share of criticism surrounding issues over its level of pornographic material and posts glorifying suicide and self-harm. Furthermore, in February 2018, **BuzzFeed** published a report claiming that Tumblr was utilized as a distribution channel for Russian agents to influence American voting habits during the 2016 presidential election. In fact, its role in American politics predates this, with Barack Obama launching a 2012 re-election campaign blog on Tumblr, following success on **Twitter** and **Facebook**.

Tumblr's unique selling point is that it emphasizes visual content over text, with gifs (graphics interchange formats) being the most popular form of imagery. Around half of Tumblr's audience is between the ages of 16 and 24, an arguably difficult to reach demographic (Smith, 2013). Media organizations have, therefore, experimented with posting content on Tumblr in an attempt to attract young audiences whom they fear are disengaged with **news**.

Unlike the abundance of scholarly research on Twitter and Facebook, Tumblr is largely unexplored, with the most notable study conducted in 2014, focusing on nine US news brands covering web, print and broadcasting (Kilgo, 2015). The findings clearly indicated that news organizations were adhering to the culture of Tumblr by posting visually oriented content, including still photos and infographics. Gifs also accounted for a significant portion of visual formats, further advancing the argument that "active news organizations in this network are tailoring their information to the platform, as GIFs are not popular image formats on many news organizations websites, nor do they translate to the analogue world" (Kilgo, 2015: 11). The study also found that news items on technology, the environment, lifestyle and health, and politics engaged readers more effectively than entertainment, suggesting that users were interested in consuming weightier topics than might be predicted.

However, despite initial enthusiasm to create accounts on Tumblr, Kilgo's research found that news organizations often failed to follow through with their endeavors and utilized the site for branding rather than informing and communicating with the Tumblr public. Indeed, by the end of 2017, many of the news organizations sampled in Kilgo's research no longer had up-to-date Tumblr feeds or simply posted content which did nothing more than link back to their legacy brand. A similar pattern can be seen in the UK, where posts from once active news brands such as the *Guardian* appear to have all but petered out.

Key Sources

Kilgo, D. 2015 "Media Landscape on Tumblr: News Organization Convergence Attributes in Youth-Oriented Social Media Networks" *Digital Journalism* 4(6): 784–800

Tumblr 2018 "About" www.tumblr.com/about

TWEET

Tweet is the name given to the 140 character (initial maximum word length doubled to 280 in November 2017) snippets of information, gossip, news, poetry or philosophy which individuals and organizations of every kind and stripe post for dissemination and sharing with other members of the **Twitter** social network. Tweets may assume the form of narrative text, a photograph or a graphic. Tweets can include **hyperlinks** that connect to cognate materials in other tweets, **social media** or other online texts. The infinitive that describes this activity of "tweeting" is "to tweet."

Readers can illustrate their approval of a particular tweet by "liking" it or "retweeting" the short message to friends or others in the network. In this way, a single tweet can be shared many times. When, for example, Miley Cyrus appeared in a video at the 2013 MTV Video Music Awards (VMA), dressed in a rather scanty outfit and "twerking," her energetic "performance" established a new record for peak tweets at 306,100 per minute. Cyrus became the number one most-searched person at **Google** for 2013 (Berkowitz and Schwartz, 2015). A different example is offered by Barak Obama's tweet on November 6th, 2012 when he declared his success in the Presidential election with a short tweet announcing "Four more years." The post was retweeted more than 810,000 times by people across 200 countries, making it the most retweeted message of 2012 (Hermida, 2013: 295)

Tweeting is popular. While Twitter is a relatively new **social media** platform, launched only in March 2006, more than 500 million tweets are posted each day, but, perhaps counter intuitively, very few of these have any direct consequence or relevance for journalism. A recent study of 1.8 billion tweets, for example, identified that less than one percent (0.7 percent) was concerned with news (Momin and Pfeffer, 2016).

Tweets may be posted by professional **journalists (freelance** and contract journalists), as well as private individuals and non-news organizations: a direct connection with journalism is more likely with journalists' tweets. Moreover, journalists increasingly use Twitter to promote their own personal brand (Hanusch and Bruns, 2016) or the corporate brand of their employing news organization (Tandoc and Vos, 2016), and as often as their editorial ambitions to achieve a wider reach and readership for their news stories.

See also **like**.

Key Sources

Berkowitz, D. and Schwartz, D. A. 2015 "Miley, CNN and the Onion: When Fake News Becomes Realer than Real" *Journalism Practice*, doi:10.1080/17512786.2015.1006933

Hanusch, F. and Bruns, F. 2016 "Journalistic Branding on Twitter: A Representative Study of Australian Journalists' Activities and Profile Descriptions" *Digital Journalism*, doi:10.1080/21670811.2016.1152161

Hermida, A. 2013 "#Journalism: Reconfiguring Journalism Research about Twitter, One Tweet at a Time" *Digital Journalism* 1(3): 295–313

Tandoc, E. and Vos, T. 2016 "The Journalist Is Marketing the New: Social Media in the Gatekeeping Process" *Journalism Practice* 10(8): 950–966, doi:10.1080/17512786.2015.10878113/7

TWITTER

The **Guardian**'s front page story on April 12th, 2016 featured a disturbing article about how women are increasingly "targeted online with racial abuse, pornography and death threats." One woman, "having made 126 crime reports to the British Police and numerous reports to Twitter declared that she felt 'destroyed and defeated'." The problem of digital stalkers, internet harassment and people who open multiple or fake **social media** accounts to make abusive threats is a problem which neither the police nor Twitter seem able to resolve (*Guardian*, 2016a: 1). In this case Twitter, the micro blogging platform which provides for disseminating and sharing news, information or any whimsical thought or significant event, using a maximum of 280 characters, seems to have been the *focus* of the **news** rather than its more usual role as a digital platform *reporting* the story.

Twitter, which is defined by Hermida as "one of a range of social networking technologies usually referred to as social media" (Hermida, 2013: 296), has its enthusiastic supporters as well as its critics. Substantial claims are (appropriately) made for the democratizing potential and effects of Twitter, given the more fulsome capacity for public debate that the platform offers. Twitter empowers people by giving them a voice in significant policy debates (Hermida, 2010, 2013, 2014). Network theorist Manuel Castells makes even stronger claims, suggesting that social media and networked global communication structures are preconditions for the growth of social movements of liberation such as the Arab Spring. Castells musters powerful, if slightly romantic, language to dub them networks of "outrage and hope" (Castells, 2015).

The emergence of Twitter, launched in March 2006, has triggered significant developments in all aspects of the gathering, reporting and reception of news, as well as for scholarly interest and research in the field of **Digital Journalism Studies**.

Most significantly, social media have posed problematic existential challenges to the identity of "journalists" and the meaning of "journalism," as online and social media enable users to become participants in a more pluralistic process of news making by posting comments below articles in online newspapers, but also by "breaking" news on social media like Twitter, whether by photographic image or text. In these ways, Twitter has increasingly blurred boundaries between professional and citizen or participatory journalists and given rise to "interlopers" in the world of professional journalism (Eldridge, 2015). Events like the London Riots in 2011 (Vis, 2013), the Paris bombings and shootings in 2015 and the attacks at Brussels airport in 2016 illustrate the particular significance of Twitter, as a **source** of news and a **platform** on which to report news, for both professional and **citizen journalists** (Broersma and Todd, 2013).

A further consequence of Twitter has been especially significant in the context of such dramatic and newsworthy events and illustrates its impact on the reach and pace at which news travels. Alan Rusbridger, ex-**editor** of the *Guardian*, observed that, since the arrival of Twitter and other social media, the average scoop now has a massively reduced shelf life of less than three seconds!

But Twitter also poses significant potential challenges for the future of a sustainable, critical and high quality democratic journalism. The **transparency** and credibility of news on Twitter, the range and reliability of sources used in its production, as well as the work experience and professional values of its **citizen journalists**, differ markedly from news produced by traditional news organizations with their tested news production protocols and professionally experienced staffs. **News** breaks fast on social media but the suggestion is that sometimes the sacrificed accuracy and credibility may be too high a price to pay for such **immediacy. Transparency**, so the argument runs, is not a wholly adequate substitute for journalists' previous commitment to objectivity. All this reminds one of American journalist and Editor A. J. Liebling's observation that, "I can write better than anybody who can write faster and faster than anybody who can write better!" Moreover, the requirement to deliver news in 280 character "sound bites" requires a capacity for tabloid compression which would test the skills of even the most professional **hack** and certainly over-reaches the skills and experience of the relatively novitiate participatory journalists.

But, despite these difficulties, Twitter's popularity has proved explosive. By its seventh birthday in 2013, it claimed more than 200 million active users, with 400 million tweets posted daily (cited in Hermida, 2013: 295); a year later, the number of daily tweets exceeded 500 million (Hermida, 2014). Twitter, moreover, is increasingly popular with professional journalists, whose uses of Twitter for newsgathering and reporting have become a "normalized" aspect of their daily work routines (Lasorsa, Lewis and Holton, 2012), although the extent and regularity with which journalists use Twitter and other **social media** in their private and professional lives varies substantially, reflecting their age, gender and their professional experience and attitudes (Hedman and Djerf Pierre, 2013).

These changes in everyday journalism – developments in digital technologies, the emergence of social media such as Twitter, shifts in journalists' professional practice and journalists' relationships with sources and **audiences** for news – have, in turn, triggered changes in **Digital journalism Studies**, in which Twitter has become a major focus for scholarly research and publication. The work of Alfred Hermida is perhaps the most outstanding single scholarly contribution here (2012, 2010, 2013, 2014). This growing prominence for Twitter and social media more generally in academic and research agendas has not been confined to particular case studies of "Tweeting the news," no matter how significant these particular studies might be (see, for example, Vis's 2013 study of the role of Twitter in reporting the UK Riots in 2011). It has, rather, extended to studies exploring and developing the methodological and research design implications of Twitter and the use of new data mining software to explore Twitter content. Momin and Pfeffer's (2016) study of Twitter and news, for example, involved the automated content analysis of an unprecedented and rather mind-boggling 1.8 billion tweets. The sheer scale of the collection and analysis of data necessary to inform scholarly studies of micro-blogging offers exciting prospects for Digital Journalism Studies.

Twitter's growth in popularity among the general public, its growing numbers of advocates and critics, as well as the scholarly and academic interest it attracts, show little signs of abating. Twitter continues to be of considerable consequence for the ways in which **digital journalism** continues to develop.

See also social media.

Key Sources

Broersma, M. and Graham, T. 2013 "Twitter as A Source of News: How Dutch and British Newspapers Used Tweets in Their News Coverage 2007–2011" *Journalism Practice* 7(4): 446–464

Hedman, U. and Djerf Pierre, M. 2013 "The Social Journalist: Embracing the Social Media Life or Creating a New Digital Divide" *Digital Journalism* 1(3): 368–385

Eldridge, II, S. A. 2015 "Boundary Maintenance and Interloper Media Reaction: Differentiating between Journalism's Discursive Enforcement Processes" *Journalism Studies* 15(1): 1–16

Hermida, A. 2013 "#Journalism: Reconfiguring Journalism Research about Twitter, One Tweet at a Time" *Digital Journalism* 1(3): 295–313

Lasorsa, N., Lewis, S. and Holton, A. 2012 "Normalizing Twitter: Journalism Practice in an Emerging Communications Space" *Journalism Studies* 13(1): 19–36

TWITTER AND NEWS

When US Airways Flight 1549 crash landed on the Hudson River on January 15, 2009, the first image was distributed to the world via Twitter. Janis Krums was on a ferry when he clicked the snapshot of the partially submerged airplane on his iPhone and shared it on his **Twitter** account thinking to himself, "that's pretty newsworthy." The image was viewed so many times it crashed the servers of TwitPic, the application that at the time facilitated photos on the micro-blogging platform. This act of **journalism** from a member of the public has now become normalized on Twitter as events are broken by bystanders, activists and citizen witnesses on a daily basis. Bruno has labelled this the "Twitter effect" (2011: 5) and suggests that **social media** tools are central to the reporting of crisis events and enable more in-depth coverage and visibility to threatened voices. More importantly, she says "it promotes an idea of a journalism more orientated to the process of news making and more open to a diversity of sources than traditional mainstream coverage could produce today" (6). In recognition of this shift towards real time, real people reporting, mainstream media have incorporated dedicated social media reporters into their news teams who constantly scour sites, particularly Twitter, for breaking news stories. As early as 2009, news organizations began "abandoning attempts to be the first for breaking news, focusing instead on being the best at verifying and curating it" (Newman, 2009: 2). Newman (2009) and Messner,

Linke and Eford (2011) recount how information about the 2008 Mumbai terror attacks and 2009 Green Revolution in Iran first broke on Twitter, while Bruno (2011) examines how journalists utilized the rapid flow of information coming from Haiti during and immediately after the 2010 earthquake. Meanwhile, the 2011 Egyptian uprising, which led to the ousting of President Hosni Mubarak, has been widely referred to as the "Twitter Revolution."

As a **news** source for journalists, Twitter is an invaluable resource with 500 million tweets posted each day, including photos and videos with verifiable geotags and theme orientated hashtags. Reporters can monitor, organize, verify and curate tweets via third party **apps** such as Hootsuite and TinEye and gauge public opinion on particular topics by searching specific hashtags which list all content using the symbol # followed by the topic, for example #brexit. By scouring Twitter, journalists are able to spot breaking news events, create stories from the tweets of public figures and curate content to put into their own news stories and packages. These sources of information may be from the public or official institutions, with public bodies such as police forces as well as corporate public relations firms increasingly using Twitter to release information and bypass traditional media. In some cases, major news stories have been innocently broken by the public before being confirmed by an official source. The raid in which terrorist Osama Bin Laden was killed by a US military operation in 2011 was live tweeted by Sohaib Ather, unbeknown to him, via his @ReallyVirtual profile. Athar posted "Helicopter hovering above Abbottabad at 1AM (is a rare event)" without realising he was tweeting about a top-secret mission. Once news broke that Bin Laden had been killed, Athar tweeted "Uh oh, now I'm the guy who live-blogged the Osama raid without knowing it."

As well as a source for news, Twitter is a popular platform for journalists and news organizations to disseminate news which is then amplified via retweets. Media commentators have also celebrated the **interactivity** of Twitter, which enables journalists to engage directly with their audiences rather than simply act as distributers of news. This can lead to powerful collaborations whereby news organizations turn to the public to share the news making process and, for instance, overcome legal restrictions. The *Guardian* used the power of the crowd on Twitter to overturn a secret injunction enabling them to legally report a story about oil trader Trafigura dumping toxic waste off the Ivory Coast in 2009.

The Guardian story announcing that it had been restricted by an existing high court order from reporting certain parliamentary proceedings had been published online for just a matter of minutes before internet users began tearing apart the gag ... blogs and the social networking site Twitter buzzed as users rushed to solve the mystery of who was behind the gagging attempt ... 42 minutes after the Guardian story was published, the internet had revealed what the paper could not ... All the while, efforts were continuing to persuade Trafigura to alter the terms of the order to allow the Guardian to report the parliamentary business, and at 12.19pm Carter Ruck emailed the Guardian agreeing to do so.

(Booth, 2009)

There has been considerable hype surrounding the collaborative and interactive nature of Twitter and its ability to bring journalists and **audiences** together in the act of news making; however, these examples tend to be the exception rather than the rule. An analysis of 1.8 billion tweets over four months in 2014 found that news organizations' accounts, across all major organizations, largely use Twitter as a professionalized, one-way communication medium to promote their own reporting (Malik and Pfeffer, 2016), thus maintaining the traditional **gatekeeping** distribution method.

See also **Twitter and personal branding, Twitter and political reporting**.

Key Sources

Bruno, N. 2011 "Tweet First, Verify Later. How Real Time Information Is Changing the Coverage of Worldwide Crisis Events" *Reuters Institute for the Study of Journalism* http://reutersinstitute.politics.ox.ac.uk/about/news/item/article/tweet-first-verify-later-new-fell.html

Malik, M. and Pfeffer, J. 2016b "A Macroscopic Analysis of News Content in Twitter" *Digital Journalism* 4(8): 955–979

Messner, M., Linke, M. and Eford, A. 2011 "Shoveling Tweets: An Analysis of the Microblogging Engagement of Traditional News Organizations" *#ISOJ International Symposium on Online Journalism* 2(1): 74–87

TWITTER AND PERSONAL BRANDING

As more and more people rely on **social media** platforms for their daily **news** supply, journalists are increasingly engaging with their audiences on an individual level, outside the boundaries of their organization. This is particularly prevalent on Twitter, where journalists **tweet** personal posts together with content promoting their professional work in what has become known as personal branding. Tandoc, Cabañes and Cayabyab (2018) suggest that in a period when trust in news organizations is seemingly declining, this kind of personalized tweeting might present a more credible alternative that sees journalism as practiced by individuals rather than by big organizations.

Within five years of the launch of the platform, UK local journalists were aware of the ability to build a personal brand via Twitter (Dickinson, 2011). In doing so, they were able to establish relationships with readers (Broersma and Graham, 2013) and stay closely connected to their audience (Dickinson, 2011), thus securing brand loyalty and legitimizing their position as a public watchdog. This individualized tweeting fulfils the dual purpose of developing a personal following for a particular journalist while also strengthening the brand of the organization they work for. Furthermore, Canter (2013a, 2014b) argues that branding and promotion on regional newspaper Twitter profiles has split into two distinct approaches with "a traditional function for news organizations and a social function for journalists" (Canter, 2013a: 492). News organization policy directs journalists to link to their legacy website but this approach is largely ignored except by those in more senior positions such as digital editors and editors (Canter and Brookes, 2016). Instead, journalists tend to promote the brand of their employer at a much more nuanced level by "indirectly building a personal brand which is engaging for users to follow" (Canter, 2014b: 16), rather than by directly driving traffic to their news website. These personal brands vary in scope from those who build a reputation for regular live tweeting, others who become celebrated for tweeting happy messages or engaging in sporting banter to a limited few who tweet family snapshots (Canter, 2014b). There is also some evidence that journalists are breaking down traditional boundaries of objectivity and professionalization by posting personal and sometimes subjective tweets commenting on the news or revealing their hobbies and interests (Hermida, 2013; Lasorsa, Lewis and Holton, 2012), using personality to create a following (Marwick and Boyd, 2011). The lack of protocol or formality around Twitter use has led to journalists creating their own tweeting style which crosses boundaries between personality and professionalism, and objectivity and comment, sometimes all within the same tweet (Canter and Brookes, 2016). Yet, the picture remains mixed, as there is still a swathe of journalists who set clear boundaries between their professional and personal persona when using Twitter as a reporting tool (Gulyas, 2013; Reed, 2013).

A more recent content analysis of the Twitter profiles and tweets of 384 US journalists (Molyneux, Holton and Lewis, 2018) revealed a tension between personal disclosure to elicit authenticity and professional decorum to maintain credibility, all while establishing a distinct voice and simultaneously promoting one's organization or the journalism profession at large. Results found that branding was common among journalists on Twitter, occurring mostly at an organizational level. However, those journalists who had been on Twitter for the longest period of time tended to share more personal information and engage in individual branding rather than organizational branding. This individual level branding involves both personal and professional content, such as speaking about one's personal life to strengthen relationships with followers and tweeting about work activities. As the following of journalists grows, these individuals may feel more able to develop personal relationships with their audience, enabling them to keep their own Twitter account if they move to a different company. Thus, personalized tweeting is preferable over organizational tweeting in the long run for journalists who hope to be transient.

Key Sources

Canter, L. 2014b "Personalised Tweeting: The Emerging Practices of Journalists on Twitter" *Digital Journalism* 3(6): 888–907

Gulyas, A. 2013 "The Influence of Professional Variables on Journalists' Uses and Views of Social Media: A Comparative Study of Finland, Germany, Sweden and the United Kingdom" *Digital Journalism* 1(2): 270–285

Molyneux, L., Holton, A. and Lewis, S. 2018 "How Journalists Engage in Branding on Twitter: Individual, Organizational, and Institutional Levels" *Information, Communication & Society* 21(10): 1386–1401

TWITTER AND POLITICAL REPORTING

Every second, on average, around 6,000 tweets are posted on **Twitter**, revealing the activities, opinions and actions of more than 326 million active users. It would, therefore, be reasonable to assume that the platform is an effective tool for journalists to gauge public opinion and reaction to the **news**. But recent political events, including the election to the US Presidency of Republican entrepreneur Donald Trump, the UK's referendum decision to leave the European Union and the rise of the far right across Europe, were not predicted by the mainstream media nor reflected in the dominant conversation on Twitter. Indeed, Twitter boss Jack Dorsey admitted in 2018 that the micro-blogging platform had a "left leaning" bias in terms of the opinions its users expressed. Journalists who turn to Twitter to source content, therefore, have to tread carefully when using it as a barometer for public opinion. Research, however, suggests that Twitter is used by political journalists as an awareness system, allowing them to keep tabs on what is happening when they are not in the **newsroom** (Parmelee, 2013). Twitter is the most consequential **social media** platform for political reporters and editors, who view **Facebook** as a secondary resource that is important for personal matters rather than politics.

Twitter is awash with political activists campaigning for social change, whether it is citizen journalists uploading **user-generated content** while risking their lives in war-torn countries or tyrannical states promoting propaganda often via **fake news** posts. All of this content is ripe for the picking for the political journalist who has become particularly popular and influential on Twitter compared to other **news beats**. Such is their status, the US social analytics firm StatSocial has created a list ranking the 1,859 most influential political journalists on Twitter. Unlike other digital reporters (Agarwal and Barthel, 2015; Canter and Brookes, 2016; Olausson, 2017), political journalists tend to preserve the traditional role of objective gatekeepers, being especially wary of sharing personal opinions (Parmelee, 2013). The same cannot be said of politicians who have shaped Twitter into their own personal mouthpieces where they can speak to the public and bypass the **agenda setting** of the mainstream media. During the 2016 US presidential elections, Donald Trump came to the forefront of political tweeting with his provocative, polemical and divisive tweets. This prolific and unvetted tweeting behavior did not stop once he was elected president, as he continued to conduct diplomacy, insult dissenters and discredit the mainstream media via Twitter, much like an unruly adolescent or petulant toddler might do. This apparent tweeting-of-consciousness has been lapped up by journalists who have turned the president's tweets into a stream of news stories that commentators lament. Ott (2017) heavily criticizes the media for using Trump's Twitter feed as a legitimate news source and castigates Twitter for treating everything one does or thinks as newsworthy rather than just opinion. "Television may have assaulted journalism" says Ott "but Twitter killed it" (2017: 66).

A content analysis of more than 2,500 tweets from @realDonald-Trump from October 2015 to May 2016 (Crockett, 2016) revealed that Trump's lexicon is simple and repetitious, using monosyllabic words such as "good," "bad," and "sad," for example: "Failing @NYTimes will always take a good story about me and make it bad. Every article is unfair and biased. Very sad!" Trump's tweets are also overwhelmingly negative and many include insults, so much so that in October 2012 the *New York Times* published a list of the 282 people, places, and things Trump had insulted on Twitter. And no one is spared his verbal Twitter attacks, with President Trump labeling the leader of North Korea, Kim Jong-un, a "madman" who "doesn't mind starving or killing his people." Trump also makes frequent use of exclamation marks and capital letters to express his anger and disgust such as "FAKE NEWS – THE ENEMY OF THE PEOPLE!" Some would argue that, using tweets as a decoy, Trump is able to control the news conversation and distract the public – and to a certain extent journalists – from his controversial policies. In doing so, Trump shifts the focus of political reporting from his politics to his personality, using Twitter as a tool for media manipulation.

See also **Twitter and news**.

Key Sources

Ott, B. 2017 "The Age of Twitter: Donald J. Trump and the Politics of Debasement" *Critical Studies in Media Communication* 34(1): 59–68

Parmelee, J. 2013 "Political Journalists and Twitter: Influences on Norms and Practices" *Journal of Media Practice* 14(4): 291–330

TWITTER AND USES BY JOURNALISTS

Journalists' uses of **social media**, including **Twitter**, differ, reflecting the influence of a range of variables. A study by Gulyas compared the impact of professional variables, including media sector, length of time working in journalism and the size of the media organization, on journalists' uses of Twitter and social media in Finland, Germany, Sweden and the UK (2013).

The study was based on 1560 survey responses to a questionnaire with 448 responses from Finland, 189 from Germany, 256 from Sweden and 667 from the UK. Gulyas found significant similarities but also differences between journalists' uses of social media in the four countries. The overwhelming majority (96 percent) of respondents used some form of social media in their professional life, with Germany (90 percent) marking one end of a continuum and UK **journalists** marking the most popular end with 98 percent of journalists using new media. Again in the UK, journalists found micro-blogging sites like Twitter to be the most useful while other journalists preferred crowdsourcing sites (Gulyas, 2013: 277). Distinctive media sector differences were also evident, with online and broadcast journalists the most active users of blogs and print journalists the least active, but these differences were apparent only in the UK and Finland.

Hedman and Djerf-Pierre's (2013) study of the "social journalists" was based on 1,412 responses from Swedish journalists to a survey distributed in collaboration with the Swedish Union of Journalists (SUJ). While all journalists used social media in their private and professional lives, only one in ten journalists "fully embraced the social media life" by "using social media at work all of the time" (2013: 373).

A striking finding was the connection between generation and social media use; in the youngest group of journalists (29 years and younger), six out of ten journalists claim to be daily users – the equivalent figure among the older group (60 years and above) was less than three out of ten (ibid.). Other factors shaping social media use by journalists include gender (although the differences here are modest), the type of workplace and the work of the journalist (perhaps predictably, social media use is greater among web/online journalists than those who describe themselves as print journalists). They found the "largest proportion of 24/7 users in the tabloid press" (2013: 377).

Based on these data, Hedman and Djerf-Pierre identified three broad categories of social media users: the "sceptical shunners," the "pragmatic confirmers" and the "enthusiastic activists" (2013: 368). The skeptical shunners "avoid Twitter" and shun any contact with social media: a stance shared by only 10–15 percent of responding journalists. They are found among older journalists in the printed press. The pragmatic confirmers use Twitter and other social media selectively and mostly to search for information online but rarely post tweets themselves (2013: 382). They feel peer pressure to use social media but are ambivalent about its value. The enthusiastic activists "fully lead a life online, being connected and tweeting or blogging continuously" (2013: 382). They are found among younger journalists working on digital and cross-media platforms and they frequently use social media for "networking, personal branding and collaboration." But it remains a small group constituting less than five percent of all journalists. Other studies of digital journalists' uses report expansive involvement of journalists with Twitter as a source of information and breaking news, as well as providing prospects for personal branding (Hermida, 2013).

Key Sources

Gulyas, A. 2013 "The Influence of Professional Variables on Journalists' Uses and Views of Social Media: A Comparative Study of Finland, Germany, Sweden and the United Kingdom" *Digital Journalism* 1(2): 270–285

Hedman, U. and Djerf Pierre, M. 2013 "The Social Journalist: Embracing the Social Media Life or Creating a New Digital Divide" *Digital Journalism* 1(3): 368–385

Hermida, A. 2013 "#Journalism: Reconfiguring Journalism Research about Twitter, One Tweet at a Time" *Digital Journalism* 1(3): 295–313

USER COMMENT THREADS

The emergence of **Web 2.0** technologies was greeted with great enthusiasm by many **journalists, editors** and the general public. The democratic **affordances** of such technologies, especially their potential for **immediacy** and **interactivity** between these communities, marked a radical redistribution of communicative power previously exercised in monopoly by journalists working in **legacy media**. In this "new age," ordinary citizens were enabled to co-create and contribute to the **news** in a number of ways, including commenting on journalists' articles, by curating **blogs**, writing and publishing in **hyperlocal** start-ups, or as "full blown" **citizen journalists** writing articles to appear alongside the contribution of professional journalists. This capacity for news to be informed by an explosive plurality of news **sources** and writers, previously excluded from **journalism**, offered the prospect of a revitalized, increasingly participative and democratic news ecology and polity.

But celebrations of the arrival of this enhanced democracy based on citizens' commentary and critique of journalists' editorial work, posted on online newspapers' comment threads, proved short-lived (Ksiazek and Springer, 2019; Santana, 2013: 18). The democratic benefits of these lengthy strings of readers' comments on news items, alongside the rapidly growing popularity of posting comments on **social media** such as **Twitter**, came increasingly to be seen to offer more nuanced and ambiguous opportunities (Greenslade, 2018).

While readers' comments offered new sources of information, opinion, stories and even interesting and engaging gossip, the anonymity afforded to those commenting on journalists' news stories, the unreliability and absence of credibility or fact checking in many of these amateur news sources, as well as the lack of civility and measure in many of the comments (Wolfgang, 2018), undoubtedly fed claims concerning the growth in **fake news** (McNair, 2018), prompted a marked deterioration in the public conversation and, on occasion, "hate speech" and threats of physical and sexual violence. Women have increasingly become the focus of such concerns, while women journalists are often targeted for particularly sexualized and violent comments (Hill Nettleton, 2019).

A woman journalist working for the magazine *Not Just Sports*, for example, triggered the following reaction to one of her articles: "I hope you get raped. You need to be hit in the head with a hockey puck and killed. You are clearly retarded. I hope someone shoots then rapes you" (cited in Hill Nettleton, 2019: 425).

Powerful women have proved a particular focus for comment, prompting women MPs to articulate their fears and concerns about these matters as well as the reluctance of media companies to take action. In March 2017, the Home Affairs Select Committee Chair, Yvette Cooper, criticized **Twitter, YouTube** and **Facebook** for procrastination in removing comments threatening violence against individually named women MPs (https://www.theguardian.com/media/video/2017/mar/14/mps-slam-social-media-companies-over-online-hate-speech-video). These developments have prompted a growing chorus of concern about how best to "clean up the fetid swamp" (Wolfgang, 2018).

Many local and regional media have been in the vanguard of dealing with this "swamp," not by cleaning it up, but by feeling compelled to close their website to readers' comments – at least temporarily. In July 2018, for example, Bradford's *Telegraph and Argus* closed its website to readers' comments because the **editor** believed that "even the most innocuous stories were being polluted with hate-filled, racist, anti-Semitic or Islamophobic tirades." The paper had initially tried to deal with such comments by "banning the worst offenders" but they returned, "Sometimes within minutes, under a pseudonym, spouting the same poison" (cited in Parveen, 2018: 8).

A year earlier, the *Yorkshire Post*, a large regional newspaper, closed the readers' comments facilities on its website (Parveen, 2018: 8). For their part, readers complained that the paper was retreating from citizen journalism, but the editor identified readers' anonymity as the cause of such intolerant hate speech. "We don't just tolerate anonymous guff," he argued. "We get and publish more readers' letters than ever, and **tweets** and *Facebook* comment. We just delete 'anon'. If you can't put your name and face to your opinion who cares anyway" (cited in Parveen, 2018: 8).

Key Sources

Hill Nettleton, P. 2019 "The Cyber Abuse of Women on the Internet" in Eldridge, II, S. and Franklin, B. (Eds) *The Routledge Handbook of Developments in Digital Journalism Studies.* London: Routledge, 425–438

Ksiazek, T. and Springer, N. 2019 "User Comment in Digital Journalism: Current Research and Future Directions" in Eldridge, S. and Franklin, B. (Eds) *The Routledge Handbook of Developments in Digital Journalism Studies.* London: Routledge, 475–487

Parveen, N. 2018 "Newspaper Website Turns Off Comments over 'Racist Tirades'" *Guardian* 26th July, 8

Santana, A. D. 2013 "Virtuous or Vitriolic: The Effect of Anonymity on Civility in Online Newspapers' Readers' Comment Boards" *Journalism Practice* 8(1): 18–33

Wolfgang, J. D. 2018 "Examining How Journalists Construct Policy and Practice for Moderating Comments" *Digital Journalism* 6(1): 21–34

USER-GENERATED CONTENT (UGC)

Content produced by the public and posted online was originally referred to as user-generated content (UGC), or user created content. It could take any form, such as images, video, text or audio, and became mainstream in the mid 2000s. UGC differentiates from professional journalistic content in its quality, rawness and lack of context. Large quantities of user-generated content were produced by the public during the 2005 London Bombings because journalists were unable to access the underground where some of the explosions took place due to security restrictions. Media organizations such as the BBC had to rely on photographs, video footage and accounts from the public, with the most newsworthy photographs being taken by the public rather than professional journalists (Allan, 2007). The BBC subsequently launched a 24-hour UGC hub to receive and verify content from the public and *TIME* magazine named "You" as the Person of the Year in 2006, referring to the rise in the production of UGC on **Web 2.0** platforms.

Back in 2008, Hermida and Thurman described UGC as content made by amateurs who published either on amateur platforms such as **You-Tube** or MySpace or had their content accepted and published within professional news organizations. The boundaries between amateur and professional content, and **platforms**, has blurred significantly since then, with most news organizations fully integrated into "amateur" sites such as YouTube and social media networks **Facebook** and **Twitter**. Although journalists were at first reluctant to use content from non-professionals and to relinquish their **gatekeeping** control, the ubiquity of such content meant that it quickly became the norm and journalists now actively seek, or crowdsource, such content on a daily basis using tools such as the #journorequest hashtag on Twitter. The term UGC is now rarely used, as journalists consider all data online as potential content and boundaries between users and producers are less distinct.

See also **citizen journalism** and **citizen witnessing**.

Key Sources

Allan, S. 2007 "Citizen Journalism and the Rise of Mass Self-Communication: Reporting the London Bombings" *Global Media Journal* 1(1) http://stc.uws.edu.au/gmjau/iss1_2007/stuart_allan.html

Hermida, A. and Thurman, N. 2008 "A Clash of Cultures: An Integration of User-Generated Content within Professional Journalistic Frameworks at British Newspaper Websites" *Journalism Practice* 2(3): 343–356

VIRAL NEWS

Obama's post-White House kitesurfing adventure, a professor being interrupted by his children during a live BBC television interview and Prince Harry's proposal to Meghan Markle were all top viral **news** stories in 2017. **Social media** has made it possible for news to spread widely and rapidly as users share content on platforms such as **Facebook** and **Twitter** to their network of friends and followers, who in turn continue the trend. This spreadable media usually contains striking or amusing video clips or photographs and often originates from news articles or television broadcasts. Virality is regarded as

> one of the mysteries of the internet era because it is difficult to know why certain songs, movies, video clips, or news articles gain sudden

and wide popularity, while other ones that are similar in quality, content, and presentation (if not better) do not become viral.

(Al-Rawi, 2017: 2)

Viral news is defined as networked news stories that spread online, predominantly via social media, faster and wider than other news stories. It involves the acts of link promotion, liking, favoriting, voting, tagging, bookmarking and most often re-posting and commenting on news items (Dwyer and Martin, 2017).

Digital native news website **BuzzFeed** has become an expert in the field of virality since its original purpose was to spot and curate viral content from across the internet. Similarly, news and entertainment company LADBible carefully constructs its content with the deliberate aim of making it "go viral." The news industry as a whole is utilizing sharing metrics, together with other forms of **web analytics**, in a bid to measure audience attention and engagement alongside story impact. Shareability is now a factor in the news selection process which journalists consider when deciding whether a story is newsworthy or not (Harcup and O'Neill, 2016). This raises questions about the pursuit of attention grabbing, potentially viral stories that will interest the public over **public service** journalism, with the emphasis simply shifting from **clickbait** to sharebait.

The challenge for journalists and editors who pursue the golden goose of viral news is that it is difficult to predict shareability factors and it is completely outside of their control. Research in the field is somewhat contradictory although the general consensus is that for content to become viral it must have perceived social value (Jenkins, Ford and Green, 2013) and be related to a user's beliefs and values (Hermida, 2014). Picone, De Wolf and Robijt also argue that news stories that go viral appeal to people's desire to connect to others, enabling news to become "a means to connect rather than merely a container of information" (2016: 929). This connection is a constructive relationship, with social media news readers preferring to share overwhelmingly positive news (Al-Rawi, 2017) despite the old adage that the public prefer bad news. News stories that contain unusual or odd events or have social significance due to the magnitude of economic, cultural, public or political events also make news more likely to become viral on Twitter (Al-Rawi, 2017).

Key Sources

Al-Rawi, A. 2017 "Viral News on Social Media" *Digital Journalism*, doi:10.1080/21670811.2017.1387062

Dwyer, T. and Martin, F. 2017 "Sharing News Online: Social Media News Analytics and Their Implications for Media Pluralism Policies" *Digital Journalism* 5(8): 1080–1100

Hermida, A. 2014 *Tell Everyone: Why We Share and Why It Matters.* Canada: Doubleday

Jenkins, H., Ford, S. and Green, J. 2013 *Spreadable Media: Creating Value and Meaning in a Networked Culture.* New York: New York University Press

Picone, I., De Wolf, R. and Robijt, S. 2016 "Who Shares What with Whom and Why? News Sharing Profiles amongst Flemish News Users" *Digital Journalism* 4(7): 921–932

VISUAL ETHNOGRAPHY

As part of the broader scholarly discipline of anthropology, ethnography is concerned with the understanding and interpretation of social organizations, attitudes, behavior, beliefs and cultures. It employs qualitative methodological approaches to research design, which typically involve interviews and lengthy periods of participant observation. Ethnography tries to achieve an understanding of "what people believe and think and how they live their daily lives" (Brennen, 2013: 159) by establishing, analyzing and interrogating research subjects' own understandings of their beliefs and behaviors. When the research design involves the use of photography, video or live streaming, it is referred to as visual ethnography. In recent times it has become an increasingly popular element in research design for at least two reasons.

First, in an important and influential article, Simon Cottle (2009) critiqued six current research approaches to **news** production studies as outdated, "out of touch" and issued a call for a "second wave" of news ethnographies to "theoretically map and empirically explore the production of today's fast-changing and differentiated news ecology" (2009: 366). Many scholars answered his call. Second, Bonnie Brennen argued that the marked increase in the popularity of ethnography in scholarly studies of media may be explained by the recent expansion in the use of digital media technologies (2013: 160). She cites the growing prevalence of surveillance cameras which observe and record people in their day-to-day public activities, the near obsessive concern with "selfies," which endlessly record our social and often private behavior on **smartphones**, while the subsequent uploading of images to **Facebook** and other

VISUAL ETHNOGRAPHY

social media necessarily blurs the boundaries between the public and private realm. In a society seemingly "fixated" with observing and recording the public behavior of others but also making our own actions and behavior a matter of public record, it is perhaps inevitable that ethnographic studies will flourish.

Gillárová, Tejkálová, and Láb's research study of the working practices of Czech **journalists** across a wide range of beats (sport, music and news) offers a "nuts and bolts" account of visual ethnographic research on photojournalists' changing working conditions and practices. The research design involved a "photo elicitation technique" in which observation was achieved by using photographs of journalists in the newsroom taken both by members of the research team and by the journalists involved as research subjects ("auto-photography") in the project. Each journalist took 25–30 photographs to capture a single representative working day, the tasks they performed and the people/colleagues they met and worked with. Journalists were subsequently interviewed about their changed working practices and conditions, using the photographs to trigger questions but also as illustrative evidence of how – as photojournalists – they actually went about the activities involved in news production (Gillárová, Tejkálová and Láb, 2012: 406).

The researchers argued that combining interviews with the photo elicitation technique offered many advantages over previous research. In interviews, the journalists served as "ice-breakers" and enjoyed greater self-confidence because their photographs allowed them to "set the topics of conversation," prompting a "greater openness and emotionality" in their answers. Interviews became "conversations" rather than "one sided interrogations" and respondents' photographs jogged their "memories and recollections" of important details otherwise likely to be forgotten. In sum, the researchers suggested that the application of visual ethnography enabled them "to overcome the disadvantages of the newsroom approaches" identified by Cottle and enabled them to "monitor the complex structure of journalists' workdays including their work routines, work environment, the spatial arrangement of newsrooms, the organizational hierarchy of their workplace as well as the influence of their work on their privacy." Visual ethnography allowed them the opportunity to gain a "richer insight into Czech journalists' everyday working life" (Gillárová, Tejkálová and Lab, 2012: 411).

Key Sources

Brennen, B. 2013 *Qualitative Research Methods for Media Studies*. Oxford: Routledge

Cottle, S. 2009 "New(S) Times: Towards a 'Second Wave' of News Ethnography" in Hansen, A., Cottle, S., Negrine, R. and Newbold, C. (Eds) *Mass Communication Research Methods, SAGE Benchmarks in Social Research Methods,* Vol. 1. London: Sage, 366–386

Gillárová, K. S., Tejkálová, A. N. and Láb, F. 2012 "The Undressed Newsroom: The Application of Visual Ethnography in Media Research" in Franklin, B. (Ed) *The Future of Journalism in an Age of Digital Media and Economic Uncertainty.* London: Routledge, 411–417

VLOGS

A video blog, or video log, shortened to vlog, which is uploaded to the internet, often on popular video sharing platform **YouTube**. The pioneers of this form of communication included Luuc Bouwman, who started a video diary of his post college travels in 2002, uploading content at internet cafes to his website back in the Netherlands, and American Steve Garfield, who launched his own video blog on January 1, 2004 declaring it "the year of the video blog" (Garfield, 2004).

What followed was a massive explosion in online video diaries as YouTube launched in 2005, becoming the fifth most popular web destination in just a year, with 100 million videos viewed daily and 65,000 new uploads per day. In recent years, the millennial generation has sought to monetize vlogging and there are now many celebrity vloggers who are worth millions of dollars. YouTube stars such as Swedish video game commentator PewDiePie, who has over 60 million subscribers and earned an estimated £12million in 2017 (Lynch, 2018), receive an income from adverts and sponsorship deals. These popular culture entertainers who often vlog on music, fashion and gaming have **social influence**, meaning they have established credibility in a specific industry via their audience and reach on **social media**. The impact on entertainment journalism is wide reaching, as younger audiences are turning away from traditional sources of entertainment **news** and seeking out these alternative voices.

Journalists themselves have experimented with vlogging, using the form to speak to camera about their thoughts, opinions or experiences, or to show what goes on behind the scenes of a news story, such as WGNO television anchor Jacki Jing. However, this has met with limited success and, as such, has not become a popular communication tool, with journalists preferring to stick to traditional blogging with the occasional illustrative video.

There is some evidence that vlogging is effective at engaging young people in political discussion, particularly around challenging normative beliefs about sex and gender, transphobia and homophobia. Rather than turn to traditional news **sources** to engage in civic and political life, young Canadians engage in social injustice issues via YouTube vlogs, which Ruby, Goggin and Keane (2017) argue is an important venue for the production and dissemination of youth perspectives.

Key Sources
Raby, R., Caron, C., Théwissen-LeBlanc, S., Prioletta, J. and Mitchell, C. 2018 "Vlogging on YouTube: The Online, Political Engagement of Young Canadians Advocating for Social Change" *Journal of Youth Studies* 21(4): 495–512

WEB 2.0

In the early stages of the web, newspapers replicated their printed publications by mirroring them online. These were simple sites with repurposed text, a few photographs and crude archives and forums that had an indirect connection to the audience. However, the arrival of Web 2.0 around 2005 brought new dynamics to newspaper websites, making them the multimedia, interactive, networked, participatory websites with a direct connection to the audience that we see today. Prior to Web 2.0, audiences could visit websites to look at the content and possibly add a comment in the forum, but their involvement stopped there.

There is disagreement over what the term Web 2.0 means, but it is most often cited as having originated from the Web 2.0 conference in 2005, created by Tim O'Reilly and John Battelle (O'Reilly, 2005). This conference was designed to rebuild confidence following the dot.com bust. O'Reilly and Battelle defined Web 2.0 as harnessing collective intelligence and building applications that literally got better the more people used them.

The impact of Web 2.0 on newspaper websites meant this community of collective users could also be harnessed for gathering news content and could actively participate online rather than passively consume their **news**. O'Reilly and Battelle (2009) also presented the notion of Web Squared, where the internet works in real time, collecting, presenting and responding to **user-generated content**. This is increased exponentially by user participation and, as such, news is driven by the collective work of users online and the ability for news to spread instantaneously in real time through social networking sites such as **Twitter**.

Key Sources
O'Reilly, T. 2005 "What Is Web 2.0?" *O'Reilly* www.oreilly.com/pub/a// web2/archive/what-is-web-20.html
O'Reilly, T. and Battelle, J. 2009 "Web Squared: Web 2.0 Five Years On" Web 2.0 Summit https://conferences.oreilly.com/web2summit/web2009/public/ schedule/detail/10194

WEB ANALYTICS

Tracking the audience has always been an integral part of **journalism** via ratings, circulation figures and audience surveys, with newsrooms receiving additional feedback via quaint methods such as letters to the **editor** and calls to the broadcasting station. However, in the past, journalists largely ignored, or rejected, audience feedback, dismissing it as inaccurate and uninformed. Web analytics, also known as web metrics, has swung the pendulum in the opposite direction, with editors now glued to wall-mounted **newsroom** screens, projecting real time data of hits, clicks and views via programs such as Chartbeat. These analytics measure, collect, analyze and report internet data for the purposes of "understanding and optimizing web usage" (DAA, 2008). This data enables journalists to get information about how many views each story is getting, how much time readers are spending on each story, what pages lead them to the homepage, and what pages they were viewing when they decided to leave the website, among others (Tandoc, 2015).

The tendency is for **news** organizations to use analytic tools to prioritize content that will attract the most traffic and, as a result, editors are displaying more popular stories more prominently on their websites (Lee, Lewis and Powers, 2012).

The measurement of audience usage has gained great commercial value for media owners, becoming the currency to negotiate fees with advertisers. And although there is much discussion over the enhanced value of engagement metrics, which measure time spent on stories rather than just counting clicks on pages, many advertisers are still more interested in clicks than counting time (Neheli, 2018). This means newsrooms often have simplistic page view targets and digital editors monitor what stories have, or are gaining, traction, and on the basis of this will choose the placement of content, develop or follow up on particular stories, share stories via social media to build traffic and then "repeat this frenetic cycle in a seemingly endless loop" (Neheli, 2018: 1041). These metrics have also been incorporated into the more traditional circulation figures in the UK since 2012. The National Readership Survey (NRS) now includes Print and Digital Data, which amalgamates data on print audiences from the NRS and Audit Bureau of Circulations with data about the online audience from ComScore. However, the ABC warns that the real number of individual users may be overstated using these metrics, since a single individual could be counted as a unique user three times if he or she accesses the same website from a home and work computer and a mobile device during the census period (Thurman, 2018).

Aside from the issue of the reliability of such metrics, there is a more primary concern that prioritizing news based on audience popularity is fundamentally flawed. Media scholars Tandoc and Thomas (2015) vehemently argue that journalists must continue to preserve their editorial autonomy online in order to meet the communitarian role of **journalism**. Rather than use web analytics to satisfy the bottom line and deliver low-cost, low-risk, low-need information, journalists should seek to understand why stories considered editorially more important, such as public affairs, do not attract as much traffic. They urge journalists to serve a purpose above and beyond the commercial, and to understand what the audience wants and use that information to balance it against what the audience needs.

Key Sources

DAA 2008 *Web Analytics Definitions* www.digitalanalyticsassociation.org/Files/PDF_standards/WebAnalyticsDefinitions.pdf

Neheli, N. B. 2018 "News by Numbers: The Evolution of Analytics in Journalism" *Digital Journalism* 6(8): 1041–1051

Tandoc, E. 2015 "Why Web Analytics Click: Factors Affecting the Ways Journalists Use Audience Metrics" *Journalism Studies* 16(6): 782–799

Tandoc, E. and Thomas, R. J. 2015 "The Ethics of Web Analytics: Implications of Using Audience Metrics in News Construction" *Digital Journalism* 3(2): 243–258

WIKILEAKS

In its brief but chequered history, website WikiLeaks has presented itself as a neutral brokering service for whistleblowers, an advocacy **journalism** platform and a collaborative source for mainstream media (Lynch, 2013). Founded in 2006 by Australian computer programmer Julian Assange, the controversial non-profit organization currently describes itself as a "multi-national media organization and associated library" which specializes in "the analysis and publication of large datasets of censored or otherwise restricted official materials involving war, spying and corruption" (WikiLeaks, 2015). To date, it has published more than 10 million documents and worked with 100 major media outlets around the world. The organization, which has won numerous awards, relies on a network of volunteers and is funded by Assange, publications sales and public donations.

WikiLeaks fiercely entered the public consciousness in 2010 when it released the Collateral Murder video, footage downloaded and de-encrypted from an American military server that purportedly showed US soldiers firing on unarmed Iraqi civilians and two Reuters employees. This was followed by a series of mega leaks that became known as the Afghan War Logs, the Iraq War logs and the Embassy Cables, or Cablegate. These consisted of 92,000 field reports from Afghanistan, 400,000 reports from Iraq and over 250,000 US diplomatic cables and 700 case reports on prisoners at Guantanamo. The material was published by WikiLeaks and its media partners, including the *Guardian*, the *New York Times* and *Der Spiegel*. The person responsible for the leaks was later identified as Chelsea Manning (born Bradley Manning), a soldier and intelligence analyst in the US Army. She was imprisoned for violating the Espionage Act in 2010 until her release under President Barack Obama in 2017. Now living as a trans woman, Manning is a public speaker and politician. Meanwhile, staff, supporters and alleged sources associated with WikiLeaks have been "aggressively surveilled, pursued, subject to harassment, intimidation, and investigated for publishing documents" in the public interest (Ruby, Goggin and Keane, 2017: 362). The future of WikiLeaks has been particularly precarious since Sweden issued an international arrest warrant for Assange in 2010 over allegations of sexual assault. He has always denied the allegations and expressed concern that he would be extradited from Sweden to the US to face unknown charges over the publication of secret documents. Assange surrendered himself to the UK police in December 2010, who held him in custody before releasing him on bail. He then absconded, breaching his bail and was granted asylum at the Embassy of Ecuador in London, where he has been living ever since. In 2017, Swedish prosecutors dropped their investigation but if Assange leaves the embassy he will be arrested by the Metropolitan Police for breaching his bail conditions. At the time of writing, the recently elected Ecuadorian President Lenin Moreno had begun talks with UK authorities to address Assange's extended asylum at the embassy.

Against the backdrop of the Assange circus, there has been vigorous debate among media scholars and journalists over the legitimization of WikiLeaks as a **journalism** platform and its role and identity within the journalistic field. Is it a media organization, as it purports to be, or is it something else entirely? Ottosen (2012) states that WikiLeaks operates in the borderline between being a collection of sources and being journalism, while Eldridge II redefines the site as a media interloper that is simultaneously an antagonist to professional journalism while claiming to belong to it (2015). In this respect, much of the digitally oriented reportage of WikiLeaks is creating a new mythology of the journalist as a complex anti-hero (Eldridge, 2017). Lynch, however, argues that WikiLeaks is a transitionary platform which has played a vital role in prompting new alliances between emerging and legacy media, helped usher in the big data revolution, spawned imitation leaking **platforms** and prompted debate over the ethics of censorship but also transparency (2013). Upon conception WikiLeaks represented itself as a whistle-blower platform and was identified by the mainstream media as a technological phenomenon, or cyber-activism. But the framing of the Collateral Murder video alongside an investigative package featuring the work of an international team of journalists placed it firmly within advocacy journalism, according to Lynch (2013). From this moment onwards, the website began to describe itself as a not-for-profit media organization and included references to **news** and journalism on its site. This evolved into large-scale collaborations with mainstream media outlets as WikiLeaks stepped back from providing its own interpretation of source documents and moved into the realm of **networked journalism** via the release of hundreds of thousands of war documents. It is here that the organization has faced its most serious criticism surrounding its ethics. These mass disclosures contained the names of military informants, which severely compromised their safety and this sensitive information could have been redacted if enough care had been taken. WikiLeaks has been accused of having blood on its hands for allowing the names of Afghan informers to remain in documents and this has been cited by journalists as an example of WikiLeaks' lack of professionalism.

See also **surveillance**.

Key Sources

Eldridge, II, S. A. 2015 "Boundary Maintenance and Interloper Media Reaction: Differentiating between Journalism's Discursive Enforcement Processes" *Journalism Studies* 15(1): 1–16

Lynch, L. 2013 "Wikileaks after Megaleaks: The Organization's Impact on Journalism and Journalism Studies" *Digital Journalism* 1(3): 314–334

WikiLeaks 2015 "What Is WikiLeaks?" WikiLeaks https://wikileaks.org/What-is-WikiLeaks.html

WIKIPEDIA

In its own amendable words, Wikipedia is a "multilingual, web-based, free encyclopedia based on a model of openly editable and viewable content" (Wikipedia, 2018). Founded in 2001 by Jimmy Wales and Larry Sanger, it is the largest general reference work on the internet, hosting more than 40 million articles in 301 different languages. By February 2014, it had reached 18 billion page views and nearly 500 million unique visitors per month. The information behemoth is owned by the non-profit organization Wikimedia Foundation and is supported by public donations.

Anyone can upload or edit content on the website which has raised considerable legitimate concerns about its reliability and resulted in many high-profile hoaxes. In 2005, it was discovered that an entry for John Seigenthaler, a retired newspaper **editor**, was false and had gone undetected for four months. An anonymous user had changed Seigenthaler's genuine biography to say that he was suspected of being involved in the assassinations of John F. Kennedy and Robert F. Kennedy (Messner and South, 2011). This is a prime example of how the wiki technology, which enables anyone to contribute or alter information on Wikipedia, is ultimately the platform's greatest strength but also its greatest weakness (Halavais and Lackaff, 2008). Wikipedia urges contributors to cite their sources, adopt a neutral point of view and follow other editorial guidelines and policies but its collaborative, open door character means that users do not have to obey the rules.

According to the website, "allowing anyone to edit Wikipedia means that it is more easily vandalized or susceptible to unchecked information" (Wikipedia, 2008). Conversely, in the same year as the Seigenthaler complaint, science journal *Nature* published a peer review comparing 42 science articles from *Encyclopædia Britannica* and Wikipedia, finding similar levels of accuracy between both.

Furthermore, analysis of journalist's use of Wikipedia as a news source at five US national newspapers over an eight-year period found that the framing of the online encyclopedia was predominantly neutral and positive (Messner and South, 2011). A content analysis of 1486 Wikipedia references in the *New York Times*, the *Washington Post*, the *Wall Street Journal, USA Today* and the *Christian Science Monitor* found that the website was increasingly being used as a **news** source, which in turn boosted its legitimacy and credibility.

Key Sources

Halavais, A. and Lackaff, D. 2008 "An Analysis of Topical Coverage of Wikipedia" *Journal of Computer-Mediated Communication* 13(2): 429–440

Messner, M. and South, J. 2011 "Legitimizing Wikipedia: How US National Newspapers Frame and Use the Online Encyclopedia in Their Coverage" *Journalism Practice* 5(2): 145–160

Wikipedia 2008 "About" Wikipedia https://en.wikipedia.org/wiki/Wikipedia: About

YOUTUBE

A young man glibly commenting on long elephant trunks at San Diego Zoo is one of the most influential videos of all time. *Me at the Zoo* was the first clip to be uploaded to video-sharing website YouTube in 2005, by site co-founder Jawed Karim. The platform, which was bought by **Google** in 2006 for $1.65 billion in shares, has subsequently become the world's second most popular website with more than 400 hours of content uploaded every minute. One billion hours of content are watched on YouTube every day as users view, upload, share, favorite, subscribe and comment on videos. It earns **advertising** revenue from Google AdSense and, although the majority of videos are free to view, it also offers subscription-based premium channels, film rentals and YouTube Premium, which gives access to advert-free and exclusive content. The site offers a wide variety of **user-generated content (UGC)** and corporate media videos, including short clips, music videos, documentaries, movie trailers, live streams and video blogging, known as vlogging. Most of the content is uploaded by individuals, but media corporations, including CBS, BBC, Vevo and Hulu offer some of their material via the YouTube partnership program. In 2010, YouTube began free streaming certain content, including cricket matches from the Indian Premier League, a question-and-answer session with President Barack Obama and the 2012 London Olympics. In October 2012, more than eight million people watched Felix Baumgartner's jump from the edge of space as a live stream on YouTube, illustrating the popularity of the online video platform and its growing dominance over legacy broadcasters.

Owing to its incredible reach, YouTube, like other platform-sharing giants, has faced fierce criticism over its handling of offensive material. The uploading of videos containing **defamation**, pornography and encouraging criminal conduct are prohibited by the company's community guidelines but YouTube relies on users to flag inappropriate content before an employee determines whether it should be removed. It has also been caught up in the Prism **surveillance** scandal, alongside telecommunications software **Skype**, allowing the National Security Agency in the US access to users' information.

The impact of YouTube on **journalism** production and distribution has been colossal, particularly as a source for eyewitness content. Major **news** events, whether human or natural, are now broken via **social media**, messaging apps and sharing networks by members of the public on the ground. These citizens are in the heart of the action hours before the professional journalists arrive. Following the 2010 Haiti earthquake, mainstream media organizations had to rely on amateur videos on YouTube to report what had happened because they were initially unable to access the Caribbean island (Bruno, 2011). Furthermore, the BBC has integrated UGC into its World News TV coverage of conflicts using YouTube as the main newsgathering source for video footage. BBC News' footage of the first six months of the Syrian conflict heavily relied on UGC for its TV reports, which led to an evolution in some journalistic roles and responsibilities, particularly processes of newsgathering, verification and dissemination (Johnston, 2016). YouTube is also host to a huge proportion of videos created by online news websites – both mainstream and digital native – as it is free to use and easy to embed into external sites. The *Guardian*, the *New York Times* and CNN all have YouTube channels, enabling users to subscribe to their video content.

Declining television news audiences have also forced media organizations to rethink their distribution methods and turn to **platforms** such as YouTube to engage younger people. This is having an impact on the types of videos that traditional news broadcasters produce, as the news values of online video differ to **legacy media**. A content analysis of 882 videos on YouTube by Peer and Ksiazek (2011) revealed that most news videos adhered to traditional production methods but broke from common content standards. Online videos repurposed from broadcast platforms experienced a spike in viewership when they broke from traditional content standards such as objectivity, suggesting that such deviations in traditional television news are especially valued by audiences.

Key Sources

Peer, L. and Ksiazek, T. 2011 "YouTube and the Challenge to Journalism: New Standards for News Videos Online" *Journalism Studies* 12(1): 45–63

REFERENCES

Abdenour, J. 2017 "Digital Gumshoes: Investigative Journalists' Use of Social Media in Television News Reporting" *Digital Journalism* 5(4): 472–492.

Adweek. 2010 "What Exactly Is a Social Media Editor/Manager?" *Adweek* www.adweek.com/digital/what-exactly-is-social-media/

AdYouLike. 2015 "Native Advertising Set to Double by 2018" PRNewswire 18 December www.prnewswire.com/news-releases/native-advertising-set-to-double-by-2018-562919861.html

Agarwal, S. D. and Barthel, M. 2015 "The Friendly Barbarians: Professional Norms and Work Routines of Online Journalists in the United States" *Journalism* 16(3): 376–391.

Ahva, L. 2017 "How Is Participation Practiced by 'In-Betweeners' of Journalism" *Journalism Practice* 11(2–3): 142–159.

Aitamurto, T. 2013 "Balancing between Open and Closed: Co-Creation in Magazine Journalism" *Digital Journalism* 1(2): 229–251.

Aitamurto, T. 2015 "Crowdsourcing as a Knowledge Search Method in Digital Journalism: Ruptured Ideals and Blended Responsibility" *Digital Journalism* 4 (2): 280–297.

Aitamurto, T. 2017 "Crowdsourcing in Open Journalism: Benefits, Challenges and Value Creation" in Franklin, B. and Eldridge, II, S. (Eds.) *The Routledge Companion to Digital Journalism Studies.* London: Routledge, 185–193.

Aldridge, M. 2007 *Understanding the Local Media.* Maidenhead: Open University Press.

Allan, S. 2007 "Citizen Journalism and the Rise of Mass Self-Communication: Reporting the London Bombings" *Global Media Journal* 1(1) http://stc.uws.edu.au/gmjau/iss1_2007/stuart_allan.html

Allan, S. 2013 *Citizen Witnessing: Revisioning Journalism in Times of Crisis.* Cambridge: Polity Press.

Allan, S., Carter, C., Cushion, S., Dencik, L., Garcia-Blanco, I., Harris, J., Sambrook, R., Wahl-Jorgensen, K. and Williams, A. 2019 *The Future of Journalism: Risks, Threats and Opportunities.* London: Routledge.

Allcott, H. and Gentzkow, M. 2017 *Social Media and Fake News in the 2016 Election* http://web.stanford.edu/~gentzkow/research/fakenews.pdf

Al-Rawi, A. 2017 "Viral News on Social Media" *Digital Journalism*, doi: 10.1080/21670811.2017.1387062.

REFERENCES

American Press Institute. "What Does a Journalist Do?" www.americanpressin stitute.org/journalism-essentials/what-is-journalism/journalist/ Accessed 31st October 2016.

Ananny, M. and Crawford, K. 2015 "A Liminal Press: Situating News App Designers within A Field of Networked News Production" *Digital Journalism* 3(2): 192–208.

Andén-Papadopoulos, K. 2013 "Citizen Camera-Witnessing: Embodied Political Dissent in the Age of 'Mediated Mass Self-Communication'" *New Media and Society* 16(5): 753–769.

Anderson, C. W. 2011a "Between Creative and Quantified Audiences: Web Metrics and Changing Patterns of Newswork in Local US Newsrooms" *Journalism* 12(5): 550–566.

Anderson, C. W. 2011b "Deliberative, Agonistic and Algorithmic Audiences: Journalism's Vision of Its Public in an Age of Audience Transparency" *International Journal of Communication* 5: 529–547.

Anderson, C. W., Bell, E. and Shirky, C. 2014 *Post Industrial Journalism: Adapting to the Present.* Retrieved from http://towcenter.org/research/post-industrial-journalism-adapting-to-the-present-2/

Anderson, F. 2009 "Mosquitoes Dancing on the Surface of the Pond: Australian Conflict Reporting and Technology" *Journalism Practice* 3(4): 404–420.

Artwick, C. 2019 "Social Media Livestreaming" in Eldridge, II, S. and Franklin, B. (Eds) *The Routledge Handbook of Developments in Digital Journalism Studies.* London: Routledge, 296–310.

ASNE 2017 "Newsroom Diversity Survey" *ASNE* www.asne.org/diversity-survey-2017

Atton, C. 2002 "News Cultures and New Social Movements: Radical Journalism and the Mainstream Media" *Journalism Studies* 3(4): 491–505.

Atton, C. and Hamilton, J. F. 2008 *Alternative Journalism.* London: Sage.

AZ Quotes.com, Marcel Proust. Wind and Fly Ltd. (accessed March 20 2019).

Baines, D. and Kennedy, C. 2010 "An Education for Independence: Should Entrepreneurial Skills Be an Essential Part of the Journalist's Toolbox?" *Journalism Practice* 4(1): 97–113.

Bane, K. 2017 "Tweeting the Agenda: How Print and Alternative Web-Only News Organizations Use Twitter as a Source" *Journalism Practice*, doi: 10.1080/17512786.2017.1413587.

Bakker, P. 2012 "Aggregation, Content Farms and Huffinization: The Rise of Low Pay and No-Pay Journalism" *Journalism Practice* 6(5–6): 627–637.

Banks, D. 2011 "A Brief Summary of Actor Network Theory" *Cyborology* 21st December https://thesocietypages.org/cyborgology/2011/12/02/a-brief-summary-of-actor-network-theory/

Barnett, S. and Seymour, E. 1999 *A Shrinking Iceberg Travelling South: Changing Trends in British Television – A Case Study of Drama and Current Affairs.* London: Campaign for Quality Television.

REFERENCES

BBC. 2011 "News Feeds from the BBC" BBC News www.bbc.co.uk/news/10628494

BBC. 2018 "Caddington Village News Blogger Sued for Libel over Fraud Claims" BBC News www.bbc.co.uk/news/amp/uk-england-beds-bucks-herts-46305141?__twitter_impression=true&fbclid=IwAR0zqaocTpgir2qJS6B WMRWdj0NDIy8rdEs3ZAGLCyNrooYjkKFD8lrv-o

BBC News Labs. 2018 "Bots" http://bbcnewslabs.co.uk/projects/bots/

Beard, M. 2009 "Is There Still Life in the List?" *Guardian* 12 December, www.theguardian.com/books/2009/dec/12/umberto-eco-lists-book-review

Bechmann, A. and Nielbo, K. L. 2018 "Are We Exposed to the Same 'News' in the News Feed?" *Digital Journalism*, doi: 10.1080/21670811.2018.1510741.

Bednarek, M. 2016 "Investigating Evaluation and News Values in News Items that are Shared through Social Media" *Corpora* 11(2): 227–257.

Belair Gagnon, V., Owen, T. and Holton, A. E. 2017 "Unmanned Aerial Vehicles and Journalistic Disruption" *Digital Journalism* published online 27 January, doi : 10.1080/21670811.2017.1279019.

Belt, D. and South, J. 2015 "Slow Journalism and the Out of Eden Walk" *Digital Journalism* 4(4): 547–562.

Bennett, A. 2016 "10 Reasons Why David Cameron Will Enjoy the EU Referendum Campaign" *Daily Telegraph* 26th February www.telegraph.co.uk/news/newstopics/eureferendum/12173413/10-reasons-David-Cameron-will-enjoy-the-EU-referendum-campaign.html

Bennett, D. 2013 *Digital Media and Reporting Conflict: Blogging and the BBC's Coverage of War and Terrorism*. London: Routledge.

Bennett, D. 2016 "Sourcing the BBC's Live Online Coverage of Terror Attacks" *Digital Journalism* 5(7): 861–874.

Berelson, B. 1952 "Content Analysis in Communications Research" in Berelson, B. and Janowitz, M. (Eds) (1966) *Reader in Public Opinion and Communication*. New York: Free Press, 260–266.

Berglez, P. 2008 "What Is Global Journalism? Theoretical and Empirical Conceptualisation" *Journalism Studies* 9(6): 845–858.

Berglez, P. 2011 "Global Journalism: An Emerging News Style and an Outline for a Training Program" in Franklin, B. and Mensing, D. (Eds) *Journalism Education, Training and Employment*. London: Routledge, 143–154.

Berkowitz, D. and Schwartz, D. A. 2015 "Miley, CNN and the Onion: When Fake News Becomes Realer than Real" *Journalism Practice*, doi: 10.1080/17512786.2015.1006933.

Berners-Lee, T. and Cailliau, R. 1990 "WorldWideWeb: Proposal for a HyperText Project" w3.org www.w3.org/Proposal.html

Blankenship, J. 2016 "Losing Their Mojo? Mobile Journalism and the Deprofessionalization of Television News Work" *Journalism Practice* 10(8): 1055–1071.

Blumler, J. G. 2011 "Foreword: The Two Legged Crisis of Journalism" in Franklin, B. (Ed) *The Future of Journalism*. London: Routledge, xv–xvii.

REFERENCES

Booth, R. 2009 "Trafigura: A Few Tweets and Freedom of Speech Is Restored" *Guardian* www.guardian.co.uk/media/2009/oct/13/trafigura-tweets-freedom-of-speech

Borel, B. 2016 *The Chicago Guide to Fact Checking*. Chicago: University of Chicago Press.

Borges Rey, E. 2015 "News Images on Instagram: The Paradox of Authenticity in Hypereal Photo Reportage" *Digital Journalism* 3(4): 571–593.

Bouchart, M. 2018 "This Is What the Best of Data Journalism Looks Like" https://medium.com/data-journalism-awards/this-is-what-the-best-of-data-journalism-looks-like-6f1713d60479

Bourdieu, P. 2005 "The Political Field, the Social Science Field and the Journalistic Field" in Benson, R. and Neveu, E. (Eds) *Bourdieu and the Journalistic Field*. Cambridge: Polity Press, 29–47.

Bowman, S. and Willis, C. 2003 *We Media: How Audiences are Shaping the Future of News and Information*. Hypergene www.hypergene.net/wemedia/weblog.php

Boyd, A. 2001 *Broadcast Journalism: Techniques of Radio and Television*. Oxford: Focal Press.

Boyd, D. 2013 "Bibliography of Research on Twitter & Microblogging" www.danah.org/researchBibs/twitter.php

Boyd-Barrett, O. 1970 "Journalism Recruitment and Training: Problems in Professionalization" in Tunstall, J. (Ed) *Media Sociology: A Reader*. London: Constable.

Brandstetter, B. and Schmalhofer, J. 2014 "Paid Content: A Successful Revenue Model for Publishing Houses in Germany?" *Journalism Practice* 8(5): 499–507.

Brantzaeg, P., Folstad, A. and Chaperro-Dominguez, M. A. 2017 "Usefulness and Trust in Online Fact-Checking and Verification Services" *Journalism Practice*, doi: 10.1080/17512786.2017.1363657.

Brantzaeg, P., Folstad, A. and Chaperro-Dominguez, M. A. 2018 "How Journalists and Social Media Users Perceive Online Fact-Checking and Verification Services" *Journalism Practice* 12(9): 1109–1129.

Brennen, B. 2013 *Qualitative Research Methods for Media Studies*. Oxford: Routledge.

Briggs, M. 2012 *Entrepreneurial Journalism: How to Build What's Next for News*. London: Sage.

Brinkhurst-Cuff, C. 2017 "MPs To Investigate Threat to Democracy from 'Fake News'" *Guardian* www.theguardian.com/media/2017/jan/29/fake-news-mps-investigate-threat-democracy

Bro, P. 2017 "Gatekeeping and Agenda Setting: Extinct or Extant in a Digital Era?" in Franklin, B. and Eldridge, II, S. (Eds) *The Routledge Companion to Digital Journalism Studies*. London: Routledge, 75–84.

Broersma, M. (Ed.) 2007 *Form and Style in Journalism: European Newspapers and the Representation of News, 1880–2005*. Leuven: Paris and Dudley.

Broersma, M. and Graham, T. 2012 "Social Media as Beat: Tweets as a News Source during the 2010 British and Dutch Elections" *Journalism Practice* 6(3): 403–419.

REFERENCES

Broersma, M. and Graham, T. 2013 "Twitter as A Source of News: How Dutch and British Newspapers Used Tweets in Their News Coverage 2007–2011" *Journalism Practice* 7(4): 446–454.

Broussard, M. 2014 "Artificial Intelligence for Investigative Reporting. Using an Expert System to Enhance Journalists' Ability to Discover Original Public Affairs Stories" *Digital Journalism* www.tandfonline.com/doi/abs/10.1080/21670811.2014.985497

Brown, M. 2010 "Why Freelancing Is Now a Dead Loss" *British Journalism Review* 21(1): 61–65.

Bruno, N. 2011 "Tweet First, Verify Later. How Real Time Information Is Changing the Coverage of Worldwide Crisis Events" *Reuters Institute for the Study of Journalism* http://reutersinstitute.politics.ox.ac.uk/about/news/item/article/tweet-first-verify-later-new-fell.html

Bruns, A. 2005 *Gatewatching: Collaborative Online News Production*. New York: Peter Lang.

Bruns, A. 2008 *Blogs, Wikipedia, Second Life and Beyond: From Production to Produsage*. London: Peter Lang.

Bruns, A. 2010 "Oblique Strategies for Ambient Journalism" *M/C Journal* 13(2) http://journal.media-culture.org.au/index.php/mcjournal/article/viewArticle/230

Bruns, A. and Highfield, T. 2012 "Blogs, Twitter and Breaking News: The Produsage Of Citizen Journalism" in Lind, R. (Ed) *Produsing Theory in a Digital World 2.0: The Intersection of Audiences and Production in Contemporary Theory*. New York: Peter Lang, 15–32.

Bureau of Investigative Journalism. 2018 "About Bureau Local" The Bureau of Investigative Journalism www.thebureauinvestigates.com/explainers/about-the-project

Burns, L. K. 2014 "Wikipedia, Wikinews and Gatewatching" https://mfjs2210win2014.wordpress.com/2014/02/13/wikipedia-wikinews-and-gatewatching/

BuzzFeed www.buzzfeed.com/expresident/pictures-that-will-restore-your-faith-in-humanity?utm_term=.uqGzOA0QAQ#.tuVgYoQrorListverselistverse.com/ Accessed 16 June 2016.

Cambridge English Dictionary online. https://dictionary.cambridge.org/dictionary/english/gatecrash

Canter, L. 2013a "The Interactive Spectrum: The Use of Social Media in UK Regional Newspapers" *Convergence: the International Journal of Research into New Media Technologies* 19(4): 472–495.

Canter, L. 2013b "The Source, the Resource and the Collaborator: The Role of Citizen Journalism in Local UK Newspapers" *Journalism* 14(8): 1091–1109.

Canter, L. 2014a "Returning to the Newsroom: A Journalism Lecturer's Tale" www.lilycanter.co.uk/academic/returning-to-the-newsroom-a-journalism-lecturers-tale/

REFERENCES

Canter, L. 2014b "Personalised Tweeting: The Emerging Practices of Journalists on Twitter" *Digital Journalism* 3(6): 888–907.

Canter, L. 2014c "From Traditional Gatekeeper to Professional Verifier: How Local Newspaper Journalists are Adapting to Change" *Journalism Education: The Journal of the Association of Journalism Education* 3(1): 102–119.

Canter, L. 2015a "Weeklies Cutting Corners in Rush to Publish on Web" Hold the Front Page www.holdthefrontpage.co.uk/2014/news/weeklies-cutting-corners-in-rush-to-publish-on-web/

Canter, L. 2015b "Chasing the Accreditation Dream: Do Employers Value Accredited Journalism Courses?" *Journalism Education* 4(1): 40–52.

Canter, L. 2017a "Media Cannibalism and Learning from Experience" www.lilycanter.co.uk/money/media-cannibalism-and-learning-from-experience/

Canter, L. 2017b "It's Not Just Commercial Media Giants, the BBC Cannabilise Too" www.lilycanter.co.uk/money/its-not-just-commercial-media-giants-the-bbc-cannabilise-too/

Canter, L. 2018 "It's Not All Cat Videos: Moving beyond Legacy Media and Tackling the Challenges of Mapping News Values on Digital Native Websites" *Digital Journalism* 6(8): 1101–1112, doi: 10.1080/21670811.2018.1503058.

Canter, L. and Brookes, D. 2016 "Twitter as a Flexible Tool: How the Job Role of the Journalist Influences Tweeting Habits" *Digital Journalism* 4(7): 875–885.

Capati, M. K. 2015 "5 Crowdsourced News Platforms Shaping the Future of Journalism" Crowd Sourcing Week 30th June https://crowdsourcingweek.com/blog/5-crowdsourced-news-platforms/

Carey, J. 2000 "Some Personal Notes on US Journalism Education" *Journalism* 1 (1): 12–23.

Carey, J. 2017 "The Magazine Market Isn't Dead, It's Different" journalism.co.uk www.journalism.co.uk/news-commentary/the-magazine-market-isn-t-dead-it-s-different/s6/a698229/

Carlson, M. 2014a "When News Sites Go Native: Redefining the Advertising–Editorial Divide in Response to Native Advertising" *Journalism*, doi: 10.1177/1464884914545441.

Carlson, M. 2014b "The Robotic Reporter: Automated Journalism and the Redefinition of Labor, Compositional Forms, and Journalistic Authority" *Digital Journalism* 3(3): 416–431.

Carlson, M. and Lewis, S. (Eds) 2015 *Boundaries of Journalism: Professionalism, Practices and Participation.* London: Routledge.

Carlson, M., Robinson, S., Lewis, S. C. and Berkowitz, D. 2018 "Journalism Studies and Its Core Commitments: The Making of a Communication Field" *Journal of Communication* 68(1): 6–25.

Carpenter, S., Cepak, A. and Peng, Z. 2018 "An Exploration of the Complexity of Journalistic Interviewing Competencies" *Journalism Studies* 19(15): 2283–2303.

Carpentier, N. 2011 *Media and Participation: A Site of Ideological-Democratic Struggle.* Bristol: Intellect Press.

REFERENCES

Carson, A. 2015 "Behind the Newspaper Paywall and Lessons in Charging for Online Content: A Comparative Analysis of Why Australian Newspapers are Stuck in the Purgatorial Space between Digital and Print" *Media, Culture and Society* 37(7): 1–20.

Carvajal, M., Aviles, J. A. and Gonzalez, J. L. 2013 "Crowdfunding and Non-Profit Media: The Emergence of New Models for Public Interest Journalism" in Franklin, B. (Ed) *The Future of Journalism; Developments and Debates*. London: Routledge, 101–110.

Carvajal, M., García-Avilés, J. A. and González, J. L. 2012 "Crowdfunding and Non-Profit Media: The Emergence of New Models for Public Interest Journalism" *Journalism Practice* 6(5–6): 638–647.

Casswell, D. and Dorr, K. 2018 "Automated Journalism 2.0: Events Driven Narrative: From Simple Descriptions to Real Stories" *Journalism Practice* 12(4): 477–496.

Castellani, S. 2016 "Everything You Need to Know about Digital Platforms" Stephane Castellani http://stephane-castellani.com/everything-you-need-to-know-about-digital-platforms/

Castells, M. 2007 "Communication, Power and Counter-Power in the Network Society" *International Journal of Communication* 1(1): 238–266.

Castells, M. 2015 *Networks of Outrage and Hope: Social Movements in the Internet Age* (2nd Edition). Cambridge: Polity Press.

Chadha, M. 2016 "The Neighborhood Hyperlocal: New Kid on the Block or a Chip off the Old One?" *Digital Journalism* 4(6): 743–763.

Chantler, P. and Harris, S. 1997 *Local Radio Journalism*. Oxford: Focal Press.

Charman, S. 2007 "The Changing Role of Journalists in a World Where Everyone Can Publish" The Freedom of Expression Project www.freedomofexpression.org.uk/resources/the+changing+role+of+journalists+in+a+world+where+everyone+can+publish

Chen, B. 2012 "How Reddit Scooped the Press on the Aurora Shootings" Bits Blog, *New York Times* July 23 http://bits.blogs.nytimes.com/2012/07/23/reddit-aurora-shooter-aff/

Cheng, Z., Golan, G. and Kiousis, S. 2016 "The Second-Level Agenda-Building Function of the Xinhua News Agency: Examining the Role of Government-Sponsored News in Mediated Public Diplomacy" *Journalism Practice* 10(6): 744–762.

Chippindale, P. and Horrie, C. 1990 *Stick It up Your Punter! The Rise and Fall of the Sun*. London: Heinemann.

Christensen, C. 2013 "The Innovators Dilemma: When New Technologies Cause Great Firms to Fail" *Harvard Business Review* November 19 https://hbr.org/product/the-innovator-s-dilemma-when-new-technologies-cause-great-firms-to-fail/1196XE-KND-ENG

Christensen, C., Skok, D. and Allworth, J. 2012 "Breaking News: Mastering the Art of Disruptive Innovation in Journalism" *Neiman Reports* September 15th http://neimanreports.org/articles/breaking-news

REFERENCES

Christensen, C. M., Raynor, M. E. and McDonald, R. 2015 "What Is Disruptive Innovation?" *Harvard Business Review* December 2015, 44–53 https://hbr.org/2015/12/what-is-disruptive-innovation

Chua, R. 2013 "The Scarecrow and the Watchdog" http://gijn.org/2013/03/28/the-scarecrow-and-the-watchdog/ (28th March)

Chyi, I. and Tenenboim, O. 2018 "What if the Future Is Not All Digital? Trends in US Newspapers' Multiplatform Readership" in Eldridge, II, S. and Franklin, B. (Eds) *The Routledge Handbook on Developments in Digital Journalism.* London: Routledge, 157–171.

Chyi, I., Lewis, S. C. and Nan, Z. 2012 "A Matter of Life and Death? Examining How Newspapers Covered the Newspaper Crisis'" *Journalism Studies* 13(3): 305–324.

Cision 2013 "Social Journalism Study" www.cision.com/us/2013/12/how-journalists-view-pr-and-social-media/

Clerwall, C. 2014 "Enter the Robot Journalist: Users' Perceptions of Automated Content" *Journalism Practice* 8(5): 519–531.

Cocking, B. 2017 "News Values Go on Holiday: The Ideological Values of Travel Journalism" *Journalism Studies* 27th January ahead of print www.tandfonline.com/doi/full/10.1080/1461670X.2016.1272066

Coddington, M. 2015a "Clarifying Journalism's Quantitative Turn: A Typology for Evaluating Data Journalism, Computational Journalism, and Computer-Assisted Reporting" *Digital Journalism* 3(3): 331–348.

Coddington, M. 2015b "The Wall Becomes a Curtain: Revisiting Journalism's News Business Boundary" in Carlson, M. and Lewis, S. C. (Eds) *Boundaries of Journalism: Professionalism, Practices and Participation.* New York: Routledge, 67–82.

Coddington, M., Lewis, S. C. and Holton, A. E. 2018 "Measuring and Evaluating Reciprocal Journalism as a Concept" *Journalism Practice* 12(8): 1039–1050.

Cohen, B. C. 1963 *The Press and Foreign Policy.* Princeton, NJ: Princeton University Press.

Cohen, N. 2016 *Writers' Rights: Freelance Journalism in A Digital Age.* McGill: Queens University Press.

Colbran, M. 2016 "Leveson's Lasting Effect on Press Police Relations" Media Policy Project Blog, London School of Economics http://blogs.lse.ac.uk/mediapolicyproject/2016/11/14/levesons-lasting-effect-on-press-police-relations/

Cole, P. 2005 "The Structure of the Press Industry" in Keeble, R. (Ed) *Print Journalism: A Critical Introduction.* Abingdon: Routledge, 21–38.

Conboy, M. and Tang, M. 2016 "Core Blighty? How Journalists Define Themselves through Metaphor: *British Journalism Review 2011–2014*" *Journalism Studies* 17(7): 881–892.

Corbyn, J. 2018 Alternative MacTaggart Lecture The full text is available at: https://labour.org.uk/press/full-text-jeremy-corbyns-2018-alternative-mactaggart-lecture/

Coskuntuncel, A. 2019 "Outsourcing Censorship and Surveillance: The Privatization of Governance as an Information Control Strategy in Turkey" in Eldridge, II, S.

REFERENCES

and Franklin, B. (Eds) *The Routledge Handbook of Developments in Digital Journalism Studies*. London: Routledge, 501–514.

Costello, E. 2018 "How Payment on Publication Is Making Life a Misery for Many Freelance Journalists" *Press Gazette* www.pressgazette.co.uk/how-payment-on-publication-is-making-life-a-misery-for-many-freelance-journalists/

Costera Meijer, I. and Groot Kormelink, T. 2015, "Checking, Sharing, Clicking and Linking: Changing Patterns of News Use Between 2004 and 2014" *Digital Journalism* 3(5): 664–679.

Cottle, S. 2009 "New(s) Times: Towards a 'Second Wave' of News Ethnography" in Hansen, A., Cottle, S., Negrine, R. and Newbold, C. (Eds) *Mass Communication Research Methods, SAGE Benchmarks in Social Research Methods*. Vol. 1. London: Sage, 366–386.

Couldry, N. and Turow, J. 2014 "Advertising, Big Data and the Clearance of the Public Realm: Marketers' New Approaches to the Content Subsidy" *International Journal of Communication* 8: 1710–1726.

Crawford, C. S. 2004 "Actor Network Theory" www.sagepub.com/sites/default/files/upm-binaries/5222_Ritzer__Entries_beginning_with_A__[1].pdf

Creech, B. and Mendelson, A. L. 2015 "Imagining the Journalist of the Future: Technological Visions of Journalism Education and Newswork" *The Communication Review* 18(2): 142–165.

Crockett, Z. 2016 "What I Learned Analyzing 7 Months of Donald Trump's Tweets" Vox www.vox.com/2016/5/16/11603854/donald-trump-twitter

Crouse, T. 1973 *The Boys on the Bus*. New York: Random House.

Curran, J. 1990 "The New Revisionism in Mass Communication Research: A Reappraisal" *European Journal of Communication* 5(2): 135–164.

Curtis, P. 2018 "A New Plan to Make HuffPost UK's Blogs the Most Desirable Place to Share Ideas, Expertise and Experiences" *HuffPost* www.huffingtonpost.co.uk/entry/huffpostuk-blogging_uk_5a5f56e6e4b0ee2ff32c4275

Cushion, S. and Lewis, J. 2009 "The Thirst to Be First: An Analysis of Breaking News Stories and Their Impact on the Quality of 24 Hour News Coverage in the UK" *Journalism Practice* 3(3): 304–318.

DAA 2008 *Web Analytics Definitions* www.digitalanalyticsassociation.org/Files/PDF_standards/WebAnalyticsDefinitions.pdf

Dacre, P. 2010 "Killing the Myths" www.editorscode.org.uk/downloads/reports/webLH_Report_2009.html

David, L. 2007 "Actor-Network Theory (ANT)" *Learning Theories* 23rd March www.learning-theories.com/actor-network-theory-ant.html

Davies, N. 2008a "Churnalism Has Taken the Place of What We Should Be Doing: Telling the Truth" *Press Gazette* www.pressgazette.co.uk/nick-davies-churnalism-has-taken-the-place-of-what-we-should-be-doing-telling-the-truth-40117/

Davies, N. 2008b *Flat Earth News: An Award Winning Journalist Exposes Falsehood, Distortion and Propaganda in the Global Media* London: Chatto and Windus.

REFERENCES

Davies, R. and Rushe, D. 2018 "World's Richest Man Delivers Amazon to $1tn Mark" *Guardian*, 5th September: 27.

Davis, N. 2019 "Seven Ways to Prevent Colds, or Get over Them" *Guardian G2*, 7 January 2019: 6.

De Haan, Y., Kruikemeier, S., Lecheler, S., Smit, G. and van der Nat, R. 2018 "When Does an Infographic Say More than A Thousand Words? Audience Evaluations of News Visualizations" *Journalism Studies* 19(9): 1293–1312.

de la Peña, N., Weil, P., Llobera, J., Giannopoulos, E., Pomés, A., Spanlang, B., Friedman, D., Sanchez-Vives, M. V. and Slater, M. 2010 "Immersive Journalism: Immersive Virtual Reality for the First Person Experience of News" *Presence: Teleoperators and Virtual Environments* 19(4): 291–301.

De Maeyer, J. 2012 "The Journalistic Hyperlink: Prescriptive Discourses about Linking in Online News" *Journalism Practice* 6(5–6): 692–701.

DeFleur, M. 1997 *Computer-Assisted Investigative Reporting: Development and Methodology*. Mahwah, NJ: Lawrence Erlbaum.

Delano, A. 2001 "No Sign of a Better Job: 100 Years of British Journalism" *Journalism Studies* 1(2): 261–272.

Deloitte 2018 "Digital Media: The Subscription Prescription" Deloitte www. deloitte.co.uk/tmtpredictions/predictions/digital-only-media-subscriptions/

Denning, S. 2018 "Why Facebook Faces a Foggy Future" *Forbes* www. forbes.com/sites/stevedenning/2018/03/29/why-facebook-faces-a-foggy-future/#2923c2104be4

Deprez, A. and Van Leuven, S. 2018 "About Pseudo Quarrels and Trustworthiness: A Multi-Method Study of Health Journalism, Sourcing Practice and Twitter" *Journalism Studies* 19(9): 1257–1274.

Dermidas, M., Ali Bayir, M., Akcora, C., Yilmaz, Y. and Ferhatosmanoglu, H. 2010 "Crowd-Sourced Sensing and Collaboration Using Twitter" IEEE International Symposium on a World of Wireless, Mobile and Multimedia Networks Montreal, QC, 2010, 1–9.

Desjardins, J. 2016 "The Slow Death of Legacy Media" *Business Insider* www. businessinsider.com/the-slow-death-of-legacy-media-2016-10?IR=T

Deuze, M. 1999 "Journalism and the Web's Analysis of the Skills and Standards in an Online Environment" *International Communications Gazette* 61(5): 373–390.

Deuze, M. 2005 "What Is Journalism? Professional Identity and Ideology of Journalists Reconsidered" *Journalism* 6(4): 442–464.

Deuze, M. 2008 "The Professional Identity of Journalists in the Context of Convergence Culture" *Observatorio* 2(4): 103–117.

Deuze, M. 2009 "The People Formerly Known as the Employers" *Journalism* 10 (3): 315–318.

Deuze, M., Bruns, A. and Neuberger, C. 2007 "Preparing for an Age of Participatory News" *Journalism Practice* 1(3): 322–338.

REFERENCES

Dewan, M. 2018 "Understanding Ethnography: An 'Exotic' Ethnographer's Perspective" in Mura, P. and Khoo-Lattimore, C. (Eds) *Asian Qualitative Research in Tourism: Perspectives on Asian Tourism.* Singapore: Springer.

Dick, M. 2015 "Just Fancy That: An Analysis of Infographic Propaganda in the *Daily Express* 1956–1959" *Journalism Studies* 16(2): 152–174.

Dick, M. 2017 "Developments in Infographics" in Franklin, B. and Eldridge, II, S. (Eds) *The Routledge Companion to Digital Journalism Studies.* London: Routledge, 498–508.

Dickinson, R. 2011 "The Use of Social Media in the Work of Local Newspaper Journalists" *Proceedings of the 2011 Future of Journalism Conference held at Cardiff University.* Cardiff: Cardiff University.

Dikkers, S. 1999 *Our Dumb Century: The Onion Presents 100 Years of Headlines.* New York: Crown Publishing Group.

Dodd, C. 2007 "Carbon Copy" *Guardian* www.theguardian.com/environment/2007/apr/09/travelsenvironmentalimpact.mondaymediasection

Dodd, M. and Hanna, M. 2018 *McNae's Essential Law for Journalists* (24th Edition). Oxford: Oxford University Press.

Doherty, S. 2014 "Hypertext and Journalism: Paths for Future Research" *Digital Journalism* 2(2): 124–139.

Donsbach, W. 2010 "Journalists and Their Professional Identities" in Allan, S. (Ed) *The Routledge Companion to News and Journalism.* Abingdon: Routledge, 38–48.

Dorr, K. N. 2016 "Mapping the Field of Algorithmic Journalism" *Digital Journalism* 4(6): 700–722.

Dorr, K. N. and Hollnbrucher, K. 2017 "Ethical Challenges to Algorithmic Journalism" *Digital Journalism* 5(4): 404–419.

Dowling, D. and Vogan, T. 2015 "Can We 'Snowfall' This? Digital Longform and the Race for the Tablet Market" *Digital Journalism* 3(2): 209–224.

Dowling, D. 2016 "The Business of Slow Journalism: Deep Storytelling's Alternative Economies" *Digital Journalism* 4(4): 530–546.

Downie, L. and Schudson, M. 2009 *The Reconstruction of American Journalism.* New York: Columbia University.

Downie, L. and Schudson, M. 2010 "The Reconstruction of American Journalism" *Columbia Journalism Review* www.cjr.org/reconstruction/the_re construction_of_american.php

Dubois, E. and Blank, G. 2018 "The Echo Chamber Is Overstated: The Moderating Effect of Political Interest and Diverse Media" *Information, Communication & Society* 21(5): 729–745.

Duffy, B. 2013 *Remake, Remodel: Women's Magazines in the Digital Age.* Chicago: University of Illinois Press.

Dutton, W. H. 2009 "The Fifth Estate Emerging through the Network of Networks" *Prometheus* 27(1): 1–15.

Dwyer, T. and Martin, F. 2017 "Sharing News Online: Social Media News Analytics and Their Implications for Media Pluralism Policies" *Digital Journalism* 5(8): 1080–1100.

REFERENCES

Ebner, C. 2016 "Language Guardian BBC? Investigating the BBC's Language Advice in Its 2003 News Styleguide" *Journal of Multilingual and Multicultural Development* 37(3): 308–320.

Eckman, A. and Lindlof, T. 2003 "Negotiating the Gray Lines: An Ethnographic Case Study of Organizational Conflict between Advertorials and News" *Journalism Studies* 4(1): 65–79.

Edmonds, R., Guskin, E., Mitchell, A. and Jurkowitz, M. 2013 "Newspapers: Stabilizing but Still Threatened" The State of the News Media 2013 PEW Research Center's Project for Excellence in Journalism http://stateofthemedia.org/2013/newspapers-stabilizing-but-still-threatened/

Edstrom, M. and Ladendorf, M. 2012 "Freelance Journalists as a Flexible Workforce in Media Industries" *Journalism Practice* 6(5–6): 711–721.

Edwards, R. and Tyron, C. 2009 "Political Video Mashups as Allegories of Citizen Empowerment" *First Monday* 14(10) http://journals.uic.edu/ojs/index.php/fm/article/view/2617/2305

Einwiller, S., Viererbl, B. and Himmkelreich, S. 2017 "Journalists' Coverage of Online Firestorms in German Language News Media" *Journalism Practice* 11(7): 1178–1197.

Eldridge, J. 2000 "The Contribution of the Glasgow Media Group to the Study of Television and Print Journalism" *Journalism Studies* 1(1): 113–127.

Eldridge, II, S. A. 2015 "Boundary Maintenance and Interloper Media Reaction: Differentiating between Journalism's Discursive Enforcement Processes" *Journalism Studies* 15(1): 1–16.

Eldridge, II, S. A. 2017 "Hero or Anti-Hero? Narratives of Newswork and Journalistic Identity Construction in Complex Digital Megastories" *Digital Journalism* 5(2): 141–158.

Eldridge, II, S. A. and Franklin, B. (Eds) 2019 *The Routledge Handbook of Developments in Digital Journalism Studies*. Abingdon: Routledge.

Engel, M. 2003 "Book Review: Hackademic Heavyweight" *British Journalism Review* 14(4): 61–62.

Evans, H. 1979 *Pictures on a Page: Photo-Journalism, Graphics and Picture Editing*. London: Book Club Associates.

Evans, H. 1994 *Good Times, Bad Times*. London: Phoenix.

Evans, R. 2014 "Can Universities Make Good Journalists?" *Journalism Education* 3 (1): 66–87.

Ewart, J. 2014 "Citizen Witnessing: Revisioning Journalism in Times of Crisis" *Digital Journalism* 2(2): 252–253.

Fallows, J. 1997 *Breaking the News: How the Media Undermine American Democracy*. New York: Vintage Books.

Favilla, E. and Paolone, M. 2018 "BuzzFeed Style Guide" www.buzzfeed.com/emmyf/buzzfeed-style-guide

Ferrer Conill, R. 2016 "Camouflaging Church as State: An Exploratory Study of Journalism's Native Advertising" *Journalism Studies* 17(7): 904–914.

REFERENCES

Ferrucci, P. and Vos, T. 2017 "Who's In, Who's Out? Constructing the Identity of Digital Journalists" *Digital Journalism* 5(7): 868–883.

Fico, F., Lacy, S., Wildman, S., Baldwin, T., Bergan, D. and Zube, P. 2013 "Citizen Journalism Sites as Information Substitutes and Complements for Unites States Newspaper Coverage of Local Government" *Digital Journalism* 1(1): 152–168.

Fink, K. and Anderson, C. W. 2016 "Data Journalism in the US: Beyond the 'Usual Suspects'" *Journalism Studies* 16(4): 467–481, doi: 10.1080/1461670X.2014.939852.

Flaounas, I., Omar, A., Lansdall-Welfare, T., De Bie, T., Mosdell, N. and Lewis, J. 2013 "Research Methods in the Age of Digital Journalism: Massive Scale Automated Analysis of News Content – Topics, Style and Gender" *Digital Journalism* 1(1): 102–116.

Flew, T., Spurgeon, C., Daniel, A. and Swift, A. 2012 "The Promise of Computational Journalism" *Journalism Practice* 6(2): 157–171.

Flickr 2018 "About" www.flickr.com/about

Forbes 2018 "Profile; Jeff Bezos" www.forbes.com/profile/jeff-bezos/

Franklin, B. 1997 *Newszak and News Media*. London: Arnold.

Franklin, B. 2005 *Television Policy: The MacTaggart Lectures*. Edinburgh: Edinburgh University Press.

Franklin, B. (Ed) 2006 *Local Journalism and Local Media: Making the Local News*. London: Routledge.

Franklin, B. (Ed) 2008 *Pulling Newspapers Apart: Analysing Print Journalism*. London: Routledge.

Franklin, B. 2009 *The Future of Newspapers*. Oxford: Routledge.

Franklin, B. (Ed) 2011 *The Future of Journalism*. London: Routledge.

Franklin, B. (Ed) 2013a *The Future of Journalism: Developments and Debates*. London: Routledge.

Franklin, B. 2013b "Editorial" *Digital Journalism* 1(1): 1–5.

Franklin, B. (Ed) 2016 *The Future of Journalism: In an Age of Digital Media and Economic Uncertainty*. London: Routledge.

Franklin, B. and Eldridge, II, S. 2017 *The Routledge Companion to Digital Journalism Studies*. London: Routledge.

Franklin, B., Lewis, J. and Williams, A. 2010 "Journalism, News Sources and Public Relations" in Allan, S. (Ed) *The Routledge Companion to News and Journalism*. Oxford: Routledge, 202–212.

Franklin, B. and Murphy, D. 1998 *What News? The Market, Politics and the Local Press*. London: Routledge.

Frayn, M. 1965 *The Tin Men: A Novel*. London: Collins.

Freer, J. 2007 "UK Regional and Local Newspapers" in Anderson, P. and Ward, G. (Eds) *The Future of Journalism in the Advanced Democracies*. Aldershot: Ashgate, 89–104.

Friedman, A. 2014 "We're All Aggregators Now: So We Should Be Ethical about It" *Columbia Journalism Review* 23rd May https://archives.cjr.org/realtalk/rules_for_ethical_aggregators.php

REFERENCES

Fursiche, E. 2013 "Lifestyle Journalism as Popular Journalism: Strategies for Evaluating Its Public Role" *Journalism Practice* 6(1): 11–24.

Gahran, A. 2008 "Skype: Why Every Journo Should Use It" Poynter www.poynter.org/news/skype-why-every-journo-should-use-it

Galily, Y. 2018 "Artificial Intelligence and Sports Journalism: Is It a Sweeping Change?" *Technology in Society* 54: 47–51.

Gallagher, R. 2013 "Skype under Investigation in Luxembourg over Link to NSA" *Guardian* www.theguardian.com/technology/2013/oct/11/skype-ten-microsoft-nsa

Galtung, J. and Ruge, M. 1965 "The Structure of Foreign News: The Presentation of the Congo, Cuba and Cyprus Crises in Four Norwegian Newspapers" *Journal of International Peace Research* 2: 64–90.

Gandy, Jr., O. H. 1982 *Beyond Agenda-Setting: Information Subsidies and Public Policy*. Norwood, NJ: Ablex.

Gardiner, B. 2015 "You'll Be Outraged at How Easy It Was to Get You to Click on This Headline" *Wired* www.wired.com/2015/12/psychology-of-clickbait/

Garfield, S. 2004 "2004: The Year of the Video Blog" https://web.archive.org/web/20041231011613/http://homepage.mac.com/stevegarfield/videoblog/year_of.html

Garrison, B. 1998 *Computer-Assisted Reporting*. Mahwah, NJ: Lawrence Erlbaum.

Getlin, J. and Jensen, E. 2003 "Caught in a Crossfire of Spin" *The Age* 27: 6.

Gillárová, K. S., Tejkálová, A. N. and Láb, F. 2012 "The Undressed Newsroom: The Application of Visual Ethnography in Media Research" in Franklin, B. (Ed) *The Future of Journalism in an Age of Digital Media and Economic Uncertainty*. London: Routledge, 411–417.

Gillmor, D. 2004 *We the Media: Grassroots Journalism by the People, for the People*. Sebastopol: O'Reilly Media.

Glasgow Media Group 1976 *Bad News*. London: Routledge, Kegan and Paul.

Glover, S. 1993 *Paper Dreams*. London: Jonathan Cape.

Goldberg, D. 2018 "Dronalism, Newsgathering Protection and Day to Day Norms" in Gynnild, A. and Uskali, T. (Eds) *Responsible Drone Journalism*. London: Routledge, 36–46.

Goode, L. 2009 "Social News, Citizen Journalism and Democracy" *New Media & Society* 11(8): 1287–1305.

Google. 2018 "About" *Google* www.google.co.uk/about/

Gorman, B. 2015 *Crash to Paywall: Canadian Newspapers and the Great Disruption*. Montreal: McGill-Queen's University Press

Goss, B. 2013 *Rebooting the Herman and Chomsky Propaganda Model in the 21st Century*. New York: Peter Lang.

Graves, L. 2007 "The Affordances of Blogging: A Case Study in the Culture of Technological Effects" *Journal of Communication Inquiry* 31(4): 331–346.

Graves, L. 2016 *Deciding What's True; the Rise of Political Fact-Checking in American Journalism*. New York: Columbia University Press.

REFERENCES

Greenslade, R. 2014 "The Reality of Digital Newsrooms: 'Copy Thrown Online with a Photo'" *Guardian* www.theguardian.com/media/greenslade/2014/jan/14/newspapers-digital-media

Greenslade, R. 2018 "Digital Revolution: Opinion Is Valued More than Fact as We Turn Full Circle" *Guardian*, 30th July: 25.

Greenwald, G. 2013 "Microsoft Handed the NSA Access to Encrypted Messages" *Guardian* www.theguardian.com/world/2013/jul/11/microsoft-nsa-collaboration-user-data

Groot Kormelink, T. and Costera Meijer, I. 2016 "Tailor Made News: Meeting the Demands of News Users on Mobile and Social Media" in Franklin, B. (Ed) *The Future of Journalism in an Age of Digital Media and Economic Uncertainty.* London: Routledge, 296–305.

Guardian 2005 "The New Commentariat" www.theguardian.com/media/2005/nov/17/newmedia.politicsandthemedia 17 November 2005

Guardian 2015 "The Guardian and Observer Style Guide" www.theguardian.com/guardian-observer-style-guide-a

Guardian. 2016a "The Dark Side of Guardian Comments" 12th April www.theguardian.com/technology/2016/apr/12/the-dark-side-of-guardian-comments

Guardian. 25 March 2016b "Editorial: The Guardian View on the End of the Independent: All News Journalism Being Turned Upside down by the Digital Revolution" www.theguardian.com/commentisfree/2016/mar/25/guardian-view-end-independent-in-print

Guardian. 2017 "MPs Slam Social Media Companies over Online Hate Speech" www.theguardian.com/media/video/2017/mar/14/mps-slam-social-media-companies-over-online-hate-speech-video

Guardian. 2017 "Freelance Charter" *Guardian* www.theguardian.com/info/guardian-news-media-freelance-charter

Gulyas, A. 2013 "The Influence of Professional Variables on Journalists' Uses and Views of Social Media: A Comparative Study of Finland, Germany, Sweden and the United Kingdom" *Digital Journalism* 1(2): 270–285.

Gutsche, R. E. and Hess, K. 2019 *Geographies of Journalism: The Imaginative Power of Place in Making Digital News.* London: Routledge.

Gynnild, A. 2014 "The Robot Eye Witness: Visual Journalism Through Drone Surveillance" *Digital Journalism* 2(3): 334–343 www.tandfonline.com/doi/abs/10.1080/21670811.2014.883184

Gynnild, A. and Uskali, T. 2018 *Responsible Drone Journalism.* London: Routledge.

Hacks/Hackers. 2018. "About" Hacks/Hackers https://hackshackers.com/about/

Hadland, A. and Barnett, C. 2018 "The Gender Crisis in Professional Photojournalism: Demise of the Female Gaze?" *Journalism Studies* 19(13): 2011–2020.

Hadland, A., Lambert, P. and Campbell, D. 2016 "The Future of Professional Photojournalism: Perceptions of Risk" *Journalism Practice* 10(7): 820–832.

REFERENCES

Hagerty, B. 2002 "Announcing the Greatest Editor of All Time" *British Journalism Review* 13(4): 6–14.

Haim, M., Graefe, A. and Brosius, H. 2018 "Burst of the Filter Bubble? Effects of Personalization on the Diversity of Google News" *Digital Journalism* 6(3): 330–343.

Halavais, A. and Lackaff, D. 2008 "An Analysis of Topical Coverage of Wikipedia" *Journal of Computer-Mediated Communication* 13(2): 429–440.

Hall, J. 2001 *Online Journalism: A Critical Primer*. London: Pluto Press.

Hanitzsch, T. 2007 "Deconstructing Journalism Culture: Towards a Universal Theory" *Communication Theory* 17(4): 367–385.

Hanitzsch, T., Hanusch, F. and Lauerer, C. 2016 "Setting the Agenda, Influencing Public Opinion, and Advocating for Social Change" *Journalism Studies* 17(1): 1–20.

Hanitzsch, T., Hanusch, F., Mellado, C., Anikina, M., Berganza, R., Cangoz, I., Coman, M., Hamada, B., Hernández, M., Karadjov, C., Moreira, S., Mwesige, P., Plaisance, P., Reich, Z., Seethaler, J., Skewes, E., Noor, D. and Yuen, E. 2011 "Mapping Journalism Cultures across Nations" *Journalism Studies* 12(3): 273–293.

Hänska-Ahy, M. T. and Shapour, R. 2013 "Who's Reporting the Protests? Converging Practices of Citizen Journalists and Two BBC World Service Newsrooms, from Iran's Election Protests to the Arab Uprisings" *Journalism Studies* 14(1): 29–45.

Hanusch, F. 2013 "Broadening the Focus: The Case for Lifestyle Journalism as a Field of Scholarly Inquiry" *Journalism Practice* 6(1): 1–10.

Hanusch, F. 2015 "A Different Breed Altogether?" *Journalism Studies* 16(6): 816–833.

Hanusch, F. and Bruns, F. 2016 "Journalistic Branding on Twitter: A Representative Study of Australian Journalists' Activities and Profile Descriptions" *Digital Journalism*, doi: 10.1080/21670811.2016.1152161.

Harcup, T. 1998 "There Is No Alternative: The Demise of the Alternative Local Newspaper" in Franklin, B. and Murphy, D. (Eds) *Making the Local News: Local Journalism in Context*. London: Routledge, 105–116.

Harcup, T. 2002 *Journalism: Principles and Practice*. London: Sage.

Harcup, T. 2003 "The Unspoken – Said: The Journalism of Alternative Media" *Journalism: Theory, Practice and Criticism* 4(3): 356–376.

Harcup, T. 2013 *Alternative Journalism, Alternative Voices*. London: Routledge.

Harcup, T. 2016 "Alternative Journalism as Monitorial Citizenship? A Case Study of A Local News Blog" *Digital Journalism* 4(5): 639–657.

Harcup, T. and O'Neill, D. 2001 "What Is News? News Values Revisited" *Journalism Studies* 2(2): 261–280.

Harcup, T. and O'Neill, D. 2016 "What Is News? News Values Revisited (Again)" *Journalism Studies* 18(12): 1470–1488.

Hardiman, A. and Brown, C. "More Local News on Facebook" Facebook Newsroom https://newsroom.fb.com/news/2018/01/news-feed-fyi-local-news/

Hargreaves, I. 2003 *Journalism, Truth or Dare?* Oxford: Oxford University Press.

REFERENCES

Harrison, J. 2010 "User-Generated Content and Gatekeeping at the BBC Hub" *Journalism Studies* 11(2): 243–256.

Harte, D., Howell, R. and Williams, A. 2018 *Hyperlocal Journalism: The Decline of the Local Newspaper and the Rise of Online Community Newspaper.* London: Routledge.

Harte, D., Williams, A. and Turner, J. 2017 "Reciprocity and the Hyperlocal Journalist" *Journalism Practice* 11(2–3): 160–176.

Hartsock, J. 2007 "It Was a Dark Story Night" *Prose Studies* 29(2): 257–284.

Hasebrink, U. 2017 "Audiences and Information Repertoires" in Franklin, B. and Eldridge, II, S. (Eds) *The Routledge Companion to Digital Journalism Studies.* London: Routledge, 364–374.

Hasebrink, U. and Domeyer, H. 2012 "Media Repertoires as Patterns of Behaviour and as Meaningful Practices: A Multimethod Approach to Media Use in Converging Environments" *Participations: Journal of Audience and Reception Studies* 9(2): 757–783.

Haughney, C. 2013 "Bezos, Amazon's Founder, to Buy the Washington Post" *New York Times* August 5th www.nytimes.com/2013/08/06/business/media/amazoncom-founder-to-buy-the-washington-post.html

Haynes, R., Hadland, A. and Lambert, P. 2017 "The State of Sport Photojournalism: Concepts, Practice and Challenges" *Digital Journalism* 5(5): 636–651.

Hays, M. 2018 "So Now *HuffPost* Decides to Pay Writers. Its Effect on the Industry Still Lingers" *Columbia Journalism Review* www.cjr.org/analysis/so-now-huffpost-decides-to-pay-writers-its-effect-on-the-industry-still-lingers.php

Hedman, U. and Djerf Pierre, M. 2013 "The Social Journalist: Embracing the Social Media Life or Creating a New Digital Divide" *Digital Journalism* 1(3): 368–385.

Heinonen, A. 2011 "The Journalist's Relationship with Users: New Dimensions to Conventional Roles" in Singer, J. (Ed) *Participatory Journalism: Guarding Gates at Online Newspapers.* Chichester: Wiley-Blackwell, 34–55.

Heinrich, A. 2008 *Network Journalism: Journalistic Practice in Interactive Spheres.* New York: Routledge.

Heinrich, A. 2012 "Foreign Reporting in the Sphere of Network Journalism" *Journalism Practice* 6(5): 766–775.

Heravi, B. R. 2018 "3WS of Data Journalism Education: What, Where and Who?" *Journalism Practice,* doi: 10.1080/17512786.2018.1463167.

Herman, E. and Chomsky, N. 1988 *Manufacturing Consent: The Political Economy of the Mass Media.* New York: Pantheon.

Hermida, A. 2009 "The Blogging BBC: Journalism Blogs at the World's Most Trusted News Organisation" *Journalism Practice* 3(3): 268–284.

Hermida, A. 2010 "Twittering the News: The Emergence of Ambient Journalism" *Journalism Practice* 4(3): 297–308.

Hermida, A. 2012 "Tweets and Truth: Journalism as a Discipline of Collaborative Verification" *Journalism Practice* 6(5–6): 659–667.

REFERENCES

Hermida, A. 2013 "#Journalism: Reconfiguring Journalism Research about Twitter, One Tweet at a Time" *Digital Journalism* 1(3): 295–313.

Hermida, A. 2014 *Tell Everyone: Why We Share and Why It Matters.* Toronto: Doubleday.

Hermida, A. and Thurman, N. 2008 "A Clash of Cultures: An Integration of User-Generated Content within Professional Journalistic Frameworks at British Newspaper Websites" *Journalism Practice* 2(3): 343–356.

Heseltine, S. 2010 "Dear Peter Preston: Universities Shun the NCTJ Too" Online Journalism Blog http://onlinejournalismblog.com/2010/05/17/dear-peter-preston-universities-shun-the-nctj-too/

Hess, K. 2013 "Breaking Boundaries: Recasting the "Local" Newspaper as "Geo-Social" News in a Digital Landscape" *Digital Journalism* 1(1): 48–63.

Hess, K. and Waller, L. 2017 "Community and Hyperlocal Journalism: A 'Sustainable' Model?" in Franklin, B. and Eldridge, II, S. (Eds) *The Routledge Companion to Digital Journalism Studies.* London: Routledge, 194–204.

Hiler, J. 2004 "Borg Journalism: We are the Blogs. Journalism Will Be Assimilated" *Micro-Content News* (1 April 2002) www.microcontentnews.com /articles/borgjournalism.htm cited in Bruns and Jacobs 2006:8.

Hill Nettleton, P. 2019 "The Cyber Abuse of Women on the Internet" in Eldridge, II, S. and Franklin, B. (Eds) *The Routledge Handbook of Developments in Digital Journalism Studies.* London: Routledge, 425–438.

Holcomb, J., Gottfried, J. and Mitchell, A. 2013 "News Use Across Social Media Platforms" *Pew Research Center's Journalism Project* November 14.

Holton, A. E., Lawson, S. and Love, C. 2015 "Unmanned Aerial Vehicles: Opportunities, Barriers, and the Future of 'Drone Journalism'" *Journalism Practice* 9(5): 634–650.

Holton, A. E., Lewis, S. C. and Coddington, M. 2016 "Interacting with Audiences: Journalistic Role Conceptions, Reciprocity, and Perceptions about Participation" *Journalism Studies* 17(7): 849–859.

Hong, J. 2011 "From the World's Largest Propaganda Machine to a Multipurposed Global News Agency: Factors in and Implications of Xinhua's Transformation since 1978" *Political Communication* 28(3): 377–393.

Howells, R. 2015 "Journey to the Centre of a News Black Hole: Examining the Democratic Deficit in a Town with No Newspaper" PhD Thesis, Cardiff University.

Hoyer, S. 2003 "Newspapers Without Journalists" *Journalism Studies* 4(4): 451–463.

HuffPost 2017 "The House Without Windows" https://housewithoutwindows. huffpost.com/#1

HuffPost 2018 "Editorial Style Guide" https://guestblogging.com/huffington-post-toolkit/editorial-style-guide/

Hurwitz, L., Alvarez, A., Lauricella, A., Rousse, T., Montague, H. and Wartella, E. 2016 "Content Analysis across New Media Platforms: Methodological Considerations for Capturing Media-Rich Data" *New Media & Society* 20(2): 532–548.

REFERENCES

Hutchby, I. 2001 "Technology, Texts and Affordances" *Sociology* 35(2): 441–456.

Hutchins, B. 2004 "Castells, Regional News Media and the Information Age" *Continuum: Journal of Media and Cultural Studies* 18: 577–590.

Influencer Marketing Hub 2018 "What Is an Influencer?" https://influencermar ketinghub.com/what-is-an-influencer/

International Federation of Journalists 2018 "Freelances' Rights" www.ifj.org/ issues/freelances-rights/

Isbell, K. 2010 "What's the Law around Aggregating News Online: A Harvard Law Response on the Risks and Best Practices" *NiemanLab* September 8th www. google.co.uk/search?q=news+aggregators+definition&oq=News+aggregator s&aqs=chrome.1.0l6.7404j0j8&sourceid=chrome¡UTF-8

Iszard, R., Culbertson, H. and Lambert, D. 1990 *Fundamentals of News Reporting*. Dubuque: Kendall/Hunt.

Jackson, J. 2017 "Channel 4 to Run Week of Programmes on Fake News" *Guardian* 19 January www.theguardian.com/media/2017/jan/19/channel-4-run-week-programmes-fake-news-lee-nelson

Jarvis, J. 2008 "Supermedia" BuzzMachine www.buzzmachine.com/2008/06/ 06/supermedia/

Jarvis, J. 2012 "Foreword" in Briggs, M. (Ed) *Entrepreneurial Journalism: How to Build What's Next for News*. Thousand Oaks, CA: Sage.

Jenkins, H. 2008 *Convergence Culture: Where Old and New Media Collide*. New York: New York University Press.

Jenkins, H., Ford, S. and Green, J. 2013 *Spreadable Media: Creating Value and Meaning in a Networked Culture*. New York: New York University Press.

Jenkins, J. and Nielsen, R. 2018 "The Digital Transition of Local News" *Reuters Digital News Report* www.digitalnewsreport.org/publications/2018/digital-transition-local-news/

Johnson, C. 2017 "Massive and Unprecedented Intrusion: A Comparative Analysis of American Journalistic Discourse Surrounding Three Government Surveillance Scandals" *Digital Journalism* 5(3): 318–333.

Johnson, J. and Forde, S. 2017 "Churnalism, Revised and Revisited" An Introduction to a Special Issue of the Journal *Digital Journalism* 5(8): 943–946 The special issue examined the impact and implications of churnalism in an age of digital media and journalism

Johnson, M., Paulussen, S. and Van Aelst, P. 2018 "Much Ado about Nothing? The Low Importance of Twitter as a Sourcing Tool for Economic Journalists" *Digital Journalism* 6(7), doi: 10.1080/21670811.2018.1490657.

Johnston, J. and Graham, C. 2012 "The New, Old Journalism: Narrative Writing in Contemporary Newspapers" *Journalism Studies* 13(4): 517–533.

Johnston, J. and Wallace, A. 2019 "Law Defining Journalists: Who's Who in the Age of Digital Media" in Eldridge, II, S. and Franklin, B. (Eds) *The Routledge Handbook of Developments in Digital Journalism Studies*. Abingdon: Routledge, 15–27.

REFERENCES

Johnston, L. 2016 "Social News = Journalism Evolution? How the Integration of UGC into Newswork Helps and Hinders the Role of the Journalist" *Digital Journalism* 4(7): 899–909.

Jones, K. 2015 "The Art and Science of Shareability from the Publisher of Buzzfeed" *Search Engine Journal* www.searchenginejournal.com/the-art-and-science-of-shareability-with-the-publisher-of-buzzfeed-sxswi-2015-recap/128204/

Jones, S. 2017 "Disrupting the Narrative: Immersive Journalism in Virtual Reality" *Journal of Media Practice* 18(2–3): 171–185.

Joust, K. and Hipolit, M. 2006 "Blog Explosion" *CQ Researcher* http://library.cqpress.com/cqresearcher/document.php?id=cqresrre2006060900

Jurkowitz, M. 2014 "The Growth in Digital Reporting" *Pew Journalism Research Project* www.journalism.org/2014/03/26/the-growth-in-digital-reporting/

Karlsson, M. 2010 "Rituals of Transparency: Evaluating Online News Outlets' Uses of Transparency Rituals in the United States, United Kingdom and Sweden" *Journalism Studies* 11(4): 535–545.

Karlsson, M. and Clerwall, C. 2018 "Transparency to the Rescue? Evaluating Citizens' Views on Transparency Tools in Journalism" *Journalism Studies* 19 (13): 1923–1933.

Karlsson, M., Clerwall, C. and Nord, L. 2014 "You Ain't Seen Nothing Yet: Transparency's (Lack Of) Effect on Source and Message Credibility" *Journalism Studies* 15(5): 668–678.

Karlsson, M. and Sjøvaag, H. 2016a "Research Methods in an Age of Digital Journalism" *Digital Journalism* 4(1): 1–8.

Karlsson, M. and Sjøvaag, H. 2016b "Content Analysis and Online News: Epistemologies of Analysing the Ephemeral Web" *Digital Journalism* 4(1): 177–192.

Karlsson, M. and Strömbäck, J. 2010 "Freezing the Flow of Online News: Exploring Approaches to the Study of the Liquidity of Online News" *Journalism Studies* 11(1): 2–19.

Karpf, D. 2012 "Social Science Research Methods in Internet Time" *Information, Communication and Society* 15(5): 639–661.

Kelly, S. 2015 *The Entrepreneurial Journalist's Toolkit*. New York: Focal Press.

Kerkhoven, V. M. and Bakker, P. 2014 "The Hyperlocal in Practice: Innovation, Creativity and Diversity" *Digital Journalism* 2(3): 296–309.

Kiely, E. and Robinson, L. "How to Spot Fake News" Factcheck www.factcheck.org/2016/11/how-to-spot-fake-news/

Kilgo, D. 2015 "Media Landscape on Tumblr: News Organization Convergence Attributes in Youth-Oriented Social Media Networks" *Digital Journalism* 4(6): 784–800.

Kim, E. 2016 "How Amazon CEO Jeff Bezos Reinvented the Washington Post, the 140 Year Old Newspaper He Bought for $250millions" Business Insider http://uk.businessinsider.com/how-the-washington-post-changed-after-jeff-bezos-acquisition-2016-5/#bezos-initially-wasnt-sure-if-he-wanted-buy-the-post-but-after-a-couple-meetings-with-former-owner-don-graham-bezos-became-intrigued-1

REFERENCES

Kirchner, L. 2014 "Why Skype Isn't Safe for Journalists" *Columbia Journalism Review* https://archives.cjr.org/behind_the_news/skype_alternatives.php

Koliska, M. and Chadha, K. 2017 "Transparency in German Newsrooms: Diffusion of a New Journalistic Norm" *Journalism Studies* 19(16): 2400–2416.

Konieczna, M. 2018 *Journalism without Profits: Making News When the Market Fails.* Oxford: Oxford University Press.

Ksiazek, T. and Springer, N. 2019 "User Comment in Digital Journalism: Current Research and Future Directions" in Eldridge, S. and Franklin, B. (Eds) *The Routledge Handbook of Developments in Digital Journalism Studies.* London: Routledge, 475–487.

Kuiken, J., Schuth, A., Spitters, M. and Marx, M. 2017 "Effective Headlines of Newspaper Articles in a Digital Environment" *Digital Journalism* 5(10): 1300–1314.

Kumar, A. and Shuaib Mohamed Haneef, M. 2017 "Is Mojo (En)De-Skilling? Unfolding the Practices of Mobile Journalism in an Indian Newsroom" *Journalism Practice*, 1–19, doi: 10.1080/17512786.2017.1389291.

Laird, S. 2012 "Instagram Users Share 10 Hurricane Sandy Photos Per Second" Mashable http://mashable.com/2012/10/29/instagram-hurricane-sandy/

Landow, G. P. 2006 *Hypertext 3.0: Critical Theory and New Media in an Era of Globalization* (3rd Edition). Baltimore, MD: Cambridge University Press.

Larsson, A. O. 2017 "Diversifying Likes: Relating Reactions to Commenting and Sharing on Newspaper Facebook Pages" *Journalism Practice* 12(3): 326–343.

Lasorsa, N., Lewis, S. and Holton, A. 2012 "Normalizing Twitter: Journalism Practice in an Emerging Communications Space" *Journalism Studies* 13(1): 19–36.

Latour, B. 1987 *Science in Action: How to Follow Scientists and Engineers through Society.* Cambridge, MA: Harvard University Press.

Lauk, E. 2009 "Reflections on Changing Patterns of Journalism in the New EU Countries" *Journalism Studies* 10(1): 69–84.

Le Masurier, M. 2015 "What Is Slow Journalism?" *Journalism Practice* 9(2): 138–152.

Lecheler, S. and Kruikemeier, S. 2016 "Re-Evaluating Journalistic Routines in A Digital Age: A Review of Research on the Use of Online Sources" *New Media & Society* 18(1): 156–171.

Lee, A. and Chyi, I. 2015 "The Rise of Online News Aggregators: Consumption and Competition" *International Journal on Media Management* 17(1): 3–24.

Lee, A. M., Lewis, S. C. and Powers, M. 2012 "Audience Clicks and News Placement: A Study of Time-Lagged Influence in Online Journalism" *Communication Research*, doi: 10.1177/0093650212467031.

Lee-Potter, E. 2017 *Interviewing for Journalists.* London: Routledge.

Len-Rios, M. E., Rodgers, S., Thorson, E. and Yoon, D. 2006 "Representation of Women in News and Photographs: Comparing Content to Perceptions" *Journal of Communication* 55: 152–168.

Lethlean, J. 2016. "Restaurant Reviews: Bloggers Don't Cut the Mustard" *The Weekend Australian* www.theaustralian.com.au/life/food-wine/restaurant-reviews-bloggers-dont-cut-the-mustard/news-story/480db526e3ff92c9264cebe7efbdd2a3

REFERENCES

Leveson Inquiry. webarchive.nationalarchives.gov.uk/20140122145147/http://www.levesoninquiry.org.uk

Lewis, J. and Cushion, S. 2009 "The Thirst to Be First: An Analysis of Breaking News Stories and Their Impact on the Quality of 24-Hour News Coverage in the UK" *Journalism Practice* 3(3): 304–318.

Lewis, J., Cushion, S. and Thomas, J. 2006 "Immediacy, Convenience or Engagement? An Analysis of 24-Hour News Channels in the UK" *Journalism Studies* 6(4): 461–477.

Lewis, J., Williams, A. and Franklin, B. 2008 "Four Rumours and an Explanation" *Journalism Practice* 2(1): 27–45.

Lewis, S. and Usher, N. 2014 "Code, Collaboration, and the Future of Journalism: A Case Study of the Hacks/Hackers Global Network" *Digital Journalism* 2 (3): 383–393.

Lewis, S. C., Holton, A. E. and Coddington, M. 2014 "Reciprocal Journalism: A Concept of Mutual Exchange between Journalists and Audiences" *Journalism Practice* 8(2): 229–241.

Lewis, S. C. and Westlund, O. 2014 "Actors, Actants, Audiences and Activities in Cross-Media News Work: A Matrix and Research Agenda" *Digital Journalism* 3 (1): 19–37.

Lim, J. 2012 "The Mythological Status of the Immediacy of the Most Important Online News: An Analysis of Top News Flows in Diverse Online Media" *Journalism Studies* 13(1): 71–89.

Linden, C.-G. 2019 "Algorithms Are A Reporter's New Best Friend: News Automation and the Case for the Augmentation of News" in Eldridge, II, S. and Franklin, B. (Eds) *The Routledge Handbook of Developments in Digital Journalism Studies*. London: Routledge, 237–250.

LinkedIn JOBS 2018 https://uk.linkedin.com/jobs/social-media-editor-jobs

Lippmann, W. 1997 *Public Opinion*. New York: Free Press Paperbacks.

Lokot, T. and Diakopoulos, N. 2016 "Newsbots: Automating News and Information Dissemination on Twitter" *Digital Journalism* 4(6): 682–699.

Lorenz, H. 2017 "News Wholesalers as Churnalists? The Relationship Between Brussels-based News Agency Journalists and their Sources" *Digital Journalism* 5 (8): 947–964.

Lynch, J. 2018 "These Are the 19 Most Popular YouTube Stars in the World – and Some are Making Millions" Business Insider UK http://uk.businessinsider.com/most-popular-youtubers-with-most-subscribers-2018-2

Lynch, L. 2013 "Wikileaks after Megaleaks: The Organization's Impact on Journalism and Journalism Studies" *Digital Journalism* 1(3): 314–334.

Lynch, L. and Sirrah, A. 2018 *Native Advertising: Advertorial Disruption in the 21st Century News Feed*. London: Routledge.

MacArthur, B. 2004 "Ego Trips Full of Passion that Set the Tone for Newspapers" *The Times* 27 February: 39.

REFERENCES

MacKenzie, K. 2011 "Kelvin MacKenzie: 'I'd Shut All the Journalism Colleges Down'" *Independent* www.independent.co.uk/news/media/press/kelvin-mackenzie-id-shut-all-the-journalism-colleges-down-2264846.html

Malik, A. and Shapiro, I. 2017 "What's Digital? What's Journalism" in Franklin, B. and Eldridge, II, S. (Eds) *The Routledge Companion to Digital Journalism Studies*. London: Routledge, 15–24.

Malik, M. M. and Pfeffer, J. 2016 "A Macroscopic Analysis of New Content in Twitter" *Digital Journalism* 4(8): 955–979.

Mari, W. 2017 "Technology in the Newsroom; Adoption of the Telephone and Radio Car from C. 1920 to 1960" *Journalism Studies* 19(9): 1366–1389.

Mari, W. 2019 *A Short History of Disruptive Technologies 1960 to 1990; Introducing the Computer in the Newsroom*. London: Routledge.

Marr, A. 2012 "Andrew Marr Says Bloggers are 'Inadequate, Pimpled and Single'" *Guardian* www.theguardian.com/media/2010/oct/11/andrew-marr-bloggers

Marshall, S. 2011 "How to Syndicate Freelance Articles Abroad" Journalism.co. uk www.journalism.co.uk/skills/how-to-syndicate-freelance-articles-abroad /s7/a545852/

Martinson, J. 2018 "How Metro Became the Most Read Paper in Britain" *Prospect* www.prospectmagazine.co.uk/magazine/how-metro-became-the-most-read-paper-in-britain

Marwick, A. and Boyd, D. 2011 "I Tweet Honestly, I Tweet Passionately: Twitter Users, Context Collapse and the Imagined Audience" *New Media and Society* 13(1): 114–133.

Massey, B. and Elmore, C. 2011 "Happier Working for Themselves?" *Journalism Practice* 5(6): 672–686.

Matheson, D. and Allan, S. 2009 *Digital War Reporting*. Cambridge: Polity Press.

Mayhew, F. 2017 "Report: Newsrooms Must Improve Source Protection in Face of Government Attacks" *Press Gazette* www.pressgazette.co.uk/report-newsrooms-must-improve-source-protection-in-face-of-government-attacks/

McChesney, R. W. and Nichols, J. 2010 *The Death and Life of American Journalism: The Media Revolution that Will Begin the World Again*. Philadelphia: Nation Books.

McCombs, M. 2006 "A Look at Agenda Setting: Past, Present and Future" *Journalism Studies* 6(4): 543–557.

McCombs, M. and Shaw, D. 1972 "The Agenda Setting Function of the Mass Media" *Public Opinion Quarterly* 36: 176–187.

McDonald, A. 2016 "Great Scott! Someone Mashed Up 'Back To The Future' And 'Westworld'" *HuffPost* www.huffingtonpost.co.uk/entry/someone-mashed-up-back-to-the-future-and-westworld-and-great-scott_us_58499e5ae4b040 02fa803e17

McGurr, L. 2010 "The Devil May Care: Travel Journalism, Cosmopolitan Concern, Politics and the Brand" *Journalism Practice* 6(1): 41–57.

McNair, B. 2001 *News and Journalism in the UK*. New York: Routledge.

REFERENCES

McNair, B. 2005 "What Is Journalism?" in de Burgh, H. (Ed) *Making Journalists: Diverse Models, Global Issues*. London: Routledge, 25–47.

McNair, B. 2010 "Why the Course at Strathclyde Pulled Out of NCTJ Accreditation" All Media Scotland www.allmediascotland.com/blog/0/123/Why%20the%20Course%20at%20Strathclyde/

McNair, B. 2018 *Fake News: Falsehood, Fabrication and Fantasy in Journalism*. London: Routledge.

McNealy, J. E. and Alexander, L. B. 2018 "A Framework for Unpublishing Decisions" *Digital Journalism* 6(3): 389–405.

McQuail, D. 2000 *Mass Communication Theory* (4th Edition). London: Sage.

Meijer, C. 2010 "Democratizing Journalism? Realizing the Citizen's Agenda for Local News Media" *Journalism Studies* 11(3): 327–342.

Mendelson, A. and Creech, B. 2016 "'Make Every Frame Count:' the Practice of Slow Photojournalism in the Work of David Burnett" *Digital Journalism* 4(4): 512–529.

Mensing, D. 2010 "Rethinking [Again] the Future of Journalism Education" *Journalism Studies* 11(4): 511–523.

Meraz, S. 2009 "Is There an Elite Hold? Traditional Media to Social Media Agenda Setting Influences in Blog Networking" *Journal of Computer-Mediated Communication* 14(3): 682–707.

Messner, M. and DiStaso, M. 2008 "The Source Cycle: How Traditional Media and Weblogs Use Each Other as Sources" *Journalism Studies* 9(3): 447–463.

Messner, M., Linke, M. and Eford, A. 2011 "Shoveling Tweets: An Analysis of the Microblogging Engagement of Traditional News Organizations" *#ISOJ International Symposium on Online Journalism* 2 (1): 74–87.

Messner, M. and South, J. 2011 "Legitimizing Wikipedia: How US National Newspapers Frame and Use the Online Encyclopedia in Their Coverage" *Journalism Practice* 5(2): 145–160.

Metzgar, E., Kurpius, D. and Rowley, K. 2011 "Defining Hyperlocal Media: Proposing a Framework for Discussion" *New Media & Society* 13 (5): 772–787.

Meyer, P. 1973 *Precision Journalism*. Bloomington: Indiana University Press.

MH Themes 2018 "Is RSS Dead? the Uses and Benefits of RSS Feeds for Websites Today and Beyond" MH Themes www.mhthemes.com/blog/uses-and-benefits-of-rss-feeds/

Miller, D. 2004 *Tell Me Lies: Propaganda and Media Distortion in the Attack on Iraq*. London: Pluto.

Miller, T. 2015 "Unsustainable Journalism" *Digital Journalism* 3(5): 653–663.

Molyneux, L. 2018 "Mobile News Consumption: A Habit of Snacking" *Digital Journalism* 6(5): 634–650.

Molyneux, L., Holton, A. and Lewis, S. 2018 "How Journalists Engage in Branding on Twitter: Individual, Organizational, and Institutional Levels" *Information, Communication & Society* 21(10): 1386–1401.

REFERENCES

Momin, M. M. and Pfeffer, J. 2016 "A Macroscopic Analysis of News in Twitter" *Digital Journalism* 4(8): 955–979.

Montal, T. and Reich, Z. 2016 "'I Robot, You Journalist: Who Is the Author?'" *Digital Journalism* 5(7): 829–849.

Moore, M. 2018 "BBC Set to Cut Back on Online Content Ignored by Its Users" *The Times* www.thetimes.co.uk/article/bbc-set-to-cut-back-on-online-content-ignored-by-its-users-w88smzhvz

Moylan, B. 2017 "Jon Stewart's Daily Show Skewered the Powerful and Pushed US Satire Forward" *Guardian* www.theguardian.com/tv-and-radio/2015/aug/05/jon-stewart-daily-show-pushed-american-satire-forward

MuleSoft 2018 "What Is an API?" www.mulesoft.com/resources/api/what-is-an-api

Murdoch, J. 2009 "The Absence of Trust" The James MacTaggart Annual Lecture at the Guardian/Edinburgh international festival 28 August www.google.co.uk/search?hl=n&source=hp&q=james+murdoch+mactaggart+lecture+transcript&meta+&aq=0&oq=james+murdoch+mactaggart=lecture

Muthukumaraswamy, K. 2010 "When the Media Meet Crowds of Wisdom: How Journalists are Tapping into Audience Expertise and Manpower for the Process of News Gathering" *Journalism Practice* 4(1): 48–65.

Myllylahti, M. 2014 "Newspaper Paywalls – The Hype and the Reality; A Study of How Paid News Content Impacts on Media Corporation Revenues" *Digital Journalism* 2(2): 179–194.

Myllylahti, M. 2016 "What Content Is Worth Locking behind a Paywall? Digital News Commodification in Leading Australian Financial Newspapers" *Digital Journalism* 5(4): 460–471.

Myllylahti, M. 2017 "Newspaper Paywalls and Corporate Revenues: A Comparative Study" in Franklin, B. and Eldridge, II, S. (Eds) *The Routledge Companion to Digital Journalism Studies*. London: Routledge, 166–175.

Neate, R. 2018 "'Too Much Power in the Hands of Too Few': The Rise and Rise of a Retail Behemoth" *Guardian*, 25th April: 8–11.

Neheli, N. B. 2018 "News by Numbers: The Evolution of Analytics in Journalism" *Digital Journalism* 6(8): 1041–1051.

Neil, A. 1997 *Full Disclosure*. London: Pan Books.

Nelson, T. 1965 "Complex Information Processing: A File Structure for the Complex, the Changing and the Indeterminate" in Winner, L. (Ed) *Proceedings of the ACM 20th National Conference*, New York: ACM, 84–100, doi: 10.1145/800197.806036.

Nesta 2012 "Million Pound Boost to Develop UK Hyperlocal Media Sector" Nesta www.nesta.org.uk/news_and_features/assets/features/1million_boost_to_develop_uk_hyperlocal_media_sector

Neveu, E. 2014 "Revisiting Narrative Journalism as One of the Futures of Journalism" *Journalism Studies* 15(5): 533–542.

Neveu, E. 2016 "On Not Going Too Fast with Slow Journalism" *Journalism Practice* 10(4): 448–460.

REFERENCES

New York Times 2017 "President Obama's Farewell Address" *New York Times* www.nytimes.com/2017/01/10/us/politics/obama-farewell-address-speech.html

Newman, N. 2009 "The Rise of Social Media and Its Impact on Mainstream Journalism" *Reuters Institute for the Study of Journalism* http://thomsonreuters.com/content/media/white_papers/487784

Newman, N., Fletcher, R., Kalogeropoulos, A., Levy, D. A. and Nielsen, R. K. 2018 *Reuters Institute Digital News Report 2018*. Oxford, UK: Reuters Institute for the Study of Journalism.

Newman, N., Levy, D. A. and Nielsen, R. K. 2015 *Reuters Institute Digital News Report 2015: Tracking the Future of News*. Oxford, UK: Reuters Institute for the Study of Journalism.

Newton, C. 2018 "Snapchat Announces a Slate of Original Programming for Discover" The Verge www.theverge.com/2018/10/10/17955916/snap-originals-snapchat-programming-endless-summer

Newton, J. and Duncan, S. 2012 "Hacking into Tragedy: Exploring the Ethics of Death Reporting in the Social Media Age" in Keeble, R. L. and Mair, J. (Eds) *The Phone Hacking Scandal: Journalism on Trial*. Bury St Edmunds: Abramis, 208–219.

Nielsen, J. 1995 *Multimedia and Hypertext: The Internet and Beyond*. London: Academic Press.

Nies, G. and Pedersini, R. 2003 *Freelance Journalists in the European Media Industry*. www.walterlima.jor.br/academico/Fiam/perfil/FinalReportFreelance.pdf

Nip, J. Y. M. 2006 "Exploring the Second Phase of Public Journalism" *Journalism Studies* 7(2): 212–236.

Noor, P. 2018 "Brands are Cashing in on Social Media Envy, and Using Influencers to Sell It" *The Guardian* www.theguardian.com/commentisfree/2018/nov/05/brands-cashing-in-social-media-envy-influencers

Norgaard Kristensen, N. and Mortensen, M. 2013 "Metasources Authorizing the News of Gaddafi's Death; New Patterns of Journalistic Information Gathering and Dissemination in the Digital Age" *Digital Journalism* 1(3): 352–367.

Nyre, L., Guribye, F. and Gynnild, A. 2018 "Taking Risks with Drones: Responsible Innovation Pedagogy for Media Education" in Gynnild, A. and Uskali, T. (Eds) *Responsible Drone Journalism*. London: Routledge, 71–84.

Ofcom. 2012 *The Communications Market Report: United Kingdom*. London: Ofcom.

Olausson, U. 2017 "The Reinvented Journalist: The Discursive Construction of Professional Identity on Twitter" *Digital Journalism* 5(1): 61–81.

Opgenhaffen, M. and Scheerlink, H. 2014 "Social Media Guidelines for Journalists: An Investigation into the Sense and Nonsense among Flemish Journalists" *Journalism Practice* 8(6): 726–741.

Oppenheim, M. "Katie Hopkins Applies for Insolvency Agreement to Avoid Bankruptcy after Losing Libel Case" *The Independent* www.independent.co.uk/news/uk/home-news/katie-hopkins-libel-insolvency-bankruptcy-jack-monroe-a8540961.html

REFERENCES

O'Reilly, T. 2005 "What Is Web 2.0" *O'Reilly* www.oreilly.com/pub/a//web2/archive/what-is-web-20.html

O'Reilly, T. and Battelle, J. 2009 "Web Squared: Web 2.0 Five Years On" *Web 2.0 Summit* https://conferences.oreilly.com/web2summit/web2009/public/schedule/detail/10194

Örnebring, H. 2010 "Reassessing Journalism as a Profession" in Allan, S. (Ed) *The Routledge Companion to News and Journalism*. Abingdon: Routledge, 568–577.

Osterberg, G. 2017 "Update on the Twitter Archive at the Library of Congress" *Library of Congress Blog* https://blogs.loc.gov/loc/2017/12/update-on-the-twitter-archive-at-the-library-of-congress-2/

Ostgaard, E. 1965 "Factors Influencing the Flow of News" *Journal of Peace Research* 1: 39–63.

O'Sullivan, J. and Heinonen, A. 2008 "Old Values, New Media" *Journalism Practice* 2(3): 357–371.

Ott, B. 2017 "The Age of Twitter: Donald J. Trump and the Politics of Debasement" *Critical Studies in Media Communication* 34(1): 59–68.

Ottosen, R. 2012 "Wikileaks: Ethical Minefield or a Democratic Revolution in Journalism? A Case Study of the Impact of Afghanistan Coverage in the Norwegian Daily, Aftenposten" *Journalism Studies* 13(5–6): 836–846.

Owen, L. 2018 "Facebook's News Feed Changes Appear to Be Hurting – Not Helping -Local News" *NiemanLab* www.niemanlab.org/2018/04/facebooks-news-feed-changes-appear-to-be-hurting-not-helping-local-news/

Pantti, M. 2017 "The Personalisation of Conflict Reporting: Visual Coverage of the Ukraine Crisis on Twitter" *Digital Journalism*. doi: 10.1080/21670811.2017.1399807.

Papa, F. 2012 "Global Media Events: Communications Strategies, Social Network Patterns and Propaganda Models – A Complex and Challenging Reconciliation" *The International Journal of the History*.

Pariser, E. 2011 *The Filter Bubble: What the Internet Is Hiding from You*. New York: Penguin Press.

Park, C. S. 2016 "Citizen News Podcasts and Journalistic Role Conceptions in the United States and South Korea" *Journalism Practice* 11(9): 1158–1177.

Parmelee, J. 2013 "Political Journalists and Twitter: Influences on Norms and Practices" *Journal of Media Practice* 14(4): 291–330.

Parveen, N. 2018 "Newspaper Website Turns off Comments over 'Racist Tirades'" *Guardian*, 26th July: 8.

Paulussen, S. 2011 "Inside the Newsroom: Journalists' Motivations and Organizational Structures" in Singer, J. (Ed) *Participatory Journalism: Guarding Gates at Online Newspapers*. Chichester: Wiley-Blackwell, 59–75.

Paulussen, S. and Harder, R. 2014 "Social Media References in Newspapers: Facebook, Twitter and YouTube as Sources in Newspaper Journalism" *Journalism Practice* 8(5): 542–551.

Pavlik, J. 2000 "The Impact of Technology on Journalism" *Journalism Studies* 1(2): 229–237.

REFERENCES

Pavlik, J. 2001 *Journalism and New Media*. New York: Columbia University Press.

Pavlik, J., Dennis, E., Davis Mersey, R. and Gengler, J. 2018 *Mobile Disruptions in the Middle East: Lessons from Qatar and the Arabian Gulf Region in Mobile Media Content Innovation*. London: Routledge.

Peer, L. and Ksiazek, T. 2011 "YouTube and the Challenge to Journalism: New Standards for News Videos Online" *Journalism Studies* 12(1): 45–63.

Perraudin, F. 2014 "Cassetteboy: 'David Cameron Won't Be Pleased by Our Video'" *Guardian* www.theguardian.com/media/2014/oct/10/cassetteboy-david-cameron-mashup-copyright

Peters, J. and Tandoc, E. 2013 "'People Who Aren't Really Reporters at All, Who Have No Professional Qualifications'; Defining A Journalist and Deciding Who May Claim the Privileges" *New York Journal of Public Policy Quorum* 34: 34–63.

Pew Research Center 2013 "Over a Quarter of Internet Users Download or Listen to Podcasts" December 27 www.pewresearch.org/fact-tank/2013/12/27/over-aquarter-of-internet-users-download-or-listen-to-podcasts/

Pfeffer, J., Zorbach, T. and Carley, K. 2014 "Understanding Online Firestorms: Negative Word of Mouth Dynamics in Social Media Networks" *Journal of Marketing Communications* 20(1–2): 117–128.

Phillips, A. 2010a "Old Sources: New Bottles" in Fenton, N. (Ed) *New Media, Old News: Journalism & Democracy in the Digital Age*. London: Sage, 87–101.

Phillips, A. 2010b "Transparency and the New Ethics of Journalism" *Journalism Practice* 4(3): 373–382.

Picard, R. 2016 "Twilight or New Dawn of Journalism? Evidence from the Changing News Ecosystem" in Franklin, B. (Ed) *The Future of Journalism: In an Age of Digital Media and Economic Uncertainty*. London: Routledge, 12–22.

Pickard, V. and Williams, A. T. 2014 "Salvation of Folly? the Promise and Perils of Digital Paywalls" *Digital Journalism* 2(2): 195–213.

Picone, I., De Wolf, R. and Robijt, S. 2016 "Who Shares What with Whom and Why? News Sharing Profiles amongst Flemish News Users" *Digital Journalism* 4 (7): 921–932.

Pool, I. D. S. 1983 *Technologies of Freedom*. Cambridge, MA: Harvard University Press.

Poole, S. 2013 "The Top Nine Things You Need to Know about Lists" *Guardian* www.theguardian.com/books/2013/nov/12/listicles-articles-written-lists-steven-poole

Pottker, H. 2003 "News and Its Communicative Quality: The Inverted Pyramid – When and Why Did It Appear?" *Journalism Studies* 4(4): 501–511.

Powers, E. 2017 "My News Feed Is Filtered? Awareness of News Personalization among College Students" *Digital Journalism* 5(10): 1315–1335.

Price, J. 2017 "Can the Ferret Be a Watchdog? Understanding the Launch, Growth and Prospects of a Digital, Investigative Journalism Start-Up" *Digital Journalism* 5(10): 1336–1350.

Primo, A. and Zago, G. 2015 "Who and What Do Journalism" *Digital Journalism* 3 (1): 38–52.

ProPublica 2018 "About" www.propublica.org/about/

Quinn, S. 2005 "What Is Convergence and How Will It Affect My Life?" in Quinn, S. and Filak, V. F. (Eds) *Convergent Journalism: An Introduction.* London: Focal Print, 3–19.

Raby, R., Caron, C., Théwissen-LeBlanc, S., Prioletta, J. and Mitchell, C. 2018 "Vlogging on YouTube: The Online, Political Engagement of Young Canadians Advocating for Social Change" *Journal of Youth Studies* 21(4): 495–512.

Radcliffe, D. 2012 "Here and Now: UK Hyperlocal Media Today" Nesta www.nesta.org.uk/areas_of_work/creative_economy/destination_local/assets/features/here_and_now_uk_hyperlocal_media_today

Radcliffe, D. 2015 "Where are We Now? UK Hyperlocal Media and Community Journalism in 2015" Nesta www.communityjournalism.co.uk/wp-content/uploads/2015/09/C4CJ-Report-for-Screen.pdf

Rafter, K. 2016 "Introduction: Understanding Where Entrepreneurial Journalism Fits In" *Journalism Practice* 10(2): 140–142.

Randall, D. 2000 *The Universal Journalist.* London: Pluto.

Reed, S. 2013 "American Sports Writers' Social Media Use and Its Influence on Professionalism" *Journalism Practice* 7(5): 555–571.

Reich, Z. 2006 "The Process Model of News Initiative: Sources Lead First, Reporters Thereafter" *Journalism Studies* 7(4): 497–514.

Reid, A. 2014 "Guardian Forms New Editorial Teams to Enhance Digital Output" Journalism.co.uk www.journalism.co.uk/news/guardian/-forms-new-editorial-teams-to-enhance-digital-output/s2/a562755/

Richardson, A. 2019 "The Movement and Its Mobile Journalism: A Phenomenology of Black Lives Matter Journalist–Activists" in Eldridge, II, S. and Franklin, B. (Eds) *The Routledge Handbook of Developments in Digital Journalism Studies.* London: Routledge, 387–400.

Richmond, S. 2009 "Telegraph.Co.Uk: 15 Years of Online News" *Telegraph* www.telegraph.co.uk/technology/6545788/Telegraph.co.uk-15-years-of-online-news.html

Ritchie, J. 2017 "What Is an Infographic? We Break It Down" www.columnfivemedia.com/infographic

Rizzo, A. 2018 "3 Facts You Need to Know about Artificial Intelligence in Journalism" Reuters https://agency.reuters.com/en/insights/articles/articles-archive/3-facts-you-need-to-know-about-Artificial-Intelligence-in-journalism.html

Rogers, S. 2013a "What Is Data Journalism at the Guardian?" www.theguardian.com/news/datablog/video/2013/apr/04/what-is-data-journalism-video

Rogers, S. 2013b "The History of Data Journalism at the Guardian" www.theguardian.com/news/datablog/video/2013/apr/04/history-of-data-journalism-video

REFERENCES

Rosen, J. 2006 "The People Formerly Known as the Audience" *PRESSthink* 27th June http://archive.pressthink.org/2006/06/27/ppl_frmr.html

Rosenstiel, T. and Mitchell, A. 2011 "The State of the News Media 2011: An Annual Report on American Journalism" *Pew Research Center Project for Excellence in Journalism* http://stateofthemedia.org/2011/overview-2/

Ross, C., Tembeck, T. and Tsentas, T. 2015 "Conflict[Ed] Reporting" *Photography and Culture* 8(2): 153–158.

Rubel, G. 2017 "Making the Embargo Work in the Era of Real-Time Communications" *PR Week* www.prweek.com/article/1431571/making-embargo-work-era-real-time-communications

Ruby, F., Goggin, G. and Keane, J. 2017 "Comparative Silence Still? Journalism, Academia, and the Five Eyes of Edward Snowden" *Digital Journalism* 5(3): 353–367.

Russell, A. 2011 "Extra-National Information Flows, Social Media, and the 2011 Egyptian Uprising" *International Journal of Communication* 5: 1238–1247.

Ryan, F., Coughlan, M. and Cronin, P. 2009 "Interviewing in Qualitative Research: The One-On-One Interview" *International Journal of Therapy and Rehabilitation* 16(6): 309–314.

Saltzis, K. 2012 "Breaking News Online: How News Stories Are Updated and Maintained Around-the-Clock" *Journalism Practice* 6(5–6): 702–710.

Sambrook, R. and McGuire, S. 2014 "We Want News on the Phone – And that Means Reinventing the TV News Channel" *Guardian* www.theguardian.com /media/media-blog/2014/aug/28/tv-news-channel-phone-digital

Sample, I. 2018 "Joseph Stiglitz on Artificial Intelligence: 'We're Going Towards a More Divided Society'" *Guardian* www.theguardian.com/technology/2018/ sep/08/joseph-stiglitz-on-artificial-intelligence-were-going-towards-a-more-divided-society

Sampson, A. 1996 "The Crisis at the Heart of Our Media" *British Journalism Review* 7(3): 42–56.

Sánchez Laws, A. L. 2017 "Can Immersive Journalism Enhance Empathy?" *Digital Journalism*, doi: 10.1080/21670811.2017.1389286.

Santana, A. D. 2013 "Virtuous or Vitriolic: The Effect of Anonymity on Civility in Online Newspapers' Readers' Comment Boards" *Journalism Practice* 8(1): 18–33.

Sapsford, R. and Jupp, V. 1996 *Data Collection and Analysis*. London: Sage.

Scanlan, C. 2002 "Beat Reporting: What Does It Take to Be the Best?" Poynter www.poynter.org/news/beat-reporting-what-does-it-take-be-best

Schaffer, J. 2007 *Citizen Media: Fad or the Future of News? The Rise and Prospects of Hyperlocal Journalism*. www.jlab.org/_uploads/downloads/citizen_media-1.pdf

Schroeder, K. 2014 "News Media Old and New: Fluctuating Audiences, News Repertoires and Locations of Consumption" *Journalism Studies* 18(11): 1343–1362.

Schudson, M. 2003 *The Sociology of News*. New York: W. W. Norton.

REFERENCES

Schumpeter, J. 1942 *Capitalism, Socialism and Democracy*. New York: Harper Perennial.

Scott, J., Millard, D. and Leonard, P. 2015 "Citizen Participation in News: An Analysis of the Landscape of Online Journalism" *Digital Journalism* 3(5): 737–758.

Sehgal, U. 2011 "'Hamsterization': The Official Term for What the Internet Has Done to Journalism" *Adweek* 13 June www.adweek.com/fishbowlny/journal ism-hamsterization/38631

Shainin, J. 2018 "How We Make the Long Read: From the Rise of the Sandwich to the Meaning of Neoliberalism" *Guardian* www.theguardian.com/member ship/2018/apr/07/long-read-how-we-make-it-guardian-shainin

Shapiro, I. and MacLeod-Rogers, B. 2019 "Who Owns the News? The 'Right to Be Forgotten' and Journalists' Conflicting Principles" in Eldridge, II, S. and Franklin, B. (Eds) *The Routledge Handbook of Developments in Digital Journalism Studies*. London: Routledge, 324–336.

Sharman, D. 2018 "Regional Political Editor to National Columnist: 'You are Not a Journalist'" *Hold the Front Page* www.holdthefrontpage.co.uk/2018/news/regional-political-editor-to-national-columnist-you-are-not-a-journalist/

Sherwood, M. and O'Donnell, P. 2018 "Once A Journalist, Always A Journalist: Industry Restructure, Job Losses and Professional Identity" *Journalism Studies* 19 (7): 1021–1038.

Shorter Oxford English Dictionary, Volume I (3rd Edition) 1973. Oxford: Clarendon Press.

Singer, J. 2006 "The Socially Responsible Existentialist: A Normative Emphasis for Journalists in A New Media Environment" *Journalism Studies* 7(1): 2–18.

Singer, J. 2019 "Theorizing Digital Journalism: The Limits of Linearity and the Rise of Relationships" in Eldridge, II, S. and Franklin, B. (Eds) *The Routledge Handbook of Developments in Digital Journalism Studies*. London: Routledge, 487–500.

Sjøvaag, H. 2016 "Introducing the Paywall: A Case Study of Content Changes in Three Online Newspapers" *Journalism Practice* 10(3): 304–322.

Slavtcheva-Petkova, V. and Bromley, M. 2018 *Global Journalism: An Introduction*. London: Macmillan.

Smith, C. 2013 "Tumblr Offers Advertisers a Major Advantage: Young Users, Who Spend Tons of Time on the Site" Business Insider UK http://uk. businessinsider.com/tumblr-and-social-media-demographics-2013-12? r=US&IR=T

So, A. 2012 "You Suck at Infographics" *Wired* www.wire.com/2012/07/you-suck-at-infographics/

Society of Editors 2014 "Advice for Aspiring Journalists" *Society of Editors* www. societyofeditors.co.uk

Sparrow, A. "Politics Live with Andrew Sparrow" *Guardian* www. theguardian.com/politics/blog/live/2016/may/25/eu-referendum-vote-leave -calls-ifs-biased-after-it-warns-brexit-would-prolong-austerity-politics-live

REFERENCES

Spiegel, E. 2012 "Let's Chat" Snap News www.snap.com/en-US/news/page/9/

Spilsbury, M. 2013 "Journalists at Work" www.nctj.com/downloadlibrary/jaw_final_higher_2.pdf

Spilsbury, M. 2016 "Exploring Freelance Journalism" www.nctj.com/downloadlibrary/EXPLORING%20FREELANCE%20JOURNALISM%20FINAL.pdf

Spilsbury, M. 2018 *Journalists at Work* www.nctj.com/downloadlibrary/JaW%20Report%202018.pdf

Staab, J. 1990 "The Role of News Factors in News Selection: A Theoretical Reconsideration" *European Journal of Communications* 5(4): 423–443.

Starkey, G. 2017 "The New Kids on the Block: The Pictures, Text, Time-Shifted Audio and Podcasts of Digital Radio Journalism Online" in Eldridge, II, S. and Franklin, B. (Eds) *The Routledge Companion to Digital Journalism Studies*. London: Routledge, 469–478.

Starkman, D. 2010 "The Hamster Wheel: Why Running as Fast as We Can Is Getting Us Nowhere" *Columbia Journalism Review* Sept/Oct 2010 www.cjr.org/cover_story/the_hamster_wheel.php?page=all

Starr, P. 2009 "The End of the Press: Democracy Loses Its Best Friend" *The New Republic*, 4 March: 28–35.

Statista 2018a "Number of Social Network Users Worldwide from 2010 to 2021 (In Billions)" *Statista* www.statista.com/statistics/278414/number-of-worldwide-social-network-users/

Statista 2018b "Number of Mobile Phone Users Worldwide from 2015 to 2020 (In Billions)" *Statista* www.statista.com/statistics/274774/forecast-of-mobile-phone-users-worldwide/

Statista 2018c "Revenue of Google from 1st Quarter 2008 to 3rd Quarter 2018 (In Million U.S. Dollars)" *Statista* www.statista.com/statistics/267606/quarterly-revenue-of-google/

Statistica 2018 "Most Famous Social Network Sites Worldwide as of July 2018, Ranked by Number of Active Users (In Millions)" *Statistica* www.statista.com/statistics/272014/global-social-networks-ranked-by-number-of-users/

Steel, J. 2011 *Journalism and Free Speech*. London: Routledge.

Steensen, S. 2011 "Online Journalism and the Promise of New Technologies: A Critical Review and Look Ahead" *Journalism Studies* 12(3): 311–327

Steensen, S. and Ahva, L. 2015 "Theories of Journalism in a Digital Age: An Exploration and Introduction" *Digital Journalism* 3(1): 1–18.

Steenson, S. and Ahva, L. 2017 *Theories of Journalism in a Digital Age*. London: Routledge.

Stenchel, M. 2016 "Global Fact Checking up 50% in Last Year" http://reporterslab.org/globsal-fact-checking-up-50-percent

Straub-Cook, P. 2017 "Source, Please? A Content Analysis of Links Posted in Discussions of Public Affairs on Reddit" *Digital Journalism* 6(10): 1314–1332.

Sullivan, A. 2008 "Why I Blog" *Atlantic Monthly* 302(4) www.theatlantic.com/magazine/archive/2008/11/why-i-blog/307060/

REFERENCES

Suran, M. and Kilgo, D. 2015 "Freedom from the Press: How Anonymous Gatekeepers on Reddit Covered the Boston Marathon Bombing" *Journalism Studies* 18(8): 1035–1051.

Sweney, M. 2018a "Leveson 2 Explained: What Was It Meant to Achieve?" *Guardian* www.theguardian.com/media/2018/mar/01/leveson-2-explained-what-was-it-meant-to-achieve

Sweney, M. 2018b "EU Copyright Law May Force Tech Giants to Pay Billions to Publishers" *Guardian* www.theguardian.com/law/2018/sep/12/eu-copyright-law-may-force-tech-giants-to-pay-billions-to-publishers-facebook-google

Tandoc, E. 2015 "Why Web Analytics Click: Factors Affecting the Ways Journalists Use Audience Metrics" *Journalism Studies* 16(6): 782–799.

Tandoc, E. 2017 "Five Ways BuzzFeed Is Preserving (Or Transforming) the Journalistic Field" *Journalism* 19(2): 200–216.

Tandoc, E. and Foo, C. 2018 "Here's What BuzzFeed Journalists Think of Their Journalism" *Digital Journalism* 6(1): 41–57.

Tandoc, E. and Jenkins, J. 2017 "The Buzzfeedication of Journalism? How Traditional News Organizations are Talking about a New Entrant to the Journalistic Field Will Surprise You!" *Journalism* 18(4): 482–500.

Tandoc, E. and Thomas, R. J. 2015 "The Ethics of Web Analytics: Implications of Using Audience Metrics in News Construction" *Digital Journalism* 3(2): 243–258.

Tandoc, E. and Vos, T. 2016 "The Journalist Is Marketing the New: Social Media in the Gatekeeping Process" *Journalism Practice* 10(8): 950–966.

Tandoc, E., Cabañes, J. and Cayabyab, Y. 2018 "Bridging the Gap: Journalists' Role Orientation and Role Performance on Twitter" *Journalism Studies*, doi: 10.1080/1461670X.2018.1463168.

Tandoc, E., Lim, Z. W. and Ling, R. 2018 "Defining Fake News: A Typology of Scholarly Definitions" *Digital Journalism* 6(2): 137–153.

Tanikawa, M. 2018 "Is 'Global Journalism' Truly Global? Conceptual and Empirical Examination of the Global, Cosmopolitan and Parochial Conceptions of Journalism" *Journalism Studies* https://doin.org/10.1080/1461670X.2018.1520610

Terdiman, D. 2018 "SmugMug Is Throwing Once-Vital Flickr a Lifeline" *Fast Company* www.fastcompany.com/40562440/smugmug-is-throwing-once-vital-flickr-a-lifeline

The Power of Citizen Journalism, 2014 Blog #3 Wordpress https://mfjs2210win2014.wordpress.com/tag/media-gatekeeping-gatewatching-gatecrashing-citizen-journalism/

Thomas, R. and Finneman, T. 2014 "Who Watches the Watchdogs? British Newspaper Metadiscourse on the Leveson Inquiry" *Journalism Studies* 15(2): 172–186.

Thorsen, E. and Jackson, D. 2018 "Seven Characteristics Defining Online News Formats: Towards a Typology of Online News and Live Blogs" *Digital Journalism* 6(7): 847–868.

REFERENCES

Thurman, N. 2014 "Newspaper Consumption in the Digital Age: Measuring Multi-Channel Audience Attention and Brand Popularity" *Digital Journalism* 2 (2): 156–178.

Thurman, N. 2018 "Newspaper Consumption in the Mobile Age: Re-Assessing Multi-Platform Performance and Market Share Using 'Time-Spent'" *Journalism Studies* 19(10): 1409–1429.

Thurman, N., Cornia, A. and Kunert, J. 2016 *Journalists in the UK*. Oxford: Reuters Institute for the Study of Journalism.

Thurman, N., Dorr, K. and Kunert, J. 2017 "When Reporters Get Hands-On with Robo Writing: Professionals Consider Automated Journalism's Capabilities and Consequences" *Digital Journalism* 5(10): 1240–1259.

Thurman, N. and Herbert, J. 2007 "Paid Content Strategies for News Websites: An Empirical Study of British Newspapers' Online Business Models" *Journalism Practice* 1(2): 208–226.

Thurman, N., Moeller, J., Helberger, N. and Trilling, D. 2018 "My Friends, Editors, Algorithms, and I: Examining Audience Attitudes to News Selection" *Digital Journalism*, doi: 10.1080/21670811.2018.1493936.

Thurman, N. and Walters, A. 2013 "Live Blogging – Digital Journalism's Pivotal Platform? A Case Study of the Production, Consumption and Form of Live Blogs at Guardian.Co.Uk" *Digital Journalism* 1(1): 82–101.

Tobitt, C. 2018 "National Newspaper ABCs: Metro Climbs above the Sun's Total Circulation as Mirror and Telegraph Titles Post Double-Digit Drops" *Press Gazette* www.pressgazette.co.uk/national-newspaper-abcs-metro-climbs-above-the-suns-total-circulation-as-mirror-and-telegraph-titles-post-double-digit-drops/

Toff, B. 2017 "The 'Nate Silver Effect' on Political Journalism: Gatecrashers, Gatekeepers and Changing Newsroom Practices around Coverage of Public Opinion Polls" *Journalism*, doi: 10.1177/1464884917731655.

Tong, J. 2018 "Journalistic Legitimacy Revisited: Collapse or Revival in the Digital Age" *Digital Journalism* 6(2): 256–273.

Tremayne, M. and Clark, A. 2014 "New Perspectives from the Sky: Unmanned Aerial Vehicles and Journalism" *Digital Journalism* 2(2): 232–246.

Tuchman, G. 1972 "Objectivity as a Strategic Ritual: An Examination of Newsmen's Notions of Objectivity" *American Journal of Sociology* 77(4): 660–670.

Tumblr 2018 "About" www.tumblr.com/about

Turvill, W. 2016. "Press Gazette Survey Finds Freelance Journalists are Happier than Staffers – but Pay Is Falling" *Press Gazette* www.pressgazette.co.uk/press-gazette-survey-finds-freelance-journalists-are-happier-staffers-pay-falling/

Tynker 2018 "How to Explain Algorithms to Kids" www.tynker.com/blog/articles/ideas-and-tips/how-to-explain-algorithms-to-kids/

UK Crowdfunding "What Is Crowdfunding" www.ukcfa.org.uk/what-is-crowdfunding/

Van Dalen, A. 2013 "The Algorithms behind the Headlines: How Machine-Written News Redefines the Core Skills of Human Journalists" in Franklin, B.

(Ed) *The Future of Journalism: Development and Debates*. London: Routledge, 144–154.

Vandendaele, A. 2018 "Trust Me, I'm a Sub-Editor" *Journalism Practice* 12(3): 268–289.

Van der Sar, E. 2017a "CBS Sues Man for Posting Image of a 59-Year TV-Show on Social Media" TorrentFreak https://torrentfreak.com/cbs-sues-man-for-posting-image-of-a-59-year-tv-show-on-social-media-171030/

Van der Sar, E. 2017b "Pirating Mainstream Media Outlets Haunted by Photographers in Court" TorrentFreak https://torrentfreak.com/pirating-mainstream-media-outlets-haunted-by-photographers-in-court-171028/

Vanian, J. 2017 "Facebook Is Testing This New Feature to Fight 'Filter Bubbles'" *Fortune* http://fortune.com/2017/04/25/facebook-related-articles-filter-bubbles/

Van Leuven, S. and Berglez, P. 2016 "Global Journalism between Dream and Reality: A Comparative Study of *The Times, Le Monde* and *De Standaard*" *Journalism Studies* 17(6): 667–683.

Van Leuven, S., Kruikemeier, S., Lecheler, S. and Hermans, L. 2018 "Online and Newsworthy: Have Online Sources Changed Journalism?" *Digital Journalism* 6 (7): 798–806.

Viner, K. 2016 "How Technology Disrupted the Truth" *Guardian* www.theguardian.com/media/2016/jul/12/how-technology-disrupted-the-truth

Vis, F. 2013 "Twitter as a Reporting Tool for Breaking News: Journalists Tweeting the 2011 UK Riots" *Digital Journalism* 1(1): 27–47.

Vogt, N. 2015 2015 *Podcasting: Fact Sheet*. Pew Research Center. www.journalism.org/2015/04/29/podcasting-fact-sheet

Von Nordheim, G., Boczek, K. and Koppers, L. 2018 "Sourcing the Sources: An Analysis of the Use of Twitter and Facebook as a Journalistic Source over 10 Years in the *New York Times*, the *Guardian* and *Süddeutsche Zeitung*" *Digital Journalism* 6(7): 807–828.

Vos, T. and Heinderyckx, F. 2015 *Gatekeeping in Transition*. New York: Routledge.

Vos, T. and Singer, J. 2016 "Media Discourse about Entrepreneurial Journalism: Implications for Journalistic Capital" *Journalism Practice* 10(2): 143–159.

Vultee, F. 2015 "Audience Perceptions of Editing Quality" *Digital Journalism* 3(6): 832–849.

Wahl-Jorgensen, K. and Franklin, B. 2008 "Journalism Research in the UK: From Isolated Efforts to an Established Discipline" in Löffelholz, M. and Weaver, D. (Eds) *Global Journalism Research: Theories, Methods, Findings, Future*. Oxford: Blackwell.

Wahl-Jorgensen, K., Bennett, L. and Cable, J. 2017 "Surveillance Normalization and Critique: News Coverage and Journalists' Discourses around the Snowden Revelations" *Digital Journalism* 5(3): 386–403.

Waldman, S. 2011 "The Information Needs of Communities: The Changing Media Landscape in a Broadband Age, Federal Communications Commission"

REFERENCES

July 2011 http://transition.fcc.gov/osp/inc-report/The_Information_Need s_of_Communities.pdf

Wall, M. 2015 "Citizen Journalism: A Retrospective on What We Know, an Agenda for What We Don't" *Digital Journalism* 3(6): 793–813.

Wall, M. 2019 *Citizen Journalism: Practices, Propaganda, Pedagogy*. London: Routledge.

Ward, S. J. A. 2010 *Global Journalism Ethics*. Montreal: McGill-Queen's University Press.

Ward, S. J. A. 2013 "Digital Media Ethics" *Media Morals* http://mediamorals.org/ digital-media-ethics/

Ward, S. J. A. 2015 *Radical Media Ethics: A Global Approach*. Chichester: Wiley-Blackwell.

Ward, S. J. A. 2018 *Disrupting Journalism Ethics: Radical Change on the Frontier of Digital Media*. London: Routledge.

Warren, R. 2015 "A Syrian Refugee Shared His Struggle to Reach Europe in Real-Time on WhatsApp" BuzzFeed www.buzzfeed.com/rossalynwarren/ a-syrian-refugee-used-whatsapp-to-share-his-journey-through

Waters, S. 2017 "The Effects of Mass Surveillance on Journalists' Relations with Confidential Sources a Constant Comparative Study" *Digital Journalism* 6(10): 1294–1313.

Waterson, J. 2018a "Cambridge Analytica Scandal and Fake News Have Left Social Media Firms Ripe for Atack" *Guardian*, 23rd August: 4.

Waterson, J. 2018b "Guardian Media Group Digital Revenues Outstrip Print for First Time" *Guardian* www.theguardian.com/media/2018/jul/24/guardian-media-group-digital-revenues-outstrip-print-for-first-time

Waterson, J. 2018c "Tax Facebook and Netflix to Fund the BBC, Says Corbyn" *Guardian*, 23rd August: 1.

Weaver, D., Beam, R., Brownlee, B., Voakes, P. and Wilhoit, G. 2007 *The American Journalist in the 21st Century: U.S News People at the Dawn of a New Millennium*. Mahwah, NJ: Lawrence Erlbaum.

Weisberg, J. 2011 "Bubble Trouble: Is Web Personalization Turning Us into Solipsistic Twits?" Slate https://slate.com/news-and-politics/2011/06/eli-pariser-s-the-filter-bubble-is-web-personalization-turning-us-into-solipsistic-twits.html

Westlund, O. 2013 "Mobile News: A Review and Model of Journalism in an Age of Mobile Media" *Digital Journalism* 1(1): 6–26.

Wheatley, D. and O'Sullivan, J. 2017 "Pressure to Publish or Saving for Print?" *Digital Journalism* 5(8): 965–985.

White, D. M. 1997 "The 'Gate Keeper': A Study in the Selection of News" in Berkowitz, D. (Ed) *Social Meanings of News: A Reader*. Thousand Oaks, CA: Sage, 63–71.

Widholm, A. 2016 "Tracing Online News in Motion: Time and Duration in the Study of Liquid Journalism" *Digital Journalism* 4(1): 24–40.

WikiLeaks. 2015 "What Is WikiLeaks" *WikiLeaks* https://wikileaks.org/What-is-WikiLeaks.html

REFERENCES

Wikipedia 2008 "About" Wikipedia https://en.wikipedia.org/wiki/Wikipedia:About

Wikipedia 2018 "Wikipedia" Wikipedia https://en.wikipedia.org/wiki/Wikipedia

Wilke, J. 2003 "The History and Culture of the Newsroom in Germany" *Journalism Studies* 4(4): 465–477.

Williams, A. and Franklin, B. 2007 "Turning around the Tanker: Implementing Trinity Mirror's Online Strategy" http://image.guardian.co.uk/sys-files/Media/documents/2007/03/13/Cardiff.Trinity.pdf

Williams, A., Harte, D. and Turner, J. 2015 "The Value of UK Hyperlocal Community News" *Digital Journalism* 3(5): 680–703.

Witschge, T., Anderson, C. W., Domingo, D. and Hermida, A. (Eds) 2016 *The Sage Handbook of Digital Journalism*. London: Sage.

Witschge, T. and Harbers, F. 2019 "The Entrepreneurial Journalist" in Eldridge, II, S. and Franklin, B. *The Routledge Handbook of Developments in Digital Journalism Studies*. London: Routledge, 64–76.

Wolfgang, J. D. 2018 "Examining How Journalists Construct Policy and Practice for Moderating Comments" *Digital Journalism* 6(1): 21–34.

Wood, S., Shabajee, P., Schien, D., Hodgson, C. and Preist, C. 2014 "Energy Use and Greenhouse Gas Emissions in Digital News Media: Ethical Implications for Journalists and Media Organisations" *Digital Journalism* 2(3): 284–295.

Woolmar, C. 2000 *Censorship*. London: Wayland.

Xin, X. 2008 "Structural Change and Journalism Practice: Xinhua News Agency in the Early 2000s" *Journalism Practice* 2(1): 46–63.

Yuan, E. 2011 "News Consumption across Multiple Media Platforms: A Repertoire Approach" *Information, Communication and Society* 14(7): 998–1016.

Zamith, R. 2019 "Innovation in Content Analysis; Freezing the Flow of Liquid News" in Eldridge, II, S. and Franklin, B. (Eds) *The Routledge Handbook of Developments in Digital Journalism Studies*. London: Routledge, 93–104.

Zelizer, B. 2004 *Taking Journalism Seriously: News and the Academy*. London: Sage.

Zimmer, M. and Proferes, N. 2014 "A Topology of Twitter Research: Disciplines, Methods, and Ethics" *Aslib Journal of Information Management* 66(3): 250–261.

Zion, L. and Craig, D. 2015 *Ethics for Digital Journalists: Emerging Best Practices*. London: Routledge.

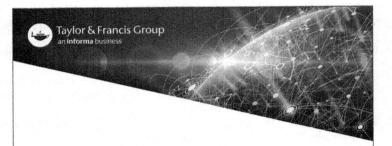

Taylor & Francis eBooks

www.taylorfrancis.com

A single destination for eBooks from Taylor & Francis with increased functionality and an improved user experience to meet the needs of our customers.

90,000+ eBooks of award-winning academic content in Humanities, Social Science, Science, Technology, Engineering, and Medical written by a global network of editors and authors.

TAYLOR & FRANCIS EBOOKS OFFERS:

- A streamlined experience for our library customers
- A single point of discovery for all of our eBook content
- Improved search and discovery of content at both book and chapter level

REQUEST A FREE TRIAL
support@taylorfrancis.com